Change Makers at Grassroots

About the Authors

Ganapathy Palanithurai, Professor in Rajiv Gandhi Chair, Gandhigram Rural Institute is an academic activist working with the people in rural areas for building the capacity of the leaders and people to reinvent sustainable grassroots democracy. He is heading the Department of Political Science and Development Administration, in Gandhigram Rural University, Tamil Nadu. His policy advocacy role at the governmental level is increasingly felt at present in all the three levels, namely, sub-regional, regional and national as he does more fieldwork than theorization. He has been associating himself with State Planning Commission of Tamil Nadu, Population Foundation of India, Rajiv Gandhi Foundation, CAPART, Ministry of Rural Areas and Employment and DANIDA (Danish-Indo Development Agency) in specific areas of activities in connection with empowerment of people. He is in the network of the Non-Governmental Organisations for Panchayat activities. He involves himself in capacity building exercise for local body leaders. He has evolved training module and manual for local body leaders. He has to his credit forty-one books, Ninty-two articles in reputed journals, twenty-three working papers, twenty-seven monographs, eighteen review articles on three major areas, namely, Legislative Behaviour, Ethnicity and Panchayati Raj System. He was a recipient of Fellowship from Sastri Indo-Canadian Institute, New Delhi and World Academy of Art and Science, USA. He has visited the US and Canada, on academic assignments. He was a visiting fellow in the MiGill University, Canada in 1989. He is a life member of Indian Institute of Public Administration, Indian Association of Public Administration, Indian Association of Political Science, Indian Association of American Studies, and Indian Association of Canadian Studies. He is a member of the expert committee constituted by the Government of Tamil Nadu, to monitor the training programme for local body leaders.

M.A. Thirunavukkarasu, the Field Co-ordinator of The Hunger Project, Gandhigram Rural Institute, is an activist working with people at grassroots level. He, along with veteran Gandhian activists Jegannathan and Krishnammal, participated in tillers movement. He is an expert in micro-planning and he has facilitated the Panchayat leaders to prepare micro plan document for their respective Panchayats. He associates himself in capacity building exercise for local body leaders and has assisted in evolving training module and manual for local body leaders training.

G. Uma, Uma presently works as the Co-ordinator of The Hunger Project in Gandhigram Rural Institute. As a Co-ordinator of the project for Tamil Nadu, she co-ordinated women leadership training programme for the elected women representatives, especially women presidents of Gram Panchayats. She has also developed a support structure to extend support to elected women representatives when they are in the field. She was instrumental in sensitizing the grassroots media to cover the struggle of the women leaders in the Panchayati Raj System.

Change Makers at Grassroots

Local Governance in Action

G. PALANITHURAI
M.A. THIRUNAVUKKARASU
G. UMA

CONCEPT PUBLISHING COMPANY, NEW DELHI-110059

Cataloging in Publication Data—DK
Courtesy: D.K. Agencies (P) Ltd. <docinfo@dkagencies.com>

Palanithurai, G. (Ganapathy), 1953-
Change makers at grassroots : local governance in action / G. Palanithurai, M.A. Thirunavukkarasu, G. Uma.
p. cm.
Case studies on panchayati raj system in Tamil Nadu, India.
Includes index.
ISBN 13: 9788180694714
ISBN 10: 8180694712

1. Panchayat—India—Tamil Nadu—Case studies. 2. Tamil Nadu (India)—Politics and government. I. Thirunavukkarasu, M. A., joint author. II. Uma, G., joint author. III. Title.

DDC 320.840 954 82 22

ISBN - 13: 978-81-8069-471-4
ISBN - 10: 81-8069-471-2

First Published 2008

Published and Printed by
Ashok Kumar Mittal
Concept Publishing Company
A/15-16, Commercial Block, Mohan Garden
NEW DELHI-110059 (India)

Phones : 25351460, 25351794
Fax : 091-11-25357103
E-mail : publishing@conceptpub.com

PREFACE

India's future looms comprehensive, diversified, pluralistic with decentralized policy making and strong grassroots level people's action characterized by strong skills, capacities and capabilities to cope with the emerging challenges of today and in the years to come due to the fast changes in the domains of polity, economy, market and technology. Yet we have registered grand failures in reducing poverty, malnutrition, hunger and increasing the opportunity for employment, access to health, education and basic facilities to the poor to the level of expectation. The entire public domain, politics, economy, public administration and market have become places for exploitation to achieve richness in any measure by abdicating all the inherited values of life from the past. Hence our polity, economy, administration and market are susceptible to manipulation, manoeuvering and devaluation for private prosperity and public loss and, as a result, marginalization of people, exclusion of communities, degradation of the environment, denigration of human life have become common practice. People who have skill, understanding, capacity, capability, aspiration and are ready for any competitive activity thrive in their respective domains of action and the others are marginalized and they are reduced to beneficiaries, petitioners and dole receivers at the mercy of the governing institutions and the dominant class. In their own homeland they are voiceless, meak and weak. They cannot claim their rights and entitlements though they are the voters deciding the fate of governments. They are the biggest contributors to fixing a government through their ballots but they are far away from the policy makers and the administrators. For each and every dole from the government, they have to rely on political brokers who get things for the poor and make a business out of it.

In India still 72 per cent of the people live in rural areas, 60 per cent of livelihoods depend on agriculture, around 30 per cent are poverty striken and 45 per cent are leading life in sub-human living conditions. Our macro picture of economic growth, rural development programmes, five year plan process, technological upgradation, scientific manpower, infrastructure facilities might have generated complacency in many who are enjoying the fruits of development. But the micro picture is grim, sordid and sorrowful. India is shining and stinking. India has two faces in terms of its richness—both the American face and the Ethiopian face. India is not one India with many faces. It has many Indias. We have Bihar India and Kerala India. We have Tamil Nadu India and Nagaland India. Conditions acutely, intensely and characteristically vary from one region to the other, and from one state to the other. Even within a state one can find variations among districts. The variations have been enhanced rather than reduced by the policy options and resource allocative decisions of the centre and the state governments. The continuous mass mobilization for political tasks helped the people to approach the political parties and their functionaries for their rightful claims on many of their entitlements. Yet providing basic minimum facilities for the people to lead a decent human life, creating conducive conditions for sustainability of their livelihood, establishing equity and equality in the socio-economic life of the people at the grassroots are still distant dreams. Appropriate constitutional provisions for equality and equity and for enabling the poor to have access to resources, health and educational facilities and livelihood opportunities remain in the text for lamentation and not for practice.

The newly advanced venture in the world, with the new nomenclature of globalization, is yet another accelerator in the mad race to exploit resources, technology and capital and thereby creates divisions, dichotomies in the humanity. Growth is fast, food is fast, life is fast, action is fast, decision making is fast, allocation is fast, and construction is fast. Degradation and depletion of natural resources are also fast. As a result, big profit, big money, big margin, big house, big facilities are available but there is no peace and no life in the home. The rich become richer, the poor become poorer. The government is unable to perform many of the accepted core responsibilities and hands over the same to the business sector. They do business under the new name of "pay and use service". Thus making profit becomes easier but governing society becomes complicated. The responsibility of taking care of the marginalized and the excluded lies with nobody and they have to take care of themselves.

At this juncture a new initiative has come from the federal government to reverse the entire paradigm of governance, development and administration through a historic Constitutional Amendment under the broad nomenclature of "decentralization of power". It has not done any magic but it provides an opportunity to the poor, the marginalized and the oppressed to claim their rights and rightful share in the resources for their development. We have seen so far that many of the constitutional provisions which are meant for achieving equity, equality and social justice have not been claimed or operationalized and still they are inoperative and hence we face all kinds of protest movements of the marginalized and the poor. As such the marginalized and the poor do not find any institutional mechanism at the grassroots to claim their rightful claims in resource allocation and rights. It is historic that a new institutional arrangement has been created constitutionally for governance at the grassroots. This new governance structure provides enormous opportunity for the hitherto excluded and marginalized to participate in governance and stake their claims and entitlements. Herein lies the challenge—the society is not positive towards this inclusion. The casteist and dominant patriarchal character of our society does not enable the excluded to become part of governance.

At this point the poor and the marginalized have to fight with the dominant to get their rights and shares and to fight with the other two governments for proper devolution of powers to the grassroots institutions. In using the rich potential of the new Constitutional Amendment, the grassroots leadership plays a crucial role. For this the grassroots leadership should have the necessary skill, capacity and capability to manage the affairs of development and to achieve equity and social development. Leadership matters much in governance at the grassroots. To realize the goals, objectives and potential of the 73rd Amendment to the Constitution of India, grassroots leaders have to be sensitized on the issues of governance and development and they have to be provided with the needed support facilities as a large number of them are drawn from Dalits and women. Creating an enabling condition at the grassroots by the civil society organization will make the grassroots institutions vibrant and capable of managing many of the development issues and governing the community.

As we see there are global resolutions and national resolutions. But the global and national resolutions have to be carried out only through local action. There should be a link between global and local action. Local problems and issues are not simple. They can be tackled very effectively only through proper governance, management and administration.

It is to be noted that leaders of grassroots institutions are not drawn from heaven. They are also drawn from the same society where from Members of Legislative Assembly and Members of Parliament are drawn. Since they are at the grassroots with the community, they can be sensitized and oriented and their mindset can be changed easily. In this context the intervention of the civil society is felt to be imperative. There may be regional variation in terms of their leadership between Bihar and Tamil Nadu or Madhya Pradesh and Kerala. Each state is unique in terms of its socio-economic conditions and devolution culture.

Our leaders at the federal level say that India should be made hunger free. India has more number of malnourished children than any other country in the world; 54 per cent of the Indian women in the age group between 15 and 40 are affected by anaemia. To tackle these problems, missions and programmes have been chalked out at national level and regional level but implementation has to be carried out by the grassroots institutions. If a leader is prepared and conscientised, a village can be made hunger free; it can also be made fully literature and malnutrition free. No one need be affected by anaemia. Many problems can be easily tackled by the Village Panchayat provided it works with the community by managing the commons and using judiciously the programmes and schemes of the government. Where are the success stories? They have to be shown to the world so that the world can see that decentralization has been impacting. After all, seeing is believing! Women leaders and Dalit leaders have created an everlasting impact in the community. We have to look for success stories to be shared with the Panchayat leaders (trainees).

In Tamil Nadu minimum powers, minimum finance and minimum functionaries have been devolved to the grassroots institutions. By building up their skill, capacity and capability, many of the leaders have carried out tremendous activities which have transformed the villages. Sometimes they are unbelievable. How these leaders, that too Dalit and women leaders, were able to struggle and achieve development and administer social justice! Their stories are captured and presented in this volume. Each one is a narrative of the exploits of a Gram Panchayat leader.

To perform this task many helped me. I have to thank many institutions and individuals for their constant help to prepare grassroots leaders for development work through training. Basically the Rajiv Gandhi Chair concentrates on capacity building and action research. It works for building a grassroots level people's movement. Preparing grassroots leaders for the movement is the prime task of the Chair. Hence training has been the constant activity of the Chair. It not only trains the Panchayat leaders but also serves as a resource centre and a supportive structure to help the Panchayat leaders who are on the job in the field. In the long drawn and arduous process, many of the leaders have emerged successful. Their successes are not mere success stories but are stories of struggles and successes.

Institutions like CAPART, Ministry of Rural Development, Government of India, the Rajiv Gandhi Foundation, the Population Foundation of India, the Ford Foundation, the UNICEF, The Hunger Project, the State Institute for Rural Development and the District Rural Development Agencies of various districts have helped us to conduct training programmes for Panchayat leaders.

There are three individuals, namely Mr.Vallinayagam, Mr. N.S. Chidambaram, and Mr. Subramaniam, who served as master trainers of the training programmes. All the three resource persons were constantly online for any help to Panchayat leaders. Since all the three resource persons are retired Additional Directors of Rural Development, Government of Tamil Nadu, their continuous assistance to the Panchayat leaders made them empowered and they were able to manage the officials at lower levels. With a sense of dedication and commitment they worked with us in our training programmes. There is yet another team consisting of Mr. M.A. Thirunavukkarasu, Dr. S. Devaraj, Mr. M. Gurusamy, Ms. G. Uma, Mr. S.P. Ramesh, Mr. V.S. Karthik, Ms. Jayashree and Mr. K. Tamilarasan, who have helped me in organizing training programmes and conducted case studies, doing training as well as fieldwork. The above institutions and individuals deserve my thanks and gratitude.

My family members, namely Mrs. Mala, my wife, my daughter P. Senthil Vadivu and my son P. Aurobindh have always been cooperative in all my academic activities. They lookafter themselves, leaving me free to pursue my work. They never not take away my time for their work. I record my sincere thanks to them. My Institute known for its committed support to the poor, Dalits and women as our founders founded it with the objective of empowering the marginalized, women, Dalits and children. As I have been training the women and Dalit leaders, I have been extended all needed support by the Institute for which I register my thanks to the authorities and my *pranams* to our founders.

G. PALANITHURAI
Gandhigram

INTRODUCTION

For the first time in independent India, an instrument has been devised constitutionally at the grassroots to govern the community and to administer development. In this regard the 73rd and the 74th Amendments to the Constitution of India are historical events to alter the paradigm of governance and administration. Even without the constitutional amendments, many states like West Bengal and Karnataka have established grassroots democracy as the respective state Chief Ministers had the political will and commitment to deepen democracy and empower the people. This new exercise radically alters the power dynamics of groups and collectivities. The whole exercise has to be done with great determination and will power on the part of the state level leaders. But one cannot expect all the Chief Ministers to have such commitment and vision to usher in the new form of democracy. Devolution of powers, in appearance, is only a simple devise but bringing it to reality needs energy, enthusiasm and a high level of courage. Devolution of powers will alter the power dynamics of individuals and groups who are in position. In the process of devolution some are lose powers and some gain powers. Those who lose power are dominant and influential in the power structure and those who gain power are the oppressed and they do not know what to do with the power.

Thus the devolution process will have more of challenges and opportunities. The challenges have to be responded to and the opportunities have to be seized. To respond to the challenges and utilize opportunities, all the stakeholders who are involved in this process have to be equipped. It is a known fact that those who are constantly moving with the government and who understand the process of governance get things done everywhere. Many of them understand the weaknesses of the governing structure and use it for their own advantage. In this context, devolution seeks to bring the people closer to governance and making the people participate in governance. To realize the basic objectives of the devolution of powers, a series of efforts have to be taken and of them the political commitment of the Chief Minister is imperative. To operationalise the spirit of the Constitutional amendment, a conformity legislation has to be enacted to conform to the spirit of the amendment. To evolve a comprehensive conformity legislation, a wide range of consultation is necessary. Proper evolving of rules and procedures is the next step in this process. The officials' mindset has to be changed to accept the implications of devolution. The skill and the capacity of the local body leaders have to be enhanced.

The masses have to be sensitized on the role of citizens in local governance in administering development and social justice. The media, research institutions, training institutions and civil society organisations have to be prepared for new initiatives and activities to create a climate for the transfer of power from the state government to the local bodies. In this devolution process it is not the institutions at different levels that get power but the different communities, when they are elected to different positions in the Panchayat system.

In Tamil Nadu, the conditions for the devolution of powers are not conducive. When the conformity act was enacted, the due process was not followed. The Tamil Nadu Panchayat Act was a hurriedly prepared document full of mistakes and weaknesses. The old Panchayat Act, which was enacted in 1958, had been diluted over a period of time. The diluted version of the old act, with the addition of the district Panchayat came into effect as the conformity legislation conforming to the spirit of the 73rd Amendment to the Constitution of India. Yet there was no inclination to conduct the elections. It was only through the election manifesto of the DMK party that the New Panchayati Raj system came into being. All hurdles were removed and elections were conducted.

After the conduct of the elections, the leaders of the three tier Panchayati Raj system were in position and they were demanding activities. Before entrusting the constitutional responsibilities, the Government of Tamil Nadu decided to share the work of carrying out the schemes of the Central and State governments on rural development. Meanwhile a committee was appointed to make recommendations on entrusting responsibilities to the three tier Panchayats. Simultaneously the First State Finance Commission had also submitted its recommendations. The L.C. Jain Committee's report is regarded as one of the best reports available in India on devolution of powers. Based on the report a number of government orders have been passed to operationalise the act. Yet substantial powers have not been given to local bodies. So a committee with Ko.Ci. Mani, then Minister for Rural Development and Local Administration, as chairperson was appointed. The representatives of all political parties were inducted into the committee. This committee also submitted its recommendations. Subsequently also orders have been passed to realize some of the recommendations. In the meanwhile the Second State Finance Commission submitted its recommendations also.

By making a realistic analysis one will find many loopholes and weakness in the system. But the Panchayat Presidents without any hesitation, have started carrying out many of the works in the Panchayats with the support of the government departments.

The bureaucracy is still dominant, with no change of mindset, and not building the skill, capacity and capability of the elected representatives. In the absence of a training policy, and poor allocation of resources for training, both the Central and the State governments have weakened the training efforts. Only a few civil society organizations took up seriously the capacity building exercise. The Gram Sabha has to be made vibrant and the citizens have to be made active participants. Mass mobilization has to be done through the media to sensitize them. The conditions in Tamil Nadu were not quite conducive to devolution of powers. Yet there was no major demand either from the political parties and civil society organisations. But Panchayat leaders were on the job. How they are able to perform is a major question. To get an answer to this question, we closely followed the Panchayat activities and studied cases. All the Panchayat leaders studied had undergone training mostly in Gandhigram Rural Institute.

With very little powers, poor resources, poor functionaries, the Gram Panchayat leaders are able to perform well. They are role models fit for emulation. How are they able to achieve such results? It is because of leadership skills, managerial competence, vision, commitment, aspiration to achieve things, sincerity, hard work, continuous updating, good rapport with the government officials, tie up with civil society organisations and interface with the media. Most of the time, the Panchayat leaders assume responsibilities and they take hold of power. If people feel that Panchayat leaders are doing well, they will be with the Panchayats and with the Panchayat leaders.

To strengthen the Panchayati Raj system the Federal Government has to give direction to the development agencies and Government Departments to carry out development activities under the programmes and schemes of the Central government by involving the local body leaders. Decentralization is a centralized drive and hence a demand has to be generated from the people for proper devolution. This demand will come only when the Panchayat leaders prove the power of local bodies and the potential of the local bodies. The caselets which we have included in this work bring to light the power of the leadership. They made a difference with their distinct quality of leadership. They are captured here.

CONTENTS

CASE - 1

WORK FOR SELF DIGNITY OF THE POOR

With a sense of commitment to work for Dalits, he started his work in water supply and transformed the life of the Dalits in his Panchayat area. His concern is the self dignity of the Dalits. By locating the sources of water at the places of the Dalits, he made them Dalits independent in getting water for their use. Their cleanliness, personal hygiene and sanitation are the other works of this Panchayat. This Panchayat has taken steps to activate the primary health centre and the sub-centre as they are the institutions of poor. He tried to provide needed facilities to public schools as they are the institutions of the poor. His transparent, innovative, technology oriented activities drew the public towards the Panchayat and the Gram Sabha. Equally he attracted the attention of the government. For the district administration this Panchayat serves as a testing ground to experiment with innovative programmes. It has emerged as a model Panchayat which attracts the attention of the other Panchayat leaders. Panchayat leaders and officials have been visiting this Panchayat in streams.

A New Brand

V. Ponnusamy, with poor (VII standard) educational background, moved over to the Panchayat, out of compulsion, from a trade union setting to work with the people to transform the life of the poor, particularly the socially underprivileged. Though he belongs to a political party (All India Anna Dravida Munnetra Kazhagam – AIADMK), he is hesitant to use the party to secure votes. According to him it is unethical to use the party as the Gram Panchayat is freed from political party based contest as per the Tamil Nadu Panchayat Act of 1994. He is of a different mould and that is why he says that the political party gets benefits from him while he does not gain anything personally from the political party. Further he feels that he has to stand on his own legs since he is working in the community. He does not want to borrow strength from the political party. He never looks at the Panchayat as a political or administrative unit. He considers it a space for social mobilization of the people for the total transformation of the poor and the underprivileged.

Moving in with Hope

He is still a worker in a spinning mill, but on leave. When elections approached after the passing of the conformity legislation in Tamil Nadu in the year 1994, he was told by the party workers that the ticket had been given to him by the political party (AIADMK) to contest for the Panchayat Union Council as Ward Member in 1996. He refused to accept the offer of the party and informed the higher level party leaders that it was a Local Body election and it should be approached as an independent candidate. Since the Local Body election is considered a community affair, the candidates have to seek the mandate of the people by projecting their own credentials and trustworthiness. Candidates cannot contest in the Local Body election as in the Assembly and Parliament elections. He filed his nomination as an independent candidate for the post of Councillor in the Palladam Block Panchayat, rejecting the offer of the party. He visited every house and every voter and promised them that he would do something for them if he was elected. All party candidates were defeated and he won the election. Having got elected as a Councillor of the Palladam Block Panchayat, he wanted to meet the basic needs of the people but he could not as the Block Panchayat can decide only the schemes sanctioned to the Block by the Central and State governments. Beyond the schemes he cannot do anything. He approached the officials for service and facilities for the people and he was informed that the Gram Panchayat has more powers and resources to do what he wanted to do. During the whole period of five years as Councillor of the Palladam Block Panchayat he got some schemes for his area and beyond that he could not meet the needs and demands projected by the people. But he demonstrated to the people that he was trying sincerely to provide facilities to the people. He approached the then President of the Gram Panchayat for delivering a few services and facilities to the Panchayat area. Being a Naidu by caste and hailing from a different place from the Panchayat area, the President was reluctant to hear the voice of the poor. He never visited the Panchayat area. Only the clerk managed everything. The above factors made Ponnusamy contest in the Gram Panchayat President election.

Further his Deep Journey

Having found the potential of the Gram Panchayat, he decided to contest the election for the post of Gram Panchayat President of Semmipalayam. Being a native of Semmipalayam, he had the distinct advantage of projecting his credibility and trustworthiness. Even in the electoral process he decided that the people can be approached directly without any political background. It was imperative that money should not be spent. He wanted to give a message to the people that he did not spend money and hence he would not take money from the Panchayat. With this determination he decided to contest in the election. There are 1656 houses in the five hamlets of this Panchayat and they can be covered within a week personally. Along with four or five members Ponnusamy visited each and every family personally and asked for their support. He promised the Dalit hamlets (two) that he would give water to the Dalit area if he was elected. In a five cornered contest he emerged victorious by a 400 vote difference. Of all the candidates he spent very little and got elected. He mostly relied on the Dalits as he gave more promises to them. Being a worker in a spinning mill, he realized the plight of the poor, that too the Dalits. He said that he knew pretty well that transforing the life of the Dalits is not so easy. It is a challenging task. Yet it will be a rewarding work as many do not venture into this kind of work.

Works Around Water

After he won the election, he realized the duties and responsibilities as a representative of the people. He wanted to fulfil the promises which he had given to the Dalits as the Dalits had cast their votes in favour of him. Of all the issues, water is their priority. Most of the problems relating to social conflict arise only in the places where water is being drawn. The Dalits are the worst affected in the water supply system as many of the water sources are located in the non-Dalit Hindu settlements. Pipelines are laid from the water sources to the Dalit hamlets through the settlements of the caste Hindus. If adequate water is available it will reach the Dalit hamlets. Otherwise the Dalits have to starve. If the Dalits compete with other caste Hindus to fetch water, the Dalits will be insulted and assaulted. The Dalits are always settled in the periphery and the tail end. By giving water to the Dalits he fulfilled his promise to the Dalits. It so happened that he attended a training programme conducted by the Rajiv Gandhi Drinking Water Mission. He considered it a boon and a gift.

Ponnusamy was determined to implement this comprehensive water supply project in his Panchayat. He decided to give water supply to the Dalit areas through this scheme. His problem was how to collect money from the Dalits who were poor. He first worked out a strategy. First a promise was given that every house would be given water connection, for which people had to deposit money under the new scheme. For every house he fixed Rs.3,200 for the pipeline and other services. Many of them agreed provided water was ensured, for which the Gram Panchayat President would be held responsible. A few families in the SC group did not commit themselves. Yet action was initiated and money was collected from the households. By depositing the money in the bank he got the project sanctioned. When the activities had been initiated, people started believing that water could be given to each and every family. Many of the SC families accepted it because their long pending demand would be met. He made water everybody's business and everybody's concern. Under this new scheme, he got sanction for Rs.45 lakhs and for this project he collected 10 per cent of the project cost from the people (Rs.4.5 lakhs). He constructed 6 overhead tanks (OHTs) and laid pipelines for water supply to all households. Apart from 6 OHTs, two ground level reservoirs and seven water pumping rooms were constructed. By doing this work he provided 100 per cent individual household water supply. There is no public tap in this village. The supply of water to all the houses to their satisfaction created confidence among the people that the Gram Panchayat President was a remarkable person who would deliver the goods. He not only provided water to individual houses, he provided water for common use also. He created two *dobhikhanas* (a place to wash clothes) meant for Dalits. In several places he provided gate valves to regulate the water supply. The valves can be opened and closed by any individual. He performed the magic of making the people owners of the water supply system by sensitizing the people on the importance of water. People who had experienced suffering in fetching water have come to the conclusion that it is a fine opportunity and this opportunity could be profitably used. People of the respective areas took responsibility for maintaining the water supply system. All storage and distribution systems are well protected and they are in the hands of people's committees. Totally there is no wastage of water. They get adequate water for both bathing and drinking purposes.

Ponnusamy made the water supply system a community affair. Everyone has access to water. The President has created a feeling among the people that they have adequate water for their use. At the same time people are sensitized to the importance of water. He provided water not only to houses, but also to primary schools (two), the middle school, the high school, the anganwadi, the church, a self help group, calf rearing shed and the temple. In all the places, regulation of water is entrusted to the respective people's groups in that area. Absolutely there is no wastage of water. From school going children to old men on the street they feel that they are the owners of the system. Ensuring water supply adequately to all has given a certificate to the Panchayat leader that he is a man of action. If he commits himself he will do it. People have started listening to him seriously. He fixed the monthly charge for water and collected the money regularly. Even the Dalits have been paying regularly without default. Defaulters are fined. They are extremely happy because they are provided water in their houses. There is no friction among the communities. One important principle that operates in the Panchayat is that leadership matters much. The powers, finances and the schemes were available in the previous period also. But the previous Panchayat leader could not do it as the present one has done.

The Panchayat President says that he has done nothing but providing a system and making the people own the system for its effective functioning. A man with fire and commitment, he has completed the task. He says that water is a mantra. Water is near and dear to the people. That is why the Panchayat President started his work with water. Through water he ensured social justice to the Dalits.

Conservation and Management of Water

He is not only interested in taking water from the earth and pumping it to the OHTs and from there giving water to individual houses, but also in conserving water through water resource management, natural resource development and conserving soil moisture. According to him people have to be conscientised on rational utilization of water and water conservation for water sustainability in the Panchayat area. He got assistance from the MLA and the MP besides the DPAP (Drought Prone Area Programme). He has created check dams numbering four at a cost of Rs.5.50 lakhs. He claims that while implementing the check dam project he distributed 3.7 tons of rice to the poor for their work in the project. He generated 528 mandays of employment. Through this work he created an opportunity for 15 wells and 5 borewells to get recharged. All the check dams are very near to the borewells from which water is lifted to the OHTs. Since he got money from the DPAP, it was imperative that watershed committees be formed through which awareness could be created about the importance of water and the severity of drought. Thus people were fully prepared and conscientised on issues of water scarcity and ways and means to avoid it.

Yet another work he carried out was the construction of rain water harvesting structure. In his Panchayat all the 1656 households have created such a structure because of the fact that the people of this village had got the needed orientation already. This work was carried out simultaneously along with the water supply system.

From Water to Sanitation

The next priority for the Panchayat President was sanitation. He knew pretty well that sanitation work in the rural area is a very tough task. His focus was on the settlements of the Dalits where the Dalits were living in sub-human living conditions. He wanted to change the entire scenario. When he started this work, the total sanitation programme was launched in Tamil Nadu. For sanitation also he adopted the same technique as in the case of water supply from the Rajiv Gandhi Drinking Water Supply Mission. He approached the district administration. The district administration responded immediately and he provided toilets to the Dalit colonies. Simultaneously he adopted a strategy to make this programme a demand driven one by removing all the bushes in the Panchayat lands which were used as places for open defecation. When all the bushes were removed people found it difficult to use the places. Thus they were compelled to go in for toilets. He provided toilets for women in several places and water connection was given to all the toilets. Women started using the toilets. He sensitized the Dalit people to the importance of sanitation. In all public places he has written slogans about the importance and implications of sanitation. In all his meetings with the Dalits, he emphasized the importance of sanitation and he blamed uncleanliness for untouchability and he advised the Dalits to follow the caste Hindus in matters of cleanliness. He cited the life of the Dalits in Kerala and how the Kerala Dalits have removed this stigma. Thus he made history of sorts. He transformed the lifestyle of the Dalits in his Panchayat area. He has provided toilet to every house. He wanted to develop a new culture among the youth. Hence he provided toilets to the high school, the balwadis and the primary schools. The appreciable part of the work was that the Panchayat provided baby friendly toilets to the anganwadi and the primary schools. He covered the anganwadi, two primary schools, one middle school and one high school. After giving water supply to all the toilets constructed in the schools he instructed the school teachers to cultivate the habit of using the toilets by the students. Thus he created a toilet culture in this Panchayat area. A centre for the production of rural sanitary material has been established by a supporting NGO (UCO, United Community Organisation) with the help of the District Rural Development Agency. This production centre supplies material to the Panchayats for the construction of individual household toilets.

Normally, when there is a scheme, the Panchayat President implements the scheme as such. But Ponnusamy is different and hence he constructed toilets not only for women and children but also for men. Whatever he carried out was based on his vision. He has a dream for his village. Like a paradise he maintains his village clean, tidy and green.

Table 1 : Sanitation Works during 2002-2003

Sl. No.	*Work*	*No.*	*Amount*
1.	Integrated Women and Children Sanitary Complex	1	2,00,000
2.	Men and Women Sanitary Complex	1	1,00,000
3.	Individual Household Latrines (Rs. 2000 per unit)	1450	29,00,000

Source : Computed from the Panchayat records.

Moreover, for the purpose of Solid Waste Management a totally mechanized unit has been installed at a cost of Rs.1.90 lakhs to serve the Panchayat. He has acquired :

Power Tiller

- a Power Tiller
- a Sewage Collection Tank (1000 litres capacity)
- a Trailer (5 ton capacity)
- One bulldozer used for clearing the bushes.

Using the mechanized unit, and with the help of well trained volunteers from SHGs, solid and liquid waste are collected and disposed of in an environment friendly way, as detailed below :

- all the households are given two separate waste bins to keep the solid and liquid wastes separately;
- the SHG members collect the wastes from

the households and separate the wastes as decomposable and non-decomposable.
- the decomposable wastes are used for producing manure and the non-decomposable wastes are used for recycling.

In this way the management of solid and liquid waste is successful and environment friendly. He collects charges for the removal of garbage.

Service with New Technologies

He is an innovator or pioneer in certain respects. He adopted a new device by which he reduced the electricity charges of the Panchayat by using a gassifier to lift water from the wells to overhead tanks. He erected a shed for this purpose. He has invested Rs.75,000 in this arrangement. The actual cost comes to Rs.1,50,000. He utilized the subsidy announced by the government. By fixing this new device he saved Rs. 2.50 per unit. All 24 hours water supply is available. In another place a windmill has been fixed to lift water from a borewell to the overhead tank for which he spent Rs.2,50,000.

Gassifier

Gassifier

Windmill

He generated biogas from the common toilets constructed for the women and men in the same place. One biogas plant was erected at a total cost of Rs.1.5 lakhs during 2003-2004. Human excreta is collected from 150 houses in a group housing scheme. The biogas produced is used for pumping borewell water for bathing and washing in the integrated sanitary complex for women and children and for cooking food and cleaning vessels in the anganwadi. This work helps to manage the human waste and protect the environment. It further reduces the electricity consumption. This gas has been used to lift water from the borewell and to light the lights in the toilets and in the balwadis. For cooking food in the Balwadi too the gas is being used. He has already planned to make use of the residual waste for vermiculture and compost making. To make the Panchayat clean, the Panchayat has purchased a power tiller with trailers to remove garbage from the street and hamlets and segregate the same and make biomanure which earns money for the Panchayat and provides employment opportunity for a few also. This power tiller is being hired out to other Panchayats by which the Panchayat earns revenue.

Plantation of Seedlings in the Panchayat Area

To make the Panchayat green, the Panchayat President has planned to plant seedlings in the Panchayat area for which he purchased a tree pit

Tree Pit Agra Machine

Agra machine for Rs.15,600 and by which he planted 2500 saplings in the Panchayat area. In several places the Panchayat has fixed electric booster to prevent electricity wastage. In this Panchayat lights are on between 6.30 p.m. and 5.30 a.m. The electric booster regulates the lights. Likewise in all the places water is being regulated through the new device he has fixed. It is known to all the users.

Electric Booster

Panchayats as they are institutions for the poor. He intervened in the group house construction and allowed the beneficiaries to have their own design and they were permitted to use their own money along with the amount given by the government. By allowing the Dalit beneficiaries to construct their houses according to their own design, the stigma attached to Dalits would go. Nobody could say that it was a government house for the Dalits. The Dalits said that hereafter they won't approach the government for repairs. Now they feel that they are the proud owners of their houses.

Dalit youths, according to him, are a potential threat to communal harmony. They must be provided education and employment opportunity. For their energy one has to provide work. He spent Rs.10,000 from the Panchayat fund for the purchase of play materials and they are kept in the building constructed for women self help groups. There are two doors to the building. One door is being used by the youth of the Dalits and the other is used by the self help group women. Since both belong to the same caste there is no problem is utilizing the same building.

Panchayat land has been given to the Dalit youth to prepare it as a playground

Walks Extramile

The headmaster of the high school informed the Panchayat President about a scheme for additional school building announced by the NABARD. Since adequate space was not available, the scheme was deferred. The President took earnest effort to give sufficient space from the Panchayat land which was adjacent to the graveyard. He constructed a small wall between the high school and the graveyard by which enough land was provided to the high school. He said government schools have to be supported by

Panchayat land has been given to the Dalit youth to prepare it as a playground. The place is fenced and the play materials are being used by the Dalits. So the Dalits, especially the youth, felt that they were being seriously considered by the Panchayat President. He enabled the Dalits to construct a small shopping complex through which the temple committee earns money and by using the money collected from the complex they celebrate the temple festival regularly. He ensured cleanliness in the temple premises. On the main road he created a park by which he attracted the children and women along with old men and women. During the evening time there is a big crowd. He earmarked an open land as a market place where rural farmers could sell their produce. It is also clean and neat. He constructed a toilet in the market place for the use of the common people.

Play Materials

Panchayat to Panchayat

On the Panchayat border there is a graveyard which is under a dispute between two Panchayats, namely, Semmipalayam and Sukkampalayam. After he became the President he approached the Sukkampalayam President and assured him of support for fencing the graveyard from the Panchayat money. The Sukkampalayam President provided a shed from his Panchayat fund. The graveyard is being used by the people of both the Panchayats now.

When Ayyampalayam Panchayat faced water shortage, Ponnusamy readily agreed to give water from his Panchayat after getting due approval from the committee and the Panchayat. Fixing a rate for the water supply he gave water to Ayyampalayam Panchayat. It is a model for leaders of both Karnataka and Tamil Nadu. He has made a fine arrangement between the two Panchayats. By giving this kind of help he maintains a friendly relationship with other communities in the neighbouring villages.

Focus on SC Women

He did another remarkable work by training the women members of SHGs in masonry. After gaining the needed skill, all the toilet construction work was entrusted to the women self help groups. They have constructed the toilets. It is another avenue of earning for the self help group members. There were only six self help groups functioning in this Panchayat. When he became the President he formed nearly twenty one SHGs. They were all from the Dalit community. They are given training in accounting, animator work and in different skills.

Building provided by District Rural Development Agency to SHGs to rear calves.

Since he organized SHGs among the Dalits and oriented them on social development activities, the district administration extended its support to him in all possible ways. According to his perception, the Dalits know the art of rearing and milch animals but are not trained in business (milk vending). Hence he decided to make them rear animals from the stage of calf to the stage of yielding calf. Four groups have been provided loan to purchase calves and they are being nurtured. A building worth about Rs.2,70,000 was provided by the District Rural Development Agency to these SHGs to rear calves. A calf is purchased for Rs.1000 and the calf will take two or three years to come to the stage of yielding calf. When it comes to this stage the value of the animal is Rs.10000 Rs.15000. From each animal they can get Rs.9000 to Rs.14000. It is a profitable work for Dalit women. He provided space for growing animal fodder. It is a remarkable achievement made by the President. All the Dalits stand behind him as he took the initiative to provide economic assistance. He argues that 10 women will get gainful employment by growing animal fodder. In the same way another 10 will get employment by rearing earthworm. The waste from the biogas plant is a very good base for preparing earthworm. Now it has become a very big business. Another 10 to 15 women can get employment. Since the Panchayat has a biogas plant, they need not get manure from outside paying money. He has enabled the SHG women to take over the PDS shops. When an opportunity was available the Panchayat leader wanted to test the service capability of the SHG women. He asked the women to take up the responsibility and they expressed their willingness. Immediately he took steps to get it for the SHG women. Through the SHG, provisions are being distributed to all the needy to their satisfaction. In the same Panchayat another PDS shop is being run by Civil Supplies Department. Comparing the performance of both the PDS shops the Panchayat leader and the people hold the view that the PDS shop managed by the SHG delivers goods properly and to the needy. It also earns a profit for the group.

Semmipalayam Gram Panchayat has five hamlets, namely Semmipalayam, Semi Goundar Palayam, Kuppusamy Naidu Puram, Sai Goundar Pudur and Semmipalayam Pudur. Totally there are 1656 households. The total population comes to 7580. There are 4335 men and 3245 women. In his Panchayat area, facilities like primary health centre, veterinary sub-centre, cooperative society, milk society, primary schools, middle school and high school are available.

He informed that house tax, professional tax and water tax are the major sources of income. He ensured total tax collection. On the Panchayat account, he has one Panchayat clerk, three scavengers and three OHT operators. Under the Rajiv Gandhi Drinking Water Mission water supply scheme he appointed one clerk, one fitter, one lady scavenger and two drivers. Analyzing the manageability taking into consideration the revenue and the expenditure of this Panchayat, this is the optimum structure and it is to be managed on its own. As an administrative structure it can sustain on its own from the resources generated from within. Basic services can be provided to the people without the aid of external agencies. Among Gram Panchayats there are thousands which are unviable in terms of manageability. That is why the Second State Finance Commission has recommended to the state government to create viable Panchayat units for easy and effective management. Semmipalayam is the best model. Even without external support it can sustain on its own and it can deliver services very effectively with the resource available with it.

A Partner

Ponnusamy carried out all the works with the support of an NGO by name United Community Organisation (UCO). He gained support from the UCO. He says that to implement many of the government's schemes the Panchayat needs support from government officials and NGO representatives as they are well versed in schemes. The Panchayat President is not a well trained person. He was not given any rigorous training. He used to attend the meetings convened by government officials and gained information. He is not aware of many of the matters pertinent to Panchayat administration. He felt that the support of an NGO is imperative. Moreover the Panchayat President is only able to articulate the problems of the people but he does not know where the solution lies. NGO officials can offer solutions as they know of a variety of schemes and programmes which the Panchayat Presidents are not aware of. Hence NGOs' role is crucial for the functioning of the Panchayats. He said that the UCO has done a commendable job in his Panchayat. He says that the NGO also has a share in his success. In the successful implementation of the sanitation programme the UCO played a major role.

SGRY Work

He is always alert in gathering information from all sources relating to Panchayat management. The SGRY is a scheme which is meant for food for work. It is very difficult to carry out the work for food. Many of the Panchayats have not succeeded in this scheme. But he succeeded in carrying out the work. By implementing this scheme he took up renovation work, construction of compound wall, drainage work, construction of training centres for women and other works.

The following works were carried out under the SGRY scheme during 2002-2003: 2 SHG training centres with 25 per cent contribution from the Panchayat fund with an outlay of Rs.2,00,000 and a PHC compound wall with 25 per cent contribution from the MLA's CDS fund with a budget of Rs.2,60,000 were constructed. A drainage system is under proposal with an estimate of Rs.50,000.

Table 2 : SGRY Works Carried Out

Sl. No.	*Details*	*No.of Works*	*Estimate Cost*	*Quantity of rice (tons)*	*No. of Mandays*
1.	Nehru Nagar Percolation Pond renovation 2002-2003	1	40,000	3.7	528
2.	Kosavankadu Percolation Pond renovation 2002-2003	1	40,000	3.7	528
3.	SHG training centre Part II	2	2,00,000	26,548	2,792
4.	SHG training centre PART I Semmipalayampudur	1	1,00,000	13,274	1,896
5.	PHC compound wall	1	2,60,000	27,344	3,906
6.	Semmipalayam AD colony drainage	1	50,000	6,637	948
7.	Individual Household Latrine	400	8,00,000	77.778	11,200
8.	Integrated Women Sanitary Complex (EAS Scheme)	1	2,00,000	—	—
	Total		16,90,000	158.981	21,798

Source : Computed from Panchayat records.

It is noteworthy that he is able to get all these schemes from the government while many of the Panchayat Presidents are lamenting that they are finding it very difficult to get schemes from the government. He says that, as he has proved that he is a performer, government officials have come to the conclusion that any scheme given to Semmipalayam Panchayat is worth it as it can be demonstrated to others. Officials can also claim it in their target reports. Hence officials are interested in giving more and more funds to Semmipalayam Panchayat. For many of the innovative schemes Semmipalayam is a testing field because the officials have found a strong and committed leader to bring success to the scheme. Whenever higher officials come from outside the state, they are brought to Semmipalayam. Thus he helps officials also. Officials need such kind of success for their survival. He works for them also. Yet another question is how it is possible for this Panchayat to get such schemes and get more funds in the context of the prevailing corrupt practices. The Panchayat President admits that corruption prevails in the administrative system. But, to escape from this ordeal, first the Panchayat President should demonstrate that she or he is honest. Second, with great difficulty, the Panchayat Presidents have to achieve something and they should emerge and attract the attention of higher officials. When they come to the level of drawing the attention of higher officials, this problem of corrupt practices will not be a major hindrance. First it is imperative that the Panchayat President should demonstrate that he is honest.

Apart from the works carried out under the schemes he carried out several works from the village fund. Various works were undertaken during 2003-2004 to the tune of Rs.5.00 lakhs.

Table 3 : Panchayat Fund Activities

Sl. No.	*Details*	*Estimate Cost*
1.	Semmigoundanpalayam Retaining Wall	16,000
2.	Kosavankadukuttai – Checkdam	38,500
3.	Anganwadi renovation and fencing	10,000
4.	Panchayat store room construction	50,000
5.	Semmipalayam bus shelter renovation	18,000
6.	Semmigoundanpalayam grave yard shed formation	50,000
7.	Semmipalayam women sanitary complex large septic tank construction	50,000
8.	SHG training centre contribution amount	50,000
9.	Semmipalayam village administrative office renovation	30,000
10.	Solid waste management project power driller, tailor and sewage water cleaning tank	96,000
11.	Panchayat office renovation	60,000
12.	Semmipalayam women sanitary complex night-soil biogas plant fencing	15,000
13.	Tree planting pit Agra machine purchased from TNAU, Coimbatore	17,000
	Total	5,00,500

Source : Computed from Panchayat records.

Resource Mobilisation

The Panchayat President has a clearcut perception about the financial status of the Panchayat. He said that the State and Central governments should give adequate resources to the Panchayat to carry out the basic responsibilities. Then only Panchayat Presidents can manage the Panchayats. At the same time the

Panchayat has to mobilize resources internally. Unless the Panchayats are equipped with financial resources, they cannot stand on their own. Hence he concentrates on increasing the income of the Panchayat and rationalizing the expenditure. He avoids wastages. He focuses on reduction of energy consumption by which a huge amount can be saved. He said that by adopting new devices the Panchayat can augment resources internally. From the Panchayat and public waste the Panchayat can generate resources. The Panchayat President should have vision and commitment. He said that the Panchayat Presidents should have a management perspective to manage the Panchayat very effectively. They cannot shirk the responsibility of providing basic services to the people by giving the reason that the Panchayat has no funds. They have to find out ways and means to augment resources. In the name of augmenting resources, the Panchayats cannot impose heavy taxes on the people. People should have the ability to pay tax also. So a viable management system has to be established.

The following are the major sources of revenue for Semmipalayam Panchayat:

1. House tax - Rs. 3,63,585 (100% collection in the past 3 years)
2. Professional tax - Rs. 2,50,000
3. Water tax - Rs. 40 per connection (Rs. 48000 p.m.)

Gram Sabha

People's participation in public programmes is an indicator of the support of the people for the activities of the Panchayat. When the Panchayat acts as a responsible and responsive body to deliver services to the people to their satisfaction, they will voluntarily attend the Gram Sabha meeting. Gram Sabha attendance is one of the indicators to judge the performance of the Panchayats. The Panchayat President says that his strength is the support of the people. In his Panchayat the majority of the people are labourers and yet they attend the meeting with the feeling that the decisions taken in the meeting will be executed and hence they attend in large numbers. He informs that he takes care of the resolutions passed in the meeting. By meeting the respective officials and pursuing matters he manages to carry out the resolutions passed in the Gram Sabha meeting. He does not send all the resolutions to the District Collector. He classifies the resolutions and writes letters to different government offices to give effect to the resolutions of the Gram Sabha. He said that he pursues such matters endlessly till they are achieved.

Table 4 : Details of Revenue of the Panchayat

Sl. No.	*Details*	*2000-2001*	*2001-2002*	*2002-2003*
1.	House tax	3,25,288.50	3,25,724.00	3,65,585.00
2.	Library tax	32,527.75	32,572.00	36,358.50
3.	Water tax	32,527.75	32,572.00	36,358.50
4.	Professional tax	2,15,100.00	2,12,670.00	2,50,015.00
5.	Building & Local development tax	30,966.00	19,122.00	82,610.00
6.	Post office deposit	16,00,000.00	16,000.00	4,50,000.00
7.	Stamp duty	61,803.00	97,301.00	83,113.00
8.	Rajiv Gandhi Public Contribution	4,60,000.00	--	--
9.	Capital tax	2,066.00	2,136.00	--
10.	2C tree tax	18.00	18.00	18.00
11.	Other income	725.00	15,716.00	48,984.00
12.	Income tax deduction	6,157.00	33,893.00	--
13.	Deposit	37,070.00	82,916.00	--
14.	State Finance Commission Subsidy	1,57,696.00	1,03,635.00	1,22,672.00
15.	Other Subsidy	5,000.00	2,400.00	--
16.	Street Light Government Subsidy	25,250.00	--	--
17.	House tax compensation	1,97,073.00	5,87,724.00	8,59,061.00
18.	Harijan death subsidy	--	2,000.00	--
19.	Post office refund	--	6,00,000.00	--
20.	Cable TV connection tax	--	1,000.00	6,900.00
	Total	31,89,268.00	21,67,579.00	23,41,675.00

Source : Computed from Panchayat records.

He did all these things to convince the people that the Gram Sabha is a powerful body. He feels that the Gram Sabha has been converted into a petition receiving forum. Panchayat Presidents collect petitions and send the same to the District Collector. In the next meeting when people raise questions about the resolutions passed in the earlier meeting, the Presidents give the answer that they have sent the papers to the District Collector and the District Collector has not acted on them. This is not the way to conduct the Gram Sabha meeting. People belonging to all castes come and sit together and discuss. What could be done at their level could be sorted out at their level. What could not be done at their level should be sent to different agencies. The Gram Sabha is an institution where people are trained and oriented in democracy and collective decision making practices. The Panchayat President is only a facilitator.

All eligible voters are the members of the Gram Sabha. All important decisions are taken in the Gram Sabha meetings, since they affect the villagers. In the year 2001 only one meeting was held, being an election year for Local Bodies. After that eleven meetings were held till October of 2003. He conducted special Gram Sabha meetings also.

As the villagers fully co-operate and participate in the Gram Sabha meetings it is so easy to convene the Gram Sabha meetings. During the year 2002-2003, five Gram Sabha meetings were held and during 2003-2004 (current year) six Gram Sabha meetings were held which include two special Gram Sabha meetings. The following table shows the details of the Gram Sabha meetings during the past 2 years:

Table 5 : Gram Sabha Meetings

Sl. No.	*2003-2004*	*2002-2003*
1.	26.01.2003	26.01.2002
2.	01.05.2003	01.05.2002
3.	22.06.2003	29.05.2002
4.	15.08.2003	15.08.2002
5.	23.08.2003	02.10.2002
6.	02.10.2003	—

Source : Computed from Panchayat records.

Health and Education

When he took over as Panchayat President, he saw the PHC in a poor sanitary condition. In front of the PHC, open defecation was practised by the people, since there was no compound wall for the PHC. Its functioning was not effective. There was nobody to ask the doctor and the other staff about their functioning. Instead of showing his power, he provided

Concrete Cement Road

a compound wall to the PHC under the SGRY scheme by spending Rs.2,60,000. He made the premises clean. On all the walls the concept of clean village was advertised. A facelift was given to the PHC by which all the staff were made to realize their responsibility. The Panchayat President said that by activating the PHC the poor are being helped. The PHC is a poor person's institution. In terms of power conferred upon the Panchayats, the PHC does not coming under the administrative purview of the Gram Panchayat and yet he made the PHC deliver services very effectively by doing service to the PHC. He says that he looked at all public institutions as institutions of the public to deliver goods and services to the public effectively for which the Panchayat has to facilitate instead of showing power. He feels that his facilitating role brings about success.

He launched a special drive for family planning and he assisted the staff of the PHC to help the pregnant women to take care of their health through the services delivered by the PHC. He frequently visited the PHC and asked the staff of the PHC about the facilities they need for effective service delivery. Even though he has no power over the functioning, he indirectly used power by assisting them in providing needed facilities. Previously no one was able to provide such facility. Hence he earned a lot of respect from the staff of the PHC.

Semmipalayam village has a primary health centre with two doctors and twelve nurses. In this PHC, 23,183 in-patients, 24,814 in-patients and 15,903 in-patients were treated in the years 2001, 2002 and 2003 (till October) respectively.

The village has 447 eligible couples and 195 have adopted family planning methods.

Table 6 : Family Planning Details

Sl. No.	*Year*	*Eligible Couples*	*FP adopted couples*	*Loop/Coper-T fixation*	*Deli-very*
1.	2000-2001	441	274	151	16
2.	2001-2002	318	160	140	18
3.	2002-2003	447	195	233	19

Source : Computed from the records of PHC.

He gives equal importance to education. Semmipalayam village has two primary schools, one middle school and one high school. All these schools get protected drinking water and have toilet facilities. Further, the literacy percentage of the village is 83.5 due to the relentless efforts taken by the Village Panchayat in terms of enrolment drives, awareness programmes. This is above the literacy average of the nation and the state.

He enabled the high school to get an additional building from the NABARD by providing additional land from the Panchayat. If the Panchayat had not given the land, the school would not have got this facility. He is always concentrating his attention on getting facilities to poor men's institutions. The high school does not come under the purview of the Gram Panchayat but he helped the high school to get such a facility because the school is helping only the poor. The rich are going to private matriculation schools. the poor are attending the Government High School. This is the reason why he helps the PHC and the high school. The details are given below :

Table 7 : NABARD 2002-2003

Name of the work	*Place*	*Amount (in lakhs Rs.)*
School building (2 class rooms, 1 girls' toilet and one science lab building)	Semmigoundan-palayam	14.00
Total		14.00

Source : Computed from the records of the School.

Observation

After analyzing the activities of the Panchayat at Semmipalayam and interacting with the President Mr.Ponnusamy, the following observations are made.

It is a well known fact that Panchayats in Tamil Nadu have several constraints, namely poor devolution of powers, functions and functionaries and yet he has been able to achieve remarkable things within three and a half years. His predecessor also had the same power, but he could not achieve things. The present incumbent has achieved these developments. It is because of his leadership, commitment and fire in his heart for service. He is not well educated and he is not so rich. He is only an ordinary mill worker. But he has a fire for service to the poor. Though he belongs to a caste Hindu family his love for Dalits and his concern for Dalit development made him devote his time to Dalit development. He is fully devoted to the cause of the Dalits. He knows the strategy to mobilize the people for development works. According to his perception the community can be mobilized on water. That is why he took up the water works first. Further he has abundant common sense. He has compassion for the poor. By his continuous mobilization of the people for Panchayat work he made the Panchayat a people's Panchayat. All activities are transparent. People see the results. When the Dalits got water, they felt that in the fifty years of democratic governance, they could not maintain self-respect, but now, through him, they feel that their self-respect is protected.

Development activities are being carried out in the corrupt administrative system. Everywhere people lament that unless bribes are given development schemes cannot come to the rural areas. It is applicable to him also. But in his case he is able to demonstrate that she/he is not corrupt and that he is a performer and as a result officials hesitate to demand bribe from him. Further he is in the eyes of all. Hence officials hesitate to demand anything from him. To avoid corrupt practices, first the Panchayat President should demonstrate that she/he is honest. Further he or she should have the capacity to fight it ought. For many of the innovative programmes officials need Panchayats to carry out such works. He demands all those innovative programmes and carries them out successfully as he has got the support of the people.

By doing things, he is conscientising the people

on development issues. People are seeing the works and repose faith in their leader. He has enormous will. It is being supported by the people. Though he is a Gounder by caste, his support base is in Dalit hamlets. He feels that basic services can be provided to all. He establishes a pucca management system to deliver services. The system is in the hands of the people. He facilitates. He sensitised the Dalits on environmental sanitation. His remarkable achievement is making the Dalit colony clean and neat on a sustainable basis. He has proved beyond that the Panchayat can work for economic development and achieve social development apart from providing basic services. What is required is a leader with a sense of commitment and a sense of honesty. Ponnusamy is having such commitment, honesty, sincerity, capacity and, above all, a fire to serve the poor and that too Dalits. Leadership matters in Panchayats.

I pay my tribute to the Panchayat President Mr.V. Ponnusamy for his dedicated service to the poor and the underprivileged. Though he belongs to the AIADMK party, in my perception he is a Gandhian worker, as he has been working for the Dalits. I express my deep sense of gratitude to him for sparing his valuable time for me by providing needed information to me from the Panchayat records. He assisted me to visit the entire Panchayat area and to interact with different segments of the people. We need such leaders for higher positions to redeem the institutions from the present malaise. He is a role model to many of our Panchayat leaders. Even the Dalit Panchayat Presidents have openly admitted that they have not done as much service to Dalits as V. Ponnusamy has done though he belongs to the caste Hindus. His leadership and vision have brought about this much of success.

CASE - 2

COMMUNAL HARMONY AND NATURAL RESOURCE MANAGEMENT

Being a Muslim woman, she is conscious of communal harmony and social and gender justice and hence she carried out many activities in Hindu temples and temple tanks. Providing water supply to the marginalised to the required quantity was her priority in her Panchayat. She removed encroachments in the common channels and water tanks forcefully and saved the water bodies from total annihilation. Her waste management is a model for other Panchayats. Her counselling to women drew women close to her. Her fight for saving the commons earned her a very good name from among all in the Panchayat area. Her grip over the Panchayat administration made her a master trainer for Panchayat training programmes. Her sharing of experience is always a thrilling experience for others.

Socio-Economic Background

Ms.Jamrud Beevi (50) is the President of Devipattinam Village Panchayat. She is a graduate and her husband is also a graduate. Her husband was in Saudi Arabia for some time. But, after a bypass heart surgery, now he is in Devipattinam, working as a bank manager. They have two daughters, of whom one is married and the other is studying in an engineering college. Her family is a nuclear one. She lives in her own pucca house with all facilities. She studied in Madurai Lady Doak College, where she realized the importance of freedom and liberty, she observed. In fact, she profoundly remembered her college days in Lady Doak College, Madurai, wherefrom she learnt leadership and realized the fullest dimensions of liberty and freedom. From her college days, she has been inclined towards public service. She was a sportsperson in school and college, spending considerable time on games. She gained openness, risk-taking ability, responding to challenges through her sports activities. She has overcome her shyness and inhibitions only through sports. This has added to her personality. She recollected that, earlier, there was a Mahalir Mandram in Devipattinam, in which women used to attend the meeting and discuss general issues of the people, particularly of women. She never wanted to be confined to her house. As a citizen, she felt that she could move with women of all castes and religions.

Her father is the Chairperson of the local Jamat, the Committee for Muslims. Her father is a good Musalman who never entertained any enmity or ill-will towards any in his village and was known to all for his positive qualities in promoting communal harmony in the village. He was the most respected person in the village for his honesty and social service. She said that she imbibed many of her father's qualities, which prompted her to move towards the public space. She said that she is plain and open, frankly sharing her ideas with others. Even after her marriage, the freedom she enjoyed was never curtailed by her husband. He is a very mature person. When the Devipattinam Village Panchayat Presidentship was earmarked for women in 1996, Muslim women as well as caste Hindu women suggested that Jamrud Beevi should contest. The Jamat of the Muslims tried to avoid any contest but the political parties did not accept the view of the Jamat leaders. So there were four candidates who opposed Jamrud Beevi. Of the four three belonged to the Muslim community and one was a Hindu woman.

The leaders of the Jamat openly supported her candidature. They accompanied her when she visited community leaders to seek their support. Even among the Hindus, most of the people promised to support her. During the campaign, people expressed their expectations, namely, provision of drinking water, streetlights, roads and public toilets. She agreed and promised that she would do the needful. The capability of the other candidates was not so sound as Jamrud Beevi's. Hence she won by 800 votes. She contested in the second election in 2001 also. She won the second election by 1200 votes. Her performance was evaluated and, based on her commendable performance, she was re-elected. Her father's service and her education and her own service were the major factors that contributed to her success in the elections.

She said that the space created for women in Local Governance is a landmark in Indian governance and Constitutional system and only because of that space she was able to come to power and do this much.

Social Backdrop

Devipattinam is a Hindu pilgrim centre but dominated by Muslim families in terms of numerical strength. Both Hindus and Muslims coexist without any difference and lead a peaceful life in this village. Even among the Hindus there are many caste divisions like Nadar, Mutharaiyar, Brahmin, Vellalar, Fisherman, Carpenter and Dhobi and they lead a peaceful life without difference and conflict. Her concern is that, in the days of communal and caste rivalry in the whole of the country, this village has to be protected from this menace and peace has to be preserved. She gives utmost importance to communal harmony. She wanted to maintain the leadership provided by her father to this village. Further she recollected the advice given by her husband and brother that the prestige of the family has to be protected at any cost and hence she wants to be objective and do justice.

According to her, the Panchayat should work on the issues of the people and, accordingly, the Panchayat should be made their institutions. Sometimes it should function as a community organization. The demands of the people have to be respected and then only people will feel that they have somebody to respond from the Panchayat. Sometimes the demand of the people may be unjust or obsolete. The leader should not regard it negatively. Either they have to be convinced that their demands are not just or the demands have to be met. The Panchayat is the people's institution. It should be a responsive institution attending to the basic needs of the community. If people come to the Panchayat, first they have to be respected and their demands have to be responded to. The Panchayat should not behave like the government. It should not be a mini kingdom. It should be a mini republic. The Panchayat should function with the participation of the people from all social and economic segments of the society. Panchayat leaders should stand by the people. We have seen the autocratic and authoritarian attitude of officials. The Panchayat leaders should not behave like the officials. They should behave like humble servants, she observed. There is yet another perception that Panchayat leaders need. The Panchayat should not be considered a space for politics. It should be perceived as a space for development. If politics enters, competition will crop up. If it is development oriented, nobody will compete.

Panchayat Management

She felt that it is essential that every Panchayat leader should have full control over the Panchayat administration. She looks at the Panchayat from a management perspective. Unless you have resources at your level, you cannot satisfy the people. Her concern is to find out resources to manage the Panchayat. What are the sources available from the State and Central governments, and what are the powers given to the Panchayats to mobilize resources on their own should be known to the Panchayat leaders. Finance gives strength to the Presidents to handle issues. She identified a source. There are plenty of buses, vans and cars coming to the pilgrim centre which is located in her Panchayat. She identified it as a potential source from which tolls can be collected. But to exercise this power she needs permission from the State government.

To get that permission the Panchayat has to fulfil certain requirements and conditions. She fulfilled all the conditions and obtained permission to levy charges on the vehicles. From this the Panchayat earns Rs.250 per day. Annually she gets Rs.90000 for her Panchayat. The house tax has been revised and she has ensured 100 per cent house tax collection by which she gets an incentive grant of 125 per cent from the SFC. She increased the house tax collection from Rs.7000 to Rs.1,70,000. She made a very interesting observation about fixing the house tax. She said that the Panchayat should assess the capability of the people to pay tax and then only the tax rate has to be fixed. She gives concession to the poor who are suffering in abject poverty.

She felt that the Panchayat should be in a position to manage the administrative cost from its own resources and then only it can sustain itself. Otherwise it will depend on the State government and State government will take away the life of the Panchayat at any moment. Panchayat Presidents should not expect that everyone will be supportive of the President's activities. As Panchayats are coming into a space which was occupied by power brokers, naturally, Panchayat Presidents have to face several barriers. To overcome all the obstacles and barriers the President has to equip herself or himself. One cannot expect that power will be devolved from above. The Panchayat Presidents have to assume powers for good work. Nobody can question the good work done by the Panchayat. If the Panchayat President is good in attending to the needs of the people, the entire community will be supportive of the President. Further the President has to be honest. If the Panchayat President is responsive to the people and honest to the core, nobody can touch him or her.

Village Economy

Agriculture and fishing are the major sources of income. Agriculture is possible if the monsoon starts in time. Many of the villagers live abroad. Fancy stores, furniture marts and other small businesses or trades are established by local Muslims as well as Hindus. Due to the regular flow of pilgrims tea shops, cold drinks centres and other petty shops are also thriving here.

Common Property Resources

There are about 12.5 acres of land meant for an orchard and in this area there is no fruit bearing tree except 69 palm trees. Three decades ago palm *gur* production was a good avocation for local people but, at present, there is no palm *gur* production on a regular basis. Most of the farmers have leased out their own palm trees for the extraction of "*pathaneer*" (a local drink prepared from palm milk). To establish an electricial sub-station, a piece of common land was given to the EB by the Panchayats. Now, anticipating the proposed Cauvery water project, 0.5 acre of land belonging to the dhargah administration has been donated. For establishing a desalination plant two acres of land has been donated. Under various categories like *oorani, salai*, footpath and cart road, there is a list of *poramboke* lands handed over to the Panchayat. Our administrative system is complicated and rules oriented which is favourable only to government officials and clerks. To overcome this difficulty one has to master the acts, rules and government orders, for which training is imperative, she observed. She attended several training programmes and refresh courses and, as a result, she is able to manage the Panchayats effectively and efficiently.

Her Perception on Panchayati Raj

She came to know much about Panchayati Raj through attending many training programmes. She has got all the literature relating to Panchayat administration. She used to attend all meetings convened by the officials, NGOs and academic institutions. She said that she has with her the Panchayat Act, Rules, Government Orders and Schemes and Programmes of the Government. She manages the office on her own. The Panchayat office is functioning from morning to evening. She said that the Panchayat should function as a people's centre. The Panchayat not only administers Panchayat matters, it should also be a guidance centre, providing guidance, information and assistance to the people. The Panchayat administration should be made responsive and responsible. The Panchayat office should be a regular functional office. Then only it can be called a system. Those who are in office in the Panchayat should realize that they are the contact persons for the people to move closer to the government at a higher level.

On Development

Jamrud Beevi said that her Panchayat is in a coastal area and so inland fishing is a good avenue of income. A fishermen's cooperative society is functioning in Devipattinam. Due to political interference, it is not functioning effectively. Agriculture is not a promising venture. About 150 families possess land and only by strengthening the irrigation sources agriculture can be made a profitable occupation. SHG activities are now picking up. Poor families of different castes join together and form SHGs. Women are now realizing the significance of the self-employment avenues available in Devipattinam itself. The Kattunaickan community (ST) is not yet reformed. She has taken earnest efforts to transform them. They engage in pig rearing and hunting birds. The women from the ST group are now coming forward to serve as helpers and maid servants. Slowly the women of that community will bring about a change in their community. She felt that people should be sensitized on development. Over a period of time people have been given an impression that the poverty of the people can be alleviated only by the government. People should be made to believe that they have to take the steps and the government should facilitate. The government never motivates the people to take the initiative for their development on their own. The Panchayat says that the people are the masters in deciding their destinies. The Panchayat provides basic infrastructure and facilities for livelihood first and then for other developments. People should be made development participants.

On Gender

Jamrud Beevi's activities are a source of inspiration to other women in SHGs. The SHG women are sensitized and now they are working against alcohol. As a woman she also supports the demand of the women that the liquor shops be removed from the village. As a result she has to face a lot of problems. There are women who forcefully resist their husbands taking liquor. The evil menace of liquor can be removed from society only through a mass struggle. It is a long drawn struggle. Anyway the SHG women have realized the implications of arrack for their family. It is coming up slowly from the women. Women groups are emerging as a movement which will one day totally eradicate this evil, she said. There are 50 SHGs functioning in the Panchayat area. When the President is a woman, family problems are brought to her notice by womenfolk and the men mend their behaviour after the advice of the President. Since she has got a family status, she is able to perform counselling also. Now women have come to discuss their problems as women have come to the public space with the assumption that women leaders will come to the rescue of women. The status of women will improve if women are made to take up responsibilities in public activities by obligatory or statutory means. The mindset of men has not drastically changed. Of course, there are some men sensitive towards gender issues. They are pro-women. When SHG members and Panchayat members meet and discuss the problems of women, nobody questions them. We have so far crossed several barriers and we have to go a long way in achieving gender equality. SHG and women leaders in the Panchayat have altered the mindset of men in society. In the democratic process women have joined together and now they are taking forward this process. The process is strenuous and painful and yet it is interesting as changes are being witnessed. Women have to face both patriarchy and caste structure. The struggle will continue for some time. Gender equity will be achieved only by partnership with men for which women have to form an alliance. Women have to work through a group. Jamrud Beevi is a boon in this regard.

On Politics

All political parties are functioning in Devipattinam, but the dominant parties are the DMK and the AIADMK. The political parties are active only during the election time. After the elections, the party leaders do not take any steps to realize the ideology or objectives of the party they belong to. Our political parties are not development oriented. They speak ill of each other. There are a number of issues to be tackled, but they are not the concern of the political parties. Political leaders at the local level act in accordance with the direction given by the party leaders. But the Panchayat leader is working on development based on the demands and the direction of the people. Panchayat leaders have to turn the agenda of the political parties towards development. All the party cadres and local leaders frequently visit the Panchayat office as the President is most of the time available at the Panchayat office. She briefs them about public issues like encroachments, drinking water project, public sanitation and other programmes carried out by the Panchayat. They seek information from the President. The President makes arrangements to get the details from the Panchayat. Totally it is transparent. As long as the Panchayats are transparent no party can interfere and influence the Panchayat administration, she observed.

Performance

There are five Wards and twelve Ward Members. Eight are men and four are women. All the Ward

Members do not attend the Panchayat meetings. Generally, only six to seven Members attend the meetings. The Members do not have vision or interest in public activities. The President can cultivate this spirit if they attend. If the sitting allowance to the Members is increased considerably, they may show interest to attend. When two women Members continuously kept themselves away from the meetings, it was verified that they were out of station. One is in Coimbatore and the other one is in Saudi Arabia. After initiating action by following procedures like sending notice to them, they were dismissed. Everybody advised Jamrud Beevi against it, but, she explained that she would go by the rule and not by her or others' personal opinions. The Gram Panchayat leaders have the onerous task of creating awareness about the new Panchayat Raj System and its implications among the people. Further the President has to train the Ward Members. Otherwise the Ward Members will act contradictory to the principle of devolution of powers.

The Ward Members who attend Panchayat meetings are very serious in their participation. They demand facilities to their Wards. Because of their faith in her they bring common people's problems to her knowledge and get her advice and help to redress them. When they proposed to construct a pucca bus stand, the Members suggested to fill the unused *oorani*, which is located at the heart of the village. She took the suggestion very seriously and initiated the process. Because of their cooperation, debris could be easily transported to the *oorani* and used to fill it. After the bus stand was established, three shops were also constructed there. Now an additional six shops are completed and from this commercial complex the Panchayat is getting Rs.550 per shop per month.

As pilgrims regularly visit the village a lot of garbage and other waste is scattered everywhere. The Panchayat decided to keep the village clean by properly monitoring the services of the sweepers. As there is no vehicle to transport the waste tractors are hired whenever necessary and the garbage is removed after the sweepers collect it.

Workers Classifying the Waste

Vehicles for Waste Collection

Public toilets have been constructed at three places and the Panchayat collects a fee of Rs.1.00 per head. Ten waste bins are provided in the bazaar and the residential area. About 60 individual toilets are provided under the CRSP. Most of the Muslims have household latrines of their own. Still the villagers prefer open air defecation and so she requested the SHG women to construct toilets in their houses and become a model to the community. She frequently monitors the services of the primary health centre. She said that the primary health centre is functioning well. Application of bleaching powder is frequent and they advice on the maintenance of public toilets. There are four wells with water fit for consumption. There are thirteen wells which are in use for other purposes. Due to more demand for water now 10 additional wells are provided. Public sanitation can be further improved by strengthening the sanitation system. She said that the cleanliness of the village depends not only on the service provided by the Panchayat, but also on the behaviour of the people. A culture has to be created among the people about decent human living, which is essential for every village. Now the SHG is an instrument and vehicle through which this culture can be promoted.

Toilets and bathrooms for Pilgrims

She promoted the clean village concept and yet she finds it difficult to maintain it as thousands of pilgrims visit her Panchayat everyday. She collects the waste from all the streets and classifies the same and puts it in a yard for compost. For this exercise she has entered into an agreement with an NGO called NACCS. Every month the Panchayat pays Rs.19500 to the NACCS to manage the waste. Of the Rs.19,500, Rs.12,000 is given as salary. She has purchased vehicles to transport the waste to the yard.

Bridge Surrounding the Shrine

Being a Muslim woman, she felt that she should evolve herself as a model among Panchayats in the days of communal conflict. In her Panchayat area there is a pilgrimage centre which attracts thousands of devotees of the Hindu religion everyday. All pilgrims visiting Rameswaram use to visit this place. There are nine deities inside the sea. The place is known as "Navabashanam". The story is that Lord Rama worshipped the "Navabashanam" to expiate to sin of killing Ravana. People who feel that they have committed sins use to go over to this place and perform *puja* in the shrine to expiate for the sin. But all the deities are in the sea. People have to cross the water either by boat or on foot, walking in the water. To reduce the inconvenience of the pilgrims, she thought of constructing a small bridge for about 90 feet, for which she approached the District Collector. The District Collector promised her that he would give sanction from the pilgrim centre development scheme fund, which is obtained from the Government of Tamil Nadu. She obtained a grant of Rs.13 lakh from the district administration to develop the pilgrim centre. She constructed a bridge around the deities, a small room to change clothes after the holy dip in the sea by the devotees, a toilet and a bath room complex. Now, without the help of a boat, one can reach that place and workship the deities. None attempted to do this work before. This enhanced her image among the people in her village. She not only constructed this bridge, but also made the entire area neat and clean by removing encroachments. She provided a sodium vapour light to the Agraharam as the Brahmins use to come to the sea to perform puja at all hours. Further the temple tank has been desilted and a boundary wall has been constructed. She provided a mercury light near the tank.

Bridge to Shrine

Shed for Pilgrim

She prepared a proposal to make this pilgrim centre more attractive and she has sent the proposal to the government. She said that she will get the sanction at any moment. If it comes, it will bring revenue to the Panchayat. Local people will get some gainful employment also.

Next to the temple her concern was to provide drinking water to everyone in the village. Her target is to provide water to the unreached. But there is no adequate water source in her Panchayat area. Geologists indicated a land with potential for water in the adjacent village which was owned by a private owner. She approached the person. The owner of the land was a Muslim woman. She was very rich and hence there was no necessity for her to sell the land. The Panchayat President pleaded that she has promised the people that she would give water if she comes to the Panchayat as President. After hearing the plea of the President the lady agreed to give the land for digging a borewell to take water. Jamrud Beevi got Rs.10.5 lakhs from the Government and spent an additional Rs.1 lakh to complete the project. By completing this work she has provided drinking water to all. She has not given water to individual houses. She has provided water through public taps. She has developed a perception that providing water through public taps will rationalise water distribution to meet the requirements. She has rejected the idea of earning

Water Harvesting Structure

money for the Panchayat by giving pipe connection to individual houses as water is precious and it is to be conserved and preserved.

According to her perception, by giving water through public taps, equality can be maintained and water could be saved. In all the houses rain water harvesting structures have been created. Yet another major work done by her in her Panchayat is a very big water reservoir. She got information about this Poovodai from the elders of this Panchayat. She interacted with the elders on the reasons for the water table going down to 90 feet. When there was a water conservation structure water was available at 5 feet depth. She asked what was the water conservation structure. The elders informed her that the Poovodai was the water structure. In 1955 there was heavy rain and, as a result, the Poovodai developed a breach and subsequently there was no repairing of the reservoir. All the years water came to this reservoir and moved away through the breach to the sea.

She started thinking about the Poovodai. When she visited the Poovodai, she found a lot of encroachments. The coverage of the area is seven kilometre in length and 100 metres in breadth. When she invited a Minister to her Panchayat, she made a presentation about the condition of the Poovodai and sought assistance. But the Minister, instead of responding to her request, craked a joke and left the place. The Minister said that the Panchayat has to think of what is possible and feasible. The Poovadai is a troublesome project which cannot be done by the Panchayat. This speech irritated her. She felt very much and made a declaration that the Poovodai will be made a reservoir to save water for the Panchayat. She approached the Collector and explained to him about the Poovadai and got sanction for Rs.25 lakhs under the SGRY scheme. She collected money from the local Jamat and the Saudhi Association for this work. They contributed Rs.75000 for this work. She removed all the encroachments with the help of the people and the district administration. The Poovodai has now been desilted, deepened and seven small inner tanks have been created. She considers it a major and memorable work done for the community. She commented that it was possible only because of the District Collector who is sincere and sensible on the issues of the rustic folk.

Yet another striking work completed by her is that a small dried up tank very near the bus stand has turned into a small shopping complex. Previously it was full of dirt and filth. Having studied the place, she decided to close the tank, for which she asked the people dump all the debris available in their area and thereby the tank was closed. She constructed a shopping complex at the site. Six shops have been constructed. She used Rs.2 lakhs from the SGRY scheme for this purpose.

Shops Constructed in the bus stand

She provided water supply and constructed toilets for all the six schools in the Panchayat area. She is the President of the SSA Committee in the school. She made it mandatory that no one should receive any money for committee meetings. Instead they should pay from their pocket to help the school. Thus she saved money and from the savings she provided a compound wall to the Higher Secondary School. She got the help of the MLA and the MP to construct needed buildings in schools. She approached all the representatives of the people and sought their help. Since she has no party affiliation, she has no hesitation to approach any leader for her village work.

Through the SSA, the tribals are being educated by sending the teachers to their area and teaching the children. An alternative school has been provided and 25 students belonging to this tribe are benefited. In all balwadis and anganwadis, kitchens have been constructed from the Panchayat fund. Water and toilets have been provided to all these centres. The tribals have been provided with house pattas. Water supply has been given to them in their locality.

Graveyard

Crematorium

Yet another major work is graveyard reconstruction. She fenced the entire area. For each and every caste a place has been earmarked for which a committee has been constituted. A small *oorani* has been created and a small well has been dug. Burial and burning can be undertaken in two different places. A road has been laid to the graveyard. A solar light has been provided.

Observing the activities of the Panchayat President, the Kanchi Sankarachariyar has invited her to his place and offered his blessings, saying that a Muslim woman has done yeoman service to the Hindu religion. This was appreciated by all Muslims.

She proudly says that she has removed nearly 600 pigs from her village. She spoke to the people who were rearing pigs. The public made several complaints against them. She repeatedly pleaded, yet nothing moved. Finally, she brought a person from outside and gunned down 580 pigs in a single day. She faced several problems on this count. But the public supported her as she did it for a good cause. She terminated the 2C patta given to an individual by the Revenue Department. By this, sand quarrying has been stopped and the commons are well maintained.

She participated in an International Conference held at Dakka from 11th to 13th June 2004. She was sponsored by the Institute of Social Sciences, New Delhi. The broad theme of the Conference was Women's Position in Local Governance, under which two main issues were taken up, namely Capacity Building and Policy Advocacy, for deliberation.

With Other Delegates in Dakka

With other Presidents on All India tour

She gives instruction to her clerk that the records and the accounts should be maintained in such a way that everyone can peruse and understand them. Her concern is to establish the Panchayat as a system. Nothing should be maintained in the house of the Panchayat President.

Gram Sabha Meeting

The Panchayat organises Gram Sabha meetings in which the community leaders and women from SHGs actively participate. Provision of drinking water, improvement to roads and extension of street lights are the major issues discussed in the Gram Sabha. The selection of beneficiaries for government schemes is finalized only in the Gram Sabha meetings. When difference of opinion emerges, the community leaders and Ward Members persuade the members. But she has made it clear that only the really poor will be recommended to avail of Government schemes. She said that she never allows political parties to determine the beneficiaries.

The SHGs seek help from the Panchayat to improve their income generation activities like mat weaving, canning, tailoring and production of fishing nets. Their requests and demands are addressed to the various departments and the President also tries to help them. The SHGs request her to attend their meetings and she attends a few meetings of the SHGs.

Provision of Street Lights

Extension of street lights is undertaken every year according to the availability of Panchayat funds and the need. After she assumed power she has provided 35 street lights along with 25 sodium vapour lights in the streets.

Other Social Development

Three additional buildings were provided to schools under the MPLAD fund, the MLA Fund and the District Primary Education Programme. She is trying to get two more buildings. As girls of the Muslim community are not encouraged to continue their studies after secondary school, she personally speaks to Muslim women about the importance of education to girls. Now more families have come forward to send their girls to school. She has another advantage in her village. She herself being a graduate hailing from the same village, she can convince them easily. She has demonstrated her ability through her performance in Panchayat administration. Medical camps, veterinary camps, and legal aid camps are effectively organized in Devipattinam. The Panchayat makes elaborate arrangements in this regard. By activating the Parent Teachers Association (PTA), four teachers were employed with PTA assistance. They conduct remedial classes in streets for school dropouts. After that the girls are encouraged to continue their studies in the regular school. As the SC community settlement is away from the school area, they wanted a separate primary school. The Panchayat gave nine cents of land belonging to the Panchayat for the construction of a school. Two teachers are now provided by the Government. The school is now functioning independently. Jamrud Beevi said that a mere petition is not enough. Matters have to be pursued continuously. Otherwise things will not materialize.

Social Mobility

Jamrud Beevi said that there is a good trend emerging in the villages, namely, that SC and other poor communities are giving encouragement to their children to continue their studies after primary and secondary levels. A competitive spirit is developing in this regard. The Muslim community, after obtaining education and exposure by getting employment abroad, have changed their traditional mindset. The SC people are acquiring new skills, particularly in the construction industry and trades like carpentry to improve their life. The consumption of alcohol or Indian made foreign liquor has also increased among the SC, Nadar and fishermen communities. Hence their economic standard is still stunted. For steady upward progress all liquor shops should be closed. Even licensed liquor shops should be removed. If the Panchayat is empowered in this regard, this menace can be stopped.

Linkage with Higher Level Representatives

The MLA, after visiting the Panchayat school, sanctioned a computer centre at a cost of Rs.8.0 lakhs.

The MP sanctioned an additional school building. The District Councillor helped to avail of funds for providing cement concrete roads and extension of street lights. The Union Councillor brought funds for school building, cement road, noon meal centre and ring wells. The works were carried out by local contractors who are very much conscious about maintaining quality. She never expects any commission or any other favour from them and so she asks them to maintain quality. She claims that she has availed of the discretionary funds from the Block Panchayat Councillor, the District Ward Members, the MLA and the MP belonging to different political parties. Since she is a non-party person, she has no hesitation to approach anybody. Further she has community support which is linked to the political prospects of the party candidates. The Panchayat President has to maintain political neutrality to attract all political parties towards Panchayat work.

Struggle with Samasthanam

The Sivagangai Samasthanam administration employed their staff and collected a toll from the vehicle owners at Navapashanam, a famous pilgrimage centre. It is not their right as the temple does not come under their jurisdiction. But the Vishnu temple in Devipattinam is under their jurisdiction. In the name of Perumal temple, they issued tickets and collected toll at Navapashanam. After she became the President, she objected to this and a case was registered with the police and the revenue officials. After verifying the tickets issued by the Samasthanam, the authorities warned them and permitted the Panchayat to collect the toll. There are shops around the temple. Earlier tax was not collected from them. But, after she became the President, a tax was fixed for them and the same was collected. The building tax is not yet fixed for the shops as the Devasthanam demanded that the tax has to be levied in its name. The dispute is not yet settled. There are 15 houses located around Chathiram for which house tax is not yet fixed. The problem is in whose name the tax has to be levied. So it is delayed. Irrespective of the reputation of the Samasthanam, the Panchayat is trying to assert its rights and authority to levy taxes and collect toll.

Her Future Plan

In many respects this Panchayat is emerging as a model. She wants to contest in the next elections also. If people favour it, she will contest. She has to contest along with men the next time. For communal harmony, cleanliness, empowerment of women, Panchayat management, sanitation, water conservation this Panchayat has to be cited, that is her dream. Though she had a desire to come to the public space, it was the people who drew her to the Panchayat. In the same way she has decided to go with the community.

Observation

Panchayat President Beevi has the fire in her to achieve something for the people. She has the needed transparency and rectitude in public life which has brought people closer to her. She has vision and, to realize her vision, she has needed commitment and energy. If she goes to the State Legislature or the National Parliament, she will deliver the goods better as she has enough skill, but she does not have such an aspiration. She derives pleasure in serving the people at the local level. She moves beyond traditional barriers. In the days of communal conflict, leaders like Jamrud Beevi are essential to save India from communal conflict.

Basic Details of Devipattinam Panchayat

President	:	Ms. Jamrud Beevi, B.A.
Vice-President	:	Ms. Josephine
Total number of Ward Members	:	11

Members Details

1. S. Nambulakshmi
2. Bhoopathi
3. V.K.S. Naina Mohammad
4. Mir Haj Begum
5. Vanniku Raja
6. Mohammad Ibrahim
7. Jasima Begum
8. Syed Noor
9. Govindan

— 2 ward seats are vacant.

Total number of Hamlets	:	2 (Gandhi Nagar, Devipattinam)
Number of Wards	:	5
Ward Members	:	Male-6, Female-4, Male (SC)-2

Table 1 : Gram Sabha Meeting

Sl. No.	*Year*	*Number of Gram Sabha Meetings*	*Date*
1.	1996-1997	—	—
2.	1997-1998	—	—
3.	1998-1999	3	(1) 25.09.1998 (2) 26.01.1999 (3) 11.03.1999
4.	1999-2000	4	(1) 1.05.1999 (2) 27.06.1999 (3) 2.10.1999 (4) 26.01.2000
5.	2000-2001	4	(1) 9.04.2000 (2) 1.05.2000 (3) 15.08.2000 (4) 2.08.2000
6.	2001-2002	4	(1) 7.06.2001 (2) 15.08.2001 (3) 11.11.2001 (4) 26.01.2002
7.	2002-2003	3	(1) 1.05.2002 (2) 15.08.2002 (3) 2.10.2002
8.	2003-2004	11	(1) 1.05.2003 (2) 30.07.2003 (3) 15.08.2003 (4) 23.08.2003 (5) 2.10.2003 (6) 23.11.2003 (7) 15.01.2004 (8) 26.01.2004 (9) 6.06.2004 (10) 26.05.2004 (11) 15.08.2004

Table 2 : Financial Status of Panchayat

Sl. No.	*Year*	*Particulars*	*A/C I (Rs.)*	*A/C II (Rs.)*	*A/C III (Rs.)*
1.	2003-2004	Income	14,21,032.10	3,44,747	11,26,735
		Expenditure	11,28,449	3,47,747	11,26,735

A/C I – Panchayat Account
A/C II – Earmarked Grant
A/C III – Scheme Fund

Table 3 : Works Carried Out with Earmarked Fund During 2003-2004

Sl. No.	*Details*	*Number of Works*	*Cost (Rs.)*
1.	Sanitary Complex	1	20,000
2.	OHT	1	68,233
3.	(a) Renovation of busstand	—	
	(b) Laying road near busstand		
	(c) Open well in the burial ground		67,683
	Total		1,55,916

Table 4 : Works Carried Out with Scheme Fund 2003-2004

Sl. No.	*Details*	*Cost (Rs.)*
1.	Indra Awas. Yojana – Construction of group houses	1,56,340
2.	Tank renovation (*Valla oorani*)	1,29,764
3.	Training centre	1,00, 000
4.	Construction of kitchen	35,000
5.	Threshing floor	75,000
6.	Gravel road	1,43,891
7.	Kitchen	50,490
8.	Upgradation of kutcha house to pucca house	50,000
	Total	7,40,485

Details of Desilting of Tank (Poovodai)

Executing Department	Department of Agricultural Engineering, Government of Tamil Nadu
Name of the Scheme	Sampoorna Gram Rozgar Yojana
Year of Execution	2002-2003 (dated 02.04.2003)
SGRY Scheme	Rs.18.60 lakhs
Small Savings Incentive grant	Rs.6.10 lakhs
Total	Rs.24.70 lakhs

Implementing Agency

1. Executive Engineer, Department of Agricultural Engineering, Ramnathapuram.
2. Project Officer, DRDA, Ramnathapuram.
3. District Collector, Ramnathapuram.

For construction of rainwater harvesting structure around Mariamman Koil oorani: Rs.80,000

Drinking water sources	OHT – 2 Open well – 5 6 feel well – 8 Hand pump – 1 Power pump – 1 Public tap – 77
EB fees	Rs.2,428 (for OHT)
Street lights	Tube light – 198 Solar light – 10 Mercury light – 2 Sodium light – 2
Street light EB fee	Rs.33,498 (once in two months)
Thaar road	—
Cement road	10 km
Gravel road	3½ km
Sanitation Facilities	
Sanitary workers	5
Panchayat toilet	2
Women sanitary complex	1
Individual toilets	856

Major Source of Revenue for Devipattinam Panchayat

House tax – Rs.1,63,820.80 (100 per cent tax collection for the past 3 years)
Professional tax – Rs.68,443 (100 per cent tax collection for the past 3 years)

Sl. No.	*Details*	*1997-1998*	*1998-1999*	*1999-2000*	*2000-2001*	*2001-2002*	*2002-2003*
1.	House tax	35169	42919.10	63540.40	92032.40	83411.50	15195.70
2.	Library tax	3489.50	4237.20	6267.10	9036.60	8170	15519.50
3.	Entry fee to the busstand	15210	1442	13829	11595	9975	8475
4.	Leasing of fishing right	1733	—	—	1825	1933	2038
5.	Professional tax	45376	52262	58240	61920	65640	64690
6.	Entertainment tax	100	—	—	3300	5400	9400
7.	Plan approval	4560	7040	—	—	4750	4960
8.	Licence fee	2214.50	3084	1908	8930	539	1833
9.	Contractor fee	200	404	1102	—	—	—
10.	Income from other sources	2500	—	—	—	—	—
11.	SFC grant	—	213645	476349	320535	337474.50	406686
12.	House tax matching grant	—	125172	64377	69120	15885	11700

(Contd.)

(Contd.)

Sl. No.	*Details*	*1997-1998*	*1998-1999*	*1999-2000*	*2000-2001*	*2001-2002*	*2002-2003*
13.	Stamp duty	–	20936	48968	–	18968	60866
14.	Caution deposit	–	10155.25	29581	–	28894	16822
15.	Sodium light	–	14700	–	8900	–	–
16.	Deposit fund from EB	–	174	–	–	–	–
17.	Local cess	–	359	–	–	5894	15276
18.	Tourism fund	–	–	75000	–	–	–
19.	Construction of bus stand shed advance amount	–	–	15000	–	–	–
20.	Toll gate fee	–	–	33082	–	–	–
21.	Other taxes	–	–	–	–	–	–
22.	Licence fee for starting hazardous factories	–	–	1192	–	–	–
23.	Rent from shops	–	–	–	18550	–	–
24.	Surcharge on stamp duty	–	–	–	52101	–	–
25.	Fine	–	–	–	1300	–	–
26.	Water tax	–	–	–	3150	270	570
27.	Fee collected from toilets near Navabhasnam and other fees	–	–	–	76444	89750	–
28.	Auctioning of tree	–	–	–	–	900	–
29.	Agreement forms	–	–	–	–	1450	600
30.	Auctioning of toilets	–	–	–	–	6500	–
31.	Rent from building	–	–	–	–	10450	19800
							1115687.00
							305345.10
							1421032.10
32.	To open account	100					
33.	Account I	70215					
34.	Account II	70128					
35.	Account III	85610					
	Opening	336605.00					
	Balance	171232.00					
	Total	507837.00					
36.	Bank interest	–	26272	36723	37272	10777	–
37.	Diwali advance	–	1660	1920	2650	–	–
38.	Deposit	–	–	–	88455	–	–
39.	Pongal Advance	–	–	–	2825	–	–
40.	GD	–	–	–	560	100	–
41.	2% & 25%						
	Total			537845.55	931276.50	876683.50	731636
				335946.00	658006.10	915824.60	470717.10
	Total			73800.55	1589282.60	1792508.60	1202353.10

CASE - 3

COMMUNAL HARMONY THROUGH SCHOOL WORK AND WATER WORK

Noor Mohammed is known for his Hindu temple activities. His concern for water conservation and his interest in working with children have earned him a good name among the Hindus. He maintains cleanliness in the village and he make's wealth out of waste. Ramanathapuram District is known for water scarcity but he has made his village water plenty. His water storage and supply system have enthused the people. His transparent Panchayat activities have moved the people closer to the Panchayat. He always mobilizes the people in large numbers for the Gram Sabha. Having seen him fulfilling promises, people repose confidence in him. His initiative of making wealth out of waste has made this Panchayat a model Panchayat. He is yet another person always on demand to share experience with Panchayat leaders.

A Leader with a Difference

Mr. Noor Mohammed (57) with the educational background of SSLC, a trader by occupation, moved over to the Panchayat setting to work for the people in order to transform the village by providing people with all basic facilities. He has five children (four boys and one girl) and of them two are doing business in Kuala Lumpur, Malaysia. He has agriculture land and cultivates rice and coconut. His economic background is very sound. Having assessed the poor performance of the officials in rural development activities for the past several years, he has taken a decision that this is fine opportunity that he can contest and set the maladies in rural development activities carried out in his village. He said that government spends every year several lakhs to each and every village through several programmes implemented for the benefit of the people. But their demands are unmet and continuously growing. Government spending is increasing every year but not solving the demands of the people. Moreover people do not have representatives at their place of residence to redress their grievances. But the New Panchayati Raj System provides this new opportunity for the local populace to take up responsibility to decide their destiny. Hence he decided to contest in the election for the post of Gram Panchayat President of Sakkarakottai. His predecessors have not done anything for the villagers. Yet he did not use this factor-poor performance of his predecessors in the election campaign. He projected only his promises. Since he identified the felt needs he put forth his election promises as provision of water supply, road for smooth transportation, street light for brighter evening and temples for worship. Of all the demands people projected only temple and water as major and basic needs in all the hamlets. Temple was projected as basic demand even in SC colony. It is a wonder that the living conditions are extremely poor in SC colony but they also project temple is a basic need. Noor Mohammed understood the reality that people could be mobilized either on the issues of water or temple. They are the basis of Indian community. There are other basic demands which were not emphasized as temples and water. He further noticed that the demand was not the demand of the uneducated, it was the demand of all. Hence he has decided to give utmost importance to these issues. Instead of making hue and cry why not we take responsibility in Panchayats and show the way to others is the thinking which prompted him to contest in the local body election. It is the usual syndrome and popular perception in India that coming to public office is to earn money. But fortunately he said that he has enough money. He can contribute money to public activities. Being a minority by religion, he was able to occupy the post of Panchayat President with the help of the majority, the Hindus. Even though the Hindus are in majority, only the people of his religion contested in the Village Panchayat President election in the first time but he was able to secure more votes with the help of the Hindus and the Jamaat also helped him to realize his dream of becoming a President. In the second election three others contested and of others one had lost his deposit. Two others are belonging to the Hindu religion and yet they could not get the votes of the Hindus. In the first election he won the election with a difference of 511 and in the second election with a difference of 476. Though he belongs to a political party, he didn't show his identity as a party member to secure votes. His idea of contesting election is to serve the community. To serve the community he need not seek the support of the party. It is not MLA or MP election. If people have faith and confidence in him, they will cast their votes otherwise they won't. Against this background he contested. All the segments helped him to get elected. As soon as he decided to contest in the election, he approached the Hindu leaders seeking their support and promised them to fulfil all their basic necessities. Construction of Hindu temple was their primary requirement and Mr.Noor Mohammed promised the people. Basically, Mr.Noor Mohammad's family is known for its philanthropy and they have assets devoted for charity. Following their ancestors, he also followed the same by concentrating his work on temple and water. A major share of his property has been spent for the temple work and providing water supply. His primary concern was to preserve communal harmony and at the same time their felt needs have to be attended to. In variably people demanded both a place for worship and regular water supply. They are the two vital demands projected by the people when he met them while doing his election campaign. Knowing fully well that Panchayat has no money to construct temples, he promised that he would fulfil their demands. Hence temple works are carried out from trust money and water works were carried out only from Panchayat money. He firmly believes that people's genuine demands could be met by the Panchayats provided Panchayat leaders have got commitment. He further feels that by providing water to their need and constructing small temples one can earn the support of the people. In his Panchayat area there are about seventeen small community temples which are being supported by the community and incidentally Panchayat President is also helping.

Works Around Water

After he got elected as a President, he started fulfilling his promises by focusing on the water. Water being a primary requirement of the people drew his attention and Ramnad District being drought hit area further motivated him to the fullest extent to solve the problem quickly. He desilted tanks, dug wells and provided the people with individual house tap connection and also common tap in each streets of the village. There was a small tank adjacent to the main road leading to Rameshwaram a leading pilgrimage centre in South India which attracts thousands of devotees all over India. Wherever the devotees go over to Rameshwaram, they use to take bath in this tank since it keeps water throughout the year. He felt that this tank has to be desilted and expanded. He deepened that tank and three sides of tank retaining walls have constructed with bathing facilities. Further he has constructed a small dressing room for women to change their dress after their bath. No Panchayat has taken such an initiative. Apart from these thing a major work done by him worth mentioning here was the desilting of *oorani* carried out by him in Vani hamlet, where the *oorani* stretches out for 22 acre. This was a major task carried out by the President. He informed that by providing water, many problems in the village could be solved. Scarcity of water for bathing, drinking and even for agriculture would create a number of social problems which disturb the harmony of the community. People should have a feeling that they can get enough water for drinking, bathing and agriculture purposes. He feels that solving the water crisis in a Panchayat many of the problems are solved. He has constructed road with the disilted sand making comfortable for the womenfolk to fetch the water from the tank. Sometimes he merges government scheme with his own money and with the help of the TWAD Board he has placed several syntax tanks near the well, so that people need not draw the water from the well instead they can get water from the tap which saves their energy. The people get adequate water for both bathing and drinking purposes.

Water Tank Desilted and Water is Stored through Rainwater

Water Tank Desilted and Bend was Constructed

Another Water Tank Retaining Wall under Construction

Focus on Education

Four primary schools are situated in the Panchayat area and they need basic facilities. After he assumed office as the Panchayat President he provided electricity facility, drinking water supply, furniture's and buildings. In order to motivate the school children, he celebrates annual day and sports day functions at his own cost and distributes prizes to the school children conducting competitions. He also achieves 100 per cent enrolment of children in schools and ensured their continuation. He has constructed school building at the cost of 2.75 lakhs with a building for library. He also concentrated his work on anganwadi by providing them pucca building facilities and all the six anganwadis are full-fledged with all facilities with proper kitchen and safe drinking water. Now the children in his Panchayat are very much happy and they are fond of him. He hasn't taken any effort for bringing high school to his Panchayat since his Panchayat is located next to the Ramnad town and students don't find any difficulty in going there. He has provided toilet facilities to the schools and requested the teachers to inculcate toilet culture among the school going children. He used to inspect the nutritive meal centres to verify whether the food served there is really nutritive. His active participation created a new atmosphere in anganwadis and schools.

Participating in School Programme

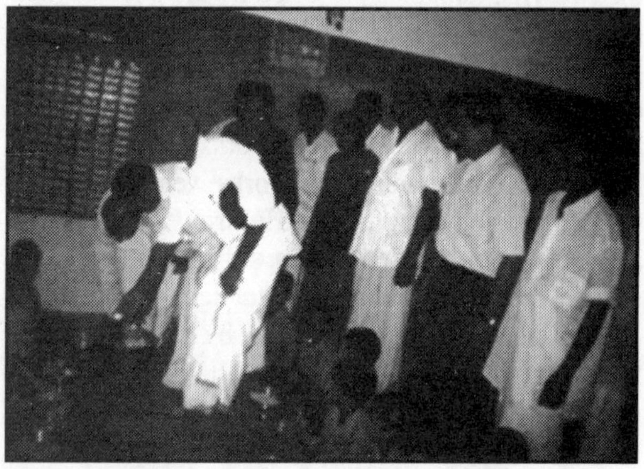

Participating in the Inspection of Noon Meal Centre

Concentration on Buildings

Next to temple and water, he concentrated on constructing community halls and has constructed five community halls which serve for many purposes. Training to SHG members are conducted in these buildings. He has utilized the community halls for training the SHG members. Moreover, currently he is modifying his Panchayat office with all modern facilities inside. The Panchayat office also depicts the essence of all the three major religions. To construct these buildings he approached two members of Parliament and he has got sanction out of their MP Constituency Fund.

Works Around Temples

He took earnest effort to contribute liberally to construct temples and takes responsibility to mobilize resources for construction of temples. He involved himself in the temple activities either for construction or for renovation or for organizing festivals. His main role is to contribute and collect and contribute. In all the Hindu temples his name has been written very prominently as prime contributor. His involvement in the following temples is immense.

Table 1 : Works Around Temple

Sl. No.	*Name of the Temple*	*Contribution (In Rs.)*
1.	Muthumariamman (Kavalar Kudiyiruppu)	80,000.00
2.	Mahasakthi Mariamman (Sivaganapuram)	45,000.00
3.	Murugan (Kuyavankudi)	15,000.00
4.	Mariamman (Pasumpon Nagar)	30,000.00
5.	Vinayagar (Prison Ramanathapuram)	30,000.00
6.	Santhana Mariamman (Sethunagar)	80,000.00
7.	Muthu Mariamman (VOC Nagar)	50,000.00
8.	Mahamariamman (Kelachothurani)	60,000.00
9.	Sidhivinayagar (Vaani)	20,000.00
10.	Vinayagar (Nehru Nagar)	20,000.00
11.	Kannan (Yadavar Kudiyiruppu)	25,000.00
12.	Sonai Kovil (MGR Nagar)	10,000.00
13.	Manchana Mariamman (Kovil Theru)	20,000.00
14.	Kali Kovil (Arunthodaiyar Colony)	40,000.00
	Total	5,25,000.00

Note : Information provided in parenthesis is the location of the temples.

He not only contributed money for construction of temple or renovation of temple or organizing festivals of temples but also to participate in the functions as a Hindu. He performs all rituals in the temples and Hindus allow him to do the same. He invites Hindus to his house during the festivals of the Muslim.

Another striking feature both a Hindu temple and a mosque in a same location and allowed the people of both the religion to pray peacefully in the same area. The importance which he gives for religious sentiments are much higher and it reflects in all his works. This kind of activity leads to the peaceful coexistence of people belonging to both the religions. Politicians in modern India plays with the religious sentiments of the people by arousing communal conflict to gain for their political upliftment. But men like Noor Mohammed who is much dignified spend his own money to secure the unity of the people of various religions which is otherwise opposed to each other and out of his own interest he protects the communal harmony of the village. He also further learns that only a leader can survive if he pays heed to the necessity of the community and interest of the people. From his exercise we can conclude that it is not the community which is communal in nature. Politicians are communal. At this juncture it is necessary for India to nurture, leaders like Mr. Noor Mohammed. He initiated temple activities in fourteen places. He has mobilized the needed resources and added his contribution and completed the task. It is strange to note that in all the temples people belonging to Hindu religion inscribed his name in either inside or outside the temple which is unique in the Panchayat. He made the people to maintain them neat and clean. He feels that he is doing a community work not the Panchayat work.

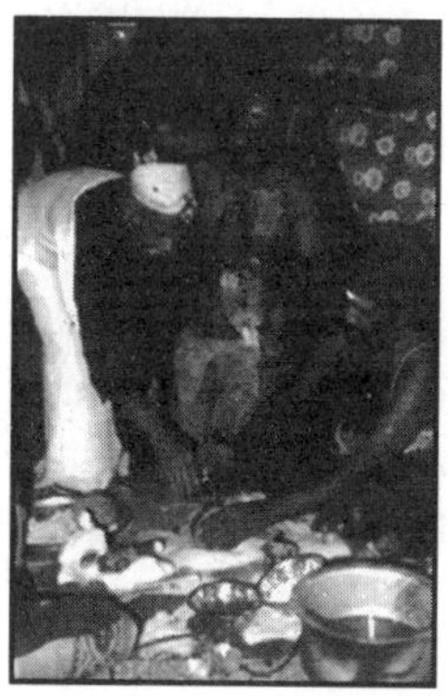

Participating in a Hindu Ritual

SC Colony Temple

Health and Sanitation

He also gave importance to the health and sanitation of the village. After undergoing a training on solid waste management he joined his hands with an NGO called Neat and Clean Service Squad (NACSS) to remove the garbage from the village. He said that it was because of the District Collector he attended a training programme he had decided to take a risk in garbage collection. His idea is to make a venture which is new which should attract all and beneficial to the people. Since his village is very near to Ramanathapuram town, it carried a heavy waste and the whole village was facing the problem of waste. Then he decided to invite the NGO to help the Panchayat in cleaning the village. The NGO has moved into his Panchayat area and started the work. He got the approval of the people for this new scheme. He created a structure for this new scheme by providing vehicle to collects the garbage and erecting two sheds for processing the waste. A very big open yard is given to the. He collects Rs.10 per house per month to remove the garbage and hands over Rs.23,500 to NACSS as their service charge. In turn NACSS through processing converts these wastes into manure and these manure is branded as "PUNYA" and sold at the cost of Rs.6 per kg. Totally 13 persons are working as a full-time member including one supervisor. These workers are paid by NACSS by the amount handed over by the Panchayat by collecting service charges from the houses. The Panchayat also earns money by selling the manure and minimum they get Rs.2000 and maximum they got Rs.3000 per month by selling "PUNYA" the manure. A shed has been constructed at the cost of Rs.60,000. In addition to these the Panchayat also gets Rs.4000 out of the service charges which they pay for NACSS. Further 13 persons, who worked early for a part-time now gets full-time job. Through this action the President has saved ecology from environmental degradation and he also earns wealth from the waste. By doing this exercise, people have been conscientized on cleanliness. President cannot make a village clean unless people of the village cooperate. The President said that he has succeed in his attempt to bring a culture among the people for cleanliness. Apart from the above activities he has concentrated on Total Rural Sanitation Programme and has constructed 600 toilets for individual houses. He has created awareness among the people through folk arts about the significance of health and sanitation and made the people to use the toilet compulsorily. One women sanitary complex is also constructed in the Panchayat and it is managed by the user group comprising self-help group members. A garden is well maintained adjacent to the complex with the waste water and drainage water from the complex.

Transforming Wealth from Waste

Workshed for Preparing PUNYA

Naming the Manure as 'PUNYA'

Concentration on SC Colony

He has provided all the facilities to the SC colony named after Gandhi. Group houses have been constructed for them and proper roads were laid. Adequate water supply is also provided to the people in that colony. At his own cost, a temple was also constructed for the Dalit for their to worship in that area. He also often visits the SC colony and enquire about their requirement. He also advices the people to take care for their health and hygiene and insists them to use the toilet properly. He has installed solar lamp in this colony and totally 17 solar lamps were installed in his Panchayat.

Gram Sabha

He draw 60 per cent of the members of Gram Sabha for Gram Sabha meeting at every time. Women's participation in Gram Sabha is more than the men members. He keeps school children also in the Gram Sabha meeting. As he fulfils many of his promises members inclined to participate in the Gram Sabha meeting. As he is a performer, people believe that whatever they discuss in the meeting that will be carried out. His crowd pulling capacity attracted the officials also.

Women

Totally 25 self-help groups are organized in the Panchayat and the Panchayat President has arranged for their earnings by giving them training on various activities and now these members are producing phenol, incense sticks, handicrafts, and some are hiring out kitchen utensils. Through this he has arranged income generating activity for women, who can look after their family better.

His Vision

He feels that a Panchayat leader can mobilize resources from within provided he or she has a commitment towards community. He or she should have resourcefulness to mobilize resources. Panchayat leader has to identify such opportunities and act on the opportunities. Being a business man by profession he finds various ways to mobilize resources. He further lamented that unless the Panchayat generates resources from within it has no future and it cannot be claimed it as self governing institution. He feels that Panchayat leader has to create an enabling environment to the people to lead a decent human living and especially for SC and ST. Still they are living in sub-human living conditions. Panchayat leader should provide needed infrastructural facilities and basic facilities to the communities. Further Panchayat should look after the vulnerable familities. All the above activities he considers as basic and must for Panchayat and that he will do the same in future also.

He will make the Panchayat accounts open for anybody's perusal. He involves the community in every action and thereby he inversed his strength and capability. He creates awareness among the people about livelihood security and how to get the works done in the government. Slowly people are empowered in his Panchayat.

Summary

Mr. Noor Mohammed by religion a Muslim respects all the religions and the secret of his success lies in the secular principle followed by him. His philanthropic character moulds him as a good leader of the people who follows two divergent religion and he made his Panchayat as a model for communal harmony. His second activity is the provision of water which is the primary requirement of the people which made him popular among the people. His concern for SC is yet another feather to his cap and his thirst for clean village earns income to his Panchayat, keeps the village clean and provided jobs to the poor people. Finally, all this character put together, Mr. Noor Mohammed emerged as a good leader serving the needs of the people at their door steps by maintaining communal harmony by providing infrastructure facilities.

District Collector and Other Hindus

Gram Sabha Participants

Gram Sabha Meeting

Dressing Room on the Banks of the Tank for Pilgrims

Profile of Panchayat

Chairperson	:	S.M. Noor Mohammed
Vice-Chairperson	:	A. Ibrahim
Ward Members	:	9 (4 male + 5 female) [G-3 + 1 SC]
Total Habitation	:	15

1. Sakkarakottai
2. Pasumpon Nagar
3. MGR Nagar
4. Manchana Mariamman Nagar
5. Sethu Nagar
6. Melachothurani
7. Kelachothurani
8. Mulla Nagar
9. Adam Nagar
10. Nehru Nagar
11. Bharathi Nagar
12. Svagnanapuram
13. Karikkuttam
14. Vani
15. Ayuthapadakaval Kudiyiruppu

Total Number of households	:	4367
Total Population	:	21292
FC & BC	:	18129
SC	:	3163
Hindus	:	13090
Muslims	:	8202

Table 2 : Details of Income and Expenditure (1997-1998)

Sl. No.	*Details of Income*	*Amount (Rs.)*	*Details of Expenditure*	*Amount (Rs.)*
1.	Opening Balance	100.00	Salary	26080.00
2.	House Tax	55589.00	TA	3525.00
3.	Library Tax	5528.00	Stationery	4009.00
4.	Professional Tax	25921.00	Electricity Charges for Street lights	35694.00
5.	Licence Tax	6101.00	Maintenance of Panchayat Office	2638.00
6.	Building Plan Approval	2350.00	Electricity Charges for Motor Pumps	9850.00
7.	Stamp Duty	24923.00	Maintenance of Street Lights	69236.00
8.	Entertainment Tax	21673.00	Expenditure of Public Health	84969.00
9.	Bank Interest	20448.00	Culverts	25947.00
10.	SFC Grant	83672.00	Funeral Grant	1200.00
11.	Other Subsidies	28323.00	New Building	60765.00
12.	Panchayat Union Fund	1119339.00	New Roads	679015.00
13.	Refund from EB	91485.00	Extension of Street Light	146526.00
14.			Extension of Drinking Water Supply	41863.00
15.			Miscellaneous	122.00
	Total	1485450.00	Total	1191439.00

Table 3 : Details of Income and Expenditure (1998-1999)

Sl. No.	*Details of Income*	*Amount (Rs.)*	*Details of Expenditure*	*Amount (Rs.)*
1.	House Tax	310720.00	Salary	29380.00
2.	Library Tax	33581.00	Bonus	2700.00
3.	Professional Tax	52514.00	President Travelling Allowance	1800.00
4.	Building Plan Approval	720.00	President and Ward Members Sitting Allowance	2250.00
5.	Vehicle Tax	183.00	Stationery	4820.00
6.	Other Tax	1506.00	Electricity Charges for Street Lights	59318.00
7.	SFC Grant	128583.00	Electricity Charges for Motor Pumps	19087.00
8.	Local Cess	620.00	Electricity Charges for Panchayat Office	8400.00
9.	House Tax Matching Grant	1334548.00	Maintenance of Streetlights	127191.00
10.	Stamp Duty Cess	36148.00	Maintenance of TV & Radio	1000.00
11.	Entertainment Tax	15736.00	Maintenance of Panchayat Office	9743.00
12.	Tender Deposit	8975.00	Maintenance of Culverts & Roads	51226.00
13.	Income From Bank Interest	16434.00	Refund of Deposit	11725.00
14.	Income from Bank Deposits	6194.00	Withdrawal of Bank Interest	36882.00
15.	Opening Balance	294011.00	Construction of Roads	186675.00
16.			Extension of Streetlights	1900.00
17.			Extension of Drinking Water Supply	4400.00
18.			Miscellaneous	19570.00
	Total	2240473.00	Total	578067.00

Table 4 : Details of Income and Expenditure (1999-2000)

Sl. No.	*Details of Income*	*Amount (Rs.)*	*Details of Expenditure*	*Amount (Rs.)*
1.	Opening Balance	1662406.00	Salary	29640.00
2.	House Tax	537521.00	TA	9300.00
3.	Library Tax	59411.00	Electricity Charges for Street Lights	89513.00
4.	Professional Tax	123220.00	Electricity Charges for Motor Pumps	18154.00
5.	Other Tax	88160.00	Electricity Charges for Panchayat Office	4013.00
6.	Stamp Duty	53391.00	Maintenance of Street Lights	215576.00
7.	SFC Grant	184845.00	Expenditure of Public Health	96000.00
8.	Income from Deposits	51704.00	Funeral Grant	8500.00
9.	Income from Bank Interest	600.00	Payment to District Library	5528.00
10.			Construction Culvert	46481.00
11.			Installation of Streetlights	79900.00
12.			Purchase of Other Instruments	10460.00
13.			Construction of Roads	2044988.00
14.			Miscellaneous	4322.00
	Total	2760628.00	Total	2673044.00

Table 5 : Details of Income and Expenditure (2000-2001)

Sl. No.	*Details of Income*	*Amount (Rs.)*	*Details of Expenditure*	*Amount (Rs.)*
1.	House Tax	766604.00	Salary	75860.00
2.	Library Tax	75359.00	Presidents Sitting Fee	2100.00
3.	SFC Grant	1494841.00	President and Ward Members Travelling Allowance	1575.00
4.	Funeral Grant	1000.00	Purchase of Paints and Salary door numbering	19525.00
5.	Building Plan Approval	4935.00	Stationery	225.00
6.	Professional Tax	136180.00	Bank Commission	75.00
7.	Income from Deposit	22321.00	Electricity Charges for Street Lights	36324.00
8.	Licence Fee	625.00	Electricity Charges for Motor Pumps	26292.00
9.	Schedule Fee	1352.00	Electricity Charges for Panchayat Office	15284.00
10.	Caution Deposit	44817.00	Installation of Sodium Vapour lamps	39365.00
11.	Fund for Sodium Vapour Lamp	17800.00	Digging of Deepwell	58790.00
12.	Fund for Play Ground	2000.00	Retaining Wall	245289.00
13.	House Tax – Matching Grant	151533.00	Funeral Grant	4000.00
14.	Mines	6903.00	Establishment Charges for Street name boards	25000.00
15.	………… Makkal Nala Paniyalar	1600.00	Construction of Roads	372792.00
16.	Opening Balance	87584.00	Construction of CC Road	159457.00
	Total	2815454.00	Total	1318818.00

Table 6 : Details of Income and Expenditure (2001-2002)

Sl. No.	*Details of Income*	*Amount (Rs.)*	*Details of Expenditure*	*Amount (Rs.)*
1.	Opening Balance	136552.00	Salary	79400.00
2.	House Tax	93841.00	Installation of Streetlights	35360.00
3.	Library Tax	84750.00	Electricity Charges	422950.00
4.	Professional Tax	49258.00	Funeral Grant	9500.00
5.	Other Tax	13650.00	Purchase of Electrical Goods	143570.00
6.	Cable Tax	9000.00	Maintenance of Motor Pumps	13760.00
7.	Cable Deposit	13650.00	Bank Commission	74.00
8.	Income from Other Source	257.00	Payment to District Library	62514.00
9.	Entertainment Tax	75164.00	Maintenance of Ponds	97500.00
10.	Funeral Grant	4500.00	Transfer to Small Savings	900000.00
11.	SFC Grant	163550.00	Expenditure on Public Health	38250.00
12.	Mines	32912.00	Purification of Drainage Water	11540.00
13.	House Tax Matching Grant	711214.00	Maintenance of Road	189643.00
14.	Bank Interest	596.00	Transfer of Account From 1 to 2	32076.00
15.	Local Cess	8307.00	Travelling Allowance	2200.00
16.	Stamp Duty	18000.00		
17.	Interest from Other Sources	4523.00		
18.	Amount from Deposit	2935.00		
	Total	2374262.00	Total	2098337.00

Table 7 : Details of Income and Expenditure (2002-2003)

Sl. No.	*Details of Income*	*Amount (Rs.)*	*Details of Expenditure*	*Amount (Rs.)*
1.	House Tax	1797896.00	Salary	98800.00
2.	Library Tax	177415.00	Removal of Garbages	183300.00
3.	Professional Tax	68687.00	Electricity Charges for Street Lights	336797.00
4.	Bank Interest	5475.00	Purchase of Electrical Goods	402560.00
5.	Other Tax	12730.00	Funeral Grant	1500.00
6.	Local Cess	4820.00	Payment to District Library	25200.00
7.	Stamp Duty	237556.00	Installation of Solar Light	50920.00
8.	Repayment from Audit Objection	110.00	Construction of Roads	45197.00
9.	SFC Grant	281832.00	Transfer from Account 1 to 2	8019.00
10.	Collection for Individual Toilet	77106.00	Establishment Charges for Street Name Boards	83000.00
11.	Interest from Small Savings	105.00	Purchase of Other Instruments	47000.00
12.	Opening Balance	273925.00	Threshing Floor	78000.00
13.			Removal of Throny Bushes	91050.00
14.			Removal of Pigs	97400.00
15.			Bank Commission	94.00
16.			Removal of Wastages from Streets	37000.00
	Total	2937657.00	Total	1585837.00

Table 8 : SGRY Works Carried Out

Sl. No	Year	Amount (Rs.)
1.	1996-1997	5,56,266
2.	1997-1998	32,000
3.	1998-1999	36,000
4.	1999-2000	80,196

Table 9 : Works Carried Out in the Scheme Fund

Sl. No.	Year	Name of the Work	Amount (Rs.)
1.	1996-1997	Retaining wall	60,000
2.	1997-1998	Shopping complex (SGRY Work)	80,000
3.	1998-1999	Group house – 10 (IAY)	51,20,000
4.	1999-2000	Latrine	25,000
5.	2000-2001	Retaining wall	1,10,000
6.	2001-2002	Cement road	1,60,000
7.	2002-2003	Retaining wall Thrashing floor Women training centre	85,000 60,000 1,00,000
8.	2003-2004	Panchayat Officer (work programme) Open well Kitchen shed	1,95,000 80,000 82,000

Table 10 : Works Carried Out in the 11th Finance

Sl. No	Work	Amount (Rs.)
1.	Road	Rs.60,000
2.	Pipeline	Rs.50,000
3.	Open Well	Rs.60,000

Table 11 : Works Carried Out in the Panchayat Fund

Sl. No	Work	Amount (Rs.)
1.	Road	6,00,000
2.	Open Well	82,000
3.	Street lights	5,00,000

Table 12 : ***Works Carried Out in the MP and MLA Fund***

Sl. No	Work	Fund
1.	Kalyana Mahal – 5	MP Fund
2.	Retaining Wall	MLA Fund
3.	Pipeline	MLA Fund
4.	Ration Shop – 1	MLA Fund
5.	Thar Road	MLA Fund

CASE-4

SYNERGY BETWEEN TRADITIONAL AND CONSTITUTIONAL PANCHAYATS

> *Rani Sathappan is a calm and very assertive Gram Panchayat leader. She had been given several awards for her good initiative and for eradicating the use of polythene material in her Panchayat area. Her transparency and democratic way of functioning have made the traditional Panchayat leaders very cooperative to her activities. Her single-handed devotion to natural resource management has drawn the attention of farmers. All tanks and water bodies are full of water during the rainy season as she has desilted and deepened the tanks and ponds. Her approach of involving all the stakeholders in the implementation of programmes has made the people participate in all the activities of the Panchayat.*

Socio-Economic Background

Ms. S. Rani Sathappan, aged 32, is the President of K. Rayavaram Village Panchayat. She is married and has two sons. Her husband is serving as an overseer in Kallal Union of Sivagangai District. She has studied up to +2. After her school final, she joined the B.Lit. course, but discontinued it as she got admission to the teacher training course. That course also she discontinued as she was married at the age of 19 years. Even though it is more than 12 years since, her interest in studying is not gone. Now she is studying M.A. History through correspondence course. She was a sportsperson during her school days. Volleyball was her favourite game. She served as a district player. Moreover she showed interest in celebrating Pongal and temple festivals along with the villagers. From these experiences she understood public affairs. She belongs to the Vallambar caste. It is one of the components in the Mukkalothor community (one of the most backward communities).

After her marriage she was away from K. Rayavaram as her husband served in various block offices for 10 years. But she and her family used to visit her own house in K. Rayavaram village frequently. Her husband, who is an engineer, showed interest in village life. Whenever he visited K. Rayavaram, he met the village elders and shared his views with them regarding the village development activities initiated by the Village Committee (traditional). Her father-in-law showed interest in village activities. He belongs to the All India Anna Dravida Munnetra Kazhagam (AIADMK). His constructive participation during the Village Committee meetings brought him a name. Due to this reputation Rani's name was suggested when the Village President's position was reserved for women (general). Rani Sathappan was a sympathizer of the Indian National Congress for long.

Recruitment

The Village Committee met to take a decision on the selection of a candidate unopposed. But there was opposition to this idea. So the Village Committee did not take any decision. Rani's father-in-law was told to field her and the majority of the members agreed to support her. The opponent belonged the Dravida Munnetra Kazhagam (DMK) Party. Though her father-in-law was a cadre of the AIADMK Party, she never projected herself politically. Moreover, the villagers openly encouraged her candidature as she was better educated than the opponent. Rani's husband readily agreed to this proposal as his wife would be a letter choice to make use of his expertise for village development. Rani had no reservations and agreed to contest in the election.

Rani and the six contestants for the Wards joined together as a group. They made two rounds and house by house and visited all the families. The opponent also belonged to her community and was also her relative. There was a tough competition, but they observed peace and so there was no untoward incident.

The villagers had a lot of expectations from the New Panchayati Raj. Earlier, during the period of officials, no one represented the village and so no development activities were carried out in the village. The Government officials did not have an opportunity to understand the socio-economic problems of the village as the village is located on the border of Sivagangai District. Moreover, there is another village named Rayavaram where the business community of

Chettiars live. Generally, if any reference is made to K. Rayavaram, officials used to remember the other Rayavaram only. So this village could not get any attention from the Government officials.

Against this backdrop, Rani's entry into the Village Panchayat might change the scenario, the villagers felt, and so there was a lot of expectations from the election. At least the name of K. Rayavaram could easily come to the memory of officials, the villagers hopefully believed.

Though her father-in-law belonged to the AIADMK Party, she was a staunch supporter of the Tamil Maanila Congress (TMC). The simplicity of G.K. Moopanar attracted her. But she could not become a full time politician. When the opportunity was given to her, she was happy to contest in the election as her husband explained to her and asked her to give the best of her ability to bring about a new name and fame to the village by serving as a good President under the New Panchayati Raj System. With this expectation the villagers elected her by a difference of 174 votes.

Leadership Sustained

The first tenure under the new Panchayat Raj System came to an end by September 2001. Rani decided not to contest again due to family responsibilities. But the villagers preferred her for the second term also, as the seat had been once again reserved for women. The Village Committee met and decided to unanimously elect the same President and Vice-President for the second tenure also. Rani respected the feelings of the villagers and accepted.

In the meantime, one of her close relatives decided to field his wife, who is an elderly woman. He came to Rani and advised her to contest for the Union Councillor's position. She frankly replied that since the villagers had decided to field her she had to respect them and so she would not withdraw her nomination. There was a straight contest. As per the advice of the village elders, she made arrangements for bringing voters who are living away from the village. The election campaign was effectively handled by Rani with the support of SHG members. She won again with a 184 vote margin — this time 10 votes more than the pervious time.

The reasons behind her success are

1. The Village Committee expected someone who would be an active President.
2. Her father-in-law is an active and constructive participant during the Village Committee meetings.
3. Her husband is educated and working in the Panchayat Union.
4. She is better educated than the opponent and her social commitment is known to other women.

Village Setup

K. Rayavaram is a small Panchayat which does not have any hamlet. About 200 families of Vallambar, 50 families of Udayar, 30 families of Valayar and 20 families of other castes like Vellalar, Velar, Asari and Pandaram are residing in the village. It is said that there is no family from the SC community. Vallambars are the dominant caste and Udayars are the second majority. They have a separate residential area just away from the main settlement. There is no caste association in the village. The youth tried to organise themselves as an association, but, due to poverty and unemployment, their spirit diminished and so they failed in their attempt.

Political Parties

The DMK, the AIADMK, the TMC and the Marumalarchi Dravida Munnetra Kazhagam (MDMK) are the parties in the village. There are no serious activities from the side of the political parties. The TMC cadres give their time for public activities as she is one of the three district secretaries nominated by the TMC Party.

Village Temples

Ayyanar Kovil and Perumal Kovil are the important temples. A Vellar and an Iyyangar are the *poojaris* in the Ayyanar and the Perumal temples respectively. The Perumal temple was renovated recently. Though it is common to all, a few families of the Udayar community spent a lot of money for the renovation. Pachaiamman and Mariamman are the Amman temples. Mariamman is common to all, whereas Pachaiamman is only for the Udayar community.

There is a Kaman Kovil in which an Asari is the *poojari*. The celebration of the Kaman festival is a popular and memorable event in the village. It draws people from nearby villages also. The Ayyanar temple celebration is facilitated by the Panchayat with the suggestion to maintain peace and to settle differences of opinion among the villagers.

Village Committee

A traditional Village Committee exists in the village. The Ambalam is the head of the Committee and there are members from the major communities. The Committee meeting is usually convened near the *oorani*, under a tree. Only men are allowed to participate in the meetings. Village affairs like organising of temple festivals, maintenance of public assets like oorani, trees in poramboke lands, conciliation between disputing parties are the major dealings of the Village Committee. When the goat rearers entered the Iyar *oorani* and the PWD *kanmai*, where a number of saplings are growing and damaged the saplings, the issue was brought to the notice of the Village Committee. The issue was discussed in the Gram Sabha meeting also. The Village Committee asked those families who rear the goats not to enter the *oorani* and damage the saplings. Rani's interaction with the Ambalam is very limited, as she is not permitted to attend the Village Committee meeting. Her husband attends the Village Committee meetings and explains the details.

Sections and groups in a village community are used to conflicts due to difference of opinion, particularly in respect of temple celebrations. K.Rayavaram is not an exception. Two different

Traditional Panchayats Appreciates Rani Sathappan

Traditional Panchayats Appreciates Rani Sathappan

groups claimed that the 'Muthal Mariathai', i.e. the first honour, had to be given to its leader. This resulted in the stoppage of temple celebration for a decade.

The Panchayat Council decided to try its best to bring the two opposing parties to a peaceful solution. Rani took special interest in this regard and she played a vital role in bringing about a settlement between those groups and, at last the temple *kumbabisekam* was performed successfully along with the festival celebrations. The villagers felt very happy about the restoration of peace and harmony.

Since then, the traditional village community started to share formally and informally with the Village Panchayat and *vice versa*. The mutual understanding and cooperation between these two institutions created a healthy working atmosphere for the Village Panchayat administration. Activities like tax-collection, selection of works, worksite and beneficiaries, protection of community assets, participation in Gram Sabha meetings, SHG functions and social control in the monitoring of drinking water supply distribution etc., are being effectively and successfully carried out to the satisfaction of the villagers and officials. Rani acknowledged that she could impress the higher officials only by good performance, for which the traditional committee extended support.

Common Property Resources

There are three ooranis and four *kanmais*. Two kanmais belong to the PWD and two *kanmais* are under the Union. Under the Social Forestry Scheme trees are planted and a watchman is employed by the Panchayat. In the oorani poramboke, velikaruvel trees are grown. As they are more than three years old, the Panchayat decided to auction the trees and approached the RDO for getting permission. Some officials expected a bribe, but Rani was determined not to give any. In the meantime, in the presence of the BDO, through an open tender, the auction was conducted for Rs.16,950. The tender was awarded. But the RDO did not respond with the sanction order to cut the trees. At last, after the transfer of the field officials by chance, Rani met the higher officials and got the order. In the meantime, more than two years had gone by. Red-tapism in the Government departments is a handicap in bringing about development. But, at the same time, people are not ready to hear excuses from the President. The people wish to achieve immediately what they want.

Desilted Channels and tanks

When there was an encroachment on the inlet channel by an individual belonging to a nearby village, the Panchayat decided to deal with the issue carefully. Otherwise there would be a clash between the two villages. They petitioned the District Collector and the Chief Minister. Rani attended the monthly grievance day and brought the matter to the attention of the District Collector. When the District Collector arranged for an inspection by the revenue officials, the revenue officials twisted the matter. They threatened that they would become enquiry officers and book the Panchayat President, if she did not obeying the officials. But the President complained against the revenue officials. Due to this difference of opinion and egoism, it was all delayed. At last the inspection was done and the officials agreed to arrange for the removal of the encroachment. As there was no action, again the issue was reported. Whenever the higher officials asked for a file/paper, the department officials used to reply negatively. As the Panchayat maintained photocopies of all their correspondence in this regard, they immediately produced them and again the issue became alive. In spite of that the encroachment is not yet removed. It is more than three years of struggle with the bureaucrats. These trials and tribulations led to her belief in the maximum "Efforts will bring about change". This slogan is printed on her official letter pad.

During the initial period, her focus was on the provision of minimum basic amenities to the villagers. In course of time she came to understand the problems of farmers. On several occasions, during the Gram Sabha meetings, the village elders and the members of traditional committee urged her to take us activities related to protection and promotion of common properties, especially irrigation tanks and ooranis in the village. Hence she was determined to work on that aspect more seriously.

Table 1 : Tanks and Ooranis in K. Rayavaram

Sl. No.	*Name*	*Category*	*Total Extent Average*	*Ayakat Average*
1.	Pappankulam	PWD	21.00.0	48.66.5
2.	Pudu Kanmoi	PWD	24.91.0	66.80.0
3.	Narathar Kanmoi	Union	9.29.0	36.66.0
4.	Sivan Kanmoi	Union	10.62.0	14.92.0
5.	Nachiar Oorani	Village Panchayat	0.54.5	-
6.	Iyyar Oorani	Village Panchayat	0.32.0	-
7.	Nambakulam Oorani	Village Panchayat	2.55.0	-
8.	Nambi Oorani	Village Panchayat	1.81.50	-
9.	Peevetti Oorani	Village Panchayat	0.49.0	-

Source : Computed.

As agriculture is the major source of the village economy, after realizing the expectation of the villagers through Gram Sabha meetings, the Village Panchayat President Rani gave priority to improving the above mentioned tanks and ooranis. Whenever there was a scope for availing of any scheme fund not only from the Department of Rural Development but also from other seectoral departments like agriculture, agricultural engineering, agro forestry, etc., the Village Panchayat made all necessary attempts to harness the fund assistance. Accordingly, desilting and deepening of tanks and ooranis, strengthening of bunds, removal of throny bushes and wild weeds, protection of standing trees and planting of more trees, maintenance of supply channels, and construction of ghat for public utility were carried out successfully, involving the village community in the planning and the execution of the works. The above mentioned activities were carried out with the scheme fund provided by the Government Departments.

Table 2 : Availing of Schemes for Protecting and Managing Common Property Resources

Sl. No.	*Source*	*Fund Assistance Total*
1.	Social Forestry Scheme Fund	250 saplings — tree planting — eucalyptus and non-fruit bearing trees
2.	NGO contribution	Rs.50,000 worth of food grain
3.	Community contribution — Namakku Naame Thittam	Rs. 50,000
4.	Community contribution	Rs.30,000
5.	NAWAPRA	Rs.66,000
6.	Agricultural Engineering Department	Rs.30,000
7.	Agricultural Engineering Department	Rs.75,000
8.	Special SGRY Fund	Rs.2.0 lakhs
9.	SGRY	Rs.33,000
10.	SGRY	Rs.50,000 (work in progress)

Source : Computed.

Village Economy

There are about 150 farmers. Most of the lands are rainfed and about 40 pumpsets are available in the village. Paddy, groundnut, black gram and sugarcane are the main crops. Sugarcane is profitable, as there is an assured price for the same, whereas the selling price of the other crops always fluctuates. The rain water stored in the PWD and the Union kanmais will be available only for three to four months. Moreover, the encroachment on the inlet channel is preventing the full flow of flood water. Due to lack of economic activities in the village, about 50 families as a whole and about 50 individual men and youth have migrated to other places. A number of youth are working in a cotton mill located at Pallathur, 10 km from the village. They go by bicycle for work. As the lifestyle is very hard, the youth prefer to take rest rather than spare time for youth association activities.

SHGs

The concept of SHGs is only now picking up in the Panchayat. There are five groups and the group meetings are convened every week on Tuesdays at their respective places. Rani is also a member in a group. After the starting of SHGs the women are training their mind to social matters. They discuss the necessity of maintaining public hygiene and the personal cleanliness of their children. The SHG members attend the Gram Sabha meetings. After understanding the poor financial position of the

Planning for Women Development

Panchayat and the availability of Government grant if the house tax is collected fully, the women are helping in the collection of house tax. Three SHGs have got bank loans. They planned a tour programme to get exposure to various self-employment opportunities along with visiting temples and hill stations. Rani assisted in finalising the places in this regard. Due to the presence of SHGs they are witnessing changes in the perception of the menfolk too. They are now coming to realize the efficiency of womenfolk.

The SHG movement has not made any serious impact in K. Rayavaram. The non-governmental organizations serving in this area organize women into SHGs but the impact was not seriously felt. It was only after her exposure trip to Raligoah Village in Maharashtra that she realized the importance of women groups and, with the guidance of block officials she initiated the group formation activity. It was possible only after convincing the menfolk of concerned families. Now there are seven self-help groups and the membership altogether is 105.

Through the initiative of The Hunger Project, the Gandhigram Rural Institute concept of preparation of Development Plan was undertaken in the Village Panchayat. To attend an orientation programme, Rani along with the SHG leaders, visited Gandhigram, where they had an exposure to various khadi and village industries. Their SHG, after returning, asked her to help them in getting training from some association. She met the district officials and succeeded in getting permission for a member of SHG members to undergo training in paper bag production. The trained women, in turn, gave training to fellow members. They made an attempt to produce but did not succeed in this venture. In the meantime, credit with subsidy was sanctioned to one group. Various trades were analysed. At last it was decided to engage in vessels/chair/furniture business, renting them out for social and home celebration. It is running at a profit as the group keeps three sets of vessels and other materials.

Planning for Women Development

As the other group members were interested in some other activities, without waiting for government assistance, they themselves contributed to get training in the production of toilet soap, washing powder and cleaning powder. They produced toilet soaps and, during the Gram Sabha meeting they sold out. Raw materials were been purchased from the Madurai wholesale market.

SHGs need professional guidance for its organizational as well as economic activities. At present she has equipped herself to fill the leadership gap. Through this exercise, she has more opportunities to move closely with the womenfolk. They used to share their family problems, personal problems as well as group issues. When she came to know that the literacy rate among the members was low, a non-formal education centre was organized by the group itself, engaging local educated young men and women. Now the SHG is her supporter. It has its impact on the village community also. If any woman President possesses determination to work with the SHGs, she can succeed, as in her case, Rani declared.

Educating the Masses

There are umpteen number of schemes available for the welfare of the marginalized sector, especially for women in the sectoral Department of Social Welfare.

Awareness creation display

SHG meeting in Progress

Even educated citizens cannot know all the details in this regard. So awareness has to be created among the public. But, creating mass awareness is not an easy task. Rani did an innovation in this regard. She met the district officials, NGOs and other concerned institutions and, with their guidance and assistance, she organized an exhibition in the village itself. Pictures, charts, photos, paintings, panels reporting the various schemes available in the Social Welfare and the Literacy Department were exhibited. The importance of women empowerment was explained with the help of field officials and educated youth volunteers. All the women in K. Rayavaram came in groups and spent a whole day there.

Performance

Rani was an ignorant women when she contested in the Panchayat election. But, during the canvassing, she came to understand the public, their expectations, the issues and the official procedures. After assuming the position, her husband regularly briefed her on the details of various schemes in Panchayat administration. He encouraged her independent leadership and so she used to meet officials without her husband. The Vice-President is a public spirited person. He personally takes up several issues and tries to meet and explain to the officials. Because of this mutual cooperation and involvement they are able to run the administration smoothly. Once the water supply seemed to become an issue as there were a lot of illegal connections and extension of pipeline in a disorderly manner. This had happened before she assumed office under the Panchayati Raj System. They discussed this issue in the Panchayat Council meetings and decided to take necessary steps to disconnect all illegal connections. The block officials were properly told of this step. They reported the matter to the police station also. As requested, the BDO accompanied them during the operation for disconnection, which went on successfully.

For smooth distribution of water supply in an equitable way, they decided to provide 22 public taps. They gave the responsibility to select the suitable places to the concerned families which live on the street. Two to three days' time was given for finalising the site. After that Rani, the Vice-President and two Members went to the people and noted down the places selected by them. Accordingly, the public taps were provided. This exercise was smoothly carried out, as they entrusted the responsibility to the concerned street. And then it was decided to give individual tap connections. As per the government order, after verifying with the TWAD officials, they provided individual tap connections to 42 houses though they had been permitted to give 70 connections. They limited the number anticipating the future need for public taps.

Interfacing with Officials

In general, officials pose as authorities. They never patiently apply their mind to understand the explanations given by the President. The authorities, without verifying the facts with the Panchayat, adjusted a portion of the SFC for the payment of arrears to the Electricity Board. But, in fact, there was no arrears as the Panchayat had properly paid the electricity bills. Rani met the concerned official, but he was not ready to give any serious attention. Rani took up the matter with the Collector and he called the concerned officer and ordered him to correct himself. Later it was done, but all this could be avoided if mutual understanding exists between officials and the President. Their mindset has to be changed.

She cited another issue as an example. It was said that a sum of Rs.30,000 was due to the Union and they proposed to deduct the same. Rani opposed the decision and so they appointed a committee to verify the earlier transactions of all the Village Panchayats. It was found that Rs.30,000 was due to the Panchayat from the Union. In spite of this the Union has not yet released the money to the Panchayat.

The problem in the payment of electricity bills in Pudukottai is always an issue. This is due to the functioning of the Thirumayam Rural Electricity Cooperative Society, which is authorised to distribute electricity to villages and to collect the bill amount. There is no office of the Electricity Board with a good system of administration and adequate staff. The Society does not seem to be an able institution in this regard. It is reported that only in Pudukottai and Kumbakonam these types of societies are involved in the distribution of electricity.

If the officials properly guide the Panchayat, they can avoid friction. During a Gram Sabha meeting, it was suggested to employ a watchman to safeguard the tree saplings planted in the oorani and the kanmai. Accordingly, a watchman was employed with a monthly honorarium of Rs.150. But the expenses incurred on the honorarium for the watchman were objected to during the audit. The official pointed out only then that a mere resolution of the Gram Sabha is not sufficient, but that the Collector has to sanction the appointment. So, from the month of August 2000, the watchman was sent off and the Rs.1,650 paid to him was objected to. The officer instructed the President to pay the amount.

A copy of the deliberations of each Gram Sabha meeting is submitted to the officials. But it is treated merely as a ceremony. The concerned officials do not give their time and mind to go through the reports and give their observations. For their failure the Panchayat President is unnecessarily punished.

The Panchayat President should be very keen and vigilant in availing of the schemes from the Government. Otherwise they will be lifted by some other Panchayat. Due to difference of opinion between the President of one Panchayat and a District Council Member who belongs to the same Panchayat, a provision for group houses to six BC beneficiaries was cancelled. Rani heard of this incident and immediately met the Project Officer and succeeded in availing of the same. Getting group houses for BCs is really a tough task. Only during the allocation to SCs a few houses can be earmarked for BCs. In Rani's village there is no SC family and so the allocation of group houses does not come to the Panchayat. At this juncture she came to know of the above incident and succeeded in getting 6 houses to the poor BC families in her village.

Maintaining linkage with the other elected representatives is essential to develop the village. In the present system of fund allocation under various schemes through different elected representatives, Rani realised the importance of each of them. She met them, shared her village's poor financial position and got allocations from those representatives. Under the allocation by the District Council, a PDS shop and a kitchen shed and a BT road were provided at a total cost of Rs. 6.75 lakhs. With the help of the Union Councillor and the Union Chairman, with whom she has a good rapport, additional school buildings, TV room and a BT road were provided at a total cost of Rs.3.65 lakhs. The MLA and the MP were also kind enough to her village. A library was constructed under the MP Fund scheme at a cost of Rs.75,000. Construction of a bus shelter and a community hall, installation of a hand pump and black topping of a road were carried out under the MLA area development scheme. The total estimate for these works was Rs. 6.20 lakhs. Under the TWAD assistance an OHT was constructed at a cost of Rs. 0.30 lakh. The Panchayat is a weak one with regard to finance. By proper representation to the Collector they got sanction for provision of one hand pump in the village.

Mobilising Community Support

Desilting of the supply channel was referred to the Gram Sabha meeting. Rani suggested that the work could be taken up through the Namakku Naame Thittam (NNT) as there was no allocation for desilting work in the Panchayat under any other head. She explained it to the farmers. Though there was no association among the farmers she met them in a group and it was decided to get contribution from each farmer. No amount was fixed in this regard but the estimate of the work and the quantum of peoples' contribution was explained. Rs.12,500 was collected as people's contribution. Even a donation of ten rupees was accepted and accounted for. By using a JCB machine the desilting was done properly. Farmers participated in the work.

Overcoming an Attempt of Block Marking on the Village

The sales of illicit liquor was totally pretended through social control in the Village Panchayat jurisdiction. To ensure its sustainability the Village Panchayat Council used to serve as a watchdog in this regard. Those individuals who had personal differences with the Ward Members schemed a plot against two Ward Members. They arranged false evidence of illicit distillation in the fields of two Ward Members and made a false complaint to the prohibition wing mobile police unit against the two Ward Members. The mobile police force entered the village and arrested the two members though it was a false complaint. It was informed to the President and immediately Rani came to the roadside and prevented the police van from moving on. The police official told her to come to police station for an enquiry and drove away the vehicle.

Rani made telephone calls to the local police officer and, as per his guidance, contacted the higher officials. Understanding the reality, they quickly moved into action. In the same day night, along with the key persons of the village, she visited the mobile police unit and explained to them that it was a false case and revealed the names of those individuals who were involved in the arrangement of false evidence. The police brought those individuals and verified the truth. At last the issue was settled amicably.

Being a woman, it was unusual to intervene in a police case, that too in a case of prohibition raid Rani felt. But to prevent a bad name for K. Rayavaram during her leadership, she stepped in boldly and succeeded in disproving the falsification attempt to first a false case.

Gender Sensitization

The Union Chairman is a woman. She encouraged the Panchayat to organise sports for women. They conducted competitions like running, musical chair, rangoli etc. Even elderly women took part in the running race. Women have also feelings and aspirations, which need an outlet. The SHG is successfully handling micro credit activities. Milch animals have been purchased and the economic standard has improved. "If the talent of women is harvested, society will develop quickly" is the realisation of the public. The respect accorded to Rani by the public is a fitting example of women's empowerment. All these changes in the status of women have happened due to two main reasons, namely, the reservation for women in the Panchayati Raj System and the drive to organise SHGs by the government itself.

Panchayat Meeting

There are only two Wards for which there are 6 Members. Of them 4 are men and 2 are women. As all are living in the village, there is no absence. All attend the meetings regularly. There is no serious issue in general. All their interest is to improve the village. Rani used to explain the efforts initiated with various sectoral departments on which she requests their opinions and suggestions. On considering the poor financial status, they have all decided not to avail of the sitting fee permissible to them. The TA of Rs.300 is not availed of by Rani. In this way the members are very cooperative.

Gram Sabha Meeting

The Gram Sabha meeting is usually convened near the oorani which is near the Panchayat office. It is the common place where the Village Committee also meets.

Proper intimation is given to the people and SHGs and so there is a good response. About 70 to 80 persons attend the meeting. They inform the people that TA and sitting fee are not availed of by the President and the Members. The various details of fund allocation are explained. Income and expenditure are explained. The people do not appreciate the efforts in availing of funds from other sources, as they know of the MLA Fund, the MP Fund and the Councillors' Fund. But a few others explain to them that even these allocations are not mandatory but it is only by the initiative of the President and the Panchayat that they are availed of.

Gram Sabha Meeting

Rani explained the efforts of the Panchayat in minimising the expenditure. The Panchayat fund is saved by proper planning and execution. Any repairs to the water supply system are attended to by local persons and there is no falsification in replacing the tube lights etc. All these are explained in the Gram Sabha meetings. There is no false voucher showing works like street maintenance or clearing of bushes. There are not many vouchers for incidental expenses in the accounts. All these details are properly explained in the Gram Sabha meeting. Due to this the Panchayat is able to find funds from the Panchayat account and the construction of three culverts and gravelling of road were carried out at a total cost of Rs.1.17 lakhs. After understanding these activities, the villagers give more respect to the Panchayat.

Social Development

Additional building, water supply, toilet, kitchen shed are provided to the school. The District Primary Education Programme is implemented in the district and the Panchayat school is also covered. Educational equipments are provided through this scheme. The Parent Teachers Association is active. When out of three teachers one teacher was shifted to another school, the Panchayat took up the issue and, with the help of the MLA, they met the DEO and succeeded in retaining the teacher. But, later in the year, due to poor strength, one teacher was shifted. About 20 to 25 children are going to a private English medium school. The Panchayat was not able to prevent them. This was reflected in the primary school strength resulting in the shifting of one teacher. At this juncture the Parent Teachers Association came forward to employ one teacher locally and the payment of Rs.250 to her was given by the Parent Teachers Association.

Rani used to meet the VHN during her visits and discuss activities like immunization. The scheme benefiting girl children, insurance coverage to SHG members, insurance coverage to marginal farmers etc. are properly explained. Rani helps in these activities. About 30 farmers are covered so far. A common graveyard is provided. A pucca approach road is provided to the common graveyard. Under the CRSP 39 toilets are provided and 50 additional toilets are going to be constructed; 18 new street lights and 6 sodium vapour lamps are also provided; and, 12 group hoses are provided to poor BC people of all castes. The selection is done in the Gram Sabha meeting. The real poor, who live in huts, are identified from each community: 6 from the Vallambar and one each from Barber, Dhobi, Valayar, Kanakkar, Udayar and Vellalar communities. One Jeevandhara well was provided to a marginalised farmer. Health camp and veterinary camps were organised. 200 RD savings accounts were opened through a mobilization drive in the post office. Rani played a vital role in this achievement.

Helping the Old

Medical Camp organised

Rani herself explained the process by which she completely eradicated polythene from her Village Panchayat. It is now a plastics free village. She has become President for a second term and is continuing her activities. She became President of the Panchayat in the first period because of the reservation of seats for women. But now she has become President on her own by projecting her achievements in the first period and seeking the mandate of the people based on her performance. She scored a breakthrough in abolishing plastics and polythene in the Panchayat because of an accident that took place in the village. Two milch animals died after swallowing polythene materials dumped in dust bins. Taking this tragedy to the Gram Sabha, she discussed this issue with the people. Having convinced the people, she evolved the norm that no one should use plastic articles in the Panchayat area and that individuals who violated it would be penalized. The people consented and the entire village has been made plastics free. For this exercise she got needed support from the SHG women leaders.

Yet another breakthrough she has scored in the Panchayat is establishing community action. There are two very big tanks in her Panchayat area. Normally such tanks are desilted and renovated by the PWD. But the PWD did not take care of the two tanks. She sent petitions to the PWD. There was no response. She convened the Gram Sabha and discussed the issue with the members of the Gram Sabha. They passed a resolution that it should be reported to the District Collector for appropriate action. In the meanwhile, they decided to desilt the tank on their own because the monsoon was approaching and before that the tank had to be desilted. The entire tank was desilted with the help of the community. The SHG women provided lunch to the people who worked in the tank. Community power was demonstrated for which the Panchayat President was responsible.

Execution of Contract Work

Three works were executed by Rani's in-laws. There was no loss and, at the same time, they ensured quality. The officials, after inspection, certified the work as the best. A loss was incurred when a culvert was constructed. The tender works were carried out as per her huband's advice. His professional knowledge and experience are much helpful in these works.

Corruption

For the Panchayat work the officials did not expect any bribe. But as per the Vice-President's advice a small amount was given to the development department officials. Rani never got any favour from the contractors. And so the contractors showed preference to undertake works in this Panchayat.

House Tax

When the Panchayat assumed power the house tax demand was Rs.6000 only. Hence they enhanced the house tax immediately from Rs.6000 to Rs.10,120. After explaining the government instructions and the financial position of the Panchayat to the people, there was no opposition to the proposal for enhancement of house tax. The whole demand is collected without any arrears.

Capacity Building Experience

Having attended the training programmes organised by the Department of Rural Development, SIRD, RETC, NGO and GRI, Rani's understanding of Panchayati Raj and its scope has improved. On 8.3.1999, when the world women's day was observed, an award was given to her as the best woman President at the district level. In the year 2000, she got the third position. After witnessing her hard work and independent nature, Rani was selected as the only

President of Village Panchayats in a team to have an exposure to a village where the watershed related activities are carried out as a model. Rani learned accounts maintenance through a clerk there. The clerk was a young woman. Now only she is picking up. She got an award of Rs.1.00 lakh for the best Panchayat in the year 1999-2000. A shopping complex is now constructed at a cost of Rs.1.50 lakhs from the award fund, adding the available Panchayat fund. A doctor, a barber and a vendor have come forward to take the shops on rent.

Receiving Awards

Yet another milestone in her Panchayat administration is settling a dispute over a tank. A tank which can store water for a year was under dispute. Nobody took responsibility and the government departments did not allow the Panchayats to take over also. Water has to be stored in the tank during the rainy season. She appealed to the District Collector and he sanctioned Rs.2 lakhs for desilting the tank but she had to get the no objection certificate from the Public Works Department. She went back and forth to get the no objection certification. At last, with great difficulty, she got the letter and gave the entire money to a committee which has done the excellent work in the Panchayat by desilting and deepening the tank. Further the committee has saved some amount and the Panchayat has decided to utilize the money for constructing toilets for the ultra-poor families in this Panchayat who are unable to give their share for the total sanitation programme. By keeping the village neat and clean she got an award from the District Collector. She received Rs.50,000.

The Suffering

The responsibility of a Village Panchayat President is tough. It needs full time attention. Visiting various offices, meeting officials, revisiting for persuasion, interacting with villagers, overseeing the works and office administration and the lists are tedious. A woman who has dual responsibilities cannot find time for all these activities. Frequently meetings are arranged in Pudukottai, the headquarters of the district. It is 40 km from the village. Sometimes they have to contact the district officials. Due to this she is not able to look after her two sons and their studies. Her younger son's standard of education is now-a-days going down and she feels sorry for this. Her elder son is studying in 7th standard and he openly criticises her functioning and he advises her to discontinue the services at least from the next time.

Her husband is very much attached to the village. He wishes to change the village into a developed one and asks for her support. He advises her to contest again, at least for another term, so that a minimum level of development is accomplished by them. In general, the officials are responsive only if the President meets them. She has to go over to all the officials. The Village Committee favours her for a third term and she hopes that they will select her unopposed.

For an Effective Panchayati Raj System

Rani suggested the following points:

As the Ward Members' involvement and

participation will strengthen the Panchayat set-up, an orientation is needed for them. There is always fear in the minds of Presidents when they are meeting or sharing with officials. This has to be dispelled by organising frequent interface between them. Enmity arises due to the election of the Chairperson to the Union and the District Panchayat. After the election the Councillor is neglected if he or she takes an opposition stand. In this dispute between the Councillor and the Chairperson, unnecessarily the Village Panchayat is also neglected. Hence the system of fund allocation should be streamlined and there should be direct election to the post of Union Chairman and District Chairman. Meetings with higher officials have to be arranged twice every month to avail of the benefit of the sectoral department schemes. The financial transactions in the Village Panchayat of K. Rayavarams are as follows:

In the year 1997-98

The major receipt was the SFC grant of Rs.25,394. The stamp duty income was very meagre, i.e., Rs.193 only. Altogether the total income was Rs.36,971 only. On the expenses side the maintenance of street lights was high at Rs.5,674. The salary to the staff was Rs.3,350 and only nominal expenses were incurred on OHT maintenance and drinking water supply. The electricity bill was Rs.2100 only. Altogether the expenses were Rs. 12,846 only.

In the year 1998-99

After enhancing the house tax, the income from the house tax was Rs.13,795. Building plan approval licence fee income was Rs.1,035. Stamp duty was a little more, i.e., Rs.1950. The major income was the house tax matching grant (Rs.21,368) and the SFC (Rs.24,994). Including the opening balance of Rs.40,987, the total income was Rs.96,727.

On the expenditure side it was found that electricity bill rose to Rs. 5956 for street lights, Rs.3400 for motor pump and Rs.1882 for buildings. The maintenance of GLR and OHT cost Rs.6733. Street light maintenance cost Rs.8924 and Panchayat building maintenance Rs.7796. Road improvement cost Rs.2400 and purchasing of new tools and furniture Rs.4570.

It is observed that the Panchayat, after saving a considerable amount during the previous year and improving the financial resources through house tax matching grant, was able to carry out a lot of works in the year 1998-99.

In the year 1999-2000

The deposit collected for individual taps generated an income of Rs.37,000 and the water tax collection was Rs.3,510. Income by way of interests was Rs.3,182 and the SFC was Rs. 49,154. From fines awarded, tree auction and other miscellaneous sources a sum of Rs.1,000 and above was received. The total income was Rs.1,16,639.

The total expenses in the year were Rs.77,229. Rs.37,000 was deposited separately as it was received as water supply deposit. The other expense was electricity bill. Altogether the bill was for Rs.13,500, of which Rs.3095 was for OHT/GLR.

In the year 2000-2001

Auction of trees (Rs.16,950) generated an additional income along with the other routine income. Rs.5,000 was received as donation. The house tax matching grant, including the previous year's balance, was Rs.34,258. The SFC grant was Rs.45,104. Rs.4450 was received as the equalization fund. The interest receipt was Rs.2923. The total income was Rs.2,07,811.75.

On the expenditure side, the highest item was the payment of electricity bill: Rs.10,567 for street lights and Rs.24,080 for motor pump. The expenditure on the maintenance of street lights was Rs.6163. Laying of new road and improvement of old road was the main work, on which Rs.53,722 was spent. There were other miscellaneous expenses. The total expenses were Rs.1,30,842 and Rs.76,794.75 was the closing balance.

The Panchayat President's strategy of close monitoring of accounts and savings is understood from the above transactions.

In the year 2002-2003

The house tax is Rs.23,910 and a considerable amount of Rs.10,104 has been collected from licence fee and house site plan approval. As stamp duty Rs.8,632 was received. The SFC grant is Rs.41,975. Altogether the income during the year 2002-2003 is Rs.95,505. The unspent balance in the Panchayat account is Rs.67,954.

Under the scheme fund an SGRY allocation of Rs.47,423 was received. Under CRSP, to construct household latrines, Rs.18,000 was received.

In the water supply account the annual receipt was Rs.32,409.

The main expenditures are construction of rainwater harvesting structure, environmental cleaning work to improve the green cover of the village, along with the routine establishment cost of salary, electricity bills, street light maintenance etc. It is Rs.58,654 of expenditure in this year under the Panchayat account. Under the scheme fund the renovation of Nambi oorani was taken up along with the construction of household latrines.

Observation

Rani is an educated, sincere and honest leader and, with her capacity, commitment and hard work, several tasks have been achieved. By her transparent activities she draws the support of the communities. She gets the needed support from her husband and family for her Panchayat works. She maintains a very good rapport with officials and this rapport helps her to achieve many things. Her vision, independent thinking, involvement of the community in Panchayat work, honesty in her dealings have made the people respect her. She is a worthy model to be emulated by many women who are aspiring for power and position.

CASE - 5

ON THE MODEL OF KUMARAPPA

A Dalit youth turned Gandhian constructive worker has taken up the major task of stopping the brewing of illicit liquor and the drinking of the same by the youth in his Panchayat area. To do the above, the village youth had to be provided with alternative employment opportunity. With great difficulty he provided such an opportunity to the youth. By evolving and adopting appropriate technology, employment opportunity was provided to the Dalit youth. By his innovative approach, he made his Panchayat hut free. He has developed a growth model by linking the activities of Koothambakkam with those of other Gram Panchayats. His Panchayat has been marked for generating employment opportunity. Though he is an educated person he has to face a lot of problems in the administration and the society. He has proved beyond doubt that a Panchayat can work for Dalits.

Background

Kuthambakkam Gram Panchayat in Poonamallee Block of Thiruvallur District in Tamil Nadu is headed by a Dalit youth, Mr. Elango, since 1996 under the New Panchayati Raj System. By profession he was an engineer earning Rs.25000 per month from a Central Government Institute meant for Research at Karaikudi. He is married to a chemist working in the ONGC. They have two daughters. He has three brothers. Being the eldest, he had the responsibility to support his family and develop his brothers. He was groomed in a social transformation movement for Dalit emancipation and empowerment. As he was oriented in the Ambedkar Movement, he was looking for an opportunity to serve the Dalits. But his family commitments made him serve the family first. To support his family, he started an industry (KSI Laboratories) with an investment of fifteen lakh rupees for his brothers. When his family was well set foot to march forward economically through his earnings, his wife's and the industry, he was drawn towards the election to grassroots institutions as it provides an opportunity to transform the lifestyle of the people, particularly Dalits. He has a firm conviction that, of all the institutions, grassroots institutions are the most powerful instrument to transform the life of the Dalits by mobilizing them for socio-economic transformation. A Gram Panchayat President can achieve many things for Dalits – more than what a Dalit MLA can achieve. All the livelihood issues can be easily addressed through Panchayats if the Panchayat Presidents are sensitive to the problems of the Dalits. His plea is that the Dalits should occupy their positions in the Gram Panchayat on their own and perform their roles and responsibilities independently. Allowing the industry to see to its own fate and resigning from his job, he contested in the election. However honest and dedicated he is, election will not spare him, as it has its own inbuilt weaknesses. As he was identified with the Dalit movement and oriented in Dalit mobilization, he was branded as a Dalit fanatic and the opponent candidate, though hailing from the Dalit community, took the political support of the Tamil Manila Congress Party. His opponent relied on the votes of the non-Dalits with the support that political party. But Elango won the election. He won the election as the people expected more from him, since he is an educated youth. He got the support of the Dalits in the first election.

Village Setting

After he was elected President of the Gram Panchayat, he observed the village scenario. There are about 1110 families, with a population of 5250, of which 52 per cent are Dalits and the rest non-Dalits, comprising Vanniars, Naidus and Mudaliars. Of the lands available in this Panchayat, 90 per cent are with the upper caste groups. Both Dalits and Vanniars are totally agricultural labourers, barring a few who have small parcels of land. The cultivable lands are with Naidus and Mudaliars. Agricultural labourers who do not find jobs most of the year started brewing illicit liquor and it became the practice of the poor. No one has come from other areas to ruin the life of the Dalits and it is the Dalits who ruin themselves by involving in the illicit arrack trade. Dalits have no other option excepting to lead a life of sub-human conditions. They had been lured to all kinds of antisocial activities under the leadership of mafia gangs from the urban areas.

When action is initiated against the ant-isocial activities, the Dalits of this village are the victims. They have no leader at their village level to show them the path to lead a decent human life. They have political leadership at the state level and no way to improve their life through their political leadership. The Dalits are being mobilized, for political struggles but their living conditions in the rural areas have not changed. They still face what they had faced all along. They live in poverty, penury and miserable conditions. The need of the hour is leadership for Dalits to achieve development. The Panchayat provides this opportunity and hope.

About Panchayats

The Gram Panchayat has four wards, nine ward members and seven hamlets. It has roads of 10,500 mts. Of them 8000 mts have been made of concrete. The total number of overhead tanks providing water is seven. There are 320 street lights. The Panchayat has 1175 households having a population of 5250. There are five anganwadis, two schools, one primary and one higher elementary. Total 530 students are studying in different schools in the village. Eighteen SHGs are functioning in the village. There are five youth groups which are very active in the Panchayat area.

On Development

In his perception and opinion Dalit emancipation is possible not through mobilizing them for political participation but through their socio-economic transformation. Unless their livelihood pattern is changed, their perception and behaviour is changed, Dalit emancipation will reamin only a pipe dream. His target is the marginalized — and the vulnerable families. He feels that the Dalits are far away from the basic facilities which have been created for livelihood security. Dalit children are deprived of development aspirations. Dalit women are the worst affected in the whole of society. By giving dolls one cannot develop the Dalits. Only by protecting their self-respect, creating awareness, upgrading their skill, linking their skill with production of marketable commodity, linking their economic activity with banks one can create an opportunity for Dalits to come up in life. Cinema, lottery and liquor are the three evils which have eaten away the vitals of the Dalits, of which liquor is the major factor which has completely ruined their life. Thus he started his work with stopping the brewing of illicit arrack. The Dalits, though belonging to his caste, started arguing what the alternative was and started opposing him. Dalit leaders instigated them to oppose him saying that he is working against the Dalits. But he successfully stopped the brewing of illicit liquor and he was in search of employment opportunities for those individuals and families who lost their jobs in this work.

On Panchayat System

He considered the Panchayat a powerful instrument for transforming the life of the rustic folk, provided powers and responsibilities are given to the Panchayat system. He regretted that, in Tamil Nadu, the Panchayat is considered only an instrument to carry out the schemes of the Central and State governments. The New Panchayati Raj System provides scope and opportunity for the deprived, marginalized and neglected to come up in life, provided good leadership is readily available at the grassroots to overcome the barriers in the institution and to work for the community. Otherwise the new system will also work for the privileged. The success of the New Panchayati Raj System largely depends on the leadership of the Panchayats and their relationship with the people. To overcome the problem which arose out of stopping the brewing of illicit liquor, he had to seek some solution in the schemes of the governments. He found out a major scheme, namely, Samathuvapuram, along with other schemes to be carried out in this Panchayat area. In his estimate, he said that he has mobilized near about one crore forty lakh rupees for various schemes implemented in the Panchayat. The Panchayat has got Rs.90 lakhs for the Samathuvapuram scheme (Housing and other infrastructural facilities for the poor of all caste groups to live together) and Rs.45 lakhs for concrete cement roads. He has determined that no work should be given to contractors and that all the works are to be carried out only by the people who have lost their job of brewing illicit liquor. He strongly believes that Panchayats have to take up works which are less skill oriented and more manual oriented, as rustic folk have only energy and not much of refined skills. Any scheme will provide employment opportunity to the rural poor if it is less skill oriented. There he found out the technology of mud block making. People are involved in making bricks through this technology and construction of houses for the Samathuvapuram. The entire construction was done by the people on their own. Likewise laying of roads was also done by the people. Their livelihood security was ensured by the Panchayat by providing jobs in the implementation of government schemes. As per his calculation, 350 families are in the vulnerable category. They need continuous manual work for their livelihood security. Yet it was not smooth sailing. Beneficiaries who got houses in the Samathuvapuram scheme raised opposition to this mud block construction as it was thought that the mud block has no strength. He tried his best to convince the people and it took near about six months. His import of mud block technology was born out of a need but people did not accept it. He took pains to convince the people. Now they have realized that they have done the right thing. He is going in for the same technology to construct 200 houses to make it a katcha-house-free village. He felt that the Dalits have a very strong mindset on all aspects of life. To break the mindset of the Dalits one has to struggle a lot. Moreover they have a strong belief that they cannot improve their living conditions.

When these works came to an end, he was in trouble as those involved in construction and road laying works would turn towards the preparation of illicit liquor. His second journey started in search of technology to provide sustainable job opportunity to the people in his village at an affordable cost. The cost of the technology should be little, it should be operated by any individual and, at the same time, it should provide opportunity to the poor people continuously for employment. He visited a number of places like Gandhigram, RTRC, Mundur, Kerala, Sevagram, Wardha, CETRI, Mysore. He found out several technologies suitable to his village, but cost reduction was needed. He thought that he could do it and improvise the technology. While looking at the type of activities that are to be undertaken and the way in which Panchayats are taking shape in Tamil Nadu he felt that all these activities cannot be done in Panchayat. Totally all Panchayats are under the control of the bureaucracy and the bureaucracy is never oriented to deliver services but oriented to look at rules and procedures. At the Panchayat level social audit is more important than the audit of the Chartered Account. In the Panchayat it is not the Chartered Accountant auditing the Panchayat but someone from the Block Development Office. This Panchayat has no space for experiments, innovations and creativity. But, to carry out all those creative works, the Panchayat has no flexibility and space and hence he started a Trust called, Trust for Village Self Governance. Because of his activities, vision and commitment, he was invited to the USA and the UK and NRIs contributed a small amount and with the small amount he improvised tools and machines. He identified mud block making as a technology and hence he got it from Auroville of Pondicherry by paying Rs.40,000. He further identified soap making, both toilet and detergent, dairying, bakery, thoordhal preparation, oil extraction, jute bag preparation, handmade paper, preparing energy efficient lights as activities to be carried out, for which technology has to be improvised. Both mud block making and jute bag preparation have been carried out.

Mud-block Making

Jute Bag and Cotton Bag Production and Training

The Panchayat President has created the following units to generate employment opportunity in his Panchayat area under the banner of the Trust.

Jute Bag and Cotton Bag Production and Training

In this unit the villagers are producing ecofriendly, value added jute bags and cotton canvas bags. One Self Help Group of 12 members is running this unit. They are producing 82 models of jute and cotton bags. Some of the models are being exported to European countries like Switzerland. This unit is functioning as a production-cum-training centre.

Rural Products

Tailoring unit to produce jute bags, cotton bags, shirts, petticoats and uniforms

Total investment needed	– Rs.1,00,000
Working capital	– Rs.1,50,000
Profit to be generated	– Rs.30,000 p.m.
Debt services	– Rs.10,000 p.m.
Profit for the people	– Rs.20,000 p.m.
No of persons employed	– 10 persons

Thoordhal Production Unit

In this unit the raw thoordhal is purchased from Vellore and Dharmapuri Districts. It is properly cleaned and soaked in water and dried. This is taken for milling where the thoordal is deskined. It is collected, sieved and sold. The skin is collected and sold as cattle feed. The thoordhal processor is purchased from the Central Food Technological Research Institute, Mysore. This is a simple model run by a HP single-phase motor. One SHG of 12 members works in this unit. This also is a production-cum-training unit.

Machinery

a. Mini Thoordhal mill (1 HP prime driver and ½ HP for classifier) - Rs.80,000
b. Soaking tanks and decanters - Rs.24,000
c. Drying yard - 800 sft
d. Working capital - Rs.1,20,000

Mini Thoordhal Mill

Capacity - 300 kgs/ day & 7 tons/month

Local market will consume 4 tons and the rest will be sold to the nearest villages.

Expected profit – Rs.28,000/- p.m.
Debt services – Rs.7,000/- p.m.

Profit for people – Rs.21,000/- per month
Employment Opportunity – 12 persons
By-product – Thoordhal dust – 2100 kgs (good cattle feed)

Soaking Tank & Decanters

Groundnut Products Unit

In this unit there are hand-operated ground-nut breaking machines available to deshell the groundnut. Each machine can crush 6 to 7 bags (40 kgs) of dry

Groundnut Products Unit

groundnut. From the broken mass the shell is removed by physical separation.

The deshelled material is sieved to separate the bigger sized kernels. The smaller size kernels are sent for oil production. The bigger sized ones are roasted and taken for burfy and chakkie production. Sometimes the bigger sized ones are sold as seeds. This also is a production-cum-training unit.

Oil Extraction Unit

Capacity —
3000 kgs Groundnut oil
4000 kgs gingelly oil
2000 kgs coconut oil

Oil Extraction Unit

Machinery

a. Rotary extractions – 3 Nos. – 1.8 lakhs
   Power – 30 HP
b. Oil filling system – Rs.20,000
c. Hand decordicators – 3 Nos. Rs.20,000

Expected profit	–	Rs.30,000 per month
Debt Services	–	Rs.8,000 per month
Profit for people	–	Rs.22,000 per month
Employment opportunity	–	12 persons
By product	–	Oil cake and ground nut shell (cattle feed)

Groundnut Processing and Eatables

Machinery

Roasters, packing machine – Rs.50,000
Profit expected – Rs.10,000 per month
No. employed – 5 persons

Soap Making Unit

Soap Making

In this unit a simple soap making system is developed. No machine and no electricity is used. Using this new device, varieties of toilet soaps are produced. This is one of the activities for the SHGs. This unit consumes coconut oil which is produced by the local oil extraction unit. This also uses the locally available herbs. This unit generates employment for 10 members. This also is a production-cum-training unit.

Production of Soap

No. of soaps – 10,000 per month

Cost of machine and materials – Rs.40,000

Raw materials – oil is obtained from oil unit – alkali and chemical from market

Expected profit – Rs.25,000 per month

Debt Services – Rs.5,000 per month

Profit for the people – Rs.20,000 per month

No. of people employed – 10 per month

Diary Processing Unit

This unit consists of mini jacketed vessel for heating and cooling the milk, a refrigerator, an open pan evaporator and stainless steel vessels for curd making and storing. In this unit 300 litres of milk can be processed per day. This gives opportunity for one SHG to work. To feed milk to this unit we are promoting groups of cattle growers. This will in turn give employment to about 60 people. This also is a production-cum-training unit.

Milk Processing and Milk Products

Capacity – to process – 300 litres milk a day

Milk Processing and Milk Products Machinery

Machinery

Baby boiler – 1
Pasteurizer – 1
Chiller – 1
Packing system – 1
Pan evaporation – 1
Trays and utensils –
Total investment – Rs.2.0 lakhs
Profit to be gained – Rs.30,000 per month
Debt services – Rs.8,000 per month
Profit for people – Rs.22,000 per month
No. of employed – 10 persons

Cattle Feed Unit

Capacity – 15 tons/month

Machinery

a. Ball mill 1 No. – Rs. 40,000
b. Grinder – Rs. 20,000
c. Packing system – Rs. 10,000
Power – 10 HP
Expected Profit – Rs.30,000 per month
Service to Debts – Rs.8,000 per month
Profit for people – Rs.22,000 per month
No. of people employed – 10

Village Bakery Unit

This is a small bakery unit to produce basic baked items – biscuits, cakes, puffs, bun and bread. This also is a production-cum-training unit.

Production of Food items

1. Sambar Powder
2. Pickles
3. Other food items

Machinery – Rs.3,00,000
Profit to be generated – Rs.35,000 per month
Debt services – Rs.10,000 per month
Profit for the people – Rs.25,000 per month
No. of persons to be employed – 10 persons

Energy Efficient Street Lights Unit

This unit produces street lights using energy efficient CFL bulbs. It produces the metal boxes, glass cover, holders, plastic components, bolts and nuts. These lights save 75 to 80 per cent of electric power. This gives employment to a group of 20 people. This also is a produc-tion-cum-training unit.

Energy efficient street light

Energy Efficient Street Lights and Electro Mechanical Gadgets

Investment on machineries – Rs.4.0 lakhs
Working capital – Rs.2.0 lakhs

Electro Mechanical Gadgets Unit

Profit generated	– Rs.50,000 per month
Debt services	– Rs.10,000 per month
Profit for people	– Rs.40,000 per month
No. of employed	– 18 persons

Construction Materials Production

a. Mud blocks
b. Ferro cement panels
c. Toilet materials
d. Roofing materials

Investment on machines	– Rs.1.5 lakhs
Working capital	– Rs.1.5 lakhs
Profit generated	– Rs.40,000 per month
Debt services	– Rs.10,000 per month
Profit for people	– Rs.30,000 per month
No. of employed	– 15 persons

His Vision of Integrated Sustainable Rural Development

He strongly feels that people-centric activities can be generated only when people are mobilized and conscientised on development. To perform the above task a strong leadership with a sense of commitment is needed. Once people are mobilized they are to be conscientised on the process of development. If they are conscientised on development, they will start critiquing the current development scenario and decide what type of development they want. Based on the awareness, the need of the people will be assessed and available skills will also be assessed. By assessing the available opportunity to meet the requirements of the society, steps will be taken at the Panchayat level to prepare a plan to achieve development. Panchayats and NGOs and CBOs will work together to address the issues of the people. Continuously people will be mobilized from assessing the need to plan and implement the same. Thus development becomes the people's subject by which government agencies will be relegated to the background.

He is of the opinion that, to generate employment opportunity, the Kumarappa model is the only solution. Many of the products coming from outside for consumption in the villages can be produced locally by introducing a new device by which money flow from the village to outside can be arrested. Products produced by the villagers have to be consumed by the villagers. Hence he feels that critiquing of the process of development is a key for village development and that, by doing so, the mindset of the people can be changed.

Panchayat Academy

He is not content with the activities carried out in his Panchayat. He is interested in and committed to creating a cadre of Panchayat leaders dedicated to achieving economic development and social justice. He considers that his Panchayat is a laboratory and all experiments successfully carried out in his Panchayat should be replicated in other Panchayats also by which his model will be emulated and a new movement can be created for development. For this kind of activities he wants to create an academy called the Panchayat Academy. It is not a mere teaching academy. It is a doers academy. Panchayat Presidents have to come to Kuthambakkam and discuss with people who are working different units of production and get to know the details. As the President, he will explain the whole process to the Panchayat leaders. He is the head of the academy and other SHG women are the co-teachers in this academy. Already he has started this work. Seeing his activities the academy is supported by the British Council. Panchayat leaders have started coming to this Panchayat in large numbers.

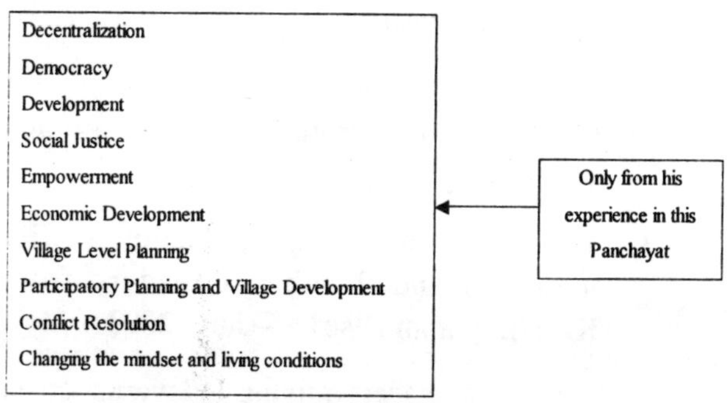

A village, by making itself a role model for total development using the Panchayati Raj System is becoming a learning centre for other villages. Based on this concept, it was decided to invite 20 to 30 Panchayat leaders from various districts to Kuthambakkam to witness the developmental process taking place here. What they are given in the programme are:

Training Programmes

Training Programmes Conducted

1. Training in village industries and sustainable development – Panchayat Leaders from Thiruvallur District.

2. Training in jute products and weaving – for women and girls from Kuthambakkam and surrounding villages – May 2003.

3. Training in toilet soap production – SHG members and Panchayat leaders from Kancheepuram District – June 2003.

4. Panchayat Leaders training and workshop on sustainable development through Panchayati Raj System – August 2003.

5. Panchayat Leaders training and workshop on sustainable development through Panchayati Raj System – September 2003.

6. Panchayat Leaders and NRIs meet on village industries and Panchayati Raj System.

7. Outstanding Panchayat Leaders meet for Pudukkottai District Panchayat Leaders-- October 2003.

8. Panchayat Leaders and NGOs joint training in sustainable village development, November 2003.

9. Outstanding Panchayat Leader meet for Thiruvallur and Kancheepuram District Panchayat Leaders, December 2003.

10. Panchayat Leaders and NGOs from Coimbatore District meeting, January 2004.

11. Women Panchayat Leaders training in village industries and women's rights, February 2004.

12. Visit to role model villages, Odanthurai and Semmipalayam in Coimbatore District. He took Panchayat leaders from his district to other areas to show other success stories.

Apart from the above programmes, meetings for youths and SHG members were organized when people visited the village industries complex. Other than this, there is an intensive research and development programme on village industries and village level marketing. Due to this a revolutionary breakthrough has happened in energy efficient street lighting and water pumping. This is going to lead to a situation wherein every Panchayat will save 65 to 70 per cent of energy in street lighting and water pumping. This will certainly liberate the Village Panchayat from the debt trap because of electricity changes. Many of the village industries programmes are successfully prototyped and the process of commercialization is going on. The support rendered by the Hunger Project and the Tamil Nadu Foundation has really helped to reach a situation wherein the Trust has gained full confidence in the village industries packages.

Photo Gallery

Influencing NRIs

By visiting various countries in the west on invitation, he sensitized the NRIs in all those countries. So far some of the NRIs have contributed their mite towards rural development activities through NGOs. Now they have started working with the communities directly with the help of the Panchayats. He helps a lot of NRIs in their activities.

Finance of Kuthambakkam Panchayat

a. Panchayat Fund Account for one year

Sl. No.	*Particulars*	*Amount (in Rs.)*
1.	House tax	2,63,000.00
2.	Library tax	26,300.00
3.	Professional tax	1,05,000.00
4.	Surcharge on stamp duty	5,55,000.00
5.	House tax matching grant	1,65,000.00
6.	Building plan approval	27,000.00
7.	Advertisement tax	10,000.00
8.	Miscellaneous	20,000.00

b. Scheme Fund Account

Sl. No.	*Particulars*	*Amount (in Rs.)*
1.	SGRY	2,36,000.00

c. Earmarked Grant Account

Sl. No.	*Particulars*	*Amount (in Rs.)*
1.	Eleventh Finance Commission Grant	63,000.00

Table 1 : Last Eight Years' Panchayat Fund

Year	*SSD*	*SFC*	*HTMG*	*LC*	*Funeral Grant*	*Thiru-valluvar Library*
97-98	3,60,066	1,20,868	40,440	-	-	-
98-99	3,46,245	1,78,830	4,01,055	-	-	-
99-00	2,98,907	3,37,454	1,33,375	6,600	2,500	5,000
00-01	5,90,811	2,58,723	2,04,990	5,783	500	-
01-02	2,31,861	2,92,889	71,615	5,847	2,500	-
02-03	11,67,761	3,88,377	1,34,670	6,077	-	-
03-04	24,69,457	3,49,218	-	6,177	-	-
04-05	1,64,560	35,694	-	-	-	-
Total	56,29,668	19,62,053	9,86,145	30,484	5,500	5,000

Table 2 : Panchayat Earmarked Grant Account

Year	*11th*	*E/Grant*	*Funeral Grant*	*11th (Toilet)*
97-98	29,020	-	-	-
98-99	-	-	2,200	-
99-00	28,208	-	-	-
00-01	43,318	23,40,000	-	-
01-02	-	-	-	-
02-03	1,21,266	-	2,000	-
03-04	-	-	-	-
04-05	60632	-	-	9,000
Total	2,82,444	23,40,000	4,200	9,000

Table 3 : Panchayat Scheme Account

Year	*IAY*	*CRSP*	*JVVT*	*JGSY*	*PMGY*	*SGRY*
97-98	3,00,000	28,000	67,122	-	-	-
98-99	7,900	-	84,000	-	-	-
99-00	4,57,075	81,364	-	1,63,761	-	-
00-01	1,39,330	-	-	7,34,433	1,66,860	-
01-02	-	-	-	65,419	-	-
02-03	2,11,911	-	-	3,52,566	-	-
03-04	-	-	-	2,41,081	-	-
04-05	-	-	-	-	-	2,07,070
Total	11,16,216	1,09,364	1,51,122	15,57,260	1,66,860	2,07,070

Special Grants		*(In Rs.)*
1.	Construction of Samathuvapuram	
	Government of Tamil Nadu	35,00,000
	Government of India (Dovetailing various Government of India Schemes)	55,00,000
2.	Namakku Namme Thittam (for laying CC roads)	44,00,000
3.	Innovative Habitat Development (hutless village):	
	Government of India, RD Department	50,00,000
	Trust for village self governance (from donations and grants)	50,00,000
4.	Solar power facilities for the Panchayat office	1,10,000
5.	Solar Street lights (from MNES and TEDA)	1,00,000
6.	Furnitures for the school children	4,00,000
7.	Computers for the school children	1,00,000
	Total	2,41,10,000

In his first tenure, he spent near about one crore forty lakh rupees through various kinds of activities. But he provided maximum opportunity to the people to use their energy and manpower. His mud block preparation was born out of this vision of providing employment opportunity. It was an ordeal for him to convince the people that mud block construction will have strength equal to chamber bricks. People accept the mud block preparation when they are employed. But they refuse to accept them to be used to construct their houses. With great difficulty he convinced the people. All his technological improvisations are made only with the aim of providing livelihood security to the poor, that too vulnerable sections of the society.

His first period was full of struggles and learning to build his vision and mission. While performing his role and responsibilities he had to face a volley of problems from many sides. Officials at lower level did not understand the works that he carried out. They issued one notice after another to book him under clause 205 of the Tamil Nadu Panchayat Act of 1994. He had to struggle a lot to convince people on each and every issue as the awareness level of the people on development is low. There is no ready made improvised technology for adoption. Working for economic development and social justice is the basic task of the Panchayats. Neither the Panchayat Ward Members nor the officials understood this. He had to work lonely as he had developed a vision. Even Panchayat ward members were not sensitized to the roles to be performed in the Panchayats. Everyone was interested in carrying out the activities if schemes and programmes were sanctioned by the government. Throughout the period his transactions were made transparent and everything was written on the Panchayat display board, including the bank balance. His transparency has brought more number of people to his fold. Equally his firm action in removing encroachment of Panchayat lands meant for the Samathuvapuram kept nearly 60 families away from him because he removed them from the Panchayat lands. The sixty families who had encroached the Panchayat lands were Dalits and hence they thought that he would not touch them in order to keep their support to him in tact.

In the beginning he was perceived as a Dalit activist and subsequently he was perceived as a facilitator of community development. One section of the people who had closely watched him admired him for his evolution from the Dalit fold to the community level. Another section felt that being a Dalit he was expected to provide job opportunity to Dalits but instead of adopting a Dalit perspective in Panchayat administration he brought community perspective to it. As a result a minor section of the Dalit families determined to defeat him in the next elections. But a major chunk who had opposed him in the first election, mostly non-Dalits, came close to him and were determined to support him in the next election. In the second election for local bodies he contested by reporting his activities and vision. Families which were involved in illicit liquor brewing and selling and families who had been evicted from encroachments joined together to oppose him. Equally the families, mostly non-Dalits, who opposed him in the first election with the perception that he was an active Dalit movement representative came together to support him since he emerged as a facilitator of community development. Four candidates contested in the election and he won the election without any expenditure. Even a handbill was prepared by some one and printed by one NGO. He said that providing job opportunity to 450 families through government schemes, keeping the Panchayat administration transparent, acting as a facilitator were responsible for his victory.

In the second period he wanted to consolidate his proposals and concretize his actions towards economic activities. He strongly believes that by proving opportunity to the people to work and earn their livelihood, the self-respect of the people could be protected.

When asked about the annual income and expenditure he said that it is around Rs. 28 lakh and Rs.18 lakh respectively. He is not interested in spending money but he is interested in studying the process of development and people's perception of their participation in the development process. He wants to change the process of development from the hands of the officials to people's hands. He said that through the Gram Sabha a healthy democratic culture could be developed at the grassroots. He gets the agenda in the Panchayat council for discussion in the Gram Sabha. He conducts the Gram Sabha on the basis of the agenda set by the Panchayat council. All issues are people centric and hence the Gram Sabha attracts the people. He has got sanction from the Central government to construct houses for the poor under the innovative housing scheme for Rs.50 lakhs.

He has developed a scheme for economic activities of the poor and it can be sustained if a cluster of villages join together. A cluster of Village Gram Panchayats have to join together to form a consortium. This can be achieved through improvised technologies. It needs lot of work with other Gram Panchayat Presidents. For the development of the poor and the well-being of all, a perspective plan is needed. He has developed a plan for the development of his Gram Panchayat. He has developed it from the beginning of the first term itself. In fact it is a plan prepared by him and it was approved by the Gram Sabha. It is not a plan document prepared with the participation of the people. It is almost a vision document prepared by the President. There are a few industries emitting waste by which they pollute the entire area and for which he has to struggle against the industries.

He has evolved this development perspective based on the writings and speeches of Rajiv Gandhi, Kundrakudi Adigalar, Anna Hazzare and Kumarappa. His belief and ideas got concretized only after his visit to Gandhian institutions. He believed that Dalit development rests not on political mobilization but solely on the mobilization of Dalits for development. Their skill has to be upgraded. Their energy has to be used productively. He concentrated his attention on the service delivered by the primary health centres and primary schools. A Parent Teachers Association has been facilitated by the Panchayat President. He provided needed furniture to the schools. He got all the furniture as donation from a donor agency. He made special arrangements for interaction with school students.

Analysis

Mr. Elango's main objective is not to work with the people in achieving economic development and social justice. His intention is to create a model in his Panchayat and the same can be scaled up. The process of development which we see today has to be reversed from the government domain to the people's domain. People should feel that they can develop on their own. He further envisages the fact that a cadre of Panchayat leaders could be created with a new mindset with a sense of commitment and honesty to perform the above task. Even in the path of development, he realistically feels that an alternative development model has to be projected which should rely on people's skill, peoples knowledge and be need based and not growth based. It should be always employment oriented, equity oriented and gender oriented.

It should have sustainability. The Panchayat cannot function in isolation. It has to work with other institutions. Now he has brought visibility to his model. To bring this model to this level of visibility he had to struggle a lot both personally and publicly. The Panchayat system which is in vogue is neither in the hands of the people nor in the hands of the elected representatives. It is in the hands of the unskilled, rusted, corrupt officials who continue to look at the Panchayat as an implementing agency. He looks at only the provisions in the Constitution, not in the system created in Tamil Nadu. People's needs and the vision of the leader cannot be addressed in the existing system. The Panchayat leaders, by building up their capacity and performing their genuine role by assuming power would generate a heat in the system which would pave the way for decentralization. As in other Panchayats, he performs the role in laying roads, providing streetlights, taking care of water supply and sanitation, and maintaining clean environment in the village. To him these are all the routine functions and no Panchayat can escape from them. He feels that Panchayats have to show the path to development for which Panchayats have to break new ground as there is enough space. But one has to understand and build the capacity to struggle against the barriers in the process of development.

He is of the opinion that social audit is the only option for creative leaders working in the Panchayats.

Conclusion

Kuthambakkam has started a movement which is a new Gandhian model of development which will gain momentum as he already started taking this model to other Panchayats. In fact other Panchayats leaders have started visiting Kuthambakkam. For Panchayats, it is Sevagram. The Panchayat leader is a neo Gandhian Worker. In the days of Dalits attacking Gandhi, a Dalit, in a convincing way, shows a practical model for the upliftment of the poor and Dalits through the model of Kumarappa. His technology driven activities will bring the needed solutions to the existing crisis in Panchayats. It is a basic question that, as he is an engineer, he can do all these technological innovations in his Panchayat, but, in other Panchayats, the leaders are not able to do the same. Here he breaks the myth and he says that anybody can use these devices. The technologies are very simple and in no way they are complicated. Already a number of Panchayats have picked up this model. For him the infrastructural facilities are very simple and, even without the Panchayats, these things could be achieved. Panchayats have to address the issues of the poor and the marginalized. The mandate of the Panchayat is to achieve economic development and administer social justice. He has addressed the two issues. He is emerging as a leader of leaders at the grassroots.

CASE - 6

PANCHAYAT LEADER TRANSFORMED TO CONSTITUTION FROM TRADITION

He emerged as a leader of the entire village. He got the support of all the communities because of his dedicated service to the people even before he became the Panchayat President. He is the President of the traditional Panchayat and the constitutional Panchayat also. His transparent activities made the people have faith in him. Having got the support of the entire village community, mobilizing the public for development work became easier for him. He took up many responsibilities from the government and carried them out in the Panchayat. The Public Distribution System was taken over by the Panchayat and it is being managed by a Self Help Group. All innovative programmes of rural development are launched in his Panchayat area as he has shown tremendous results in all Panchayat activities. Nallukottai Panchayat is a household name among development functionaries and workers. It is also a model Panchayat. For interface programmes of Panchayat leaders, this Panchayat serves as a model.

Socio-Economic Background

Mr. Ramanathan, aged 65, belonging to the Kallar community, is the President of Nallukottai Gram Panchayat. He has completed SSLC. His family is a joint family. He lives with his wife and three sons who are all married. They help in his agricultural activities. Four acres of dry land and four acres of wet land are the properties owned by him. There are two pumpsets in the land and so he cultivates cash crops like banana and sugarcane. He lives in his own pucca house with facilities like electricity, toilet and individual water supply tape.

His Socialization Process

During the 1960s the village administration was vested with the Ambalam, the traditional head of the village. Once the Ambalam was asked by the Government to desist from carrying out the responsibilities of village munsif temporarily for some reasons. Ramanathan was asked to complete the revenue collection and he promptly attended to the work. After that he was relieved from that responsibility. The villagers appreciated his sincere service and honesty during his temporary tenure.

The teachings of Mahatma Gandhi attracted him and he actively involved himself in the Congress Party's activities. In 1965, when the election to the Village Panchayat was announced, his friends and well wishers advised him to contest in the election. The ex-President, who was his paternal uncle, did not keep himself away from the contest. But the villagers predominantly supported Ramanathan. After realizing the trend prevailing at that time of the election, his uncle came forward for a compromise and Ramanathan was elected unopposed. Since then the villagers have elected him again and again in spite of some opposition to him.

Recruitment Process

In the 1996 election, on behalf of a DMK minister who hails from Sivagangai, a young person who was the secretary of the youth wing of the DMK Party contested against him. Ramanathan put up a notice pointing out his earlier performance and appealed to the voters to cast their votes according to their conscience and not on party basis.

Moreover, after the split in the Congress Party in the year 1977, he dissociated himself from any political party and became apolitical. This is known to all. Hence, irrespective of caste and political parties, he won more number of votes. The opposing candidate was the ex-clerk of Nallukottai Panchayat. He was dismissed from service for malpractice in accounting for the rent collected for the community well. Later he joined the DMK Party. He contested against Ramanathan. But the people rejected him. Ramanathan holds the opinion that it is better to contest than be elected unopposed, because an unanimously elected person has to be a shadow of the electorate and so he cannot command respect in the Panchayat. Ramanathan successfully completed his tenure during 1996-2001. He brought name and fame to his

Panchayat. Nallukottai got the best Village Panchayat award at the district level consecutively for two years 1998-1999 and 1999-2000. A cash award of Rs.1 lakh was received each year with a citation and a memento.

Receiving award from District Collector

During the second tenure under the New Panchayati Raj System, Ramanathan declared that he was going to contest again. Villagers, cutting across castes decided to elect him unopposed. Moreover, the public in general came to a realization that the Village Panchayat was for development and not a place for controversy. Hence they proposed unanimous election to Ward Members also. There are six Ward Members. But one youngster firmly demanded that he should be one of a Ward Member. Hence election was held for only one Ward Member. Ramanathan has become a celebrity, being the President of Nallukkottai Village Panchayat since 1965 to till today.

His Comments on Politics

The political scenario was undergoing an immense change after 1967. The entry of the Dravidian parties opened the gate to even unqualified persons to dominate public affairs. The people's perception of leadership has also changed. They prefer rowdy elements and anti-social elements. The respect commanded by those individuals who honestly engaged in public affairs has been reduced. Corruption is visible everywhere. Earlier the elected representatives like MLAs and MPs offered their car for the benefit of others and fulfilled the demands of the villagers without expecting any return whereas the situation now is an ugly one. MLAs and MPs are bargaining with the people for works to be given on the basis of commission. *Percentage* is a very ordinary word. Against this backdrop how can one expect quality of work or honesty in administration? Having realized the situation, Ramanatham does not expect any recognition from the public. They just demand that their grievances should be addressed. He understands that one cannot swim against the current. He says that he is answerable to his conscience. He believes in the maxim "service to humanity is service to God". Hence, in spite of no income from public life, he has sustained his spirit in serving the people. But the common people do not have this maturity.

Village Setup

Nallukottai is a middle sized village. Its population is 3000. In the 1996 election, there were only two Wards from which 6 Members were elected and, of them two were women and four were men. The Kallars are the dominant caste. There are Agamudaiyars also but their number is very limited. Chettiars, Vellalars and Velars are the minority communities. There are many SC families in the village and it is the second major community. About 55 SC families availed of the special scheme of patta land and other benefits implemented in the year 1967 with the guidance of Ramanathan. The SCs are progressing well as they engage in agriculture and other employments also. There is a problem of non-availability of adequate agricultural labour. In the year 1986 an exclusive settlement named Indira Nagar was established, in which 50 SC beneficiaries were provided with 50 housing units through the efforts taken by Ramanathan.

The SC community is now an empowered one as there is no caste discrimination. Earlier they called the upper caste landlords/owners "Ejaman" (i.e., Lord), but nowadays they sit equally with other castes and fearlessly share their opinions. Regarding the economic status of the other communities, Ramanathan observed that in general all families have improved their life standard as the Government is providing loans for various activities, implementing welfare programmes like housing. Employment opportunities have also increased, as for instance works under the EAS, the food for work scheme, the JGSY. These schemes were periodically implemented in the village and gave benefits to all. The Periyar dam irrigation water is available to the farmers of this village. If the irrigation water is brought in time agriculture will be an intensive activity by which the village economy will improve. All the activities initiated by the various Government departments facilitate the development of farmers as well as landless labourers in Nallukottai.

There is no caste association in the village. But there is a Village Committee under the Nattar system. There are two villages under the jurisdiction of the Nattar system of community management. Organising a one day event, namely *Mandagapadi,* in the Chozhavaram temple on the fifth day is the biggest assignment undertaken by the Nattar. All other social problems like family disputes, disputes between communities and villages are dealt with by the Nattar system. Ramanathan is one of the personalities in the Nattar of Nallukottai Village.

Ramanathan observed that, in general, the present generation in all communities do not prefer to work in the field. Many of the youths gained skills especially in the construction sector and became masons and reinforced cement concrete structure manufacturers. Ramanathan himself served as an instrument of this change of avocation, especially among the youths belonging to the SC community. He once engaged in the construction of houses for a real estate promoter. At that time he encouraged the youths of the SC to learn the skills in the construction industry and many of them now independently work as masons and a few of them have gone abroad also.

Youth Group

The youth are having Cine Fans' Associations in the name of Rajinikanth and Vijayakanth. They organize sports and distribute sweets and prizes. During the time of the Ayyanar festival the youth play an active role in preparing the grounds and the approach roads to the temples. When the Panchayat undertook maintenance work in the inlet channel of the oorani, the youth contributed their labour. An NYK unit is also active in the village. The youth belonging to the NYK contributed money to provide a slide in the Children's Park established in the campus of the Panchayat office.

Village Temple

In the Angalamman temple the *poojari* is a Kallar. In the Putheri Karuppiah temple the *poojari* is from the Pillai community. Generally the families of these two communities respectively administer these two temples. Athi Untha Varda Ayyanar is the common temple. It is the "Gram Deivam". A Velar is the *poojari.* A three-day celebration is organized in this temple. Each family contributes for the celebration. If a poor family is not able to contribute the fixed amount they are permitted to donate half of the amount fixed. The Panchayat makes the arrangements for making available drinking water and takes care of environmental sanitation during the festival time. Moreover all the Ward Members, youth group members and women are involved in the bandobust activities. Their presence itself is like that of a police force.

Common Property Resources

There are 5 acres of poramboke land under various heads like oorani, grazing land, threshing floor and pathway. None of the above sites are under encroachment now. But, in 1996, a large number of families had encroached up ten acres. The Panchayat met them and persuaded them to remove themselves. At the same site Social Forestry was undertaken after properly fencing round the area. About 50 families who reared goats were advised not to rear goats at least for 4 years. In the meantime the tree saplings planted would grow well. Those families adhered to the decision. The tamarind tree saplings are now well grown.

Community Hall

There are 9 ooranis and 14 kanmais. Due to non-availability of adequate water fishery is not possible. The Union does not take necessary steps to protect the trees. The public cut down the trees. If the same property is given to the Panchayat the Panchayat will properly protect them and enjoy the income from selling the trees. As it is the Panchayat has to undertake a cumbersome procedure to auction, to cut and to sell the trees and corruption is an acute problem in the process. As only public tender is permitted a lot of licence holders come for bidding but they form a syndicate among themselves so that no one attempts a high bid. Due to this the Panchayat does not show interest in maintaining the Union tanks. Generally for Rs.10 lakh worth of trees, 50 per cent is spent as corruption in the process from tender to transportation. From VAO to RI, Tahsildar, Zonal Tahsildar, RDO, DRO, Forest Department and Union all have rights and authority in this process. It is a difficult task.

Once fish were reared in the tanks. Rs.400 was spent for the purchase of fingerlings. Rs.4000 was the income from the sale of the grown up fishes. Due to lack of adequate water it is not a viable programme now.

As the monsoon of 2004-05 did not fail, there is adequate water in the ooranis and tanks. Before the advent of the monsoon, needed works like desilting, deepening, maintenance of bunds and clearing of inlet channels were undertaken under drought relief work and Sampoorna Gramin Rozgar Yojana. Moreover three new fish ponds were dug. Ramanathan said that he has made arrangements to procure fingerlings to grow fish in all the water bodies in the Village Panchayat.

Performance

In the first week of every month the Panchayat Council meeting is convened. Refreshments are provided to the Members. Members, Wardwise, explain the expectations of the Ward people. The availability of funds in the Village Panchayat is explained to the Members. After consulting the Members, Wardwise works are finalized and works are carried out accordingly. Gram Sabha meetings are also promptly organized. Even before the announcement by the Government, Ramanathan organized the Gram Sabha as he has read the rules. People responded well. He talked to them and got their suggestions. The problem is that there is no recognition given by the Government to the activities planned in the Gram Sabha. He openly explained to the participants the efforts he had made to get funds from various sources. He used to share the practical problems in this regard. The Panchayat arranges refreshments to the participants during the Gram Sabha meetings. The public do not have vision to develop the village. They just demand drinking water, street lights and drainage facilities whereas he always dreams of how to create self-sufficiency in the village. The SHG members show interest in attending the Gram Sabha. The women from Dalit areas also attend and voice their needs in the Gram Sabha meeting.

Nallukottai as an Innovative Panchayat

Augmenting resources to improve the finances of the Panchayat is one of the innovations attempted by Ramanathan. CPRs are rich resources if properly managed and give a regular income. Under Social Forestry, 2000 tamarind trees have been planted in 10 acres of land. A watchman is employed to protect the saplings. Along the roadside, for a distance of 5 km, 1250 tamarind trees have been planted and another watchman is employed to protect these saplings. Now, after 3 years, all the trees are ready to yield. By auctioning the trees, the Panchayat can earn a considerable income. The community hall-cum-marriage hall, constructed in an earlier period, is an income generating asset. Rs.500 day is the rent collected by the Panchayat. Every year an average of Rs.5000 is the income from the rent. From 2003-2004 the rent has been enhanced to Rs.550.

Bathing and Dressing Room

Community Hall

Two community wells meant for irrigation are properly maintained by the Panchayat. For more than 10 years the water has been adequate for about 60 farmers. Recently the ground water level fell. In one well the motor is in a state of disrepair and there is no efficient mechanic to repair it. Rs.15 is collected as rent per hour for the water. An average of Rs.4000 is the annual income earned by the Panchayat.

Road Facility

A hand pulled cart is made available for rent to the public. Families make use of the cart for transporting their commodities to the field like rice, milk and so on as bullock-carts are a costly. An average of Rs.200 per month is the income to the Panchayat. For carrying the dead bodies of poor families, on several occasions, volunteers are not available. Having sensed this problem, Ramanathan shared this problem in the Gram Sabha meeting. After discussing with the participants, it was decided to make an "Amarar Oorthy". Rs.75 is collected as rent. For the customary blowing of the conch and beating of bell plate, the two equipments were purchased and they are rented out at Rs.10 per day.

To improve the environmental sanitation 19 public toilets have been provided in different places which are convenient to the public. Sufficient water supply is also provided. People now understand the necessity of the toilets. A new sanitary complex was constructed during the second tenure where biogas is produced from the nightsoil. This is the first linked biogas plant in Sivagangai District. An SHG is entrusted with the management of the complex. About 75 women are making use of the complex. By the biogas produced here, the motor pump installed for lifting water from the bore well is operated. Thus a saving of Rs.2,000 per month is effected from the EB charges paid by the Panchayat.

Biogas Plant

Further a bathing tub for men and a drinking water tank for cattle are provided. A community centre with a television set is provided where the public sit and spend their leisure time happily.

Clean Village Campaign

When the government advised to give much attention to improving the sanitation of the village, Ramanathan determined to make his Village Panchayat a clean one. His effort to provide toilet to all families materialized after the construction of the new sanitary complex. When a few men failed to desist from the habit of open defacation, the Village Panchayat formed a monitoring committee. Two individuals were caught in this regard. The issue was brought to the notice of the Gram Sabha and, as per the decision of the Gram Sabha, a fine of Rs.100 each was collected from them.

Concrete Cement Road

With regard to the drainage system, a pucca drainage has been installed in all the streets where CC road is provided. Further, along the main road, a pucca drainage system was provided to drain all the sewage water. The depth of the drain is only one and a half feet so that the cleaning of the same is easy. Solid wastes are collected daily and biodegradable waste is segregated in a yard. Vermiculture is undertaken from the biodegradable waste. One kilogram of earthworm is bought from a private farm. A Vermicompost manure tank has been constructed and two members from an SHG are involved in the vermicomposting. Rs.1,000 is earned from the sale of vermicompost. Due to heavy rain continuously during the current monsoon, the work was disturbed. Now it has been resumed. Villagers are told to minimize the use of polythene bags. For compost manure also a separate yard has been constructed and put into use.

Periodical cleaning of streets, pruning of grass along the roadside, clearing of thorny bushes and protection of all avenue trees are undertaken promptly. The village roads and streets are very neat and clean. The drains are kept clean. One can feel the visibility of cleanliness everywhere. The Village Panchayat of Nallukottai was declared the best Village Panchayat under the clean village campaign and Ramanathan got the prize money of Rs.5 lakhs from the President of India for the year 2003-04.

Solar Light

At a cost of Rs.1,75,800 eight solar lights have been provided. Rs.72,000 were availed of as a subsidy in this regard. Out of the 8 lights, four have been installed in Indira Nagar, two on the Panchayat office road and two on the west street.

Ramanathan said that for his attempt to create self-sufficiency in finance in the Village Panchayat, a considerable amount, i.e Rs.75,000 to 80,000, per year could be saved from the EB charges.

To create awareness on the importance of Siddha medicine, 17 varieties of herbal plants have been planted in the campus of Village Panchayat office.

People's Participation

A weekly market has been established near the Public Distribution shop. About 10 vendors bring their commodities every Saturday. An average of Rs.100 is collected every week as toll from these vendors. Ramanathan said that he himself used to spare his time for the collection when the Panchayat clerk was not available for some reason.

Under the food for work scheme and the SGRY around Rs.10.83 lakhs were utilized. Villagers have been engaged in the works undertaken under these schemes. About 100 workers got regular employment for about 100 days in these works. Rice was kept in storage and distributed immediately to the workers.

When the public distribution system faced problems due to the maladministration of the staff, people reported the matter during the Gram Sabha meeting. The staff of the PDS shop demanded a higher price than the fixed rate. The matter was reported to the District Collector and he conducted an inspection and took action against the staff. The

Collector suggested that the PDS shop could be run by an SHG. As the suggestion was good and very useful to the people, Ramanathan personally involved himself in influencing the SHG members. The district officials also encouraged the SHG members. An SHG came forward and it was oriented in the management of the shop. Now the SHG has been successfully running the shop for the past 10 months. An average of Rs.2000 is the monthly income, of which Rs.1000 is the salary to the women staff who are looking after the Public Distribution System shop. All the problems that existed earlier at the PDS shop have disappeared now.

There are four SHGs among the BC people and one SHG among the SC people. They convene their meetings in the campus of the Panchayat office. If necessary they have been permitted to use the community hall also. If any problem like shortage in allocation of any PDS commodity is reported to Ramanathan, he contacts the district officials and sets things right. ASSEFA and the Department of Animal Husbandry are the key facilitators of the SHG which runs the PDS shop. Ramanathan maintains that, compared to the earlier system, the President of the Village Panchayat is an empowered person under the new system of Panchayati Raj. The executive power given to the President is a good arrangement. The fund allocation is proper and regulated now whereas, earlier, only by influence or proximity the President could get money from the Union. The SFC, JVVT, 10th Finance Commission Funds are finalized at the top tier itself in which the other two tiers can not interfere in anyway. Now opportunities are available to those Presidents who are really determined to serve the people. Moreover, the new system is popular among the people and officials by which the President gets more recognition if he/she is sincere. The newspapers publish a lot of news on the various schemes that are earmarked for Panchayati Raj Institutions. He used to learn a lot of details from the newspapers. Hence he has arranged to provide newspapers in the hamlets, namely, Thirunarayanapuram and Indira Nagar.

Samathuvamayanam

Earlier the SCs and the caste Hindus had separate graveyards. When the Samathuva Mayanam scheme was announced, Ramanathan immediately met the District Collector and got the sanction. RC building, funeral platform, approach road, hand pump, vehicle for carrying the dead body (Amarar oorthy)—all these facilities are now provided at a site which is about 4 acres in extent. Now both SC and BC communities commonly use this graveyard. A total of Rs.1.86 lakhs was spent on this.

When some caste groups tried to make use of other sites convenient instead of the Samathuvamayanam, Ramanathan strictly opposed it and even told them that legal action would be taken against those families. Then the villagers realized the power and authority of the Village Panchayat in handling these irregularities and all adhered to the rules and properly made use of the newly established Samathuvamayanam.

People Yet to be Changed

Under the NNT, it was decided to form a cement concrete road. He hopefully took efforts to collect contributions from the public. The cost of the work was estimated at Rs.2.00 lakhs. As 1/4th contribution, Rs.54,000 was needed he started mobilizing resources from the people. In spite of repeated appeals, people did not come forward to contribute. But the district authorities sanctioned the Government grant. As there was no wayout he contributed a part and managed the rest by undertaking the contract work himself. But he did not compromise on quality. The work was executed to the satisfaction of the authorities, who acknowledged the same even during the Gram Sabha meeting. People's mindset has not yet changed. They are still in a dream that the Government will provide everything. Planned awareness activity is to be taken up to bring about a change in the mindset of the rural masses.

The villagers, after witnessing the hard work undertaken by Ramanathan, came forward to contribute their share when a metal road work was sanctioned recently. The village Temple Committee donated Rs.20,000 as its share and the work is going to be commenced in the month of December 2004.

Scheme Fund Works

Under the JVVT allocation, a TV room, bus shelters, street maintenance, approach road to graveyard maintenance, AD colony road improvement and cement road laying were undertaken. Under the 10th Finance Commission grant retaining wall, bridge, hand pump and compound wall were provided. Under the EAS oorani maramathu and construction of Panchayat office were done. Under the CRSP, so far 300 household toilets have been provided.

Threshing Floor

Building owned by Panchayat

From the Union fund, desiliting and maintenance work were carried out in two ooranis. IAY group houses have been constructed for both SC and BC people. As most of the SCs got houses earlier, BC beneficiaries were selected from among poor families and 28 housing units were given to BC beneficiaries. Jeevandhara wells have been provided to 15 marginal farmers.

CC road, thrashing floor, drainage, metal road, SGRY works of desilting of tanks, 4 toilets to school and balwadi, construction of shopping complexes and provision of solar lights are the major activities undertaken in Nallukkottai during the second tenure under the New Panchayat Raj System.

Panchayat Committees and their Functions

The Panchayat has formed a Work Committee, a Peace Committee and a Monitoring Committee. The Ward Members who are in these committees do not show interest in their effective functioning. They even fail to attend one or two meetings. They think that the President will do all things and most of the Members do not have the spirit to serve the people. They are not assertive even in the matter of their own entitlements. Hence the Committees exist only in name.

Linkages

The representatives of the other two tiers, namely, the Union Council and the District Panchayat, never bother to visit the Panchayat or to attend the Gram Sabha meetings. Their mind is on the calculation of the percentage of commission they can collect. They do not have any development vision. The desilting and other kudimarmathu works carried out massively with a considerable amount as estimate are executed by the PWD. The ruling party is unnecessarily interfering in this work. The MLA and the MP are in some way or the other enjoying the privilege of getting money from the contractors. The works are not under the monitoring control of the people and so the Panchayat is helpless in this regard. Unless a statutory linkage is created among the PRIs most of the benefits from the schemes implemented by various departments will be siphoned off by others.

The Education Department is not under the jurisdiction of the PRIs. It is an independent department. Though the Panchayat can interfere the decisions makers are the officials of the Education Department. Hence Ramanathan tried to involve himself deeply in this issue. He spoke to the Headmaster. Any further interference will result in unexpected turns and the ultimate sufferer will be the President as he has to lose his self-respect. The Revenue Department unnecessarily delays the request of the Panchayat to convert the oorani poramboke into natham poramboke so that the site earmarked for a health subcentre could be approved. The Panchayat does not claim the whole extent but only 0.08 cent, which is owned by the Panchayat. But the Revenue Department has taken more than a year to process this request. The department officials raised fresh questions every time and because of this red tapism it was getting delayed.

IRDP and its Success

Under the old IRDP, loans have been given to 60 poor families. The Indian Bank officials who extended these loans used to conduct monthly reviews regularly. Ramanathan also advised the beneficiaries to take necessary steps to repay. Most of the farmers realize that only after prompt repayment they can avail of further loans. So they come to the Panchayat office and entrust their installment dues to the Panchayat clerk along with the pass book. After promptly paying the dues the books are returned. Ramanathan is very serious about getting back the loan money from the beneficiaries. Otherwise the Panchayat's name will be damaged. In this regard the villagers are very much cooperative.

Relationship between the President and the Village Health Nurse

Personally, Ramanathan feels that close relationship with women staff is not good for the President. Matters like pregnancy, child birth and other women related activities are entirely looked after by the nurse. Unnecessary interference by the President will create unnecessary problems and so he keeps a distance. Health check up campaign and eye clinics are successfully organized. There is a good response and the patients properly adhere to the advice of the doctors and continue the medicine or visit the hospitals referred to by the doctors.

Tax Revision

Once in five years house tax revision is effected. In the year 1996, the house tax demand was Rs.5000 and, after revision, it was Rs.20,000. Now it has again been revised to Rs.35,000. Most of the houses are tiled houses. There are only six or seven huts in this Panchayat. Within a year these too will be replaced by tiled houses and the village will become a village without huts. It has been achieved now.

Children's Park

Golden Jubilee Children's Park and Sports Ground

When Ramanathan proposed a park for children all the members of the Gram Sabha approved of it. Now a park within the name *Ponvizha Poonga* has been established on 0.60 cents at the Panchayat office. Play equipments like swings, sea-saw, slide, merry-go-round and jungle-gym have been provided.

For the youth a sports ground has been prepared near the school. Sites for long jump, high jump, tennis, volleyball, cricket and *kabadi* have been provided. A carrom board has also been provided. Both student and non-student youth are playing in the sports ground.

Award for Achievement

In the years 1998-99 and 1999-2000 this Panchayat was adjudged the best Panchayat at the district level. Each year Rs.1.00 lakh was given as award money. From the award money, cement road, drainage and compound wall for the Panchayat office campus were provided. Provision to employ a chartered engineer for the civil works of the Panchayat is a good arrangement. Undue delay by the Union official is now avoided by engaging the chartered engineer.

The district level officials give due importance to PRIs only if the District Collector gives importance to them. Earlier "Panchayat medai", the monthly interface meet between the Village Panchayat Presidents and Government officials in the presence of the District Collector was promptly organised. Day-to-day problems were brought to the notice of the

Collector. The activities of various departments in the village were also shared. The Collector's orders with regard to the requests of the Panchayats were well taken by the officials. After the transfer of that Collector the significance of the "Panchayat medai" has diminished. Unexpected delay in releasing funds is not properly taken care of by the authorities. Earlier the District Collector immediately contacted the department officials and instructed them to carry out the activities to fulfil the demands of the Panchayats. This type of quick and serious attention is now not available. The "Panchayat medai" should be a permanent feature. Otherwise the gap between the District Collector and the Panchayati Raj Institutions, particularly the Village Panchayat, will widen.

Information Dissemination

The Panchayat has three display boards through which all the details of Panchayat activities are published. An audio equipment system is also available in the Panchayat. Once in 15 days necessary information on the Panchayat, oorani and drinking water supply is announced through the public address system. Ramanathan displays the income/expenditure statement. But the villagers do not pay any attention to the accounts as they witness the activities carried out in the village. If proper awareness is given in a systematic and planned way people's knowledge will improve.

Links with officials are needed for achieving things. Ramanathan frequently meets the officials and shares the village problems. Finally, he seeks their advice and help. When a transformer burst, he contacted the EB over phone and it was immediately attended to. Officials are positive towards the Panchayat Presidents who are honest and sincere.

Ramanathan equipped himself and developed his leadership by newspapers and Gandhiji's books. He attended training programmes at Gandhigram Rural Institute and the SIRD. He attended the All India Panchayat Parishad meeting in New Delhi and he shared his experience through AIR talks. In any meeting of Village Panchayat Presidents convened by the district officials his talk used to cover all matters, issues and problems of Village Panchayats as a whole. It is always welcomed by both officials and Presidents. He said that his approach is not to merely find fault with anybody but to understand and take necessary steps to get things done.

Future Options

Ramanathan will contest again in the election and is determined to provide more cement roads, to strengthen the Farmers' Association and the SHGs, to give attention to further resource mobilization for the Panchayat and to construct a health subcentre. He proposes to get an SHG to undertake vegetable gardening in one acre of land available in the Panchayat.

He is of the opinion that only a motivated leader with dedication and vision can transform the villages. He explained that he got recognition from the government by his consistent work and so became a member in various committees constituted at the district level. He is serving as the Chairperson of the District Village Panchayat Presidents Association.

Nallukkottai is now a place for learning, he said happily. His strength is continuous learning. He says that he promptly attends all training programmes and other meetings meant for Panchayats. His visit to SIRD, NIRD, RETC, Gandhigram Rural Institute and his periodical meetings with state level officials are the learning experience, he felt.

His desire is to make the Panchayat self-sufficient to meet its expenses without depending on the Government. If micro level model planning is undertaken with the help of the District Planning Committee he will try his best to draft the plan. EB charges increase year by year and maintenance of street lights, TV sets and water supply system is expensive. The Panchayat must equip itself to meet all these expenses from its own resources. Hence he did his best to mobilize the income of the Panchayat. There are 100 street lights, 7 sodium vapour lamps (AMT has paid for the provision), 11 hand pumps, 41 public taps, 2 OHTs, 3 TVs, 1 community well and community assets like office building, PDS shop, community hall, public toilets, ponds, roads etc. All these need proper maintenance. The President has to be committed to his work. Otherwise these will be underutilized. His public life is a successful one but he cannot properly look after his family. He sold about

3 acres of dry land due to limited income from these lands.

Conclusion

The Nallukkottai Gram Panchayat President, though old and hailing from a traditionally dominant family and community of the Panchayat, is a transformed individual with an extraordinary will power, coupled with a sense of commitment to transforming the village by changing his and the people's attitude, beliefs, views in favour of development and democracy. He demonstrated his rectitude in managing public affairs, which earned him the support of the public. He made the Panchayat laboratory for testing many innovative practices and schemes which, in turn, attracted the bureaucracy to move towards his Panchayat. His conceptualization of the Panchayat institution made him work for making the Panchayat a self-reliant institution. The Panchayat has to be made self-reliant in terms of its resources and economy. He is known in the whole of Tamil Nadu, both among the Panchayat leaders and the bureaucrats. His Panchayat has become a Mecca for Panchayat administrators. He earned his name among the people by serving them selflessly and this is perhaps due to the influence of the writings of Gandhiji. Though he laments that the existing system of polity and administration is corrupt and non-performing, he is of the firm view that it can be changed from below and that the Panchayat is the right place to establish good governance. Honest Panchayat leaders can change the entire paradigm. Working with the people is not easy but, once this exercise is set in a decisive direction, achievement in not difficult either.

CASE - 7

GREEN PANCHAYAT ON THE MAKING

This Gram Panchayat President had a dream of making the entire Panchayat area green with the active participation of the community. With this dream he approached the district administration and made it possible. His engagement with government officials yielded good results and in the same way his engagement with the community helped him to carry out many activities with the active participation of the people. He engaged not only the government officials and the community but also school going boys and girls. He made the Gram Sabha an instrument for adult education. His energy saving device saved his Panchayat money. His clean village campaign, with the active involvement of school children, yielded good results.

Mr.Shanmuganathan is the President of Rajendrapuram Village Panchayat of Aranthangi Union in Pudukkottai District. In the midst of many Village Panchayat leaders who are yet to be oriented in the concept of development, Shanmuganathan has conceptualized development from the perspective of ecology and environment and he is boldly making attempts to conscientise the people on development as he perceives it. He firmly believes that ecology, environment and natural resource management, are the vital activities of the grassroots institutions at present. By undertaking these the poor can be saved from marginalization and vulnerability can be reduced. The commons have to be saved and they are to be enriched. By doing so employment opportunity could be created. Economic growth, economic development and industrial development are essential for the development of the country. For security of livelihood and to provide opportunity to the poor to earn their livelihood, the local resources are very important. Water, soil, flora and fauna and livestock are the lifeline of the rustic folk.

Shanmuganathan belongs to a backward community, the Senaithalivan caste. He is now 50 years old. He ran an oil extraction unit after he completed his SSLC. But, as he could not compete with modern mega units, he discontinued his business. His association with service organizations and his basic interest in understanding the ecological and environmental impact on agriculture and his links with sports clubs provided an opportunity to him to realize the scope of the New Panchayati Raj System in delivering developmental services to the rural community.

Shanmuganathan perceives the New Panchayat Raj System as an instrument of grassroots democracy and the village community as the right unit for inculcating democratic values and principles. Panchayats are the right instruments to achieve development and social justice. With this hope he contested in the Panchayat election and won the election held for the Gram Panchayat President's position under the New Panchayat Raj System in 1996. "Panchayati Raj Institution in practice is different from what I perceived," Shanmuganathan says. In the existing system of allocation of tied-up funds, bureaucratic control, political interference, lack of people's participation and with the limited financial sources, the development of a village is a stupendous task. Shanmuganathan firmly says: "I realized these constraints within a period of six months of my entry into the Village Panchayat office. I understand that there is no systematic approach by the district administration. Most of the time the activities are moved according to the whims and fancies of the head of the district administration," Shanmuganathan observes. Frequent visits to various sectoral departments and establishing good rapport with the staff and officials of sectoral departments sustained his voluntarism as officials cooperated with the President to meet the needs of the people. Further he read many of the writings of Gandhiji and he understood his vision of the village community. Hence he frequently visited all habitations and interacted with the people, listening to the villagers. In these interfaces he tried his best to explain to the people his vision and plans to transform the village. His basic premise is that people should be given an opportunity to plan for their development. The concept of schemes has to go. Government schemes have belittled the people and the same schemes have given the impression to the people that poverty can be eliminated by the officials of the government. The government schemes have made the people not to think and act. People should be allowed to develop their own plan, based on their own vision.

About the Village Community

Rajendrapuram is the revenue village as well as the Village Panchayat. In Rajendrapuram Panchayat, there are three habitations, namely, Erukkalakottai, Kurunthirakkottai and Kakkakadu. They are the hamlets. Ambalam is the predominant caste. Muslim families are present in considerable number. Yadava, Chettiar, Senaithalaivan and SCs are other communities. The total population is 3295, male 1754, female 1541.

There are nine Ward Members, six men and three women. The Vice-President is a youth from the Muslim community. The Village Panchayat Council members are working in harmony and extend their cooperation to the President. He feels that as long as the President is honest, sincere and committed, he or she can get the support of the Ward Members and the people. First the leader should demonstrate his or her integrity and commitment.

Mobilizing the Community

After realizing the limitations of the government machinery in providing basic amenities to the villagers, Shanmuganathan decided to go back to the original system of village development, i.e., kudimaramathu. This system was in vogue for several centuries in Tamil Nadu. Many of the common facilities were created and sustained by the active participation of the people.

Hence he wanted to revive the old practice for which he wanted to mobilize the people. He spent a lot of time to interact with the community members, especially farmers, on the importance of voluntary service and self-help with regard to the upgradation/maintenance of village roads. As almost all roads in this Panchayat were narrow in size and in the category of cart road, during the agricultural season, the villagers suffered a lot to transport the agriculture inputs as well as the products.

People's Participation for common welfare

Hence the people expected that the Village Panchayat should come to their rescue. Altogether the length of the approach roads is 7 km. To make necessary improvements in these roads, there was neither any special scheme with the government nor adequate finance with the Village Panchayat. This issue was propeply explained to the villagers and the only alternative, kudimaramathu, was understood by the community. They came forward to give their labour free of cost. People of the concerned habitations joined together, levelled the existing mud road, and extended the width. When it was found that the approach road to the burial ground in the SC habitation was too narrow a few farmers were persuaded to part with their piece of land to widen the road. 80 per cent of the village mud road was leveled by kudimaramathu. People who engaged in this task were provided with only light refreshment by the Village Panchayat. These works were undertaken ahead of the declaration by the Government of Tamil Nadu of innovative scheme named Namakku Naame Thittam. The District Collector was apprised the contribution made by the people, which made the district administration supervise, visit and verify the works done and then the district administration sanctioned money for gravelling of 60 per cent of the mud roads improved under the kudimaramathu. The farmers were happy because the time required to transport their agricultural inputs/ products was lessened. The district administration, which gave sanction for gravelling the roads, increased the image of the President among the people.

The next step was to clean the wild bushes and weeds which grossly covered the surface of the water in the tanks and lakes. To eradicate these wild weeds Shanmuganathan availed of the assistance of agricultural experts and obtained a chemical weedicide. The villagers, both men and women, joined together and sprayed the chemical using hand sprayers. The wild weeds are now controlled in many tanks to a certain extent.

Though Shanmuganathan claimed all these as success, he has a sorrow to share. Fund was obtained from the MPLADS to maintain the bunds of irrigation tanks involving the ayacutdhars. But the fund was inadequate and there was an unexpected delay in mobilizing the people's contribution. When the Member of Parliament was approached to allocate additional fund it did not materialize. The fund was refunded. Shanmuganathan felt that it was a defeat not only to himself but to the villagers also.

Linkage with Sectoral Department

The link roads in the Panchayat, to an extent of 6 km, were in a very bad condition. They were like channels, deep and muddy. Shanmuganathan, through the proper channel, contacted the Chief Engineer of Rural Roads. He used to contact the office and pursued the matter, but, at the time of decision making, the engineer was transferred. When a new engineer came, he raised querries and the President tried to reply. Afterwards, the file was put up for decision making. Again the engineer was transferred. A novel can be written in this regard. He maintained the file in this regard intact. There was delay at the Chief Engineer's office due to frequent transfers of the Chief Engineer too. For meeting the Chief Engineer the travel and other related expenses were met from his own pocket. He told the Chief Engineer that his interest was not a selfish one like that of a contractor or personally motivated politician. He begged to consider his genuine attempt to serve the real poor villagers. He finally succeeded. A BT road was laid under the RR scheme for 6 km in Rajendrapuram Village Panchayat. To get things done in government offices is not so easy. It is the attitude of the officials who work in the government offices that they are giving alms to the people as if the people are the receivers receiving government benefits. They feel that they are the owners of government. Unless this attitude is changed, it is very difficult to do service to the people.

Improvement in the Supply of Drinking Water to the Villages

Provision of drinking water, that too protected water, is really a challenge in rural areas. The source should be adequate and the villagers must cooperate with the Village Panchayat. In Rajendrapuram Panchayat there are 5 OHTs, of which three tanks are having 30,000 litre capacity each and two tanks have 60,000 litre capacity each. The supply from four OHTs is interlinked so that if there is any damage in one OHT supply need not be interrupted. There are 125 public taps and 60 household connections in the Village Panchayat. To ensure equal quantity of water to all and to prevent the misuse of water, control valves and ferule system were installed in all distribution links. He carried out a water audit personally and provided water to all. He took a bold decision to use this new device of using ferule for water distribution. He earned the wrath of a few families who continuously misused water. He says that the Panchayat President should be bold enough to take such steps to ensure equity.

SHG Activities

Shanmuganathan reads all newspapers. He says that he used to understand many things through television and newspapers. Further his contacts with the staff and officials of the government departments enable him to comprehend the ways and means available in the government to improve the village. After understanding the details of the SGRY scheme and the significant role earmarked for NGOs in this regard, he himself involved with an NGO in the formation of SHGs among womenfolk. There are 15 SHGs, but only three are very active, as he regrets. The M.S. Swaminathan Research Foundation trained SHGs in the production of micro organisms which are used as pesticide successfully in sugarcane farms. The production can be easily marketed to M/s EID Parry Sugars Limited, which is running a sugar factory in this area.

Being a sensitized environmentalist, Shanmuganathan sees an immense scope for popularizing the products of organic farming. He says that, apart from sugarcane, the micro organisms could control pests in vegetables, flowers and paddy also. He proposes to equip one SHG to establish a unit in the Village Panchayat. After a period of three months, the production will fetch Rs. 60 to 70 for each member, he says.

Shanmuganathan regretfully share the hardship encountered in orienting the SHG members towards non-conventional economic activities. Though he took steps to avail of the gas retail dealership from Bharath Gas to one of the SHGs in the Panchayat, the group members were not ready to takeup the challenge. Shanmuganathan says that rural women prefer to go in for rearing of milk animals rather than taking risk in other commercial ventures. He emphasizes the important role of the NGOs and the government in this regard.

SHG Women at Work

Prevention is better than cure. But the rural masses do not attach seriousness to this concept due to lack of awareness. Shanmuganathan says that rural families are travelling by cycle 7 km. to market their milk for a meagre income. They fail to understand the nutritional importance of food. Villagers in general do not keep the milk for themselves. They sell all the milk. But the majority of them are in an anemic condition. To educate them he organized a health camp exclusively for women and adolescent girls. He explained the medicinal value of herbal plants which are locally available.

Gram Sabha as a Forum for Education

Shanmuganathan conceived the concept of Gram Sabha as a forum to educate the villagers. He brought experts in various fields during the Gram Sabha meetings and educated the mass. He used to collect various details of schemes implemented by many sectoral departments and distributed them to the villagers in the form of notices, phamplets and other publications. He tried his best to improve sanitation by creating awareness involving experts in this field. He regretted that he was able to achieve only 30 per cent success in the task of individual household latrine construction. Construction of toilets can be achieved by the Panchayat Presidents. The difficulty lies in making the people use the toilets. Many of the Presidents have attained the target of 100 per cent toilet construction but not 100 per cent utility of the toilets. He feels that a toilet culture has to be created.

Educating People

Education Development

There are three middle schools in this Village Panchayat. For high school the students are going to the nearby village of Silattur as well as Aranthangi Town. He has given importance to the enrolment of all eligible children. The VEC and the PTA are not effective but, with the help of a few teachers and villagers, Shanmuganathan was able to draft an annual plan for the welfare of the school students.

- Essay and oratory competitions were organised.
- Educational tours were arranged for students.
- Prizes were awarded to the outstanding students.
- Teachers from among State Awardees and National Awardees were invited to address the student community.
- To ensure protected drinking water supply to the students, the required vessels for boiling, filtering and storage were provided to all the three schools. In each class room a vessel is provided to store purified drinking water for the students.
- With the help of the Tamil Nadu Foundation, the Ajim Premji Foundation and the MSSRF computer education was given to the students.
- A nail cutter was provided to each class to maintain cleanliness.
- Toilet facilities were provided in all three schools.
- Water was provided to the toilets.
- Enough care was taken to ensure that the toilets are being used.
- Parents were motivated to send their wards at least upto the eighth standard.
- Youth groups among men are entrusted with responsibilities in the plan implementation of student welfare activities. The Youth Club of Erukkalakottai donated the cost of one power pump for the school.
- Students are encouraged to engage in village welfare activities like clearing of thorny bushes along the roadside, assisting in transporting of tree saplings for planting, arrangement of fencing and awareness programme on rain water harvesting.

Awareness Generation

Yet another problem in the village is the spread of used polythene in the entire village — how to clean and how to dispose of the same. He first sensitized the masses on the implications of polythene for the environment of the village. He further started acting on it. Villagers helped the Panchayat to clear polythene bags from the entire village. Students have been educated to keep wastes in three different bags. Thus he made waste management easy by educating the people.

SHG

SHG

Adoption of Energy Saving Technology in Street Lighting

In Rajendrapuram the street lights have not been functioning properly due to voltage fluctuation. The tube lights used to burn on only after 10 p.m. Further there were frequent failures. Shanmuganathan came to know the innovation undertaken in Kuthampakkam, one of the model villages in Tamil Nadu, where the street lights were replaced by florescent tube lights of 18 watts. The cost of one set of the florescent tube is Rs.650 only. The energy saving is expected to be to the extent of 60 per cent and material saving upto 10 per cent. Shanmuganathan got the approval of the Panchayat Council to make use of Rs.35,000 sanctioned to the Panchayat by the district administration from the equalization fund and Rs.30,000 collected as plan approval given to a private college authority. Shanmuganathan is keen on the mobilization of resources to the Panchayat but very strict in spending. The Panchayat building is yet to be electrified. He is managing without electricity in his office. At the same time he is giving priority to the public interest.

With regard to our enquiry about the scope of planned development through Village Panchayat, Shanmuganathan explained that there is a plan with the Village Panchayat. But due to paucity of funds, activities are prioritized according to the availability of funds. In this context he felt that unless there is sufficient devolution of finance to the Panchayati Raj Institutions, planned development cannot be achieved in villages.

Greening of Village

Shanmuganathan has created history in promoting micro-climate impact on the environment. He developed interest in understanding the ecology and environment during the 1980s when drought and the failure of monsoon were experienced in consecutive years. Shanmuganathan explained that agriculture in Rajendrapuram village never met with failure. He attributed this to a reason, namely, that they used to get at least some rainfall which was properly harvested and stored in the irrigation tanks and shared. He further said that the flora and fauna are totally disturbed and thereby the rainfall has been reduced. Farmers have not been well oriented in managing the micro ecosystem. At the same time the village farmers have to be oriented in effective water irrigation management also.

Nursery

After realizing this concept of green effect, Shanmuganathan consistently lobbied with the district administration to allocate fund for afforestation in his village. He used to plea for even a small fund of Rs.25,000 to Rs.50,000. The district authorities especially the then District Collector Mr. Makwana firmly believed the leadership of Shanmuganathan and selected Rajendrapuram village for the implementation of IWDP where the Panchayat was permitted to plant 1550 trees in its area of jurisdiction. Shanmuganathan considered it as a boon to the village.

Shanmuganathan, in consultation with the IWDP Committee members as well as forest officials identified 42 varieties of trees suited to plant in his village area. It was proposed to plant these tree saplings along the roadside, the tank bunds, sides of the canals, poramboke sites, school and temple campuses. Saplings were collected from the social forestry nursery and brought to the village where a nursery site was established. The saplings brought from the forest department were replaced with local soil, enriched with manure and kept for a period sufficient enough for transplanting. This special approach helped in ensuring 95 per cent survival rate after transplantation. The village roads in Rajendrapuram are less in width and so the planting of saplings have been done on the edge of the private land sites. Special meetings have been arranged to convince the private landholders in this regard. Except two or three individuals all gave permission for planting of tree. Villagers themselves involved in digging of pits, transporting of saplings, arranging for fencing and refilling of pits. They developed a positive mindset and voluntarily involved in the protection also. SHG members were engaged in watering the plants. They collected water from various sources in pots and buckets and irrigated the saplings. Though the wage is less they happily involved in this activity. Thus the whole activity of greening of village has become a people's programme.

Activities in Integrated Wasteland Development Programme (IWDP)

Understanding the seriousness shown by Shanmuganathan, the IWDP was sanctioned during the year 2003-2004. As referred earlier the tree planting activity is one of the component. There are other activities also under this IWDP. The SHG formed under this programme had the opportunities to undergo training in tailoring, agarbathi and candle manufacturing. There was training in poultry also. Three women got sewing machine and three are being involved in poultry activities.

The villagers, men and women, were exposed to various rural developmental activities when they were taken to Dharmapuri, Kodaikkanal, K.V. Kuppam and Hyderabad for an educational tour under the IWDP. In two tanks, namely Pallivasalkulam and Chettikulam, repair and maintenance works have been carried out. As a token of service to the educational sector, one of the schools got barbed wire fencing under this scheme.

One hand sprayer has been to a landless agriculture labourer. Shanmuganathan is the President of the IWDP Committee. He won the confidence of the committee members and successfully implemented the planned activities under this programme.

Innovative Rainwater Harvesting

Pudukkottai District is famous for its number of ponds and tanks. Rajendrapuram Village is also surrounded by many tanks and lakes. There are five PWD tanks and seventeen ponds/tanks under Village Panchayat jurisdiction. Two ooranies are under the enjoyment of private parties. Villagers are always vigilant in their maintenance. Altogether the total ayacut of these irrigation tanks is about one thousand acres.

Innovative Rainwater Harvesting

When the Government of Tamil Nadu emphasized the establishment of RWH structures in all buildings, public and private, Shanmuganathan introduced a novel method. There is a tile manufacturing factory near the village of Rajendrapuram. Broken tiles are dumped there. He proposed to install a drainage system to drain the rainwater from the roof top of individual houses effectively by paving

Innovative Rainwater Harvesting

the broken tiles in the front and backyard, and, to collect the drained rainwater, a soak pit was dug at the side of the dwelling units. Scientifically it is a sound idea.

But transporting the huge stock of tiles to each habitation in all four hamlets .is expensive. Though the public were ready to give their labour for loading and unloading the cost of loading could not be borne by them. He approached an NRI and, with his financial contribution, he engaged a lorry and transported the broken tiles.

In about 80 per cent of the dwelling units the RWH structure, i.e. a drain and a soak pit, were established successfully. People joined together and worked as a team in this regard. This innovation attracted the attention of the district authorities and an incentive of Rs.35,000 was given to the Panchayat.

The villagers, after witnessing the honest efforts of the President to improve the villages; slowly came to recognize his leadership. The house tax demand during the period of 2002-2003 was Rs.7,000. Shanmuganathan, without waiting for the guidance of the officials, enhanced the house tax to Rs.16,000. When the District Collector appealed to the Village Panchayats to fix the house tax as per the guidelines of the State Government, it was enhanced to Rs.50,070. People were told about the necessity. 80 per cent of the demand has been collected so far and he is confident that 100 per cent collection can be done as the public understand the financial position of the Village Panchayat.

Conclusion

The Panchayat leader has a vision but he finds it very difficult to translate his vision into reality as there is a gap between the leader and the people in the thought process. But, to win over the confidence of the people, he proved his honesty. He is always different from others in doing things. To him ecology and environment are very important for the livelihood security of the poor. He is not a leader to reach the target fixed by the government. He firmly believes that by conscientizing the people on development many things can be achieved with the active participation of the people. He carries out activities according to the needs of the people. He feels that the weakness is in the governance system and the community. People do not have development aspirations. Equally they do not have the needed awareness to lead a decent life in human living conditions. People generally want to be beneficiaries to receive benefits. It is necessary to create awareness among the people about their role in the process of development as development participants. The Panchayat President has proved that people can be mobilized and made to participate in any development activity as owners of development. He says that whatever success he has achieved is due to the whole hearted support extended by the people. In his opinion every Panchayat leader should have a vision for his/her Panchayat area. To translate the vision into reality the Panchayat leader should have needed commitment and capability. Of all the qualities the Panchayat leader should have the tendency of respecting the people and maintaining high moral authority and rectitude. The Panchayat leader should not indulge in achieving targets like government officials. Panchayat leaders should study the process of development and they should go with the people. Each village is unique, each block is unique, each district is unique. Understanding the uniqueness, Panchayat leaders have to work accordingly. Shanmuganathan is a model in the above aspects.

CASE - 8

NEW MANAGEMENT WITH TECHNOLOGY

This Panchayat is also a model for effective management of Panchayat finances. All the activities of the Panchayat are technology based. His concern for the poor and his commitment to action enabled the Panchayat to get more number of schemes and programmes. His effective Panchayat management yielded good results. For many of the visitors this Panchayat is a showpiece as it has helped the poorest of the poor. It is a self reliant Gram Panchayat. Innovative schemes are experimented within his Panchayat. A leader with a development vision he took the initiative to transform the life of the tribals.

Odanthurai is a Village Panchayat of modest size in Karamadai Panchayat Union of Coimbatore District. There are nine members in the Village Panchayat Council and, of them, six are male and three female. Among these Ward Members two are from the Scheduled Tribe Irular community, one male and the other female and one is from the Scheduled Caste. Odanthurai Panchayat consists of 9 villages, namely, (1) Oomapalayam, (2) Uppupalayam, (3) Naripallam Road, (4) T.A.S. Nagar, (5) Vinobaji Nagar, (6) Gandhinagar, (7) Kallar Pudur, (8) Thooripalam, (9) Alamarathur. Oomapalayam is the mother village in Odanthurai Village Panchayat. This Village Panchayat is a multi-caste and multi-religious one. Families belonging to Backward, Most Backward, Scheduled Caste and Scheduled Tribe communities are living here. They are Hindus, Muslims and Christians, who all live in harmony. Okkaliga Goundar is the dominant caste. Valayar is the next in numerical strength. Arunthathiyar a sub-group of the SCs and Irular (ST) are also in good number. There are totally 1050 dwelling units in the Village Panchayat of Odanthurai.

Odanthurai Village Panchayat Office Building

Location of the Village Panchayat

The Panchayat is situated on the northern bank of the river Bhavani, opposite Mettupalayam on the southern bank. It lies on the Coimbatore-Ooty highway. The mega water-sports entertainment centre "Black Thunder" is located within the jurisdiction of this Village Panchayat. There are other business firms like fruit processing units, cold storage units, tanneries, automobile units and saw mills functioning in the jurisdiction of Odanthurai Village Panchayat. A decade ago, the Village Panchayat was a most backward area. There were no basic amenities for the residents. The Scheduled Tribe families were bonded labourers without even a piece of land to build their huts on. Almost all SC families lived in huts in penury. The primary school functioned in a single building without any basic facility and with little space for play. The vision of the Village Panchayat President under the new Panchayat Raj System changed the destiny of the people of Odanthurai. Within eight years, Mr. Shanmugam, the President of Odanthurai Village Panchayat, made the Panchayat the best among the 389 Village Panchayats in Coimbatore District and the first in the entire country in the implementation of various innovative programmes to improve the socio-economic life of the villagers.

Evolution of his Leadership

Shanmugam, aged 49, belongs to the Okkaliga Goundar community. Basically he is a farmer, owns a large extent of coconut grove and banana plantation. He lives with his wife and two children. His son is studying engineering and his daughter is in high school. He belongs to a family traditionally reputed for its concern for the cause of the villagers. One of his close relatives served as the President of Odanthurai Village

Panchayat from 1961 to 1965. His paternal uncle was the President in the next term, i.e., 1965 to 1970. Once again his close relative who was the President during 1961-1965 served as the President from 1970 to 1977. After a gap of a decade, his father become the President from 1986 to 1991. His father, being aged, involved Shanmugam in managing the Panchayat activities. Shanmugam, after his school final, did not continue his studies due to his involvement in looking after the farming activities. He gained inspiration from Mr.M.G.Ramachandran. When assisting his father in the Panchayat administration, he used to visit various government offices to perform Panchayat work. He said that there was no linkage between the district administration and Village Panchayat. He realized that people expected a lot from the Village Panchayat leaders whereas the Village Panchayat system was dependent on the government's grant. His family was known for public service and his father created a track record in service through the old Panchayat system. He was groomed by his father in Panchayat activities. He cultivated the officials at all levels when his father was President of the same Panchayat. Hence his image was up in the public domain when election was announced.

Dawn of New Panchayati Raj System

Being literate, Shanmugam understood the significance of the new Panchayat Raj System. When the election was declared for Panchayati Raj Institutions in the year 1996, his father himself advised him to contest. Shanmugam said that he had also a perception that development could be achieved through the New Panchayati Raj System.

Shanmugam is a sympathizer of the AIADMK. But he did not claim his political identity with the AIADMK when he contested in the election. There were two opponents during the 1996 election. He won in the election by a margin of five hundred and eighty five. His family background, his sociability and his public image worked as factors for his success.

His Performance

Shanmugam understood that only by improving the financial position of the Panchayat the immediate felt needs of the villagers could be fulfilled. He identified that the most important felt needs of the villagers were the provision of drinking water and housing for the poor. There was no distribution of protected drinking water in the Panchayat. The public used to walk two kilometres to fetch drinking water. There was no scheme of water supply implemented by the TWAD board in Odanthurai Panchayat. With a proposal to sink a borewell for drinking water, he started augmenting the Panchayat income through house tax and the same was revised in the year 1997 from Rs.23,000 to Rs.1 lakh. Adding the grants received from the government and other sources of income, one borewell was sunk in each of the nine hamlets.

Though borewells were provided, the villagers expected supply of water from the Bhavani river as in the case of the nearby municipality, Mettupalayam. The villagers, due to non-availability of river water for drinking, went to the riverside to collect water directly from the river though it was not purified. Hence the demand for a protected water supply scheme was raised again and again with the district authorities. The district authority arranged for a proposal in this regard.

The district authority proposed to develop a plan of water supply to cover six hamlets leaving out the areas of the STs in Kallar Pudur, the hutments of SC and the proposed new layout of Gandhi Nagar. Shanmugam directly intervened in this proposal, interacted with the TWAD officials, and persuaded them to include these areas also in the proposal. At a cost of Rs.30 lakhs an estimate was drafted by the TWAD. Yet fortune did not favour Odanthurai as allocation was delayed due to financial crisis.

New Opportunity

During the year 1999-2000, the government of India announced the new scheme of Rajiv Gandhi National Drinking Water Mission (RGNDWM). It was an innovative scheme as it demanded public contribution to the implementation as well as the maintenance. It is not so easy to mobilize the public and collect their contribution for a drinking water scheme in the context of the supply driven system of government administration. But Shanmugam tried his best. He visited each habitation and explained the scope for availing of the RGNDWM scheme as the TWAD scheme was delayed due to financial crunch. As the borewells provided from the Panchayat fund became dry during the summer, the public came forward to contribute.

Rajiv Gandhi Drinking Water Mission

Water Filter Plant

A committee was formed in this regard, and a proper register was maintained to register the details of individual contributions. Commercial firms gave donations to the Panchayat. The rich families were the major contributors. When Shanmugam improved the road facilities, widened roads, undertook maintenance works and provided BT road, the rich and the middle class families felt happy over the improved facilities as it could be better utilized for transportation of their agricultural commodities as well as driving of their personal vehicles comfortably. About two lakhs of rupees were donated by these rich families.

The cost estimate for a full-fledged drinking water system covering all nine hamlets, one treatment plant, laying of pipeline for a distance of 13 kilometres, five overhead tanks (4 tanks of 30,000 litre capacity, and one tank of 1,00,000 litre capacity) and one booster station all put together was forty eight lakh rupees of which the public contribution was to be 4.8 lakh rupees. There are 225 house tap connections and sixty five public taps to ensure adequate drinking water to all throughout the year. Water is tested and it is certified as fit to drink. Odanthurai became the first Village Panchayat in the entire country to implement the RGNDWM scheme. The national inauguration of the scheme was celebrated in Odanthurai for which ministers and higher officials from State and Central governments came over to that village. Odanthurai became a place for learning. Elected representatives of Panchayati Raj Institutions and government officials from all over the country made visits to Odanthurai to understand the strategies adopted in mobilizing the community and collecting contribution and the technology of the treatment plant.

Management System in Water Supply

Shanmugam said that, with the guidance of the TWAD officials, an audit was made of the water supply system. It was found that, at the rate of 280 litres per minute, totally 2.30 lakh litres are collected each day. The population is 5,500. At the rate of 50 litres per head the required quantity of water is 2,75,000 litres. Besides this human consumption there are the needs of the cattle and commercial firms. Hence it was decided to provide a separate line to distribute drinking water from this new system to the main village Oomappalayam as there are more number of households there. Here the filtered water is supplied only through public taps. Everyday, for about two hours, water supply is available for the public through this new line. After this borewell water is made available to the public. A gate valve system is strictly adopted to ensure water to all families. Proper care is given to the maintenance of power pumps. Shanmugam said that the maintenance cost is only nominal as the OHT operators keep vigil over the distribution system. Hence the annual maintenance cost is around rupees thirty six thousand only. The deposit from 225 households is promptly collected and Rs.2,25,000 is held as fixed deposit. An annual interest of Rs.10,247 is earned from the deposit amount. The monthly water tax is collected and the annual income from the water tax is Rs.80,040. The overall annual expenditure for electricity charges is Rs.84,000. To reduce the electricity charges, a bio mass gasifier plant has been erected. The gas produced from the plant is utilized to run a generator and in turn the power pump. Hence the cost of electricity charges is reduced considerably, i.e., from Rs.84,000 to Rs.30,000 now. The bio gasifier plant is in operation for the past one year. It is found from the separate account maintained in the Panchayat for water supply that Rs.2,41,635 is available as in the month of November 2004. When thousands of Village Panchayats are not able to come out from their debt to the TNEB and make their grant money from the government to the TNEB, Odanthurai is one of the few Village Panchayats not only having cleared the arrears but also saving a large amount. Hence the SFC grant of Rs.1.20 lakhs received from the government is available for development in Odanthurai. Shanmugam shared that his wish for providing purified river water to all his villagers was fulfilled within a tenure under new Panchayati Raj System.

Achievement in Rural Housing

Shanmugam said that after fulfilling the basic need of water supply to all, his aspiration to improve the welfare of the poor can now be attended to. He was of the opinion that the mindset of poor could be transformed towards development if only the individuals live in a house owned by them. The self-respect of any individual could be improved if people live in their own house. Owning a house is a matter of pride in a society of poor people. Hence Shanmugam was keen on availing of the housing scheme for the poor. During 1997-98, through the IAY, 45 houses were constructed for 45 SC families._

Yet there are many poor families living in huts not only among SC but also among the MBC and the Backward Communities also. Moreover the families of STs do not have a piece of land. Hence land had to be acquired for the STs from the private land owners as there was no unreserved forest land available for distribution to them. Having witnessed the abject poverty and plight of the landless Scheduled Tribes, Shanmugam approached the district officials and urged them to take the initiative for land acquisition. Actually it was his first attempt before he worked for the provision of protected drinking water supply to all. But, as various procedures had to be adhered to in land acquisition, there was a delay in this regard. A layout was proposed to provide 119 house sites to 119 ST families and notice was served to acquire 6.50 acres of land from a private land owner. The concerned land owner was a business magnate who was not ready to lose his estate as the market value of the property was around fifty lakh rupees. Hence he went to court and obtained a stay in the high court and stalled the proceedings for land acquisition. In the meantime, in consultation with the district authorities, through the public prosecutor, a counter petition was filed and the stay was vacated successfully. Shanmugam, anticipating the move of the land owner to approach the Supreme Court, appraised the district authorities and pressurized them to obtain a caveat. By his constant vigil and timely action in consonance with the law, a caveat was obtained successfully.

Shanmugam moved his coins very quickly and calculatingly. The stay obtained by the landholder having been vacated and a caveat obtained against any appeal, he approached the District Collector to take immediate steps to issue house site pattas to the ST families. Accordingly a mass contact programme was conducted and on that day itself free house site pattas were distributed to 119 ST families. The families immediately occupied their allotted sites.

In the process of providing houses to ST families, the first step of house site allotment was successfully achieved in spite of legal hurdles. Then Shanmugam persuaded the district authorities to approach the Scheduled Tribes Development Commission for the provision of 119 pucca houses. The fund allocation of Rs.40.46 lakhs was made available and the work was immediately commenced.

When the progress of the construction was at the lintel stage, the land owner got an order of *status quo* ante from the Supreme Court. Shanmugam personally corresponded with the government pleader, supplied all the needed records, details and supportive factors related to the case. Within a period of four months, the stay obtained from the Supreme Court was lifted and the house construction was completed successfully.

ST Colony Kallar Pudhur

The Scheduled Tribe families of the Irular community who so far lived without a piece of land now possess their own houses. They have a sense of pride as they themselves were involved in the construction. The private land owner finally attempted to bribe Shanmugam. But Shanmugam's integrity and determination to work for the welfare of the suppressed won. The new settlement is a model. The ST women are organized into self-help groups. To ensure regular income to each family, milch animals have been distributed. To sustain this economic activity a Scheduled Caste milk producers' society was established. Adult men, especially youths, have also been organised into self-help groups. They expected daily wage income and demanded to arrange for a factory or some industrial activity in the Panchayat. Shanmugam felt that the government and the non-governmental organizations must work together for the development of the suppressed communities. The Panchayat administration alone cannot work in this regard.

Shanmugam is now making efforts to have a hostel for the ST students to improve their standard of education. He proposes to make arrangements for the provision of computer education to ST students as information technology is becoming the order of the day.

Implementation of Katcha Housing Scheme

The katcha housing scheme is one of the useful rural housing schemes. Instead of construction of a new house by spending a huge amount, a poor household could be provided with the minimum facilities, especially fire proof roofing, ventilated room and toilet facilities at a minimum expenditure of Rs.10,000 from the government grant. With the contribution of labour and other odd things, a katcha house could be easily and quickly constructed. Shanmugam was able to avail of funds under the katcha housing scheme and 65 katcha houses were constructed successfully. Poor families belonging to SC, ST and Most Backward Communities were benefited by this. By proper planning and promoting participation of beneficiaries the Panchayat was able to construct twelve katcha houses at the cost of ten houses, Shanmugam said.

Innovative Group Housing

Shanmugam, when making efforts to augment income to the Panchayat in addition to enhancement of house tax, gave attention to increasing the property taxes from commercial firms. He also met the officials of government institutions like forest college and private matriculation school, and collected the professional tax promptly. In the meantime, the share of the entertainment tax collected from Black Thunder was also received. Hence the Panchayat's finance is on a sound footing. Basic facilities like drinking water, road, street lights etc., were provided during his first tenure. In this context Shanmugam had an innovative proposal of rural housing for the poor from the Panchayat fund.

Innovative Group House

He approached the District Collector and requested him to grant permission to utilize the Panchayat's own fund for the construction of 60 group houses for poor families. Altogether there were 135 poor families who needed housing. But, as the available fund in the Panchayat account was inadequate for the construction of 135 houses, he further pleaded with the Collector to exercise his influence to provide the scheme fund for the remaining poor families. The Collector wondered how a Village Panchayat could earn that much money and questioned Shanmugam in this regard. The major income that Shanmugam referred to was the house tax matching grant at the rate of 300 per cent of the total house tax demand as the collection of the same was cent-per-cent all in three years since 1996. The matching grant received from the government for three years itself amounted to about Rs.11.50 lakhs. The District Collector took it as a serious effort of the Village Panchayat in delivering of social justice to the poor. During the visit of the nodal officer (who had been deputed to facilitate development) the District Collector brought him to Odanthurai. After witnessing the new settlement established for the Scheduled Tribes, the nodal officer positively replied to the proposal of another new settlement for all eligible poor families in Odanthurai.

The total project cost was estimated at Rs.45.90 lakhs for the construction of 135 houses. There was no special scheme with the government in this regard. The only option was the SGRY scheme but it was a procedure that only public assets could be created using SGRY fund. Provision of housing was also a labour intensive activity and, further, in the establishment of a new settlement of 135 houses, site improvement, drainage facilities, approach roads, street pavement, construction of nightsoil linked bio gas plant etc., could be treated as common facilities.

Night Soil Linked Biogas Plant

Gram Sabha Meet

Considering the nature of the project the government sanctioned the construction of 135 houses provided the Village Panchayat contributed the fund earmarked for the construction of 60 houses. Shanmugam was happy because, instead of sixty houses, the Village Panchayat was fortunate to have a hundred and thirty five houses. Immediately he convened the special Gram Sabha and selected 60 poor families from the BC, 20 from the MBC, 35 from the SC and 20 from the ST. The project was successfully completed. The quality was commended as the best by the Parliamentary Committee for Urban Development when it visited Odanthurai.

Achievement in Education

At present there are two primary schools and one middle school in Odanthurai Panchayat. Further there are two matriculation schools run by private managements. The primary school located at Oomapalayam functioned in an old building where there were only two classrooms without any other basic infrastructure facilities. The villagers demanded to make improvements in the school so that it could be upgraded to a middle school. Shanmugam came to know that there was no common land available to extend the facilities of the school. The issue of non-availability of common land always struck in his mind and, in consultation with the VAO, he tried his best to find a common piece of land. In that attempt he came to know that under 'natham' classification an extent of three and a half acres of land had been allotted to an ex-serviceman in the year 1942. The concerned beneficiary, instead of holding the land himself, let it out to a third party, which was a violation of the rules. Shanmugam tookup the issue with the Collector and succeeded in bringing the RDO for a personal inspection and verification. The RDO recommended cancellation of the allotment. The ex-serviceman appealed to the DRO and the issue was delayed.

School

School Compound

In the meantime, the ex-serviceman went to court. The court very quickly heard the case and reitreated that the decision taken by RDO was correct.

Shanmugam, realizing the need of the hour, acted quickly and the eviction was executed. On the same day the foundation for a school building was also laid after cleaning away the banana plantation which stood there. During the construction of the school building, the ex-serviceman appealed and obtained a stay in a writ petition. The writ petition was dismissed and the Collector was authorized by the court to proceed. In the meantime the then Collector was transferred and Shanmugam met the next Collector and briefed him of the nature of the issue. The Collector was very kind. He not only took immediate action but also sanctioned funds under various schemes like Employment Assurance Scheme, Sampoorna Gram Rozgar Yojana, Sarva Siksha Abiyan. A new school with adequate buildings, all necessary infrastructure like toilet, drinking water system, kitchen shed, playground and compound wall etc., came up. Further the primary school was upgraded to a middle school. All those activities were successfully completed within a period of one year. Shanmugam said that he was able to achieve all this because of the positive mindset of all the concerned officials. His tireless efforts, including spending his own money to periodically visit the district officers and Chennai to meet and appraise the lawyer, also counted in this regard. The Parent Teachers Association mobilized about one lakh rupees and in all classes from first standard to eighth standard, furniture was provided to the students. There was a proposal to provide two computers to train the students. With regard to balwadi centres the Village Panchayat arranged for the provision of toilets, drinking water supply. Further, in one Balwadi, the flooring was upgraded with tiles, spending Rs.15,000 from the Village Panchayat fund. It was proposed to provide a lot of toys and other play materials to the children in the balwadis.

Adoptation of Appropriate Rural Technologies

Shanmugam is a progressive farmer. His interest to learn new things was useful to the Panchayat Administration. His consciousness of the income and the expenditure of the Village Panchayat drove him to consult professionals in various sectors of development. When solar light technology was popularized by private entrepreneurs he approached them and arranged for the installation of 25 solar lights. There was a subsidy but the subsidy amount was given to the commercial firm at that time.

Solar Lights

Shanmugam calculated the profit in this regard and directly approached the authorities of the Non-Conventional Energy Development Board and succeeded in availing of the subsidy directly by the Village Panchayat. Further, instead of agreeing to the price of solar lights that prevailed in the market, Shanmugam directly contacted a few companies and negotiated for a lesser price. One company came forward to reduce the cost of the solar lights as the payment was immediate as well as directly by the Panchayat instead of routing through the government machinery. Suppliers in general feel it hard to get orders and supply through the government department as there is a lot of procedures as well as unnecessary

Bio-mas Gasifier Plant

delay in addition to commission to the officials. Hence, at a considerably less cost per set, Shanmugam was able to procure forty five sets of solar lights. Totally there are sixty five solar lights, which save an expenditure of about fifty thousand rupees annually to the Village Panchayat.

Shanmugam adopted other appropriate technologies like biomass gasifier by which electricity is produced from the bio-fuel of wood pieces to run the generator in the pumping station under the Rajiv Gandhi Drinking Water Mission. There he fitted an equipment to mix the solution to purify the water even after the filter beds to ensure maximum purity. The 135 toilets constructed in the innovative group housing colony is being linked with a plant. The nightsoil linked biogas plant is successfully functioning as the households are advised to utilize the toilet. At present about 20 householders get gas from the plant. It is said that an average of one hundred rupees is saved by each family due to the provision of bio-gas. Otherwise they would have to purchase fuelwood every month.

New Lead

Yet another new technology that Shanmugam proposed is the establishment of a windmill. It was said that at Sulthanpettai near Palladam in Coimbatore, there are many windmills being erected and energy is produced successfully as the flow of the wind is at the required speed. Shanmugam said that the total cost of the plant including the cost of site and other equipment was Rs.1.53 crore. The capacity of a production plant is 350 KV, which may produce an average 9.0 lakh units of energy in a year. If the sales price of one unit is Rs.2.30, the annual income is around twenty lakhs, he projected. He planned to avail of a loan and the loan amount could be repaid within six years. He felt that there was a lack of vision among the development officials with regard to the concept of Rural Development. He further said there were only a few officials at higher levels who have the fire to work for innovation instead of mechanically implementing the schemes and programmes. He is of the opinion that in any Village Panchayat whether it is financially sound or poor, by a calculated vision building exercise of the Village Panchayat Council and the enabling guidance and encouragement of the concerned government officials, could plan the phases of development in major sectors like education, health, poverty alleviation and rural housing. He emphasized that the Panchayat Presidents should dream to make the Village Panchayat a self-sufficient entity and should be a honest and committed leader so that he or she could gain support and assistance from every corner.

Development Administration should be a coordinated effort of all concerned. At present there is only a limited coordination among the various partners, namely, government, non-government and public. Taking the initiative in this regard is the responsibility of the grassroots leadership, Shanmugam said.

About the Future Vision

Shanmugam remarked that in the context of the New Panchayati Raj System, a lot of development is possible. During the first tenure provision of basic amenities was successfully attempted in his village and in the next phase provision of housing to the poor and improvement in the educational activities were achieved. Simultaneously, attention was given to equip the women. This kind of activity has to be strengthened in future, Mr. Shanmugam said.

Farming activities in the area are changed now-a-days, Mr. Shanmugam said. Hence the employment opportunities to rural landless labour is very limited. His focus in future is to equip the youths, especially students, in terms of education. Imparting computer education and encouraging students to move further from the school education into various vocational and technical and professional education have to be ensured, Shanmugam emphasized.

When the election was announced for the second tenure under the New Panchayati Raj System, the villagers in general and the women in particular compelled him to contest again. He agreed after their persuasion. There was opposition. But he won by a margin of 1250 votes. Shanmugam said that he did not make any special efforts in the election campaign, like door to door canvassing. He just published pamphlets where he listed the achievements and the proposed works to be done further. People reposed faith in him and reelected him. His leadership is getting improved, he shared. Year by year he has learned a lot by involving himself in various development activities and through interaction with various personalities, he added.

His exposure visit to northern states like Rajasthan, Madhya Pradesh, Maharashtra and New Delhi was very useful, he remarked. The state of Tamil Nadu is emerging as a developed state in the transformation of rural areas, Shanmugam said. In spheres like all weather road, school infrastructure, provision of protected drinking water, SHG activities, creation of other infrastructure facilities, rural electrification, rural housing to the poor, Tamil Nadu is ahead of all other states, Mr.Shanmugam said. What the most Village Panchayats of Tamil Nadu have to focus on is the proper and committed activities under rain water harvesting system as the ground water level in the major portion of Tamil Nadu is going down. He is correct in his vision as the development experts also emphasize the protection and promotion of ecology and environment, which have a major share in the achievement of sustainable development.

Odanthurai has become a lighthouse pointing to the right direction in the concept of rural development. Elected representatives from all over Tamil Nadu and other states of India, development officials, non-governmental organizations' managers are coming to Odanthurai. Shanmugam was invited by the training institutions like SIRD, RETC, KILA, Gandhigram Rural Institute, to share his views and activities.

Progress and advancement of rural India is a challenging task in the context of several obstacles. But in the New Panchayati Raj System a new trend has emerged in many villages. There are leaders coming to assume responsibility to lead. These leaders know the mindset of villagers, the system of bureaucracy, the status of politics and the inbuilt deficiency in the Panchayat Act. But they are determined to make an honest attempt, a step by step progress and steadily attract the attention of all concerned. These leaders are pathfinders who find ways and means within the existing system of governance as well as influence the system for innovations also. Shanmugam of Odanthurai belongs to this list.

Conclusion

He worked on three major areas, namely water, housing and energy. He involved the people in all the activities not only in terms of mere physical participation but also in terms of material contribution. He conducted the Panchayat administration in a transparent way. Further he challenged the moneyed to serve the poor. His concern for social justice brought name to him. His innovativeness, commitment and sincerity have drawn the attention of officials and they cooperated with this Panchayats in all its activities. In a corrupt system, the government machinery works without any favour from the Panchayat leader for which the Panchayat leader paves way if he is honest and committed. His determination to make the Panchayat self-reliant has started yielding results after he successfully mobilized the resources from the Panchayat area itself. He created many such leaders in Tamil Nadu. Of them the Semmipalayam Panchayat President is one.

CASE - 9

STRUGGLE FOR ENVIRONMENT

The three Gram Panchayat leaders are fighters. They have been waging a relentless fight against the mafia taking sand from the Panchayat area. This struggle is going on for the past five years and these leaders are fighting with the active support and participation of the community. Saving the natural resources from excess exploitation is the major work in these Panchayats. By exhibiting their honesty, they have kept the community with them and faced severe hardships. Police, bureaucracy, politicians, and the mafia joined together to harass these Panchayat leaders. So they went up to judiciary to safeguard the interests of the community.

Introduction

The following three case studies are the best examples to demonstrate how elected women and men representatives are struggling at the grassroots to protect the environment and natural resources. Like these three Gram Panchayat Presidents there are innumerable Gram Panchayat Presidents fighting against the industrial mafia who are polluting the rural areas and illegally exploiting natural resources like water and sand. The existing bureaucratic set up favours exploiters and does not help the Panchayats and the people. The Panchayat Presidents have to mobilize the community to wage a relentless struggle against such exploitation. These leaders with their vision, commitment, leadership and honesty, are able to manage the Panchayats as well as protect the environment and natural resources. Of course, they are being supported by the people and some of the supportive civil society organizations.

I. Appipalayam Gram Panchayat in Karur District

Ms. Eswari, aged 46, belongs to the MBC. She has studied up to pre-university course. Her husband is one of the four traditional leaders who constitute the traditional Village Committee. Her husband has been looking after the day to day administration and the annual celebration of the village temples for the past 30 years in the Village Panchayat of Appipalayam. Ms. Eswari has been the President of Appipalayam Panchayat consecutively for two tenures since 1996.

Village Setup

Appipalayam is a modest village in size. Its population is 2694 — 1364 men, 1330 women and 248 children and adolescents. The total number of families are 860. It is said that for the past two decades the villagers are strictly adhering to the small family norm. Among the communities of Appipalayam, the Kongu Gowders are the dominant caste and Naickers, SCs and Nadars are less in numerical strength. There are 10 hamlets, of which Appipalayam is the mother village. The Village Panchayat Council consists of 9 Ward Members, 6 men and 3 women. Agriculture is the main occupation in the village. The village is covered by the irrigation system of Amaravathi Dam. It is located at the tail end of the irrigation system. A check dam is constructed near the village, from which the Thiruma Nilayur Rajavaikkal, the main channel, waters the 900 acres of ayacut spread across Appipalayam and the nearby Village Panchayats of Karuppan Palayam and Sanappirattu.

Farmers cultivate paddy, banana, sugarcane and turmeric. Some raise fruit trees (sappota). There are coconut plantations also in Appipalayam Panchayat area. Despite the vagaries of the monsoon, agriculture is successfully carried on in this area. The landless labourers get regular work throughout the year. Moreover as the Village Panchayat areas of Appipalayam and the nearby Panchayat of Karuppan Palayam are located on the side of the Dindigul-Bangalore National Highways and also lie on the banks of the River Amaravathi, dyeing industries are also coming up. There are about one hundred units in Karuppan Pallam Panchayat and 13 units in Appipalayam Panchayat. As the nature of the work demands many manual labourers, many local landless labourers get work regularly in the dyeing units.

Her Recruitment

When the election was announced under the New Panchayati Raj System, the villagers of Appipalayam Panchayat preferred Ms.Eswari as the Presidentship was reserved for women. The villagers felt that, being an educated lady who also hails from the traditional community, she would be the best choice to manage the Village Panchayat. But there were two opponents. One was from the Naicker community and the other from the Gowder community. Provision of drinking water facility, road improvement and transport facility were the issues raised by the villagers. Ms.Eswari promised to fulfil these demands of the people. She won the election by a margin of 166 votes.

The Issue of Water Pollution

As a large number of dyeing units are located in Karuppan Palayam Panchayat, it was estimated that about five lakh litres of polluted water is drained out through the public drainage into canals and on to the streets. It stagnates all the time and mosquitoes breed. The ground water has become unfit to drink. The public complained but their Panchayat President did not pay attention, Ms.Eswari said. But, in course of time, the ground water of Appipalayam also got polluted as the dyeing units located in Appipalayam also let out waste water into public places. Ms. Eswari said that the dyeing unit proprietors dug borewells and, in the case of failure to strike water, they let the waste water without treatment into these bores. Hence five borewells meant for drinking water purposes have become polluted; the water has become rose/dark coloured and also more saline. The villagers of Appipalayam suffer from stomach ache, fever, diarrhea, jaundice and discoloured teeth.

The Primary Health Centre is functioning at Karuppan Palayam where many patients with the above mentioned symptoms reported for treatment. The Medical Officer advised the Presidents of both Panchayats, Karuppan Pallam and Appipalayam, to make arrangements for testing the drinking water. The water sample from Appipalayam was sent by the Village Panchayat for testing to Salem as the facility is available only there. The report was received. It mentioned that the water was unfit to drink. Ms. Eswari said that the officials of the Pollution Control Board failed to respond immediately to the demands of the public. They delayed taking action against the dyeing units. Only after a continuous struggle by the public the issue was brought to the notice of the District Collector. The District Collector visited the village to verify with the public. The dyeing units' administration bribed their workers whose habitations are located along the roadside and made them reply favourably when the Collector questioned them about the quality of the water. The District Collector, instead of visiting the whole area to verify the truth, believed the statements of those who lied, called Eswari and advised her not to unnecessarily make complaints against the dyeing units. It was only after going through the report of the water test that the Collector came to realize the cheating by the dyeing units. The issue was highlighted in the media and the Pollution Control Board compelled the managements of the dyeing units to construct effluent treatment plants. There are eight treatment plants in Karur, of which two plants are located in the area of Appipalayam and Karuppan Palayam. The managements of the dyeing units do not run the effluent treatment plant as per the specifications of the Pollution Control Board. Instead of insulating the solid waste in the dyeing units with polythene to prevent the soiling of the earth or mixing with water, they keep the heaps of waste open and directly on the earth. It is a great danger and, during rains, the wastes are drenched and mix with the earth, polluting ground water. The government authorities are not taking any serious action against this unlawful activity of the managements of the dyeing units. Now the water is unfit to drink. The district authority is planning to get water from the Cauvery river, Ms.Eswari added, though the villages are located on the banks of the river Amaravathi.

In the meantime, to provide protected water to the public, Ms.Eswari made arrangements for directly pumping water from the river Amaravathi. Two wells have been dug inside the riverbed and, using two 10 HP motors, water is pumped to OHTs supplying protected water to the main village of Appipalayam and Chettipalayam hamlet. For the residents of Chokkampatti, Attanparappu, Raika Gowndanputhur, Muthusoli Palayam and Kaliappan Gownder Puthur, a separate bore has been dug at the check dam on the Amaravathi and water is pumped from there. At present there is adequate water in the river but, during summer, the water supply will not be adequate and so scarcity will occur.

Getting water from the river Amaravathi will not be a permanent solution, Ms. Eswari observed. The dyeing units of Appipalayam and Karuppan Palayam are not strictly adhering to the safety measures and do not show real interest in running the effluent treatment plants as per the norms specified. The solid wastes heaped like a hill in each dyeing unit pose a threat to the ground water including percolation into the river Amaravathi. One kilogram of waste of chemicals like bromium/chromium is enough to contaminate one lakh litres of water, Ms.Eswari pointed out. In this context the water of the Amaravathi river is in danger. Now itself thousands of acres of wet lands are affected and in the near future the water of the river Amaravathi will become unfit for any use. In the name of promoting export of high quality fabrics, the life of the villagers of the riverside has been endangered. The Government can bring Cauvery water for drinking purposes but what is the way to get irrigation source for farming activities, she questioned. At present the dyeing units of Appipalayam are letting out their waste water into the downward area of Karuppan Palayam. Mrs.Eswari is not happy in this regard though her villagers are protected from ill-health due to the consumption of contaminated water. She felt that the villagers, especially poor families of the nearby Village Panchayat of Karuppan Palayam, are the victims. As the President of Karuppan Palayam himself is running a dyeing unit he never complains to the authorities about the quality of the drinking water supplied by the Panchayat. But the villagers of Karuppan Palayam agitated against the President and so, without informing Appipalayam Panchayat, the officials made arrangements to dig a borewell in the jurisdiction of Appipalayam Village Panchayat, Ms. Eswari said.

But the farmers of Karuppan Palayam, who own borewells, got their water tested and in the report it was noted that the water was unfit to drink. As the villagers agitated, with the support of the district officials, the President of Karuppan Palayam, instead of taking action against the dyeing unit managements, made an attempt to dig a borewell in the jurisdiction of Appipalayam. The villagers of Appipalayam mobilized themselves and appealed to her to prevent them. Ms. Eswari, along with Ward Members and the public, opposed the officials digging a borewell. The issue was highlighted to the district authorities and Ms. Eswari and her husband were warned that they would be booked in a case of preventing public servants from doing their duties and further section 205 of the Tamil Nadu Panchayats Act would be imposed on her to take the initiative to suspend/dismiss her from the Presidentship. Ms. Eswari did not yield to the threat. Hearing of the threat of action invoking section 205, the villagers joined together and told the officials that even after the dismissal of Ms. Eswari they would elect her again and again. Understanding the situation, the officials effected a compromise in the presence of the Project Officer, DRDA, that the dyeing units of Appipalayam should not let out their waste water in the jurisdiction of Appipalayam, either in public places or in their own places, so that the groundwater of Appiplayam will not get polluted. The managements of the dyeing units functioning in Appipalayam were instructed to connect with the effluent treatment plant located at Karuppan Palayam. Then only the sinking of borewells was permitted.

Issue of Sand Quarrying

When the issue of water pollution due to dyeing units was successfully handled and the Appipalayam Panchayat arranged for the supply of protected water from the well dug in the riverbed of the Amaravathi, a new threat came in the form of quarrying of sand in the riverbed of the Amaravathi, Ms. Eswari said.

The riverbed of the Amaravathi is located within a half kilometre from Appipalayam. The river sand of the Amaravathi is of a higher quality than that of the Cauvery, it is said. Hence hundreds of cart loads of sand are illegally quarried from the Amaravathi riverbed near Appipalayam Village. The wells for drinking water are constructed on the riverbed. The illegal sand mafia did not spare even these areas. Unmindful of the negative impact on the system of drinking water supply as well as the system of irrigation they continued their illegal quarrying of sand. Ms.Eswari met the Presidents of those Village Panchayats for which the drinking water wells are constructed on the riverbed and explained the scope of the damage to the percolation due to the sand quarrying. She succeeded in convening the Gram Sabhas in four Village Panchayats including Appipalayam and a resolution was passed demanding the intervention of the District Collector so that the illegal sand quarrying could be stopped at once. The Collector came to the spot and inspected the damage caused. The PWD officials informed that permission was given for quarrying only at Thalapatti which is far away from the wells of Appipalayam and so there won't be any problem. But Ms. Eswari said that though the PWD officials restricted sand quarrying to a place, the selfish sand mafia never adhered to rules and regulations. Hence she and the villagers refuted the PWD officials and pleaded with the Collector. When the Collector announced that at a depth of three-four feet, sand could be taken, the villagers expressed their shock saying that they would lie down before the vehicles and sacrifice their life instead of living as dead people without adequate source of water for drinking as well as irrigation. At last the Collector agreed to stop all the mining activities in the riverbed of the Amaravathi near Appipalayam. The mass action became a success thanks to the determination and firmness of Ms.Eswari when the other Presidents of the concerned Village Panchayats did not courageously argue with the Collector. At present the sand quarrying has been stopped.

Emergence of Farmers Association

In the context of the contamination of water and sand quarrying, the farmers of Appipalayam and the nearby Village Panchayat joined together and institutionalized their solidarity. To fight legally against the managements of the dyeing units and the sand mafia, those farmers whose lands were getting damaged created an association to protect the groundwater and to obtain compensation from the proprietors of the dyeing units. They filed a case in the year 2003 in the Green Bench of the High Court, Chennai. Villagers in general, especially farmers and the poor who realized the value of the village commons and its protection, enthusiastically joined together in the struggle.

Her Support Structure

The training and orientation given by Gandhigram Rural Institute and NGOs like the Human Rights Foundation and AREDS helped her in understanding the significance of the village commons and link of livelihood with the village commons, Ms. Eswari observed. The support and guidance extended by these institutions are her strength. Now that the farmers have got awakening the struggle cannot be defeated by the selfish elements, she said hopefully.

"I strongly believe that the Village Panchayat needs support from many sources to bring about development," Ms. Eswari said. She clearly made use of the opportunity when some NSS students camped at Appipalayam. Through them she established contact with St. Joseph's College of Trichy and, with their guidance, she took about sixty villagers, farmers, young men and women to Kodaikkanal Anglade Institute of Natural History for an orientation and awareness in ecology, environment and protection of nature. After attending the orientation classes, the vision of her village farmers became sharp, Ms. Eswari claimed. To the question of how she got more interested in the issue of water pollution and sand quarrying, Ms. Eswari replied that, as a woman in a family of farmers, she realized the importance of protected drinking water and sustainable water for irrigation. Being the President, she determined to ensure the same to one and all.

Conclusion

The reservation for women in Panchayati Raj Institutions is questioned by many who have failed to visualize the potential of women leadership. Indian women, especially rural women, prove their strength by upholding the family and culture in spite of many obstacles and challenges. Elected women leaders of local bodies, after getting oriented in the concept of decentralization, social development and development administration, easily swim across the current of opposition, criticism and even threat to their self and consistently work for the betterment of the village as a whole as they are mothers in families.

II. Vanduvancheri Gram Panchayat in Naga-pattinam District

Socio-Economic Background

Ms.Rani Muniyakannu, aged 39, is the President of Vaduvancheri Village Panchayat. She belongs to the Most Backward Community. She has studied upto the higher secondary course. Her family is a nuclear one, consisting of her husband, one son and one daughter. Both the children are studying in school. Her husband is the former secretary of the local unit of the DMK Party and the President of the Cooperative Society. The family has 10 acres of wet land and 10 acres of coconut plantation. They live in a tiled house but have now decided to construct a new house this year. The present house has all facilities like electricity, toilet and drinking water tap connection. Rani is an active member in the federation of women leaders. She is the Secretary of the eastern region, covering four districts, namely, Pudukkottai, Thanjavur, Nagapattinam and Thiruvarur. She is also an active woman leader in the DMK since 1996, serving as the Union level women's wing convener. She used to deliver speeches effectively during the DMK Party's public meetings.

Recruitment

A cousin of Rani's was a former member of the Gram Panchayat. Her husband wished to contest in the elections but the position was reserved for women. The DMK Party proposed Rani for the post as their family is a reputed family and their affluence and honesty is known to all. Moreover, Rani is an educated woman. Earlier she served as a balwadi teacher in her native village before her marriage. She used to show her boldness in dealing with family issues. Since her husband was involved in settling disputes in the village she also participated in the conflict resolution process and through these incidents she earned a name among the public. Against this backdrop she was fielded in the Panchayat elections.

There were five candidates in the fray including Rani. Except Rani all the rest had political backing. Though Rani's family belongs to the DMK Party, the DMK Party men supported the candidate fielded by the Congress Party. Even the lone SC candidate in the fray was supported by the Communist Party of India. But except Rani the rest were less educated, older than her and economically weak. During the election campaign Rani promised all essential services to the needy. Individuals who belong to the Thamilar Bhoomi Party, close relatives, both men and women, and the labourers who were working on her farm accompanied her during the campaign. The expenditure was less than Rs.10000 as only notices and wall posters were printed. Rani won the election by a margin of 300 votes. Her husband's social involvement, her caste, her family reputation, in addition to her education and age were the contributing factors for her success. There was no untoward incident but the defeated persons did not continue their friendship with her. But she used to visit their houses to attend social functions.

Village Setting

Vanduvancheri is a multi-caste village where Ambalam, Thevar, Konar, Reddiar, SC, Naicker, Muslim and Nadar communities live. The Ambalams are the majority caste. The village has six hamlets, namely, Sarubojaramapuram, Dulasiapattinam, Vanduvancheri, Periya Thidal, Panchankulam and Vellikkidangu. The Panchayat is situated along the costal area and the backwaters flow through it.

Village Temples

Avvaiyar, Kollathu Mariamman, Sivan and Ayyanar temples are considered common to all but the SC people cannot enter them. Vandurai Mariamman temple belongs to the Ambalams. Nowadays the SC men come to this Mariamman temple and offer the kavadi during the festivals. The Thevars will not come to the Amman Kovil and the SC women cannot come into the Mariamman temple. But they are permitted upto the statue of the Nandhi in the Sivan temple. The village temple celebration is organised by the Village Committee consisting of representatives from the major castes. People donate money to the Village Committee to conduct the celebrations.

The Committee members are mostly involved in other public activities including the Panchayat's.

Usually the Ambalam community's decision is upheld by the others. A Muthirayar caste association once functioned actively. But, after its transformation into a political party, namely the Thamilar Bhoomi Party, the caste association lost its significance. Moreover, the Ambalam allies of the Muthirayars switched over to the then ruling party, the DMK. There is one mosque in the Muslim street.

Political Parties

The DMK is the dominant party and the AIADMK is almost equally strong. Other parties like the CPI, CPI(M), BJP, Thamilar Bhoomi, Makkal Tamil Desam are also present in the village. The office bearers of all the political parties used to meet and share their concerns and opinions on the Village Panchayat activities. Mostly the men belonging to the DMK evince keen interest and enthusiasm in public issues. The youth wing of the DMK Party is an active body. The members show their involvement whenever needed to tackle issues. At the time of the issue of silicon sand misuse, the youth mobilised themselves and participated in programmes like *dharna*, demonstration and fasting to protect the environment.

Women's Association

With the guidance of an NGO, a women's association is functioning in the Panchayat for the past six years. About 15 SHGs are functioning in this Panchayat, out of which seven have got the revolving fund. Obtaining land for lease, obtaining fishing rights by tender, extending micro credit among themselves are the prime activities of the SHGs. Handicrafts training-cum-production has also been organised by one group. The NGO, the President of the Village Panchayat and the SHGs maintain good relationship among themselves. The SHG women attend the Gram Sabha meetings. They extended their support during the mass action in connection with the misuse of silicon sand. A retired headmistress is engaged in organising the women's association and awakening the womenfolk. The SHGs are picking up well as the women show interest in public activities and come out boldly to criticise the mistakes in the government's activities.

Village Economy

The village land is mostly sandy and so trees like coconut, mango, palm, casuarina, and cashewnut are growing. Most of the land is owned by Muslim farmers. The other castes get these lands on lease from the Muslims. Near the backwaters area the drainage canal brings flood waters upto a depth of 12 feet. The water is good for irrigation and so paddy is being cultivated. The paddy variety is a good and traditional one and it can withstand floods also. The paddy is liked by Kerala people and so it is being sent to Kerala. There are around 50 acres of common land lying on the two sides of the backwaters canal. The poor farmers are cultivating paddy in those lands.

As the village is a remote one the Agriculture Department officials do not visit and provide guidance. Due to lack of professional guidance in agriculture the yield of the cashewnut is nowadays reduced. The Department of Horticulture has a scheme but it is not suited to the local farmers. To improve agriculture the government sectoral departments must visit and interact with the farmers and help them in farming activities. There is potential for inland fishing for which the farmers need orientation as, for about five months, from July to November, it is a good season for fish culture in the backwaters. During the rest of the year the native fishermen community has the right to catch fish. During this season fish is available in plenty. Farmers and fishermen have maintained this agreement traditionally. Due to non-availability of cold storage and market access most of the fish caught by the fishermen goes waste or is used as manure in groves. So the government must come forward to properly help both the farmers and the fishermen community.

Due to the non-availability of adequate grazing land the cattle population has been reduced now. The poor who availed of government loans misused the loan assistance but those who availed of them from the Society regularly repaid the loan. To improve the village economy modernization of fish farming and proper marketing access is necessary. Value added production from mango, coconut and cashew nut will also improve the economy of this area. There should be a provision to give a large sum to develop the land by mortgaging it as the farmers mortgage the land to individuals and waste the money on non-productive items of expenditure. To avoid any default in repayment the registered document can be kept in the possession of the lending institution.

Social Problems

Suspicion and mistrust between Hindus and Muslims resulted in a communal dispute during 1999-2000. Some Muslim youth hailing from other area pasted posters in the streets where Hindus were living. Usually the Muslims never entertain any advertisement in their street. So there was a dispute between the Hindu and Muslim youth in which two Hindu young men suffered injury. Cases were registered and a Peace Committee was formed. As the two communities usually never entertained any ill-will they wanted to settle it amicably. The Hindus advised the Muslims not to encourage outsiders in the village as they do not understand the relationship among the various communities. At last the Muslims sent away the youth who had come from other areas to this village for jobs. The Panchayat played an active role in this peace process.

Alcoholism is nowadays increasing and illicit liquor is freely available as the distillers are not controlled by the police in spite of complaints made against them. The Panchayat cannot do anything against the culprits as the police do not support the Panchayat.

On Common Property Resources

In the Vanduvancheri Panchayat and in two nearby Panchayats, silicon, the rare earth, is available in plenty. The silicon sand is fit for export to foreign countries as raw material used in glass and software industries.

Three companies established near Vanduvancheri own four acres, two acres and five acres respectively and have got a licence to quarry the silicon. But they take the silicon even from outside their land and cause damage to the sub-soil and so soil erosion takes place. When the farmers complained to the Panchayat, a resolution was passed to refer the issue to the Government's Pollution Control Board. As nothing happened, the people decided to stage a demonstration and to prevent the transportation of the silicon. The police came and arrested Rani with other women and the youth. All the people mobilised and sat in front of the Police station. By evening all were released as the Superintendent of Police ordered to do so. When the matter was brought to the notice of the District Collector he felt unhappy over the activities of the Panchayat President.

The matter was further referred to the Additional Collector of Mines. Then, fasting was observed by the villagers. When the problem became serious, the President met the Rural Development Minister and asked for his intervention. He said that the licence is issued by the Central Government. A high level official visited from Chennai and inspected the site and verified the complaint against the Panchayat. The sites belonging to the companies were marked and they were advised not to quarry sand in other areas. The NGO, SNEKA, rendered counseling, guidance and assistance in this regard. Moreover the media blew up this issue. The MLA, when contacted and asked to extend his support, advised Rani that it was not possible to prevent quarrying as the companies had got licences. After the struggle, when Rani had succeeded in regularising the activities of the companies, the MLA himself paid a visit to the village and felicitated her.

There are two cases in the High Court for which Rani has to frequently go over to Chennai to meet her lawyer. The NGO, SNEKA, provided legal guidance and helped to engage a lawyer in this regard, Ms. Rani said. There is no permission to utilize the Panchayat fund in this regard. Several times, to bring things to the notice of the district officials, the villagers are mobilized and visit the district headquarters. Expenses in this regard are a large amount, Ms. Rani said. Moreover due to this issue, "I and my family lose peace of mind; and even my security is in threat," Ms. Rani explained.

Silicon sand quarrying should not be permitted in residential areas. Silicon sand functions as a soaking agent retaining water. The ecology and the environment of Vanduvancheri and the nearby Village Panchayats are protected and promoted by the silicon sand filter system, Ms. Rani said. By permitting mining in this area, without considering the damage to the environment as well as the resident population, the government officials who project developmental activities fail to address the local environmental issues. The Village Panchayat is not treated as a stakeholder in this regard, Ms. Rani complained.

Ms. Rani sustained her struggle against silicon mining irrespective of all the hurdles she faced. There was an attempt to damage her character. Recently, during the local festival season, bit notices without the address of the printers were distributed to the public in which her character was belittled in unparliamentary words. Though the villagers realized the damage caused by the silicon sand quarrying, they were poor and unable to contribute other than their moral support to the Village Panchayat. Hence the expenses were met by her for which she had to sell her property.

There is a garden site of 57 acres belonging to the Panchayat, with 200 mango trees, 300 cashewnut trees, 100 coconut trees and casuarina trees. There are also 30 small ponds. The garden is properly maintained as two watchmen are employed by the Panchayat. The Panchayat President in the previous period took no action when the villagers cut the trees. Even now his family members cut trees and sell them without the knowledge of the Panchayat. The incident was reported to the Union officials and the police. None of them came and took action. Once a villager stole a cashewnut tree. He was caught and punished by the Panchayat and after that such theft has declined.

The garden can be fenced with barbed wire if the Government permits the Panchayat to utilise the seed money from the income. But only 10 per cent of the total income is allowed to be spent by the Government. There are about 36 palm trees, 27 ponds and 2 acres of poramboke, where individuals grow coconut trees. A sum of Rs.8 per tree is collected by the VAO and paid to the Panchayat. Earlier the amount was Rs.50 per tree but the Government reduced the rate. About Rs.50000 is earned from the garden. From the auction of ponds Rs.15000 is received and from the palm trees Rs.250 is received. About Rs.4000 is the income from the 2C trees. There is enough scope for planting more trees, particularly mango, and the Panchayat is planning to plant new saplings in the garden year by year.

Government Officials *Vs.* Panchayat

Provision of drinking water is an essential activity in the Village Panchayat but any repair to the motor pump cannot be immediately attended to as there is a rule that the work estimate has to be approved by the TWAD engineer. Due to this unnecessary delay is experienced and the public get angry with the Panchayat. Due to the unexpected transfer of engineers and other officials the work sanctioned by them or monitored by them is put to unnecessary scrutiny by the new staff. If the work is being executed anticipating sanction for the same, due to the transfers, it is delayed. There are 27 electric posts in a damaged condition and so fitting of lights on these posts is not safe. When the same was informed several times to the officials of the Electricity Board they failed to take action. Usually most of the officials give oral instructions and refer to other officials. So there is unnecessary misunderstanding. The Forest Department officials expect personal benefits when the Panchayat approaches them for getting permission to cut and sell the casuarina trees grown in the garden.

Gram Sabha

Usually the public do not come to the Gram Sabha in large numbers. About 100 men and two hundred women attend the Gram Sabha meetings. The NGOs create awareness among the people in respect of the Gram Sabha. As per the communication received from the Chief Minister it is important to invite the women to the Gram Sabha.

Issues like bringing the VAO's office nearer to the Panchayat and his shortcomings, alcoholism and desilting of tanks are discussed. The public take the opportunity to comment on all activities during the Gram Sabha meetings. Once, in the very presence of the VAO, they demanded the passing of a resolution to transfer the VAO for his shortcomings. The Ward Members regularly attend the Gram Sabha meetings.

When the problem of alcoholism was discussed in the Gram Sabha, the public suggested forming a committee and, accordingly, a committee was formed with 25 members from all the hamlets. In spite of this the people expected the President to take a leading role. When the Youth Sports and Recreation Committee was formed as per the suggestion of SHG women, four women members were enrolled in the committee. If proper orientation is given to the public, they will enhance their participation.

Panchayat Meeting

Once a month the meeting of the Panchayat is convened. All the Members attend regularly. The Members give more attention to drinking water supply and proper functioning of street lights. A few Members used to take care of the EB staff and ensure the replacement of old bulbs promptly. When one Member was absent for two meetings he was pulled up and then he attended regularly. He explained that as he had gone out on business he could not attend and requested to be excused. The fund available is informed to the Members and they suggest the work. The priority is also determined by them. Accordingly the resolutions are passed. The Muslim and Dalit members are very serious in their intention to do service to their areas and are always dominating the discussions. There are nine members, six male and three female. Only one SC male represents the SC community but he is an active person.

Works Carried-out

In the year 1996-97 there were no major expenses other than the maintenance of drinking water source from the Panchayat fund. In the year 1997-98, from the Common Property Resources, the Panchayat got an income of about of Rs.47000 and so a lot of activities were carried out like hand pump maintenance, street light maintenance, TV maintenance, and repair work in the Village Panchayat office. Under the scheme fund, materials for the TV room were purchased. During the period 1998-99 the major expense was the electricity bill of Rs.23000. Maintenance of OHT and hand pumps and street lights was undertaken from the Panchayat fund at a cost of Rs.34000. Under the JVVT, during 1998-99, TV room, road improvement, CRSP, retaining wall were provided. Two group houses were also constructed. Under the earmarked fund a new hand pump was provided at a cost of Rs.20000.

In the year 1999-2000 sanitation was given due attention. Dustbins were provided to streets to collect waste. Bathing ghats were provided at the village tanks. Under the 10th Finance Commission allocation drinking water pipeline extension was undertaken at a cost of around Rs.40000. During 2000-2001 maintenance expenses for hand pumps, street lights, passenger shelter, pipeline extension (II phase) were carried out from the Panchayat fund.

More money is needed for maintenance of street lights and hand pumps, whose functioning is frequently disturbed. If only the Panchayat has its own source of income it will be possible to maintain the drinking water system and the street lights. Otherwise it is really a problem. During 2000-2001, under the JGSY, a culvert, a bus shelter and a cement road were provided at a cost of Rs.168000. Graveyard approach road maintenance in all hamlets, hamlet approach road maintenance, construction of culverts in the approach roads leading to the graveyards, establishment of library and sports and recreation centre for the youth were the other activities carried out in the Village Panchayat. Most of the work was executed by contractors who were very prompt in their work as they did not need to give any commission to the Panchayat. But the undue delay in the settlement of the bills by the Union discouraged them.

Social Development Activities

School building, balwadi buildings, laboratory in Government High School, toilet in school, borewell in school were provided from the Union as well as the MP area development fund. From the allocation under the MLA constituency development fund, a bridge, five sodium vapour lights, a BT road and a PDS building were provided. Twelve biogas plants were provided to eligible farmers. Rani is the Honarary Chairperson of the Parent Teachers Association. She actively engages in the activities of the PTA and the students are encouraged to improve their standard of education. Prizes and trophies are awarded to the best students for which she used to mobilize resources. As the residents of the Muslim street demanded proper sanitation, dustbins were provided and the waste was stacked for manure. Under the CRSP 20 toilets were provided to 20 families.

Rani maintains a good relationship with the VHN and helps her in her activities. The nurse used to provide details of communicable diseases like cholera to the public. The higher secondary school is far away from this village and so most of the girl students discontinue their studies after school final. As most of the SC families do not possess pattas the Panchayat is taking efforts to get pattas for all the SCs. About 120 persons got pattas last year due to the initiative of the Panchayat.

Conclusion

The position of the Village Panchayat President is very significant and needs full time attention. So Rani and her husband spend a lot of time improving the Village Panchayat. As their time is spent on public activities they cannot spare adequate time for agriculture, which has resulted in a heavy loss. Being a honest person she has to face a lot of problems in the Panchayat administration. She has to incur the displeasure of the officials and the high caste elite. She will not contest again in the Panchayat but, in consultation with the NGO, she plans to work for women's development.

Observation

It is unequivocally clear that the women leaders are sensitive to the issues of livelihood and natural resources. They feel that the natural resources and that too the commons are the lifeline of the poor and the women. Hence, with abundant common sense, the women leaders give enough attention to protect the water sources and bodies. The same sensitivity and sensibility are not found in the higher level officials and people's representatives. As a result the grassroots level leaders are alone. Natural resources are exploited and polluted by the industrial houses. They are powerful and they come to do exploitative work with the active but invisible support of the officialdom. To overcome this menace, grassroots leaders have to mobilize the people to fight against the industrial houses. Legal procedures are violated by the industrial houses but they are not taken to task. When the people fight against such violations, they are taken to task. Women have come to power with an array of barriers and obstacles. Yet, they have to fight against such exploitation. The above two case studies demonstrate the intensity and gravity of the issue. There are innumerable leaders at the grassroots fighting against such kind of exploitation. In the era of globalization, natural resources are one of the major casualties which are being exploited by the industrial houses. To overcome this issue the people and people's representatives have to be very alert and empowered. It is the women leaders who are very serious about the protection of the environment and natural resources. In the whole process of the struggle, the women leaders are empowered.

III. Thiruvasi Gram Panchayat in Tiruchirappalli District

Mr. Cheran is the President of Thiruvasi Gram Panchayat in Manachanallur Union of Tiruchirappalli District. He belongs to the Muthuraja community, which is recognized as backward. His age is 33 and he is yet to be married. His responsibility as the President of Thiruvasi Village Panchayat demands his whole days and nights and so he purposely delays his marriage. His father is a traditional Panchayat leader as well as a senior party worker in the DMK party. His parents own more than 10 acres of land on which they have a banana plantation.

Cheran had his primary schooling in his native village of Thiruvasi itself. But for his high school studies he was put in a government aided private management school situated at Puthanampatti, 25 kilometres away from his village. His hostel life made him come to the public space.

About the Village

Thiruvasi is popular for its Siva temple, which attracted the Nayanmars of Saiva philosophy. The temple was visited by the four forerunners among the Nayanmars—Appar, Sundarar, Thirugnana Sambandar and Manickavasagar. The temple is still an attracting feature.

Thiruvasi is a multi-caste village consisting of Muthurajas, Vellalars, Adi Dravidars and Servais. These are the major communities in Thiruvasi as well as Thudaiyur, the hamlet of the Thiruvasi Panchayat. Agriculture is the main occupation of many and quite a number of families in Thudaiyur are engaged in the avocations of gem-cutting and mat-weaving. The village is situated on the banks of the river Cauvery and Mukkombu, the tributary of the Cauvery. The fields of Thiruvasi have been under the irrigation of the Ayyanvaikal of Mukkombu.

The village communities are living together peacefully. Among the communities of Thiruvasi, the Muthurajas are numerically dominant. Cheran's father was the President of the Parents Teachers Association. He once served as the Chairperson of the trustees of the Siva temple of Thiruvasi.

Public Orientation of Cheran

During late 1980s the Government of Tamil Nadu took a decision to rename places which had been changed meaninglessly by improper pronunciation or by cutting down on letters for easy spelling. Cheran said that, under the impact of the World Tamil Conference held in Thanjavur during the late 80s, the name of his village Thiruvasi was changed into Thiruvasai and a gazette notification was also issued by the government in this regard. The villagers of Thiruvasi did not accept the decision of the government and decided to agitate against the government. In this struggle all joined together and the participation of youths was noticeable. Cheran participated very seriously and on the occasion of the visit of the revenue officials in connection with the agitation over the name change, Cheran boldly questioned the officer whether he would accept it if his name was subjected to a change. The villagers congratulated him on his boldness. At last the government withdrew the decision and the earlier name Thiruvasi was retained. Cheran, after enjoying the taste of success of the struggle, involved himself further in other public issues affecting the villagers. The sluice of the irrigation cannal meant for Thiruvasi was defunct due to lack of periodical maintenance on the part of the PWD. The usual demands of the villagers could not make any impact on the mindset of the concerned officials. At last an agitation was organized and it was successful. The government did all the needed works and the sluice became functional. Further a bed-dam was also constructed to ensure the storage and flow of sufficient water to be conducted through that sluice. Cheran played the role of youth organizer in that struggle.

The experience gained from the above public events shaped his understanding of public life. Slowly he built his leadership by engaging himself in monitoring public events, offered his comments courageously and, when the opportunity was provided, he readily accepted the responsibilities. There was an opportunity which Cheran successfully handled.

There is a High School run by the Department of Adi Dravidar Welfare in Thiruvasi. The villagers of Thiruvasi and nearby villages proposed to bring Higher Secondary classes to the High School. But the authorities of the Education Department refused to oblige saying that there was not enough strength of students and also citing the absence of sufficient space needed for building the infrastructure for a Higher Secondary School.

Cheran's father held the position of the Chairman among the trustees of the Siva temple. The Trust Board of the Siva temple identified a suitable site owned by the temple and resolved to give the land for the school. The Higher Secondary School came up there. Though the father of Cheran supported these activities, he personally did not encourage Cheran's social activities. His parents felt that public activities took time and energy along with money. But Cheran was determined to go his own way.

New Panchayati Raj Election

During 1996, when elections to Panchayat bodies were declared, Cheran was just 23 years old. Many youths and elders advised Cheran to contest. There were four candidates from the main village of Thiruvasi and two from the hamlet of Thudaiyur. Among the candidates a mutual understanding was reached and all except Cheran withdrew their nomination so that there would be a straight contest between Thiruvasi and Thudaiyur. But Cheran's father compelled him to withdraw from the election. To avoid any further clash between parent and son, Cheran also withdrew his nomination. It was a surprise to note that the father of Cheran himself filed his nomination just for name's sake but he did not engage in any campaigning activities. The candidate from Thudaiyur won in the election.

Cheran felt very much that he was denied the opportunity to serve the villagers with power and authority as President at the behest of his own parents. Cheran left Thiruvasi and stayed in another village Thiruvanaikaval. In the meantime, an unexpected event, namely, the expulsion of the leader Vaiko from the DMK party occurred. Cheran was attracted by the charismatic leadership of Vaiko and joined his MDMK party despite opposition from his father, who is a staunch supporter and a senior cadre in the DMK. Steadily Cheran became an active cadre of the MDMK. He became the Deputy Convener of the students wing at the district level in 1993, became a state level general body member in 1997 and became the Union Secretary in 2002. Cheran's public and political orientation steadfastly gained momentum in due course.

The Function of Village Panchayat Council (during the period 1996-2001)

The elected President failed to deliver the expected services to the public and the Council Members accused him for his various misdeeds. At last the President was removed and the administration was handled by the Vice-President. These happenings influenced the thinking of Cheran and he decided to prove that an honest administration was possible under his leadership, if he became the President.

The Elections of 2001

In 2001 there were four contestants including Cheran. Cheran issued a manifesto promising fair and impartial administration and honest dealings. Cheran won by 124 votes. It was the first time that a candidate from the main village of Thiruvasi won in the Panchayat election. For mutual understanding, the demand of the Thudaiyur public that the Vice-President could be from their village was accepted and a woman member from Thudaiyur was elected Vice-President.

The Illegal Mining of Sand

Immediately after assumption of office, the Village Panchayat Council of Thiruvasi discussed the illegal sand mining carried out in the Thiruvasi-Kollidam river belt. Cheran explained to the public in this regard and they advised him to take necessary steps to prevent the illegal sand mining. The youths of Thiruvasi extended their solidarity. Those who were involved in the illegal sand mining, for name's sake, availed of a legal permission for sand mining in a patta land but illegally made all arrangements to transport lorry loads of sand from the bed of the river. They even constructed a bridge for their convenience. When they illegally entered the bed of the river to mine sand, the villagers of Thiruvasi prevented them. It was decided to discuss the issue at the village level. It was proposed by the illegal sand miners that a handsome amount would be given to the village community of Thiruvasi if the preventing of the mining was withdrawn. The public in general were prepared to yield but the Village Panchayat Council was steady in its decision of demanding legal mining through proper tender so that the legal share of revenue in this regard could be availed of by the Village Panchayat. The Panchayat Council collected vehicle tax for about 10 days but the district authorities instructed the Village Panchayat not to collect any vehicle tax from the illegal sand miners. The Village Council demanded legal tender for mining. In the meantime, there was a change in the proprietorship of the firm. A new firm entered the illegal sand mining and successfully influenced the villagers of Thiruvasi by offering more than a lakh of rupees as a monthly dole to the community, Cheran explained.

To counteract the efforts of the illegal sand miners, Cheran and his Ward Members took the support of Thudaiyur villagers and agitated against the illegal sand mining. The illegal sand miners influenced the villagers of the Thudaiyur also. The Village Panchayat Council of Thiruvasi became a lonesome entity. In course of time, out of six Members, four joined hands with the villagers. But Cheran took the issue to court.

The so-called illegal sand miners had a legal permission for mining sand in the nearby Village Panchayat, namely Melapathu-Kilyanallur. But, in reality, there was no mining activity there. In the meantime, there was no distribution of money from the illegal sand miners to the communities of the two villages. They realized that they had been cheated. All came to the Village Panchayat and, during the Gram Sabha meet in October 2002, it was decided to challenge all concerned. A public interest litigation was filed against all concerned—the sectoral department authority and the party involved in illegal sand mining, Cheran explained.

The accused replied that there was no sand mining at Thiruvasi but only at Melapathu-Kilyanallur. The Village Administrative Officer certified that there was illegal sand mining in the revenue jurisdiction of Thiruvasi and the Village Panchayat of Melapattu--Kiliyanallur passed a resolution that as the sand mining was done only at the Thiruvasi Panchayat, it was doubtful whether Kiliyanallur Panchayat could legally avail of the revenue share from the sand mining. These references were submitted as additional evidence by the Thiruvasi Panchayat. But the court directed the District Collector himself to verify and submit a report. Based on his report, the court did not take any action against the accused.

Threat to Presidentship of Cheran

In the meantime, there was a scheme to displace Cheran from the Presidentship, designed by his opponents. Four Ward Members levelled charges against Cheran and, based on their complaint, the officials concerned took away all records and account books without giving any acknowledgement. There was an audit of all accounts and twelve charges were levelled against Cheran and he was asked to submit his explanation. In the meantime, the power of cheque operation was denied to Cheran and, under section 205, an enquiry was announced. A case was filed by Cheran against that attempt at removal under section 205 and, after a period of eight months, the power of cheque operation was restored to him.

The opposition to the illegal sand mining still continued in spite of the threat to kill him. A handbill was sent to Cheran in which he was asked to adjust with the sand miners or prepare to die. Though the anonymous handbill issue was reported to the police authorities no action was taken against the culprits.

In the meantime, there was a lorry accident in which two of Cheran's close friends who fearlessly joined hands with Cheran in his struggle against illegal sand mining died.

The Impact of Illegal Sand Mining

The river water is available for irrigation for a period of six months only. As the majority of the farmers grow banana, which is a one-year crop, the farmers irrigate the crop through borewells. There are one hundred and forty borewells in Thiruvasi Village Panchayat. Due to illegal sand mining the ground water level went far below and 10 to 15 feet depth had to be dug further in all borewells to get water for the remaining six months so that the farmers could save the banana plantation.

Further, due to the mining activities throughout day and night and the plying of hundreds of lorries the geography of the area was damaged. Earlier there were green bushes and small plants in the vicinity of the area on which the cattle population grazed. Now-a-days it is all completely destroyed.

There are hundreds of workers who have migrated from nearby districts and who are engaged in the loading and transportation of sand. To cater to their need for alcohol, illegal arrack business was started. Yet another issue of sexual exploitation and the public nuisance of prostitution cropped up. In spite of all these issues, there was no fruitful action initiated by the concerned sectoral authorities.

The Support of the Print Media

Cheran's struggle has been sustained in spite of his being let down by his own village community. The media helped him in his struggle. Newspapers, weeklies and other periodicals featured the details of the struggle waged by the young rural leader Cheran. The response from the electronic media was not so encouraging. Cheran wondered why unnecessary popularity and coverage are given to other minor issues in the electronic media but not to this.

The Silence of Political Parties

Cheran expressed his disappointment that there was no encouragement extended by the political parties to his struggle. Many of the local leaders of various political parties kept silence rather than comment on the illegality of the sand mining.

In the midst of mental agony, Cheran, the young man, sustains his hope in the judiciary as two cases filed by him are yet to be decided upon. In the meantime the share income from sand mining of rupees sixty nine lakhs has been distributed to the nearby Panchayat Melapathu Kiliyanallur. He has appealed for the stay of the allocation of share from the mines to that Village Panchayat.

His Immediate Agenda of Action

Cheran's immediate agenda has five items. The first is to take necessary steps to speed up the cases filed in court. The second is to complete the left out activities initiated for the development of the villagers. The third is to empower the women Self Help Groups in their micro-economic activities. Taking steps to rejuvenate the defunct cooperative milk society is the fourth item. The fifth one is the welfare of the marginalized. There are about one hundred poor families who dwell in small huts. They have to be provided with pucca houses.

Being a young and a knowledgeable person, with the strength of the youths, Cheran proposes to work for brining various tiny industries to his village and to nearby villages where the parts and accessories for small and large scale industries can be produced by village youths after necessary skill training.

Cheran's leadership is a hope to all who repose faith in grassroots democracy. His vision on the natural resources and human resources has sharpened through his leadership in the Village Panchayat Council. He acknowledged the encouragement given by Gandhigram in equipping his leadership consistently.

Conclusion

The above presented three cases are only examples to portray the intensity of exploitation of natural resources for the benefit of a few individuals in the era of globalization and liberalization. But ultimately the over exploitation of the natural resources would result in affecting the livelihood security of the poor. It is an established fact that natural resources are the lifeline of the poor. When natural resources are deleted and polluted the worst affected are only the poor. Further dyeing industries waste water have polluted the entire area of certain villages. The Panchayat Presidents have to struggle with all kinds of challenges and face volley of problems as those individuals who take sand illegally activities would invite trouble to the people who are desirous of fighting illegal activities. To oppose all kinds of illegal activities community support is needed. In the above cases the Panchayat Presidents have responded the challenges with the support of the communities. Since natural resources are money spinning factors, mafia who does this work would oppose any resistance powerfully.

The three Panchayat Presidents are brave, committed and honest and they fought against such kind of exploitation. But they have mobilized the people to resist such kind of exploitation. It is proved through these case that decentralization of power can work for protecting the livelihood security of the poor. However limited the powers they enjoy, with the limited powers, the Presidents are able to perform their duties and responsibilities in protecting the natural resources. The above cases are worthy models to be emulated.

CASE - 10

PRESIDENT ATTRACTS PRESIDENT

Keerapalayam is known for its innovative sanitation activities. Each and every house, whether it is a hut or a pucca building, it has been provided with toilet facility with the active participation of the people. This Panchayat sowed the seeds of the sanitation movement in Tamil Nadu. The Panchayat President has mobilized a lot of money internally as people's contribution for many works. Self Help Groups have been assisted to create more of production units to manufacture products. The Keerapalayam health service is considered a model for other Panchayats since health governance is very strong in this Panchayat. His rapport with officials, other tier Panchayat leaders, political party leaders is fine and positive and hence he is able to mobilize huge resources for his Panchayat activities.

Brief History of the Panchayat

"Keerapalayam" is an ancient village of Keerapalayam Block near the Heritage City of Chidambaram of Cuddalore District in Tamil Nadu. Cuddalore district, which was earlier called South Arcot District, lies along the North Western coast of Tamil Nadu and the district is a four hours' drive south of Chennai along the East Coast Road. Keerapalayam Village lies across the bank of the Vellar river, which is a seasonal river flowing through the district.

It is said that since the Vellar river divided the Chola and Pallava kingdoms during the earlier periods and Keerapalayam village lay along its boundary, it became a divider or a "cross-mark" between the two kingdoms. The literary word for the cross-mark or divider between two areas is "keeral" in Tamil. "Palayam" indicates habitation. Hence, the people living in this area came to be known as residents of "Keerapalayam".

Panchayat Profile

Keerapalayam Village has a population of 5347 (3012 Men and 2335 Women). The Village Panchayat has 1160 households and has two habitations, namely Thirupaninatham and Chettikulam. The Village Panchayat has today become a model village of not only in the district but also of the entire State because of its pioneering efforts in the field of total sanitation, drinking water availability and assets maintenance, Self Help Group movement, public participation in community projects, Rain Water Harvesting, greening up activities and efforts in the field of education and health.

Out of eight, 3 are women and 3 of the Panchayat Members belong to the Scheduled Caste community. The Village Panchayat has been visited by senior officials of the Government of India and the Government of Tamil Nadu in the last few years to see and believe the unique experiment of Keerapalayam Panchayat, a role model in successfully implementing various governmental schemes and projects. The total length of roads is 6 kms, of which 4 kms are black topped and 2 kms cement. For education there are 2 balwadis and a public library. The other facilities are market, butchery shed, 2 bus shelters, 2 PDS shops, community hall, 5 TV rooms, cinema theatre, post office and street lights (181 in number).

100 farmers possess lands and their only crop is paddy. The major source of irrigation is a lake. Besides 200 people are engaged in rearing of goats and milch animals. A veterinary centre is functioning in this Panchayat.

Socio-Economic Background

Mr. K.P. Paneer Selvam is the Panchayat President of Keerapalayam Village Panchayat. Aged 54, he belongs to the BC community and lives in a joint family. He is a graduate. His occupation is agriculture and he possesses 15 acres of land. The land income is Rs.50,000 per year. He has good housing facilities with tap connection.

Village Setting

A number of government and financial institutions are functioning in this Panchayat, of which schools, bank, health centre and PACB help the Panchayat development activities. The major castes are Vanniar, SC, Naidu, Pillai, Chettiar, Viswakarma (Paneer Selvam's caste), Mudaliar and ST. For health and sanitation drainage facilties are available in both the villages and toilet is available in all the houses. A public toilet is available for both men and women attached with bathrooms. The AIADMK and the DMK are the dominant parties in this Panchayat.

Caste organizations function very actively in this Panchayat and 12 SHGs have been recently started. Their savings total Rs.30,000. An NGO helps in the formation of SHGs and is involved in women's development activities. It has developed good relations with the Village Panchayat.

Recruitment Process

Before 1996 there were no basic facilities and this Panchayat had to be considered a weak Panchayat. For this reason Paneer Selvam contested in the elections. Two persons contested against him. They were a Vanniar and an SC person and their age was 60 and 35 respectively. During the canvassing the youth accompanied Paneer Selvam and he promised to provide the basic facilities. Paneer Selvam belongs to the AIADMK Party and so his party members supported him. Besides the youth and the elders also supported him because they considered him a sincere man. For this reason he was elected President of this Panchayat in the 1996 elections. For election expenditure he spent more than Rs.15,000 for notices and other expenses. His caste is in the minority. Yet he won the election.

Perception

He has a clear understanding of the role of the new Panchayat Raj System in Tamil Nadu as per 73rd Amendment to the Constitution of India. But as per the Tamil Nadu system he says that the Panchayat is an effective implementing agency. He perceives that the Panchayat can do well even if it is only an implementing agency. His perception is that one has to work effectively as per what is of hand instead of talking too much on what is not available on hand.

Development

Changes are essential for the development of society. People have to voluntarily participate in village development activities. At the same time officials should support the demands of the people. There should be a synergy between the needs of the people and the supply from the government.

For village economy agriculture is the base but today there is no regular rain and diseases affect the crops. In certain areas drought continues. Though there is a hospital for animals there is no adequate medicine in the veterinary centre. The villagers do not have adequate awareness about the various diseases of the crops. Hence training is needed for the farmers. For employment there is no regular job in this area but the people go for coolie work. Even coolie work they do not get regularly. These are the major problems in improving the village economy.

Politics

The AIADMK is the dominant party in this Panchayat and the others are DMK, TMC, Congress, BJP, CPI, MDMK. For Panchayat activities parties are kept away. Paneer Selvam himself sets an example in this regard.

Gender Issues

Paneer Selvam suggested that women should participate in Panchayat development activities through Gram Sabha meetings. Adequate social security is not available for women and this is a primary factor for economic disempowerment of the women. Women could be empowered through training. The training programme should be oriented towards self-employment. Women should be trained into artisans and entrepreneurs. In this way SHG women will be empowered in all aspects. More opportunity is to be given to women because everywhere men drive the society.

Performance

The Ward Members attend the Panchayat meetings regularly due to transparency in the Panchayat activities. Transparency is essential in all aspects of Panchayat development.

In Gram Sabha meetings women participate more than men, particularly SHG members, and ask questions related to their own development, patta and loan. These are the people's expectations in the Gram Sabha meeting. For improving the Gram Sabha meetings transparency is essential both at Panchayat level and official level. Government grants are to be increased and regular employment sources should be provided for all people. In the past five years the following works were done:

Under the IAY 93 group houses were constructed for the SC people and 10 group houses for other people. Maintenance of group houses (20 in number) was undertaken. In 1997-98 under the IRDP 80 beneficiaries were selected and under the TRYSEM 10 people were trained for self-employment. The other works undertaken were as follows:

1. Bus shelter
2. Drainage near Indian Bank
3. Retaining wall for school
4. Public toilet
5. Small plants distributed to houses
6. Sports material purchased
7. Free site given for marriage hall
8. Free land given for constructing drainage system.
9. The following works were also carried out:
   (i) Toilets programme under DANIDA
   (ii) Maintenance of water works under DANIDA
   (iii) Drainage system
   (iv) Metal road formation
   (v) Conducting medical campaign

Sanitation Works

1. Individual toilets under DANIDA (454 persons)
2. Under CRSP 50 persons were benefited
3. Drainage system (from MLA and Union funds)
4. Public toilet under JVVT scheme
5. CRSP school toilets
6. Garbage pit

New Buildings

1. Village Panchayat office
2. School Building
3. Commercial complex
4. TV rooms
5. Kitchen shed
6. Hospital

Namakku Naame Thittam

1. Maintenance of community hall
2. Irrigation works for agricultural development
3. New metal road formation
4. Medical Campaign

DANIDA

Drinking water works and others (Rs. 854 lakhs and people's contribution of Rs.1.28 lakhs).

Under EAS

1. Deepening pond in 2 places Under JVVT
2. Commercial complex building
3. Culvert and drainage system
4. Fruit plants were supplied to the SC families
5. Goats were provided to physically disabled persons

District Collector's Fund

1. Construction of marriage hall
2. Maintenance of well

General Works

1. Sub-station for electricity in the Keerapalayam Panchayat
2. Special coaching classes in the Ayyan Library hall for students every Monday after 5 pm
3. Pension for widows and the elderly
4. Marriage assistance for the poor

5. Government grants and other facilities for physically disabled persons
6. Maintenance of kovil
7. Rs.2000 collected for Kargil scheme and given to the Collector

From Panchayat funds the following works were done:

1. Maintenance of community hall
2. Cement road near Indian Bank
3. Footpath work
4. Desilting work
5. 50th Independence Memorial Arch
6. Maintenance of colony roads
7. Mechanic shed for women

From the MLA Fund sodium vapour lamps, drainage system and marriage hall were provided. From the MP Fund marriage hall and maintenance of roads near colony were provided.

The Village Panchayat has close association with youth associations and NGOs. Hence the following works were undertaken:

1. Medical campaign
2. Pulse polio programme
3. Immunization for animals
4. Awareness on small savings
5. AIDS awareness through cultural programmes
6. Committee formed for arrack eradication.
7. Sanitation works through NSS students
8. Workshops for farmers
9. Drainage cleaning

DANIDA assisted Water and Sanitation Project

To improve the status and condition of rural water supply and sanitation, an innovative project was carried out by DANIDA in collaboration with the Government of Tamil Nadu in Villupuram and Cuddalore Districts. The project was considered significant. It was demand driven rather than supply driven in approach and, sharing the burden of the project, the beneficiaries themselves had to meet one seventh of the cost of the scheme meant for them. Moreover the scheme formulation was participatory. After the creation of the asset the same was handed over to the Village Panchayat itself for the sustainability of the scheme. There is another sector, sanitation, in the project: household latrines and institutional latrines could be constructed by the needy. Beneficiaries have to contribute their share towards the cost of HHL and IL construction.

DANIDA-WS in Keerapalayam

As a part of introducing the concept and activities of the project, DANIDA mobilized the Presidents of Village Panchayats Unionwise. The President of Keerapalayam, Panneer Selvam, was also invited and he attended the meeting. The concepts of demand driven, cost sharing and participatory approach were explained. Panneer Selvam was the first to react against that in the meeting. He said that as the villagers were already drenched in the dependency syndrome, these ideas would not be taken well. The project administrators persuaded him and others by explaining the ways and means to educate the masses in this regard and the availability of field staff including engineers to carry out the programmes under the project by the Village Panchayats.

Further a two day orientation training was arranged for all the Presidents of Village Panchayats in this regard, involving the Gandhigram Rural Institute. The DANIDA-WS Project took off well in course of time. Keerapalayam led ahead of all the other project villages, because of the able leadership of Panneer Selvam.

Orientation to Public of Keerapalayam

A public meeting was organized to explain to the villagers the project and its various components. People gathered in good number but most of them were menfolk. Their perception was that it was not wise to build the toilet in the house/campus as sufficient open fields existed away from the habitations. It was decided to bring more women and then to decide to do further. When the next meeting was convened, a good number of women turned out and they accepted that the toilet was very much necessary. A third meeting was held in which many women came forward to talk of the scheme. Here and there the toilets have come up. Witnessing the physical structure and its utility the scheme was speeded up. The villagers spent additional amount for better facility in the toilet. About 500 household latrines have been constructed under DANIDA. And through the Central Rural Sanitation Programme (CRSP), an additional 300 toilets have been provided to the rest of the villagers.

The inhabitants of small houses expressed their inability to find adequate space for the construction of toilets in their houses. A public toilet was constructed with the assistance of the DRDA where six toilets and six bathrooms have been provided. About thirty families are utilizing this toilet.

Utilization of Toilets

The mindset of the rural masses with regard to personal habits of health and sanitation seemed to be underdeveloped. The modern system of life and society has brought several new things like pucca drainage, cement concrete road, public toilets etc., to the rural areas. But the concept of operation and maintenance has yet to be realized by the public. With much drive toilets were constructed but all of them were not put to use. To ensure cent-per-cent utilization the message was spread through school students, Panneer Selvam said.

Youth volunteers, both men and women, came forward to take the message from door to door. The operation and maintenance of toilets was demonstrated to each and every stakeholder. The students raised their voice and influenced their parents for necessary behavioural change. Toilets are now utilized but not by all the members in the family. Still a few elders and other persons prefer open-air defecation. Though they are negligible in number, the Village Panchayat has proposed to completely ban open-air defecation. The cultural barriers in the family system in this regard have to be targeted. In urban families changes are brought about quickly whereas in rural areas it takes time, Mr. Panneer Selvam said.

The Concept of IEC and its Significance

Sanitation is a way of life. It starts with the baby. Inculcation of necessary behaviour and practice in maintaining personal hygiene and public sanitation by each individual has to be ensured for total rural sanitation. The toilet is a part. Safe disposal of solid and liquid waste, tree planting for pure environment, keeping common places neat and clean, equipping the villagers in health awareness and practice of better preventive care system, avoiding stagnation of rain water/waste water by rainwater harvesting system, ensuring potable drinking water, toilet facilities in educational institutions, upkeep of roads, all these activities are the components of total rural sanitation. The villagers of Keerapalayam realized this in course of time after they got household latrines, Mr. Panneer Selvam said.

Construction of drainage is an expensive work for which there is no adequate budget allocation to Panchayat bodies. Through the participation and contribution of people and with DRDA and DANIDA assistance, drainage facilities were provided to streets and lanes in Keerapalayam main village. In the bazaar of Keerapalayam, the solid wastes are spread along the highway. It gives an awkward look and creates an unhealthy atmosphere. Hundreds of people used to gather in the bazaar and the bus stop. There is no sanitary worker in the Village Panchayat. Wastes were heaped high. The issue was frequently raised by the people/ Ward Members/ youth groups. A meeting was organized to sort out the problem. The SHG women and youth groups came forward to do maintenance work periodically. They demanded baskets and a cart to transport away the solid wastes. To each house two baskets were distributed, one for organic wastes and the other for inorganic wastes. Each household was ready to pay Rs.5 as monthly contribution. A bullock cart was provided with a driver by the Village Panchayat. Once a week or twice a week, the solid wastes are transported away safely. A manure yard is proposed to convert the organic wastes into rich compost manure. The Dr. M.S. Swaminathan Research Foundation is giving guidance in this regard.

Temples and observance of religious and auspicious days play a vital role in the inculcation of personal hygiene as well as public sanitation. There are 11 temples in Keerapalayam Village Panchayat. Ganesh Temple, Amman Temple, Murugan Temple, Ayyanar Temple and Kannan Temple have been renovated. The local public as well as philanthropists from outside munificently donated to temple renovation works. Panneer Selvam took the initiative for the renovation works in all these temples. Periodical lamp worship by women brought a behavioural change which made an impact on the environmental sanitation also, Panneer Selvam felt.

Tree planting was undertaken on roadsides and in public places. Shady trees were planted. To each house, tree saplings of guava, sappotta, mango, coconut, lime, and papaya were distributed and most of the saplings have survived as care was given by the householder. Medicinal plants were also distributed. The villagers of Keerapalayam are now well aware of the importance and the role of trees and green coverage in the promotion of total rural sanitation.

Medical camps and eye camps were organized in association with non-governmental and governmental institutions. Necessary referral was made to the district hospital. Panchayat Ward Members ensured proper follow-up of these cases. The health officials undertook a survey in Keerapalayam and the number of persons suffering from general diseases has now decreased, anemia cases are reduced and water borne diseases are completely eradicated.

Provision of institutional latrines in the primary and the high school of Keerapalayam was carried out by the Parents Teachers Association. Students are properly oriented to make use of the school latrine. Water facility was provided by the Village Panchayat.

Streets and lanes were widened by removing the encroachments. Earlier the narrow streets and narrow lanes failed to ensure a clean environment. After widening these passages, the householders and the traders are trying to maintain the front area of their buildings clean and neat, Panneer Selvam said.

A public park was established near the Panchayat office campus. Though it is a small one, the concept of park touched the inner sense of the seer.

Rainwater harvesting has now-a-days gained the attention of the government and the public. In general there is a perception that it has a limited scope in the case of hutments. But, in consultation with village elders, the youths made arrangements to collect the run-off water at a point so that it could be stored or let down into the ground for percolation. A movement was initiated in rainwater harvesting and in 500 houses, 200 hutments, 150 tiled houses and, 150 pucca houses rainwater harvest structures were installed by the owners themselves. The Chartered Engineer of the Village Panchayat helped in this regard. He offered technical guidance to the villagers. SHG members and youth association members spread the message to each house. The personal advice and attention of the Chief Minister in the promotion of rainwater harvesting is the chief source of inspiration and so the activities rolled on in five hundred houses, Panneer Selvam happily shared.

Lessons

To ensure total rural sanitation the following steps have to be undertaken, Panneer Selvam pointed out:

1. Effective sensitization and proper follow-up.
2. Personal visit/motivation.
3. Availability of various types/models of toilet.
4. Institutional latrines — appropriate models.
5. Efforts to use the toilet facilities.
6. Knowledge/skill in proper operation and maintenance of toilets.
7. Supplementary components of sanitation like drainage, safe disposal of solid wastes, tree planting, rainwater harvesting etc., should also be targeted.
8. Provision of necessary infrastructure facilities meant for environmental sanitation.
9. Involvement of all stakeholders.
10. Orientation to Village Panchayat President and all Ward Members.
11. Convergence of relevant schemes and programmes of the governments in the improvement of sanitation.
12. Integration of all relevant activities under the total rural sanitation programme, involving private institutions also.

3. (i) Performance under Rural Development Department Schemes

(a) Sanitation

Keerapalayam Panchayat has 1160 households. The Panchayat lies across the National Highways from Chennai to Chidambaram. Earlier, in the early mornings and late nights, the people used the roadside for open defecation. This used to be an amazing sight even for the foreign tourists going to the heritage town of Chidambaram nearby.

When the Government of India and the State Government launched the Central Rural Sanitation Programme and when the DANIDA Assisted Sanitation Programme was also launched, Keerapalayam Panchayat grabbed the opportunity to transform itself into a totally sanitized Panchayat. The present Panchayat President, Panneer Selvam, who became President in 1996, sought assistance from the district administration for construction of individual toilets through the CRSP scheme and the DANIDA scheme. Gradually, individual household toilets were built one by one in each of the households of the Village Panchayat. Within a span of one year more than 600 toilets were built. At present all the 1160 houses have got individual toilets. A split up is given hereunder:

(i)	Under assistance of DANIDA	–	563
(ii)	Under assistance of CRSP	–	50
(iii)	Construction along with Group Houses	–	184
(iv)	By individuals	–	373
	Total	–	1160

Open defecation has been totally eradicated in the village. The present stage of sanitation in the village is that one public latrine, which was constructed to cater to some individual households of the village, has been abandoned by the villagers since all of them have got toilets in their own houses. Now the above public latrine is used only by persons visiting the local market.

Sanitation in the village — A Unique Transformation

In fact, Keerapalayam Panchayat has got the unique distinction of being declared the First Totally Sanitized Village Panchayat in the whole of Tamil Nadu in September 1998. The above experiment of total sanitation was verified by the then Secretary, Rural Development Department, Tamil Nadu, Dr. R.C. Panda, IAS. This success story was highlighted by even the national newspaper *The Hindu* in its news entitled "A Success Story in Rural Sanitation," on 24.9.1998.

Total Sanitation in Institutions also

There are two primary schools and one high school in the village. The primary and high schools have been provided with sanitation facilities by the Village Panchayat and the concept of teaching the sanitation concept at the school level itself is followed in Keerapalayam Panchayat.

Village Cleanliness — A Role Model for other Panchayats

The sanitation of a village does not end with the construction of toilets in individual houses and in the schools and other Government buildings. For a village to look clean, its streets should be cleaned and there should be proper disposal of drainage/sewage in order to ensure model cleanliness in the village. This has also been ensured in the Panchayat :

- By dovetailing the amount available in the Rural Development schemes like JGSY and SGRY schemes, the Village Panchayat has so far laid cement concrete roads across 12 of its village streets. Due to this the village streets look clean and free from village garbage and slush.
- The Village Panchayat President has introduced household collection of garbage within the village. Two separate garbage bins are available in each household.
- The collected garbage is separated as degradable and non-degradable wastes and this is collected by means of tri-cycles by the villagers themselves and the above effort can also be labelled as 'Self Help Efforts'.
- Big garbage pits have been constructed in various parts of the village to compost the degradable wastes. The Village Panchayat has ensured that the highways and roadsides

which were earlier heaped with piles of garbage are now free of any such ugliness.

- The Village Panchayat has also now started conversion of the degradable wastes into compost by using the composting process.

Village Greening up — A Way to Sanitize the Environment

Keerapalayam Village Panchayat has ensured that the village looks clean not only on its surface but also in its environment. The Panchayat President and the Members have in the last few years planted more than three thousand trees in various parts of the village. In fact, Keerapalayam Panchayat boasts of a beautiful *Village Park* in which trees have been planted by the Village Panchayat Members as well as many of the VIPs who come to see the wonderful initiative of the Panchayat. The Panchayat President has taken special efforts to put up a number of trees within the campus of the three schools of the village and the Panchayat also ensures regular watering of the above trees through the efforts of the villagers.

To add cream to the cake, Keerapalayam Panchayat has the unique distinction of having a fountain in its green park, which has been built by the voluntary donations of the villagers and which oozes sparkling water churning out a melodious sound in the evenings when the fountain is switched on for the amusement of the villagers.

(b) Rainwater Harvesting: A Cent-per-cent Transfomation

(i) Private Households

Keerapalayam Panchayat became a role model for the entire district by being one of the first Panchayats to be totally covered by rainwater harvesting structures.

The Village Panchayat has two hamlets

(i) Thirupaninatham
(ii) Chettikulam

There are a total of 1160 houses. All the households have rainwater harvesting structures. The details are:

(i) Tiled Houses	164
(ii) R.C.C Houses	123
(iii) Thatched Houses	689
(iv) Group Houses	184
	1160

(ii) Government Buildings

The Village Panchayat President and the Members have ensured that not only individual households, but also government buildings have rainwater harvesting structures. The following government buildings available in this Village Panchayat also have rainwater harvesting structures:

1.	Panchayat Union Office, Keerapalayam	1
2.	Additional Educational Officer's Office	1
3.	Self Help Group Building	1
4.	Community Hall	1
5.	Library Hall	1
6.	Anganvadi Centre	1
7.	T. V. Rooms	5
8.	School Buildings	3
9.	Panchayat Shopping Complex Building	2
10.	Fair Price Shop	1
11.	Agriculture Development Office	1
12.	Post Office	1
13.	Electricity Board Office	1
14.	ICDS Office	1
15.	Civil Supplies Paddy Procurement Centre	1
16.	Primary Agriculture Co-Operative Bank	1
17.	VAO's Office	1

(iii) Religious Structures

Rainwater harvesting structures have also been provided in the following religious places in this Village Panchayat with the full co-operation and participation of the local people:

1. Arulmigu Selliamman Temple
2. Arulmigu Murugan Koil
3. Arulmigu Sapthakannigai Temple
4. Arulmigu Somanathar Temple

Desilting of all village ponds has been undertaken fully. The Panchayat now goes with the vision that not even a single drop of water should go waste.

(c) Water Harvesting Structure, Desilting of Village Tanks

Keerapalayam Panchayat has utilized the government scheme to ensure that all village ponds are desilted on a regular basis.

In Keerapalayam Village there are 6 village ponds. Out of these five village ponds were desilted last year at the initiative of the Panchayat. For the sixth village pond, Nalla Thanneer Pond, desilting work has been carried out under the SGRY II in this current year 2003-2004, at an estimated cost of Rs. 1.00 lakh and the work has been completed.

All the village ponds which are the main source of water recharge for borewells and also the direct source of water for animals, desilting is carried out regularly to receive maximum rainwater.

(d) Efforts Taken to Provide Drinking Water Facilities to the Villagers

In 1996, Keerapalayam Panchayat had two OHTs. At that time one of the two OHTs was leaking and the borewell of the other OHT had dried up. The Village Panchayat decided to take efforts to ensure easy drinking water availability to the villagers. The following steps were taken in this regard through the efforts of the President, Panneer Selvam.

- A new borewell was sunk to replace the failed borewell source by providing 1/7th of its cost as public contribution to the DANIDA Assisted Project.
- The leaking OHT was repaired through the DANIDA assistance fund by providing 1/7th of its cost through public contribution.
- Four new OHTs were constructed by representing to the district administration and the Tamil Nadu Water Supply and Drainage Department through the Village Panchayat. The Village Panchayat is now a proud possessor of six OHTs, 108 public taps and 176 household connections. One OHT (60000) is under construction.

Drinking water is given to the villagers regularly twice a day. There are 12 Mark-II Hand Pumps and 32 Shallow Hand Pumps. All the water sources work even during summer due to the following two reasons:

(i) Successful rainwater harvesting has ensured that the ground water does not deplete even during summer.

(ii) Women plumbers have been trained to repair any hand pumps if they malfunction.

The average water supply to the villagers is 80 lpcd. The village boasts of sufficient water supply even when other villages reel under drought conditions during summer.

Safe drinking water is ensured and for this periodical testing of water supply is made.

(e) Swajal Dhara

Swajal Dhara has been taken up in the village for provision of water supply to the Government High School at Keerapalayam by collecting a contribution of Rs.25,000 from the public for taking up a Rs.5.00 lakhs project for construction of an OHT with borewell for the High School that caters to 531 school students.

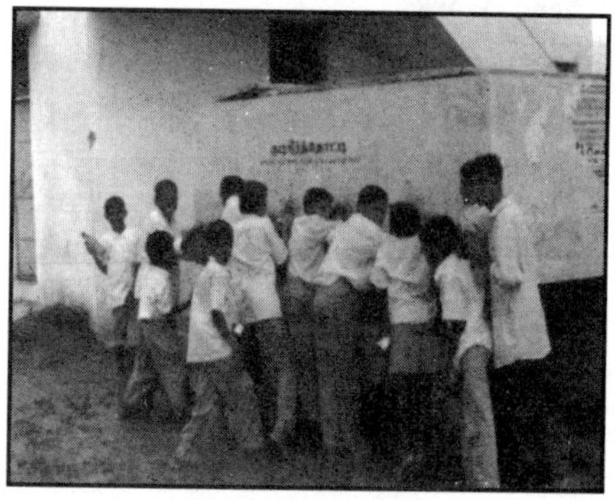

High School Students

3. (ii) (a) Initiative in Rural Health — Keerapalayam Model

The Village Panchayat has got a Health Sub-centre within the Panchayat limits. There are a number of instances in the district when the Village Health Nurse does not reside at the Health Sub-centre where she is supposed to reside and only visits the Sub-centre during the day-time. However, the proactive Keerapalayam Panchayat President and the Members have ensured

Under JGSY and SGRY the following works are taken up and completed and are put to use

Year	*Name of the work*	*Name of Scheme*	*Estimate amount Rs.*	*Expenditure Rs.*	*Mandays generated*
2000-01	Tree plantation	JGSY	9630	9630	1070
	WBM Road	JGSY	37597	37597	418
2001-02	Culvert	EAS	47000	47000	522
	30 Household latrines	JGSY	30000	30000	333
	Cement Road	JGSY	102000	102000	1133
	WBM Road	JGSY	24000	24000	267
2002-03	Self Help Group Building	SGRY II	100000	100000	111
	Gravel Road work	SGRY II	21000	21000	233
	Community Centre Additional Room	SGRY II	120000	120000	1333
	Threshing Floor	SGRY I	60000	60000	667
2003-04	Desilting of Village Pond	SGRY II	100000	100000	1111
	Cement Road	SGRY II	50000	50000	556
	Culvert	SGRY II	45400	45400	504

SGRY the following centrally sponsored schemes have been implemented in this Village Panchayat

Year	*Name of the work*	*Scheme*	*No.of works*	*Estimate amount Rs.*	*Expenditure Rs.*	*Mandays generated*
2000-01	Group Houses	IAY	1	32000	32000	356
2001-02	Group Houses	PMGY	25	800000	800000	8889
2002-03	Upgradation of houses	IAY upgradation	3	30000	30000	333
2003-04	Group Houses	IAY	9	288000	288000	3200
	Upgradation of Houses	IAY Upgradation	15	150000	150000	1667
Other Scheme Works						
	Gravel Road to Kuravar colony	Small Savings	1	120000	120000	
	BT high school road	Incentive		300000	300000	
	BT Indian Bank road street	SFC		200000	200000	
	Flushing of OHT Bores	CRF	5	40000	40000	
	Flushing of HP Bores	CRF	2	8000	8000	
	Extension of Pipe line village to Narikuravar colony	CRF		44000	44000	
	Mark II H.P at IB street	CRF		71000	71000	
	Anganwadi latrine ICDs Keerapalayam	TRSP		4000	4000	
	Construction of drainage at Indira Nagar			300000	300000	
	Repair to Pt. Building for use by SHG	SGSY		36000	36000	

The following works are sanctioned during 2004-2005 and are in progress

Sl. No	*Name of the work*	*Name of the scheme*	*No.of units*	*Estimate amount Rs.*
1.	Group House	IAY	10	340000
2.	Cement road colony	SGRY II		130000
3.	Drainage colony			50000
4.	BT road to BC street			33000
5.	BT road	SGRY I		100000
6.	Repair to GH		8	54000

that the Village Health Nurse does stay in the Health Sub-Centre premises and is available for all vaccinations, routine check-ups and emergencies. The Panchayat has taken the following efforts to promote the health of the villagers:

- Vaccination has been provided to each and every child in the village in the last 5 years.
- Cent-per-cent vaccination for pregnant mothers has been ensured and the progress is also reviewed in the Grama Sabha meetings.
- The Village Panchayat President and the Members have ensured that polio drops are given to the children on cent-per-cent basis during every yearly polio camp.
- The Village Panchayat has also taken up a drive to give DFA tables for curing elephantiasis/filariasis.
- The Village Panchayat requested and succeeded in persuading the health authorities to distribute iron tablets to all children and women, especially girls of adolescent age.
- In the last 7 years, the Village Panchayat has conducted annual health camps by utilising the services of Government doctors and also the doctors of the medical college of Annamalai University. Similarly, yearly eye camps have been conducted at the persuasion of the Village Panchayat.
- The Village Panchayat President has also proudly conducted free acupuncture camps for the patients.
- The services of the Anti-Leprosy Unit of the district has also been utilised by the Village Panchayat to detect and cure leprosy within the village. 5 villagers (2 women and 3 gents) who had initial symptoms of leprosy were cured through the above timely efforts of the Village Panchayat.

- The Village Panchayat has also been actively involved in detection and treatment of sexually transmitted diseases amongst the villagers.

3. (ii) (b) Efforts Taken for Success of Family Welfare

In Keerapalayam Village Panchayat the Government policy of two children has been adopted throughout the Village Panchayat. Family welfare is stressed through visual media, cable TV, posters, public address system, campaigns etc.

35 Family planning operations were carried out in 2002 (from January 2002 to December 2002) and 33 operations were done in 2003 (from January 2003 to December 2003) and 17 operations were done from January 2004 to June 2004.

Totally 12 babies were born during 2003 (from January 2003 to November 2003).

All family planning measures of the Government of Tamil Nadu are followed in this Village Panchayat and by this the birth rate is reduced considerably.

T.B. Awareness Camp in the Village Panchayat

3. (ii) (c) Innovative Step of the Village Panchayat in Education

In 1996, Keerapalayam Panchayat had only one school building which housed both the Panchayat Union Elementary School and the Government High School. The Village Panchayat President and the Members felt that Chettikulam hamlet also needed its own Elementary School building in order to ensure that all the children receive elementary education. The Village Panchayat also felt the necessity of having a separate High School building since the building of the Elementary School did not suffice for the High School. The above vision of the Panchayat led to the following :

- A new Panchayat Union Elementary School at Chettikulam was opened 4 years back and this caters to 52 children who predominantly belong to the downtrodden sections of the society.
- The Village Panchayat elders voluntarily vacated six acres of land for the construction of a new Government School building for Keerapalayam Panchayat.
- Generally a new school will get a 3-classroom building under the Sarva Siksha Abhiyan scheme through the special sanction of the District Collector. However, since the land was gifted by the Village Panchayat elders for the Government High School, Keerapalayam, the then District Collector allocated two additional buildings in the same year under the Sarva Siksha Abhiyan scheme for the Government High School, Keerapalayam, and hence the above school has five classrooms now. This is a unique gift given to the Village Panchayat by the district administration for its proactive role in the promotion of school education.
- The Village Panchayat also collected a sum of Rs.25,000 and deposited it under the Swajal Dhara scheme and hence a water supply scheme, including construction of an OHT and a borewell, have been undertaken under the Swajal Dhara scheme for provision of drinking water supply to the 561 students of the Government High School, Keerapalayam.
- The Village Panchayat also took efforts to enrol the school students in the School Recurring Deposit Scheme of Small Savings in order to promote the habit of small savings. As a reward to the Village Panchayat for these efforts, the present District Collector sanctioned a sum of Rs.3.00 lakhs from the Collector's Discretionary Small Savings Fund for laying of a pucca road from the main road to the Government High School.
- The Village Panchayat has also got about 20 families of Narikuravas who are erstwhile nomadic people and who now do the business of selling ornamental beads etc. The Village Panchayat President and the Members took efforts to ensure that all the 16 children of the Narikurava families were enrolled in the local Elementary School. This effort has been highlighted in the press also.

The above effort of enrolling the children of erstwhile nomadic families in school has really been a wonderful achievement of Keerapalayam Panchayat.

3. (iii) Revenue Mobilization by the Panchayat in Past 3 Years

The main revenue of this Village Panchayat is from house tax. All the houses are enrolled under house tax. The demand under house tax for the year 2003-04 is Rs.33,366. The Panchayat has collected cent-per-cent tax in the previous year. However, Keerapalayam Panchayat doesn't rely on only house tax for its income.

Besides the house tax this Village Panchayat is collecting the following taxes and fees and all these are the revenue sources of the Village Panchayat:

(i) Professional tax from employees
(ii) Licence Fees
(iii) Building plan approval fees
(iv) Rent for Panchayat owned Community Hall and Shops
(v) Daily Market tax through annual tender

In fact the uniqueness of the Panchayat is that it was sanctioned an amount of Rs.15 lakhs (Rs. 5 lakhs under MPLAD plus Rs. 5 lakhs under MLACDS plus Rs.5 lakhs under JGSY), when it was declared the first totally sanitised village of the state. The community hall now fetches a regular income to the Panchayat. The Village Panchayat also gets income through the daily market.

The revenue for the last three years 2000-01, 2001-02, 2002-03 and 2003-2004 is furnished hereunder.

Community Centre of the Village Panchayat

Keerapalayam Panchayat for the Year 2000- 2001

Panchayat Account – I

Sl. No.	*Category of revenue*	*Total revenue collection Rs.*
1.	House Tax	23507
2.	House Tax Matching grant	33867
3.	Library Tax	2388
4.	Professional Tax	42270
5.	Miscellaneous Tax	41840
6.	Building Plan approval Fees	2594
7.	Shopping complex rent	9638
8.	Local Cess	-
9.	Local cess surcharge	-
10.	Deposit	-
11.	S.F.C. grant	204831
12.	Waste paper sale	-
13.	Fishery rights Lease	525
14.	Community centre rents	550
15.	Stamp duty	32704
16.	Entertainment Tax	11329
17.	Deposit for house connections	47356
18.	Cycle stand Lease	1240
19.	Daily Market	12238
20.	Water Tax	4110
	Total	470987

Account - II

Sl. No.	*Category of revenue*	*Total revenue collection Rs.*
1.	Subsidy for funeral rites	4455
2.	25% Panchayat contribution fron A/c No. 1	-
3.	10th Finance/11th Finance grant	38305
	Total	42760

Account - III

Sl. No.	*Category of revenue*	*Total revenue collection Rs.*
1.	JGSY/SGSY	92328
2.	IAY	15895
3.	PMGY	-
4.	Kutcha	-
	Total	108223

Keerapalayam Panchayat for the Year 2001- 2002

Panchayat Account - I

Sl. No.	*Category of revenue*	*Total revenue collection Rs.*
1.	House Tax	31807
2.	House Tax Maternity grant	-
3.	Library Tax	3125
4.	Professional Tax	28710
5.	Miscellaneous Tax	-
6.	Building Plan approval fees	4068
7.	Shopping complex rent	14582
8.	Local cess	-
9.	Local cess surcharge	-
10.	Deposit	-
11.	S.F.C. grant	81060
12.	Waste paper sale	-
13.	Fishery rights lease	5320
14.	Community centre rents	12150
15.	Stamps Duty	34982
16.	Entertainment Tax	45622
17.	Deposit for house connections	25000
18.	Cycle stand lease	-
19.	Daily Market	5592
	Total	292018

Account - II

Sl. No.	*Category of revenue*	*Total revenue collection Rs.*
1.	Subsidy for funeral rites	6940
2.	25% Panchayat contribution fron A/c No. 1	-
3.	10th Finance/11th Finance grant	13281
	Total	20221

Account - III

Sl. No.	*Category of revenue*	*Total revenue collection Rs.*
1.	JGSY/SGSY	72043
2.	IAY	1930
3.	PMGY	-
4.	Kutcha	-
	Total	73973

Keerapalayam Panchayat for the Year 2002-2003

Panchayat Account - I

Sl. No.	Category of revenue	Total revenue collection Rs.
1.	House Tax	47466
2.	House Tax Matching grant	6198
3.	Library Tax	4704
4.	Professional Tax	51820
5.	Miscellaneous Tax	
6.	Building Plan approval Fees	4096
7.	Shopping complex rent	9590
8.	Local Cess	-
9.	Local cess surcharge	-
10.	Deposit	-
11.	S.F.C. grant	235810
12.	Waste paper sale	-
13.	Fishery rights lease	1180
14.	Community centre rents	6200
15.	Stamp Duty	37269
16.	Entertainment Tax	14306
17.	Deposit for house connections	7000
18.	Cycle stand lease	-
19.	Daily Market	2500
	Total	428139

Account - II

Sl. No.	Category of revenue	Total revenue collection Rs.
1.	Subsidy for funeral rites	14869
2.	25% Panchayat contribution fron A/c No . 1	-
3.	10th Finance/11th Finance grant	107269
	Total	122138

Account - III

Sl. No.	Category of revenue	Total revenue collection Rs.
1.	JGSY/SGSY	101974
2.	IAY	270000
3.	PMGY	-
4.	Kutcha	29870
	Total	401844

Keerapalayam Panchayat for the Year 2003- 2004

Panchayat Account - I

Sl. No.	Category of revenue	Total revenue collection Rs.
1.	House Tax	33816
2.	House Tax Matching grant	-
3.	Library Tax	3382
4.	Professional Tax	55321
5.	Miscellaneous Tax	578
6.	Building Plan approval Fees	11774
7.	Shopping complex rent	23000
8.	Local Cess	5066
9.	Local cess surcharge	-
10.	Other receipts	5442
11.	S.F.C. grant	186730
12.	Waste paper sale	-
13.	Fishery rights lease	500
14.	Community centre	13875
15.	Stamp Duty	20602
16.	Entertainment Tax	17957
17.	Deposit for house connections	-
18.	Cycle stand lease	-
19.	Daily Market	-
20.	San quarry	19500
	Total	397543

Account - II

Sl. No.	Category of revenue	Total revenue collection Rs.
1.	Subsidy for funeral rites	-
2.	25% Panchayat contribution fron A/c No. 1	33953
3.	10th Finance/11th Finance grant	53622
	Total	87575

Account - III

Sl. No.	Category of revenue	Total revenue collection Rs.
1.	JGSY/SGSY	112519
2.	IAY	111000
3.	Kutcha	120000
4.	TRSP	149765
5.	Other schemes	170000
	Total	543284

Works Done by Public Contribution

1.	Bus Stop	Rs.40,000 Thiru D. Adiyapatham Live-Stock Assistant
2.	Indian Bank Street Sewage Water Canal	Rs.60,000 Thiru. Vijayaragavan, Engineer (Rtd.)
3.	School Compound	Rs.50,000
4.	Garbage Collecting Cart	Rs.5,000 Thiru. A.K. Ramasamy, Ex-Village President
5.	Public Toilet (2)	Rs.80,000 DANIDA
6.	School Toilet	Rs.40,000 Thiru. Krishnamoorthy
7.	Thirumathi Manimen-galai Rtd. Teacher gives	Rs.500 to the first rate student annually
8.	Chidambaram Assembly of the group of number in Thiru.K.S.Alagiri B.A., given distributed saplings to the whole village worth	Rs. 3,000
9.	Village Extension Work	Rs.20,000 Thiru. K.Santhanam, Driver, Government, TNSTC
10.	Library Donation	Rs.20,000 Village People
11.	Sports Goods	Rs.50,000 Thiru. D. T. K. Pandian
12.	Community Hall Plot	Rs.10,000 Thiru. D. T. Kalia Perumal Naidu
13.	Plot for Sewage Water Canal	Rs.10,000 Tmt. Krishnammal, Mettu Street
14.	Television	Rs.15,000 Thiru. Adiyapatham, Rtd. Lie Stock Assistant

Works Done by Public Contribution

1.	Individual Toilet under DANIDA Assistance	Rs.2.44 lakhs
2.	Drinking water under DANIDA	Rs.1.28 lakhs
3.	CRSP Individual Toilet	Rs.025 lakhs
4.	Chettikulam community hall	Rs.0.06 lakhs
5.	Water canal for cultivation	Rs.0.04 lakhs
6.	Blue metal road	Rs.0.45 lakhs
7.	Medical Camp	Rs.0.20 lakhs
8.	Water canal for cultivation	Rs.30,000
9.	Poor widow Krishnammal donated 1 cent land	Rs.50,000
10.	Thirumathi Neela, belongs to Adhi Dravida Community gave 3 cents lands to the road of Burial Ground	Rs.25,000
11.	Individual toilet by DANIDA and Public contribution for 408 persons	Rs.2.44 lakhs
12.	Individual Toilet Central Local Fund for 50 persons	Rs.0.25 lakhs

3. (iv) (a) Grama Sabha Meetings

As per the provisions laid drawn in section 3(2) of the Tamil Nadu Panchayat Act, 1994, Grama Sabha meetings are conducted in Keerapalayam Village Panchayat on the dates specified by the State Government, viz. January 26th, May 1st, August 15th, and October 2th, and special meetings for selection of beneficiaries under schemes whenever ordered by the Government/District Collector by adopting the guidelines prescribed by the State Government from time to time.

In these meetings the development activities proposed to be taken up under state and centrally sponsored schemes, various activities going on in the Village Panchayat, its action plan are discussed; views are obtained and, accordingly, schemes/activities are taken up, the accounts of the Panchayat are made known to the public in the above meetings.

Gram Sabha

District Collector and Project Officer DRDA Participating in the Grama Sabha

Sl. No.	*Year*	*Date of Meeting of the Gram Sabha*	*Required No. of participants for the Meeting*	*No. of Participants*
1.	2000	26.1.2000	287	450
		1.5.2000	287	407
		15.8.2000	287	419
		2.10.2000	287	346
2.	2001	26.1.01	287	389
		6.5.01	287	319
		24.6.01	287	452
		15.8.01	287	405
		11.11.01	287	377
3.	2002	26.1.02	287	324
		15.2.02	287	330
		14.4.02	287	464
		1.5.02	287	490
		15.8.02	287	351
		2.10.02	287	305
4	2003	26.1.03	287	360
		28.4.03	287	368
		1.5.03	287	343
		8.7.03	287	370
		15.8.03	287	351
		23.8.03	287	316
		2.10.03	287	325
		23.11.03	287	380
		26.1.04	287	308
		6.6.04	287	315

3. (iv)(b) Identification of Beneficiaries for Various Development Schemes

Year	*Date of Gram Sabha*	*Name of the Scheme*	*No. of Beneficiaries identified*
2000	26.1.2000	IAY Group houses	33
		Crediting Subsidy	33
2001	24.6.01	IAY Group houses	86
		IAY Kutcha	13
2002	14.4.02	IAY Group houses	150
		Kutcha	100
		GH Repairs	75
2003	8.7.03	IAY Group houses	26
		Kutcha	15
2004	26.1.04	IAY	35
		Kutcha	10

Additional Director of Rural Development and Project Officer Visiting the Grama Sabha of the Panchayat

3. (iv)(c) Preparation of Village Plans

The Panchayat Council of Keerapalayam Village Panchayat has prepared and approved the draft annual village plan for every financial year and has executed the schemes in the same year.

The Panchayat Council has prepared and approved the draft annual village development plan for the year 2002–03 and has started the works.

Sl. No.	*Name of the Scheme*	*Name of the work*	*Estimated cost Rs.*
1.	IAY upgradation	Upgradation of 3 kutcha houses	30000
2.	SGRY II	Self help group building for women	100000
3.	SGRY II	Road work (gravel)	21000
4.	SGRY II	Community centre	120000
5.	SGRY I	Threshing floor	60000

Cement Road Executed Under SGRY II 2003–2004

In a similar manner, the Panchayat Council prepared and approved a draft village development plan for the year 2003-04. Accordingly following works were taken up and all the works were completed by November 2003 itself (4 months ahead of schedule).

Sl. No.	*Name of the scheme*	*Name of the work*	*Estimated amount*
	2003-2004		
1.	I AY	9 group houses	288000
2.	I AY upgradation	15 kutcha houses upgradation	150000
3.	SGRY II	Desilting of village pond	100000
4.	SGRY II	Cement road	50000
5.	SGRY II	Culvert	45400
	Plan for 2004-2005 approved by Pt.		
1.	IAY	Group House - 10	340000
2.	SGRY II	Cement road colony	130000
3.		Drainage colony	50000
4.		BT road to BC street	33000

The Village Panchayat is preparing plans properly and executing the works within the time stipulated. All works including current year work are completed.

Before Execution

After Execution

Upgradation of Kutcha House Under I.A.Y. 2003-2004

Group House Under I.A.Y. 2003-2004

3. (iv)(d) Maintenance of Assets and Properties: The Unique Way

1. Keerapalayam Panchayat is unique in the state in terms of having lady plumbers for repair of hand pumps. The repairs to the hand pumps and power pumps are carried out then and there by the Village Panchayat. This Village Panchayat has trained lady plumbers amongst the women of the Panchayat itself who attend to the hand pump repairs and who are nominally paid by the Panchayat.
2. All the street lights are burning. The Panchayat President has in fact kept a *Complaint Box* for the public to inform him of any non-burning street light or non-functioning hand pump so as to take immediate remedial action.
3. The water resources like village ponds are renovated every year by the Village Panchayat under various schemes.
4. All the roads vested with the Village Panchayat are maintained properly and improvement done through the funds allotted under the SGRY and other schemes.
5. All the buildings owned by the Village Panchayat are maintained properly and all the buildings are in good condition.
6. This Village Panchayat has a community centre and a shopping complex. The buildings are maintained properly and rent is being received regularly by the Panchayat.
7. Keerapalayam Panchayat proudly owns a *Village Library* also.
8. Perhaps this is one of the very few Panchayats to own a park with a fountain.

3. (v) Innovative Initiatives of Keerapalayam Panchayat

(a) Women Plumbers/Attending to Repairs to Hand Pumps

Keerapalayam Panchayat, with the assistance of DANIDA, has trained a group of village women to repair hand pumps. This women's group is attending to hand pump repairs in this Village Panchayat and also other Panchayats in the Keerapalayam Panchayat Union. They have been provided with necessary tools and equipments for repairs. The women plumber group of this Village Panchayat are a proud asset of the Panchayat and are formed due to the sole efforts of the Panchayat President and the DANIDA project. One is astonished to see the women, who once knew only child-rearing and cooking, now repairing hand pumps, which their menfolk can't even think of doing. Using the trained group as resource persons hand pump repairing is organized for all the Keerapalayam Block Village Panchayats.

Women Plumbers Attending Repairs

Training Programme Participation by Project Officer, DRDA.

Participants of the Training Programme

(b) Women Mason Groups

Similarly the Village Panchayat, with the assistance of DANIDA, has given mason training to a group of ladies from this Village Panchayat and this group has constructed the latrines of this Village Panchayat. This group is now also doing mason work in and around the Village Panchayat. Keerapalayam Panchayat leads the state in real women empowerment.

Women Mason Group

(c) Clean Village Campaign/Rural Sanitation

This Village Panchayat was, as earlier mentioned, the first village in Tamil Nadu to have cent-per-cent self-sufficient sanitation under the Rural Sanitation Programme. This Village Panchayat has also been assisted by DANIDA in water supply and sanitation programme. Open defecation in the entire Panchayat has been fully arrested. All the houses are having household latrines. Roads are kept clean. This Village Panchayat is among the few Village Panchayats selected for implementation of the Clean Village Campaign. Pucca drainage facility has been provided. 3000 seedlings have been planted and are taken care of. Garbage pits are constructed along roadsides and decomposed waste is farmyard manure. A women Self-Help Group is also formed now for collecting plastic wastes and for using it for laying plastic roads in future. The entire atmosphere is kept clean by the multi-pronged activities of the Village Panchayat administration.

(d) Samathuva Mayanam

In Tamil Nadu, cremation/burial grounds have traditionally been different for people of different castes/communities. However, Keerapalayam is different in this aspect too. By the action of the Village Panchayat President, a common Samuthuva Mayanam (common burial ground) is maintained for all the communities/castes. This has been done with the approval of all the public in the Gram Sabha.

(e) Rain Water Harvesting Structures in Houses

All the 1160 houses including all the offices in this Village Panchayat have rainwater harvesting structures.

View of Rain Water Harvesting Structure

Tiled Houses	-	164
RCC Houses	-	123
Thatched Houses	-	689
Group Houses	-	184

The President of this Village Panchayat has taken good steps and has achieved 100 per cent rainwater harvesting structures.

The Panchayat President has taken effective steps and has also installed open space rainwater harvesting structures along the roadsides.

(f) Rainwater Harvesting Under SGRY

There are 6 village ponds in this Village Panchayat. Desilting of the ponds is being done regularly. Desilting of the "Nalla Thanneer Pond" has been done in the current year 2003-04 at an estimated cost of Rs.1.00 lakh.

Desilting of the village ponds has enabled the Panchayat to receive additional rainwater and this has raised the ground water level considerably.

(g) Execution of Works by Public Contribution

The Village Panchayat has the uniqueness of taking up works through public contribution in a number of cases. Some such major works taken up through public participation are:

- The Community Centre of the Village Panchayat has been constructed across a site which is valued at Rs.13.98 lakhs as per the market value and it was donated by the public free of cost. The Community Centre constructed at a cost of Rs.15.00 lakhs is now a source of income for the Panchayat.
- The present High School building of Keerapalayam Panchayat has been put up in an area of about six acres which was donated by the villagers for promotion of school education.
- The fountain in the village park has been built with cent-per-cent contribution by the village public.
- One woman, Tmt. Neelavathy, belonging to the SC community, has donated one cent of

land free to the Village Panchayat for extending the burial ground road.

- Another lady, Tmt. Krishnammal, has donated one cent of land free of cost to the Village Panchayat for the construction of a drainage across the BC street.
- The Village Panchayat also mobilized public contribution worth Rs.40,000 for putting up a gymnasium for the youth.
- The former MLA, Thiru. K.S. Alagiri, who is a resident of the Village Panchayat, has donated 2000 tree seedlings for greening up the Panchayat roads in Keerapalayam Panchayat.
- One bus shelter has been constructed across the National Highways through cent-per-cent public contribution.
- A school latrine in the Panchayat Union Elementary School has been constructed through voluntary public contribution.
- A drainage across the Indian Bank Street has been constructed by the Village Panchayat through the assistance of some village individuals on a voluntary basis.
- The compound wall and gate to the Panchayat Union Elementary School, Keerapalayam, was built through public donations.
- Two thatched sheds have now been constructed for the newly built High School through public contribution in order to cater to the rising strength in the Government High School at Keerapalayam.
- A sum of Rs.21,000 has been collected by the villagers as contribution for the latrine constructed in the Government High School, Keerapalayam, as part of the public contribution to the DANIDA project.
- All the books in the Village Panchayat Library have been mobilized by the present Panchayat President through voluntary donations from the villagers.
- Some health campaigns conducted in the Panchayat previously, including an acupuncture campaign were organized on a voluntary basis by the villagers through the efforts of the Keerapalayam Panchayat.
- The TV in one of the common TV rooms of the Village Panchayat has been donated to the Village Panchayat by one of the villagers based on the request of the Keerapalayam Panchayat President.
- Unique coloured dresses has been bought for all the 13 Self Help Groups by the villagers themselves to give encouragement to the Self Help Group women members.
- A veterinary camp has also been conducted in the Village Panchayat by getting donations from the Rotary Club.
- The public have contributed Rs.60,000, being 1/5th of the amount for drainage and, accordingly, a drainage at a cost of Rs.300000 has been sanctioned under the Total Sanitation Programme in 2003-04 and the work is completed.

(h) Self Help Group Activities

There are 13 active Self Help Groups of women in this Village Panchayat. All the groups are doing innovative trades like coir making and jute products.

Now the Panchayat has formed one group for waste plastic materials. The waste plastics will be collected, cut into pieces, mixed with bitumen in heating process and used for laying of plastic bitumen roads. The plastic wastes will be disposed of by the above method and will provide income to the SHG group. Similarly one group is given training for making rural sanitary pans. The sanitary pans produced by the group will be utilized for individual household latrines built in the block.

Secretary to Government Rural Development and Driector of Rural Development Inspecting the Coir Making Unit

Jute Products Making Groups

(i) Bio-Gas Linked Toilets

Keerapalayam Panchayat is now propagating households latrines linked to bio-gas. Such toilets get bio-gas from both human and animal gas and the gas generated is used for cooking. This has gained popularity. Many villages are coming forward to adopt the process.

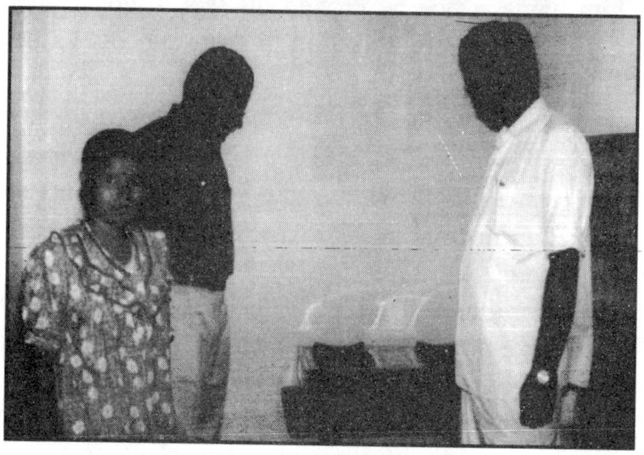

Project Officer Inspecting Bio-Gas Linked Toilets

(j) Encroachment Evictions: A Common Decision

Keerapalayam Panchayat has also taken up encroachment eviction through the assistance of the district administration on a regular basis. In its latest efforts, 57 structures were evicted in November 2003 along the highways land. In fact the present VAO's office was built by the Panchayat only after eviction of encroachments there.

Seeing is believing. Nothing can be better described about Keerapalayam Panchayat than seeing it with one's own eyes. The latest visit was by the Secretary to Government, Rural Development Department, Government of Tamil Nadu, Tmt. Santha Sheela Nair, IAS, and Dr. M. Rajaram, Director of Rural Development, Government of Tamil Nadu, on 4.12.2003. The visitors to the Panchayat also included the previous Secretary, Dr. R.C. Panda, IAS, and a number of foreigners, including officials from the embassy of Denmark and the DANIDA project related officials.

Various District Collectors have given awards and certificates to the dynamic President of the Village Panchayat, Panneer Selvam, for leading the Village Panchayat in pioneering efforts. In fact, an amount of Rs.2.00 lakhs was given as an additional incentive reward to the Village Panchayat by the then Collector of Cuddalore District for its efforts in total sanitation. A sum of Rs. 3.00 lakhs was granted by the present Collector Shri Gagandeep Singh Bedi, IAS, to the Panchayat for its efforts in involving school students in the Small Savings Scheme. The Village Panchayat President, Panneer Selvam, has been included as an honorary faculty member in the State Institute of Rural Development at Chennai by the Government of Tamil Nadu to disseminate practical tips relating to Rural Development to other Panchayat Presidents and Councillors of various local bodies of the State of Tamil Nadu.

Secretary to Government Rural Development and Director of Rural Development Inspecting the Bio-Gas Plant

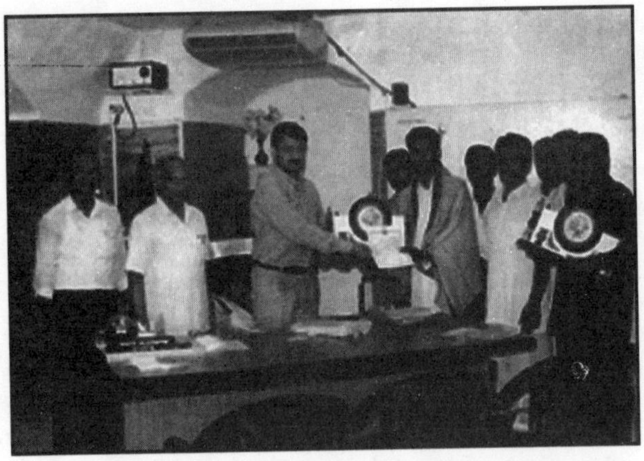

Panchayat President Receving Best Panchayat Reward of Rs. 2 lakhs from the then Collector

Panchayat President Receiving Certificate and Reward of Rs.50000 for Best Panchayat under Clean Village Campaign from District Collector

Visit of President of India

The Keerapalayam Panchayat President met the President of India and briefed him about his activities in the Panchayat. Evincing keen interest, the President of India promised to visit his Panchayat. As per his promise he visited the Keerapalayam Panchayat and attended the Gram Sabha meeting and made an appeal to the people and the Panchayat Members on what they have to do in their Panchayat further. It becomes a message for all Panchayat leaders.

Evaluation

The Panchayat President does have no special powers to carry out so much of works in his Panchayat. He has got powers like other Gram Panchayat Presidents but has won the attention of all, including the President of India. How is it possible for him to do so much of works and how is he able to mobilize this much of resources are the basic questions. He clearly perceived that the Panchayat has to attend to the needs of the people as they have not been attended to by the government agencies in the past several years. He is aware that in the context of the poor resources available and less powers devolved, it is very difficult to fulfil the responsibilities. But he was determined to respond to the challenges. He started his work in a most difficult sector, sanitation.

Bringing about a sanitation culture is not easy, but he took up the task. He is very clear about one aspect of the dynamics of development, namely that development can be achieved only through mobilizing the people and making the people participate in the process of development. He succeeded in sanitation. Having achieved success in sanitation, he projected his image as an achiever. Once an impossible task was achieved the whole officialdom moved towards him to experiment with several innovative programmes.

Yet another strength is mobilizing the Self-Help Group women for economic development activities. He stood with them in their activities. He further evinced keen interest in using many of the new technologies for generating employment opportunities apart from the traditional activities. When the agencies were ready to test many of the new technologies, most of the Presidents hesitated to take risk and face challenges. He took the challenges as opportunities and turned them into success, which actually brought him name. Once he proved his worth, government departments were after him to show success in their schemes through Panchayats. Further he touched upon all segments by providing assistance to them which, in turn, helped him to mobilize the people.

He has mobilized resources from all segments and tapped needed money from the appropriate agencies. He demonstrated his capability and commitment by achieving things in the Panchayat, which, in turn, made the people believe that the Panchayat has the potential to achieve and people started believing the Panchayat leaders. Officials who were on the lookout for potential Panchayat leaders to carry out certain challenging new schemes approached the President of Keerapalayam Panchayat.

Since he demonstrated his ability in making certain things a reality in his Panchayat, people started believing the Panchayat and the Gram Sabha. Hence his Gram Sabha meeting was always vibrant, with the active participation of youth and women. It was not the powers, finance and functionaries which made the Panchayat active. It was only his performance and leadership which made the Panchayat active and vibrant.

When the implications of all the activities were seen visibly, officials, NGO representatives, other Panchayat leaders started visiting this Panchayat to learn how the Panchayat worked. It became a model for others.

Further he demonstrated his commitment and honesty in Panchayat administration which is yet another reason for the confidence reposed in him by the people. He attracted all the segments of the people. He is known for his risk-taking. Many innovative technologies have been introduced in his Panchayat. He prepared the youth and the women for the regeneration of the village communities.

Though he belonged to a political party (AIADMK) and had the aim of getting a chance to contest in the Assembly elections, he abdicated the desire after he became the President of the Gram Panchayat. Panchayat Presidents are struggling to mobilize the people for community development action. But he is able to mobilize them because he slowly moved away from the party affiliation. He feels that he is more than an MLA or MP, because, when people are with him, the MLA and the MP come to him. Such kind of support he has gained from the people as he attends to the needs of the people. All his activities are carried out with the active participation of the people.

He worked in such a way that in each and every programme people had to contribute their share. At the same time he has not disturbed the poor and the marginalized. In the first period, he projected his ideas as promises to the people and got elected though he belonged to a minority community in the village. In the second period, he projected his performance. By keeping himself away from the party he belongs to, he drew support through his transparent transactions in Panchayat activities. His performance changed the attitude and perception of the people towards his leadership. There is yet another aspect one has to consider, namely, that the leadership can create several changes. It is not the money but it is the leadership that makes changes. If a leader is sincere, honest, committed, humble, she or he can do any work in society for which the cooperation and the support of the people is assured. The leader need not take shelter under caste or class or religion.

Conclusion

A Panchayat leader clearly understood the Panchayati Raj System and started acting with a sense of commitment and responsibility. He openly says that today the Panchayat is considered an implementing agency and hence the Panchayat has to carry out a whole lot of government programmes. On that basis he carried out all the schemes and programmes more effectively and efficiently in his Panchayat with the participation of the people than a contractor. At the same time, he proved his worth as a leader, showing the way to the people. His honesty, commitment and sincerity attracted the people and government officials towards him. By carrying out activities, he demonstrated to the people that he will do things and his words are believed.

At the same time, he made it a point that stakeholders should be made owners of the projects and programmes. He further demonstrated that, for all the activities, he made the people contribute their share.

It is a well known fact that our administrative system is in the thick of corrupt practices. Even in this corrupt administrative system how is he able to achieve this much of results is a big question. He says that, as long as Panchayat leaders are honest, sincere, capable and committed, the corrupt officials won't disturb the entire process of development activities. Further he says, by the honest activities of the Panchayat President, even the corrupt system can be changed. He has unequivocally demonstrated that honest Presidents can achieve results provided they have the capability. Honesty without capability cannot achieve anything in the Panchayat system.

His Panchayat becomes a model for many Panchayats. For Panchayati Raj training, his Panchayat is a centre for fieldwork. It becomes the Mecca or Medina for Panchayati Raj management. Many departments of the government are in search of good Panchayats to achieve their target of activities. He said that if Panchayats demonstrate that they are good Panchayats, government officials will come to the Panchayat leaders. Many of the Panchayat leaders make themselves reliable and they attract the government officials. They never plead for schemes and programmes, but programmes and schemes come to their Panchayats. A man committed to a party has abdicated his political ambition for the cause of the community. His dedicated services to the community have attracted the attention of the President of India. His invitation to the President of India was promptly responded to by him and he visited his Panchayat. He appreciated the Panchayat's activities.

He developed an aspiration to become a MLA but now he feels that he is more than a MLA. He is happy and contented with what he has and what he has achieved.

CASE - 11

INNER TRANSFORMATION TRANSFORMED THE VILLAGE

She was persuaded into the President's post by her husband. She took up the responsibilities vigorously when he passed away. She first transformed herself into a selfless dedicated servant of the community and the entire community extended her its support. Her activities were centred round sanitation, water supply and primary education. By her dedicated activities she attracted the attention of the Canara Bank. Now it is an adopted village of the Canara Bank. Her honesty, transparent administration, responsiveness, contact with the community, linkage with government officials have made it possible for the Panchayat President to transform the entire Gram Panchayat area. Being a widow, she is able to administer the Panchayat effectively.

Socio-Economic Background

Ms. S. Siddeswari is the President of Koonavelampatti Village Panchayat. She is 50, a widow and has two sons. Her husband was the former Panchayat President of Koonavelampatti Panchayat of Rasipuram Union, Namakkal District, from the year 1983 to 1990. She has studied upto the 7th standard. She belongs to orthodox Goundar community and was married at the age of 17. Her family is a nuclear one and their occupation is agriculture. Both of her sons are lorry drivers in a private concern and have completed their 10th standard. Her house is located amidst their agricultural land (farm house), which is also maintained by her.

Her husband belonged to a rich family and had extensive property in Koonavelampatti. As Panchayat President he spent his own property for the welfare of the people. In Palapalayam he dug a well upto 600 feet with the support of the District Collector and provided water supply to the entire community and created a rain water harvesting belt (in the nearby hill area) in Kulakkadu, which not only provided drinking water but also raised the ground water level. He constructed public latrines for women and laid tar roads. He earned the goodwill of the people. He belonged to All India Anna Dravida Munnetra Kazhagam (AIADMK).

When the 73rd Constitutional Amendment announced the reservation for women, he thought of making his wife the President and planned to handle the administration in her name. After she was elected President, he did all the work. She was confined to the home as a housewife and looking after agricultural activities.

Even in the first elections of 1996, she merely contested as a candidate while her husband promised the people that he would provide drinking water, roads, streetlights, public latrines and a proper drainage system for the village. With one woman as opponent, she won by 450 votes. One year later, her husband died of a heart attack.

The entire village was shocked at his death. As an innocent woman, always seeking and following the words of her husband as a sincere wife, she was not able to manage. She wanted to resign her post as President and decided to send her resignation letter to the Collector. She confined herself at home for nearly three months and never came out. The District Collector, the Block Development Officer, the Project Officer, the members of AIADMK Party, the elderly people of the village, the Union Chairman and everyone encouraged and convinced her that they would support her and guide her in every Panchayat activity. The clerk of her Panchayat, named Ramamoorthy, aged 60, who had 40 years of experience, assured her of assistance and explained to her the Panchayat administration. She was very much afraid of taking the position of leadership and felt timid to take up the activities as a widow. She feared how the people would treat her, how she could involve herself in public activities, outside the home, as a widow. But the entire community urged her to attend to the Panchayat work.

She came out of the house after three months and went along with the Panchayat clerk to the Collectorate, the Block Office and the DRDA and learnt about Panchayat management. Within six months, she learnt about every activity of the Panchayat. She first wanted to solve the drinking water crisis of her Panchayat. When she was thinking of seeking assistance from the Government she came to know about a new scheme called the Anna Marumalarchi Thittam. She tried and got it. Under the Anna Marumalarchi Thittam, her Panchayat got Rs.1 crore for village development activities (out of the 18 persons who applied for the Anna Marumalarchi Thittam, she was the only woman who got the scheme). By using this scheme she undertook the following activities: tar roads, building for ration shop, bridges, Panchayat office building, 42 group houses for all communities, bore wells for drinking water supply, public latrines for men and women, proper drainage system, cement roads, etc. This brought her name and also boosted her self-confidence. She developed a healthy trend of consulting all Ward Members on each and every work and issue formally and informally. She further made it mandatory that all activities have to be carried out in a transparent way. She never assumed power and she acted as a responsible person. She is always polite and courteous to all, which attracts everyone and everyone cooperates with her in her activities.

She wants to take the people with her and she makes them be with her by explaining the details of every issue. She demonstrates herself as a model to other poor women Panchayat leaders. She in fact motivates others by citing her case. She started attending all the functions and programmes organised by the government. Her interaction with officials and others provided the needed input to stand on her own. She transmitted that experience to others also. She is respected by the district administration as a curious woman President of good performance. She was honoured by the SIRD as the best performing woman of Namakkal District. Now she serves as a resource person for various programmes organized by government departments.

Sanitation

Koonavelampatti Panchayat has a large population, but the scavengers appointed for the Panchayat are only two—one woman and one man. The Panchayat has a large number of drainage channels and they are not properly cleaned. In most places the solid wastes are scattered because no waste pits or drums are provided for garbage collection. The garbage is collected by a tractor once in a month and disposed of in the outer area of Koonavelampatti.

Total Rural Sanitation Campaign

The Panchayat is now involved in creating pits, for classifying the solid wastes as non-compostable and compostable wastes. The special measures taken for cleanliness are due to the effect of the training undergone by the President and the Ward Members (on the request of the President, the Ward Members were allowed to participate in the training programme organized by SIRD, Krishnagiri, in the month of October 2004). The training oriented them and made them concentrate on total sanitation and created confidence in them and they have seriously aimed at getting the reward which is given by the government for the cleanest village and they want to make the village a model Panchayat. Under the MLA fund, Rs.5 lakhs was sanctioned for cleanliness under the total sanitation programme (but it has not yet been received). A private site was purchased for Rs.10,000 for the construction of a drainage channel. The site was cleaned by the Thiruvalluvar College students under an NSS campaign.

The President, along with school students, organized clean village campaign rallies and tried to make the people aware of the destruction caused by garbage. The people in Koonavelampatti Puthur disposed of the garbage close to the noon-meal centre of the school and it created unhygienic surroundings, especially for the school. The President, along with the Members, tried to highlight the importance of cleanliness, but nothing happened. The PTA discussed the matter and placed a board near the noon-meal centre of the school, which warns that anybody disposing of garbage there will be punished. The headmaster is very much supportive regarding this issue and the people who disposed of wastes were caught and made to clean the same. The President is confident that the people will surely change their mind if she convinced them with proper alternative measures. At the request of the Presidents of Namakkal District, the District Collector passed an order that individual water connection should be provided to houses only on the condition that the house must have individual toilet and proper rain water harvesting structure.

Provision of Drinking Water

The entire village was provided with sufficient water sources like overhead tanks, bore wells, hand pumps, street taps, individual water connections, wells, etc. Both drinking water and water for other purposes are sufficiently given to the people. Most of the problems arise due to individual water connection and street taps. A few opponents try to install illegal connections.

Once a person established 7 illegal connections in his house and surroundings. The President asked him to remove those connections, but he refused. The people of that area squatted on the road with plastic containers and engaged in a demonstration. The Collector, the police officials and others accompanied the President in the elimination of such illegal connections.

The street taps provided by the Panchayat are made of plastic, the reason behind this being the prevention of rusting and easy maintenance. The people who cause damage are asked to replace the same.

The Panchayat decided to provide equal distribution of water by supplying on alternate days. This was approved by the Gram Sabha. Regarding the maintenance, the Panchayat has decided to get approval from the Gram Sabha for the collection of Rs.10 from the people as water maintenance charges.

This Panchayat, under a collective drinking water scheme—the Edapadi Rasipuram Water Scheme—supplies water to another Panchayat named Kurukkapuram. The electricity charges for this water supply, the motor maintenance charges and the operator's salary are paid by the Koonavelampatti Panchayat. As approved by the Commissioner and the Engineer of Rasipuram Union, Edapadi paid Rs.18,262 to Koonavelampatti Panchayat as maintenance charges.

Village Economy

Agriculture, poultry, animal husbandry and power loom units are the major sources of income. Seasonal agricultural activities are undertaken by the land owners. Most of the people are engaged in weaving through power loom. Agricultural labourers go to other nearby villages also. Cotton, rice, turmeric, onion, sugarcane, ragi are the major crops cultivated here. Every Thursday a weekly market is set up in Koonavelampatti Puthur, where vegetable vendors from Kurusamipalayam, Annaikattipalayam and other nearby villages come for selling vegetables. This market is run by the Panchayat through some private contractors. Grocery shop, STD booths, petty shop, small stationery shop are also available here. A few people have migrated to Namakkal and Erode and are working as labourers in textile mills and as construction workers. There was one textile cooperative society from where the power loom owners purchased thread for weaving. Some persons go to Namakkal and purchase raw materials there and the finished goods are sold to big shops. Towels, *sarees* and *dhoties* are manufactured here through power looms. Many women are engaged in precision work and men are engaged as machine operators. A few women power loom owners are also here.

An agricultural association has been formed and they have discussed the cultivation pattern, methods of irrigation, pesticides, etc. Special free veterinary camps are also organized by the President with the help of the Animal Husbandry Department.

Village Set Up

Koonavelampatti is a Village Panchayat which has 9 hamlets. The total population is 5050. Most of the people belong to Goundar and Mudhaliyar communities. 175 families belong to the SC community and the other communities are Nadar, Chettiyar and Pandaram. The SC community have a separate colony and some of the families are also living within the villages. There is no caste association in the village. A common graveyard is available for all the communities.

Political Parties

The AIADMK, the DMK, the Congress and the BJP are the parties in the village. But the majority belong to the AIADMK party. The Rasipuram constituency is always in the hands of the AIADMK party. The party people provide full support to the Panchayats of this area. Most of the MLA/MP funds are utilized for the development of this Village Panchayat. Her husband earned a name among the AIADMK party members, as he was a serious follower of the AIADMK party.

Youth Groups

The village youths actively participate in the Panchayat activities. They belong to the Nehru Yuva Kendra, the SMK Ilainger Mandram, the Vanavil Mandram and Men's Self-Help Groups. Under the Nehru Yuva Kendra the youths from the SC community are provided with sports inputs and have a play ground in the SC colony.

They are enthusiastically engaged in organizing awareness programmes for the villagers. They have enacted street plays on rain water harvesting, sanitation and cleanliness, the importance of the utilization of latrines, etc. They have also engaged in the construction of RWH setups in houses, individual toilets, sanitary complex, proper drainage, etc. They actively participate and render service during Panchayat meetings. They have also collected relief funds and donations for helping the people suffering due to calamity. The damage caused during the rainy season was cleared by these youth groups. Most of the youths in the SC colony have completed their degrees, but, due to poverty, they are not able to engage themselves in any work or business. The President approached several institutions for providing income generating training programmes to these youth groups. Some of them are taking tuition for students under the advice of the President.

Educational Institutions

In Koonavelampatti and Palapalayam there are one primary and one secondary school and one management matriculation school is situated in Karayanthinniputhur. The children of the Panchayat are studying here. A proper noon meal centre building is newly constructed near the schools and the food is provided under the supervision of the teachers. Toilet for the students is available in a nearby sanitary complex, but due to lack of water connection, it has not been opened. The headmaster asked the President for the construction of toilets especially for the girl students and it was accepted by the President also. Parents Teachers Association meetings are frequently held and the required needs are immediately fulfilled. At the request of SHGs, the PTA recommended the extension of teaching hours for the students and one woman teacher was appointed by the PTA. The newly appointed headmaster of the school actively participates in the Panchayat activities voluntarily. The President motivates the students by distributing prizes during competitions. She has already planted trees near the school and has also decided to plant more trees in the surroundings of school buildings with the help of the students and the teachers of the school.

Forty-four dropouts who are working in power looms are educated under the SSA Scheme, which is handled by two women teachers. Due to insufficient buildings these classes are held in a building which was constructed for SHGs. The Headmaster and the President take full responsibility for the education of these students and have made several arrangements

Motivating School Children

for getting government aids like bags, books, food, etc.

Three Anganwadis are working under this Panchayat. The Village Health Nurse (VHN) frequently visits these villages and provides iron tablets to teenage girls and instructions to mothers. A Primary Health Centre is situated in another Panchayat, Kurusamipalayam. A sub-centre is in Puthur. Women go to this sub-centre and get prescriptions from the lady doctor, which helps them to clarify their doubts without any hesitation.

Her Village Panchayat Adopted by Canara Bank (Year 2003-2004)

As a woman President, she always went along with another woman Panchayat President, Mrs.Vijaya, who is also a widow. She belongs to Murugapampatti Panchayat. Both of them approach every department regarding their issues. They both visit many places and attend training programmes. She is also a second term President. Her village population is 920.

When both of them visited the Canara Bank for some personal transactions, the manager discussed their scheme of village adoption. She convinced the manager by telling about her village population, their basic needs and their expectations. She clearly highlighted the low economic condition of her village. The manager was very impressed by the active involvement of the President, her clear explanation and her courageous attitude. He declared that Canara Bank would adopt her Village Panchayat. This made her confident that her village would become economically sufficient.

The Canara Bank adopted Koonavelampatti for one year. It sets up an office with an agricultural consultant. Financial assistance like various loans were provided for income generating activities like tailoring, animal husbandry, power loom, feeds for cattle. Likewise various loans were given to the people who had less than Rs.5000 as annual income. Six tractors were distributed to farmers. An overhead tank for drinking water supply, with a bore well, was constructed for the SC community in the colony. The power loom owners and poultry owners received Rs.30-40 lakhs for their business. The loans received were properly repaid by the people without fail and they got further loans. A blood checkup camp, organized by the Canara Bank for this Panchayat, was inaugurated by the President.

Gram Sabha

The Gram Sabha meetings are organized in various villages of the Panchayat as preferred by the people. With the help of tom tom or through distribution of bit notices, the venue and the time of the Gram Sabha meeting is informed to the people. It may be held at the school or else in the open ground under a tree. 70 per cent of the people attend the Gram Sabha meeting. All the Ward Members and SHG women members also participate without fail. Each and every subject is approved by the Gram Sabha. The agricultural association and the youth groups are the supporters of the Gram Sabha. The SC community clearly discusses every issue and asks the President to fulfil their demands. The allocation of funds for the Panchayat, the proposed expenditure, the schemes to be implemented, the provision of more drinking water etc., are clearly explained by the President. The opposition that emerges can be handled by her and the Members of the Panchayat. The SHGs actively participate and demand income generating activities. The recent Gram Sabha meeting proposed to focus upon the cleanliness of the entire Panchayat, removal of wastes, solid waste management, removal of sewage water, use of individual and public toilets, maintenance of rain water harvesting structures, etc. Proper water supply, water for all were the subjects discussed in the Gram Sabha meeting. The sitting fees of the Ward Members is directly transferred to an

RD (recurring deposit) as per the decision taken by the President and accepted by the Ward Members. With the approval of the Gram Sabha, all the people of the village, including SHG members, desilted the Kulakadu pond in the year 2004.

Gram Sabha

SC Colony

There are 175 families belonging to the Dalit community. Cobblers, sweepers, agricultural labourers, powerloom labourers — these are the occupations of the SC colony. They have developed a good relationship with the President. She frequently visits their colony, receives their hospitality and hears their problems. Group houses, OHT, roads, threshing floor, play ground for youths, community hall, proper drinking water supply, works under several schemes especially allotted for the SC community, etc., are the works done for these people. Hollow block individual latrines are yet to be constructed in the homes of the SCs (Rs.900 is provided by the government, the Panchayat adds from its fund Rs.100. The total amount of Rs.1000 is spent for the construction). There is no differential treatment between the SCs and the other communities.

Water Sources

In Kulakadu, there is a hilly area which was under the control of the Forest Department. After discussing with the Panchayat, the Forest Department has decided to construct a pond at the foothills of Kulakadu. The work is estimated to cost Rs.4 lakhs.

This pond will surely fulfil the agricultural requirements of the Panchayat. It is 1 km away from the Panchayat pond created by the President's husband. These water sources will not only fulfil the agricultural needs, but also raise the ground water level as rain water harvesting structures and provide drinking water to the entire Panchayat. Hence they play a multipurpose role. In Palapalayam, 3 check dams have been constructed. On the Alagarmalai Odai and in Kulakadu lake area 2 check dams have been constructed.

Health Camps

The President organized various health camps for the welfare of the people with the help of NGOs and the government Health Department for polio drops, skin disease, eye checkup, sexually transmitted diseases and disorders relating to reproductive health. Veterinary camps for cattles were also organized.

Ration Shop

Three ration shops are situated in this Panchayat. All the provisions are distributed without fail, which is frequently supervised by the President. Free *dhotis* and *sarees* were first distributed to the people below poverty line (the list was made by the President, who instructed the Ward Members to supervise the distribution) and then to others. Hence the distribution was held smoothly without any rivalries.

Tree Planting

The President has shown great interest in tree planting. The Forest Department provided saplings of neem, gooseberry, tamarind and mango and these saplings were planted in the Ayakoil area, on the sides of the pond, roads and agricultural lands and they are maintained by the people of the Panchayat. Trees were also planted around the schools.

Group-House

Forty-two group houses were constructed under the Anna Marumalarchi Thittam for all communities. The beneficiaries are highly benefited by these houses. They were of the old type, with latrines inside the house. Now 6 sanctioned houses are being constructed in a new model, wherein the toilets and bathrooms are constructed outside the house. The government provided Rs.34,000 and the beneficiaries contributed their own resources say, Rs.15 to Rs.20 thousand. The beneficiaries whole heartedly thanked the President for getting them own houses. The katcha house scheme is not preferred by the people, because of the conditions laid down by the government for the scheme: the amount sanctioned for the scheme is Rs.10,000 and, with this, they have to construct toilets and install a solar stove. The people are not aware of the utility of toilets and solar stoves. The President supervises the area frequently and checks the drainage system and insists on the beneficiaries maintaining cleanliness.

Street Lights

125 street lights are provided in the entire Panchayat. Among them 12 are solar vapour lamps and the rest are tube lights. 12 lamps are provided to the SC colony. Due to the consumption of more electricity, two solar vapour lamps have been altered by the President to tube lights. Nearly Rs.40,000 is spent on electricity charges.

Self-Help Groups

There are 19 SHGs formed under this Panchayat. They have done several income generating activities with the financial aid provided by the Canara Bank. In Palapalayam one group started a power loom unit, in Rasipuram another group run a Xerox shop, two mini tempo autos are rented by two groups and another group runs a shop. The sanitary complex which is maintained by one Self Help Group, has collected Rs.10 from each house as maintenance charges. The women of that area fully utilize the toilets. The school students also utilize them. Due to water crisis, they allow the women to utilize the toilets and bathrooms but do not permit them to wash clothes.

SHG

In front of the sanitary complex, the compound wall depicts the importance of rural sanitation. The entrance floor is constructed of cement. On either side of the cement floor, they maintain a garden with plantain trees, neem trees and some floral plants. The ground is covered with grass and it appears like a park. The plants are safely placed inside a fencing and the waste water is used to grow these plants.

Close to the sanitary complex, a bio-gas plant is constructed. The bio-gas from the unit is utilized for pumping water to the sanitary complex. Electricity supply is also setup as an alternative. A solar lamp is installed in front of the sanitary complex. This setup has greatly reduced the electricity charges. The SHG women members have appointed a sweeper who frequently cleans the toilets with bleaching powder, checks the tanks for water, watches the surroundings and is always conscious of keeping the surroundings clean.

If any problem arises, the SHGs come and meet the President. The President also takes immediate steps for rectifying the problem. Preference is given to them. A building is constructed for SHG activities. The President also attends their meetings whenever she finds time.

The SHG which got the power loom unit needed space for their work. The President assured them that they would be surely provided with a building for the power loom unit with the approval of Gram Sabha, which was going to held in the month of January 2005. She also decided to arrange some training programmes for the SHGs in order to undertake more income generating activities through self-employment programmes. She wants to link up with some supportive institutions for providing income generating training programmes.

In this Village Panchayat, all women Self Help Groups are provided with numbers instead of names. Group No.1 was formed in the year 1997. It has fourteen members. The group members met frequently and discussed their activities like accounts keeping, savings, revolving funds. All the groups meet every Monday regularly and discuss the reproductive health care of women, child health, early age at marriage and its impact, abortion, violence against women, village development activities, income generating group activities, sanitation, sanitary complex, etc. Then two members from each group collectively meet once a month in the SHG building constructed by the Panchayat. The President attends this meeting wherein the SHGs discuss the Panchayat's needs and their contribution. 5 groups have received the revolving fund and the other groups fulfil their needs from their own savings.

The SHGs have contributed maps, sports items and prizes to the school and a Rs.10,000 worth silver crown was provided by these SHGs to the Panchayat temple. During periods of water scarcity, vehicle-delivered water was distributed by the SHGs through a token system. Health and eye-donation camps were also conducted by them through supportive institutions. After the sanctioning of the construction of the sanitary complex, these members removed the thorny bushes and stones and assisted during the construction. They have planted tree saplings in the school surroundings. Iron tablets were distributed to teenage girls with the help of the VHN. Relief fund during natural calamity has also been collected by them. These SHG women were trained in pipe repair mechanism, maintenance of sanitary complex and sanitation. Minor pipe repairs were rectified by these group members. The President solved many family problems created by in-laws and other family members with the help of the SHGs. The Mudhaliar community widows always wear white sarees. The SHGs tried to change this trend. They urged them to wear coloured *sarees*. Two widows accepted their request and started to wear coloured *sarees*. Along with the President they celebrate March 8th and demonstrate against the following issues on March 8: female infanticide, familial violence, dowry, abortion, sex discrimination, etc., and urge 1/3rd reservation for women in Parliament.

Two SHG members rented two mini tempo autos. They appointed two drivers. Cement bags, silk materials, thread were loaded in these two vehicles and a good profit (Rs.9,500 per month) was gained from these vehicles. But due to the carelessness of the drivers, the vehicles were not properly maintained. The profit fell low. Hence the maintenance charges and the drivers' salary have not been met. After consulting the President, the vehicles were put up for lease and the women now receive Rs.5,000 per month.

The SHGs have assured the President that they will render their full support for making the village clean and work hard for making their village a model Panchayat.

House Tax

In the beginning of her leadership the Panchayat had to manage debts of Rs.60,000. At first the collection of house tax was only Rs.7,500. The Panchayat administration decided to hike the house-tax with the Gram Sabha's approval to Rs.15,000 and then to Rs.35,000. Now they have collected Rs.65,000. It has now been decided to increase the house tax upto Rs.90,000 with the approval of the Gram Sabha in January 2005. The people have been convinced by the President and the Ward Members. The President is very sure and confident because most of the basic needs are fulfilled.

Future

Her main aim is to make the Panchayat very clean and create awareness among the people about sanitation. She has decided to construct an overhead tank for Koonavelampatti Puthur, which will surely relieve the water scarcity. By way of lending support to SHGs, she wants to create a building for their powerloom unit.

Observation

The President of Koonavelampatti actively participates in and performs the Panchayat activities well. She is always zealous to get income from supportive departments/institutions. She does not want to contest in the next elections, because she wants to make room for youngsters. She has decided to support them in every activity.

The main income source for the village is house tax. But the village has a chance for creating other income sources—from quarry, management schools, powerloom units, poultry farms, etc. But she doesn't have the relevant government orders and other related information, because she has not undergone any training like the training organized by Gandhigram Rural Institute. Moreover, she thinks that the people may create problems when she tries to collect these taxes. Many common properties are encroached upon. No action against these encroachments has been taken yet.

Reasons Behind Success

After her long-term experience she mentioned the following reasons for her effective Panchayat administration as a second term President:

- Entire village people's support.
- Eager to gather information.
- Support of clerk, Union Councillor, political party, SHGs, Collector and other district officials.
- Having a good partner and having friendship with the woman Panchayat President of Murugampatti.
- Treating the Panchayat as a family.
- Enhancement of decision-making power.
- Full support from the Ward Members of the Panchayat.
- Visiting several departments for gathering information regarding financial resources.
- Attending all the programmes wherever they are held.
- All the works are carried out with the approval of the Gram Sabha.
- Becoming familiar with everyone.
- Good communication and transparent administration.

Details of Koonavelampatti Panchayat

President	:	Ms. S. Siddeshwari
Vice-President	:	Mr. A. Ramasamy
Number of Wards	:	9
Total Numbers of Ward Members	:	9
Details of Members	:	1. V. Sivakumar 2. R. Thenmozhi 3. K. Venkatachallam 4. C. Vijaya 5. R. Athyappan 6. R. Subramaniam 7. S. Chellappan 8. R. Athyappan 9. P. Saroja
Ward Members	:	Male - 5 Female - 3 SC - 1 (Male)
Total Number of Hamlets	:	9 1. Koonavelampatti 2. Koonavelampatti Puthur 3. Palapalayam 4. Karayanthinniputhur 5. Thonamedu 6. Adhidravidar Street 7. Arunthathiyar Street 8. Poyar Street 9. Anikattipalayam

Koonavelampatti Village Panchayat—Population Details (1991 Census)

Sl. No.	*Names of the Hamlets*	*Male*	*Female*	*Total*
1.	Koonavelampatti	256	330	586
2.	Koonavelampatti Puthur	938	845	1783
3.	Palapalayam	568	557	1125
4.	Karayanthinnipatti Puthur	237	273	510
5.	Arunthathiyar Street	186	177	363
6.	Anaikattipalayam	224	201	425
	Total	2409	2383	4792

SC Community

Male	:	390
Female	:	360
Total	:	750

2001 Population

Male	:	2566
Female	:	2484
Total	:	5050

Revenue Details of the Panchayat

Sl. No.	*Details*	*1995-96*	*1996-97*	*1997-98*	*1998-99*
1.	House Tax	10,530	13,951	21,654	22,547
2.	Library Tax	292	2,158	2,166	2,261
3.	Professional Tax	6,597	9,318	13,356	15,924
4.	Water Tax	-	-	92	2,034
5.	2C Tree Tax	6,867	6,966	16,577	68,838
6.	House Tax Matching Grant	9,088	8,863	-	1,07,423
7.	Surcharge on Stamp Duty	79,936	28,250	3,379	3,837
8.	Interest	896	-	3,885	1,875
9.	Lisence Fee	1,215	-	-	4,422
10.	Local Cess	600	400	-	-
11.	Graveyard incentives	2,090	4,910	3,315	4,973
12.	Auction income from market	48	24	-	-
13.	Vehicle Tax	-	6,504	-	-
14.	Tax on sales tax	-	-	-	-
15.	Miscellaneous income	-	-	794	-
16.	Advance	-	-	10	-
17.	SFC	-	-	1,34,946	1,31,946
18.	Income from the auction on waste goods	-	-	340	2,925
19.	1996-97 library tax	-	-	1,282	-
20.	Income from auction	-	-	17,763	-
21.	Miscellaneous lease (vehicle charges)	-	-	-	1,479
22.	Income from scheme (S.A.) fund	-	-	-	4,200
23.	Deposit	-	-	-	560
24.	Balance income from Panchayat Union Fund	-	-	-	1,38,782
	Total	1,22,995	81,344	2,19,559	5,14,026
	Last year balance	45,813	26,847	—	2,935
	Total	1,68,808	1,08,191	2,19,559	5,16,961

Sl. No.	*Details*	*2000-01*	*2001-02*	*2002-03*	*2003-04*
1.	House Tax	29,131	29,912	30,548	41,716
2.	Library Tax	2,913	2,991	3,054	4,174
3.	Professional Tax	20,670	14,550	16,110	20,535
4.	Water Tax	8,850	44,040	29,730	-
5.	Lisence Fee	417	2,255	5,555	1,555
6.	Miscellaneous lisence fee	1,550	200	500	1,200

(Contd. Table)

(Contd. ...)

Sl. No.	Details	2000-01	2001-02	2002-03	2003-04
7.	Plan approval fee	4,825	5,100	3,290	13,645
8.	Market lease	4,420	6,135	4,765	4,450
9.	Miscellaneous lease (vehicle charges)	6,3000	62,164	83,936	2,08,977
10.	Surcharge on stamp duty	2,000	6,600	6,960	-
11.	Entertainment tax	2,230	2,230	2,230	2,495
12.	Local cess	3,056	3,040	1,110	3,176
13.	2C Tree tax	2,400	-	-	-
14.	Other grant	2,400	-	-	-
15.	Caution Deposit for water	1,41,000	14,000	10,990	1,400
16.	Expenditure income from play ground board	975	-	-	-
17.	SFC Grant	1,99,482	1,45,259	3,29,582	2,65,902
18.	Playing centre grant	3,000	-	-	-
19.	House tax matching grant	22,484	67,659	98,322	35,828
20.	Bank Income from interest	2,713	1,953	1,045	-
21.	Other grant (Natural Calamity Relief Fund)	-	50,000	-	-
22.	Other grant – Incentives	-	5,050	-	-
23.	Income from the Auction on waste goods	-	9,442	2,703	4,914
24.	Graveyard incentives (grant)	-	-	8,000	-
	Total	5,56,246	4,77,100	6,41,400	6,12,932
	Last's year balance	69,009	65,700	66,645	12,634
	Total	6,25,255	5,42,800	7,08,045	6,25,566

Major source of revenue for Koonavelampatti Panchayat
House Tax – Rs.1,99,989
House tax Matching Grant – Rs.3,27,659

Details of Wells

Sl. No.	Name of the Village	Location	Nos.
1.	Koonavelampatti Puthur	Near Panchayat office	1
2.	Koonavelampatti Puthur	Chettikadu	1
3.	Koonavelampatti Puthur	Thonamedu (small)	1
4.	Koonavelampatti Puthur	Thonamedu (big) not in use	1
5.	Palapalayam	Near stream	1
6.	Palapalayam	Near graveyard	1

(Contd. ...)

(Contd. ...)

Sl. No.	Name of the Village	Location	Nos.
7.	Palapalayam	-	1
8.	Palapalayam	Big well	1
9.	Adidravidar Street	Near Mariamman Koil	1
10.	Adidravidar Street	GLR	1
11.	Adidravidar Street	Located in the north side	1
12.	Arunthathiar Street	Big well	1
13.	Arunthathiar Street	Located in north side	1
14.	Karayanthinniputhur	Located in the south side	1
15.	Koonavelampatti	Near Perumal Koil	1
16.	Poyar Street	Located in the north side	1
17.	Anaikattipalayam	Near Mariammal Koil	1
	Total		17

Public Latrines

Sl. No.	Name of the Village	Location	Nos.
1.	Koonavelampatti Puthur	Near sanitary complex	1
2.	Koonavelampatti Puthur	Sanitary Complex	1
3.	Palapalayam	Near stream	1
4.	Palapalayam	Near OHT	1
5.	Adhidiravidar Street	Near OHT	1
6.	Adhidiravidar Street	-	1
	Total		6

Hand Pumps

1.	Koonavelampatti Puthur	-	1
2.	Palapalayam	-	1
3.	Karayanthinniputhur	-	1
4.	Koonavelampatti	-	1
5.	Anaikattipalayam	-	2
6.	Poyar Street	-	1
	Total	-	7

Mini Power Pumps

1.	Koonavelampatti Puthur	-	1
2.	Palapalayam	-	1
3.	Karayanthinniputhur	-	1
4.	Poyar Street	-	2
	Total	-	5

Power Pumps

1.	Koonavelampatti Puthur	-	1
2.	Palapalayam	-	1
3.	Adidiravidar Street	-	2
4.	Arunthathiar Street	-	1
5.	Koonavelampatti	-	1
6.	Thonamedu	-	1
7.	Karayanthinniputhur	-	1
8.	Anaikattipalayam	-	2
	Total	-	10

Street Lights

Sl. No.	Name of the Village	Tube Light	Sodium Vapour Lamp	Total
1.	Thonamedu	9	1	10
2.	Kooonavelampatti Puthur	34	4	38
3.	Palapalayam	22	1	23
4.	Adhidiravidar Street	11	1	12
5.	Arunthathiyar Street	8	1	9
6.	Karayanthinniputhur	7	1	8
7.	Koonavelampatti	2	1	3
8.	Kulakadu	2	1	3
9.	Anaikattipalayam	10	1	11
10.	Perumpalli	6	1	7
	Total	111	13	124

Two sodium vapour lamps altered into tube lights in Adhidravidar street

Koonavelampatti Puthur – sanitary complex – solar lamp - 124 + 1 = 125

House Tap Connection

Sl. No.	Name of the Village	Issued Connection
1.	Koonavelampatti Puthur	93
2.	Palapalayam	17
3.	Adhidiravidar Street	16
4.	Karayanthinniputhur	2
5.	Koonavelampatti	2
6.	Thonamedu	21
	Total	151

Overhead Tank

Sl. No.	Name of the Village	No	Capacity
1.	Chettikadu	1	60,000 litre
2.	Palapalayam	1	60,000 litre
3.	Arunthathiyar Street	2	10,000 litre, 60,000 litre
4.	Karayanthinniputhur	1	10,000 litre
5.	Koonavelampatti	1	10,000 litre
6.	Perumpali Poyar street	1	10,000 litre
7.	Anaikattipalayam	1	10,000 litre
8.	Adhithiravidar	1	20,000 litre
	Total	9	

Gram Sabha Meetings

Sl. No.	Year	Number of Gram Sabha Meetings	Date
1.	1996-1997	-	-
2.	1997-1998	-	-
3.	1998-1999	13	1. 16.04.1998 2. 05.05.1998 3. 06.05.1998 4. 27.05.1998 5. 22.06.1998 6. 25.06.1998 7. 03.07.1998 8. 13.08.1998 9. 15.08.1998 10. 09.10.1998 11. 30.12.1998 12. 26.01.1999 13. 05.02.1999
4.	1999-2000	5	1. 16.08.1999 2. 02.10:1999 3. 09.12.1999 4. 26.01.2000 5. 09.02.2000
5.	2000-2001	4	1. 12.04.2000 2. 15.08.2000 3. 02.10.2000 4. 26.01.2001
6.	2001-2002	4	1. 24.06.2001 2. 15.08.2001 3. 11.11.2001 4. 26.01.2001
7.	2002-2003	4	1. 01.05.2002 2. 15.08.2002 3. 02.10.2002 4. 26.01.2003
8.	2003-2004	6	1. 01.05.2003 2. 15.08.2003 3. 02.10.2003 4. 02.10.2003 5. 23.11.2003 6. 26.01.2004
9.	2004-2005	3	1. 06.06.2004 2. 15.08.2004 3. 02.10.2004

Work Details Under Panchayat Fund (1999-2000)

Sl. No.	Work Details	Estimate	Received Amount
1.	Drainage Channel in Puthur	22,000	19,965
2.	Drainage Channel in Palapalayam	50,000	46,000
3.	Drainage Channel in Palapalayam	45,000	43,120
4.	Drainage Channel in Palapalayam	20,000	14,888
5.	Bridges over channels in Koonavelampatti Puthur	45,000	41,160
6.	Renewal of roads in Karayanthinni Puthur	15,000	13,073
7.	Maintenance of Roads in Koonavelampatti Puthur Streets	9,000	8,820
8.	Drainage Channel in Palapalayam	21,500	20,976
	Total	2,27,500	2,11,002

2000-2001

Sl. No.	Work Details	Estimate	Received Amount
1.	Construction of public toilets for women in Palapalaym AD street	22,000	20,461
2.	Construction of gravel roads around the women public toilets in Arunthathiyar Street	16,000	15,264
3.	Construction of concrete roads in Koonavelampatti Puthur	50,000	47,850
4.	Extension of pipelines	20,000	18,937
5.	Pipe connection for new borewell in Thonamedu	30,000	29,234
6.	Renovation of GLR in AD street	20,000	16,774
	Total	1,58,000	1,48,520

2001-2002

Sl. No.	Work Details	Estimate	Received Amount
1.	Extension of pipelines in Palapalayam	24,800	11,730
2.	Extension of pipelines for women toilets in Koonavelampatti Puthur	18,000	15,000
3.	Extension of pipelines in Koonavelampatti	19,000	12,033
4.	Construction of platform in drinking water board in Thonamedu	6,100	6,075
5.	Construction of public women toilet in Palapalayam	50,000	48,350
	Total	1,17,900	93,188

2002-2003

Sl. No.	Work Details	Estimate	Received Amount
1.	Maintenance of roads in Koonavelampatti Puthur	12,000	11,125
2.	Maintenance of roads from Thonamedu to Koonavelampatti Puthur	7,000	6,685
3.	Maintenance of public women toilets in Koonavelampatti Puthur	6,000	5,280
4.	Establishment of borewell with electricity connection in Arunthathiyar Street	16,000	14,067
	Total	41,000	37,157

2003-2004

Sl. No.	Work Details	Estimate	Received Amount
1.	Construction of bridge over drainage	6,000	5,850

2004-2005

Sl. No.	Work Details	Estimate	Received Amount
1.	Construction of small bridge over the channel in Karayanthinniputhur	8,000	7,650

Details of Self Help Groups

Sl. No.	Name of the Village	No. of Groups & total Members	Fund Received	Name of the Supportive Institution	Income Generating Activities
1.	Koonavelampatti Puthur	Group I – 19	Revolving Fund	C.S.G.	Min Auto Tempo
		Group II – 15	-	C.S.G.	
		Group III – 16	Revolving Fund	C.S.G.	
		Group IV – 19	-	C.S.G.	
		Group V – 20	-	C.S.G.	
		Group VI – 14	Revolving Fund	C.S.G.	
		Group VII – 14	-	C.S.G.	
		Group VIII – 16	-	C.S.G.	Panchayat Union (BDO)
2.	Perumpali	Group I – 20	Revolving Fund	C.S.G.	-
		Group II – 20	Revolving Fund	C.S.G.	-
		Group III – 13	Revolving Fund	C.S.G.	-
		Group IV – 18	Revolving Fund	C.S.G.	-
		Group V – 16	Revolving Fund	C.S.G.	-

(Contd. ...)

(Contd. ...)

Sl. No.	*Name of the Village*	*No. of Groups & total Members*	*Fund Received*	*Name of the Supportive Institution*	*Income Generating Activities*
3.	Thonamedu	Group I – 16	Revolving Fund	C.S.G. C.S.G.	- -
4.	Palapalayam	Group I – 15	Revolving Fund	C.S.G.	-
		Group II – 19	Revolving Fund	C.S.G.	-
		Group III – 14	Revolving Fund	C.S.G.	Xerox Machine
5.	Anaikatti-palayam	Group I – 15	Revolving Fund	C.S.G.	-
6.	Karayanthinni-puthur	Group I – 17	Revolving Fund	C.S.G	Mini Auto Tempo
7.	Palapalayam Colony (Arunthathiyar Street)	Group I – 14	-	Magnam	
Total Women SHGs			-	19	
Total Men SHGs			-	4	
Total			-	23	

Supportive Organizations for the formation of SHGs	**Funding Institutions**
1. C.S.G	P.A.C.B., Koonavelampatti
2. Magnam	Canara Bank, Pilla Nallore
3. Panchayat Union Office, Rasipuram	

Evaluation

The elected woman representative accidentally emerged as a leader by proving her worth after the death of her husband. Her husband, though a person committed to social work and social service, also believed in patriarchy and he decided to operate the Panchayat through his wife. Thus she was only in position as Panchayat President for some time. But she is not a novice in management. When her husband was Panchayat President, she was looking after the agricultural activities of her family. She had ability and skill in management. Even after her husband's death, she was made President only by the community. It is a prevailing custom in our political system that if a male MLA or MP dies, immediately his wife is given the ticket and she wins the election on sympathy. Likewise people extended support and she was convinced to take up this assignment. But having taken over this position, with her abundant common sense, she made it a point that she did not want to get the support on sympathy. She started moving about to get schemes and programmes sanctioned to her Panchayat. She got the Anna Marumalarchi Thittam and carried out all the activities under the scheme. By the above activities she created hope among the people that she will deliver the goods to the people. She also gained the confidence that she can manage the Panchayat.

She provided a different type of leadership. She is very simple, unassuming, transparent, honest and sincere in all her activities. As a result she commands respect. It increases her faith in herself.

When the Canara Bank was in search of a Panchayat for adoption, she was determined to get it for her Panchayat. She was enthusiastic and ably provided the needed information to the Bank Manager. Further she gave hope to the Manager of the Bank that she was a good and respectable leader with a sense of honesty and commitment. Hence the Bank Manager decided to adopt her Panchayat. This again boosted the image of the leader.

Knowing the full pain of a widow, she started helping other widows in her area who have taken up the Panchayat President's post and responsibility. She helps not only them but also other women Panchayat Presidents.

She has developed a healthy relationship with all the social segments of the population in her Panchayat area whether it be women groups or SCs or any other group. By giving a patient hearing to any problem of any group she has developed a good rapport with the people. She used to apprise the people of the activities of the Panchayat in the Gram Sabha meeting. Her maturity in handling Panchayat activities and her tactics in managing the bureaucracy have earned a good name for her.

Though she is not much aware of the full implications of the New Panchayati Raj System, she perceives it as an opportunity to serve the people. She feels that if the Panchayat is a government, it has to serve the people like the other two governments. She has enormous patience in handling difficult situations.

She has developed a good approach, namely, that she has to win the confidence of the people and hence she used to apprise each and every section of her activities. She is always in search of programmes and schemes for her Panchayat area. She is of the opinion that a Panchayat leader can be a good person by carrying out the existing government programmes to the fullest extent possible with all sincerity.

She has demonstrated to other women Panchayat leaders that any one can become a good Panchayat leader provided she has commitment, sincerity, honesty and capability. According to her, self-confidence is the first indicator of a capable leader.

CASE - 12

PLASTIC FREE VILLAGE

Konamoolai Gram Panchayat is known for its initiative in preparing a perspective plan for the development of Konamoolai. Her activities range from sanitation, removal of encroachment, keeping the village free from plastics, natural resource management to linking SHGs with Panchayat activities. Her presence in the Panchayat office provided opportunity for the people to get their grievances redressed. Constant monitoring of the Panchayat activities with the support of the Ward Members is the secret of her success.

"Every woman should be economically independent and equip herself with confidence and courage to meet any kind of situations, each and every village would become economically well developed and sustainable when it has healthy environment" observed by Ms. Padmini, Konamoolai Panchayat President of Erode district. Her age is 49 and her educational qualification is SSLC. Her husband Mr. A. Shanmugam was a retired person, who served as a clerk in Erode Municipal Office. Due to ill health, he got his voluntary retirement from his service. Her son who has completed his diploma course in Civil Engineering and serves as a contractor in Sathyamangalam, and her daughter is also studying her post graduation. She belonged to a big family, which did not allow her to complete her school days fully. But her maternal uncle supported her for school education. When she wanted to work outside, her family members restricted and warned her that woman need not to go outside for jobs. They have criticized her when she got job opportunities in government departments like police department but withdrew from several opportunities.

Then she was married to Mr. Shanmugam, who was a close relative of her parents. Her father-in-law was a patriot, follower of Congress party. Being a traditional panchayat member, he was the managing trustee of a temple in her village. Her mother-in-law also served as a Panchayat Ward Member in 1980s. But the whole family engaged in business. They had started one restaurant in Sathyamangalam. In 1996 election, she was motivated by her mother-in-law for contesting in the election. Hence she contested independently, but defeated only by 36 votes. Most of the family members belonged to AIADMK party, hence they sought party support but the party members refused to support, because her community has no mass base in that village. Majority of them were Telegu Chettiars, Vellala Gounder and Okaliha Gounder. Even though she was the Erode District Secretary of AIADMK Party Women's Association, she could not get the support of her party.

But being a serious party member, her husband approached MLA and MP for funds to carry out activities for community welfare of their village (at that time she was not in the position of Panchayat President). Under the MLA and MP fund one huge canal was constructed and one big over head tank for drinking water supply has also been constructed. This service made by her husband drew the attention of the other communities. In the next term people from other communities compelled her to context in the election. In a five corner contest, she won the election by 364 votes. The people demanded, for construction of one pucca concrete road and provision of drinking water from the Bhavani river.

Village Profile

Konamoolai Village Panchayat of Sathyamangalam Union has 11 hamlets, and they are Konamoolai, Anna Nagar, Gandhi Nagar, Sennimoopanputhur, Nanjappa Goundanputhur Colony, Nanjappagoundanputhur, Akkarai Negamam, Akkarai Negamam Puthur, Udaiyar Colony, Karumariamman Nagar, Shakthi Garden Avenue. The total area of the Panchayat is 418.66.5 hectares. Total number of households are 1516 and total population of the Panchayat is 4698.

The Panchayat has situated on the river banks of Bhavani and closure to the western Ghats. The main occupation of the people are agriculture and weaving. The major agricultural crops were paddy, sugarcane, turmeric and plantain. For irrigation purpose, the farmers utilized well water, river water and borewell water. Rice mill, textile mill and handloom units are also in this area and many labourers were engaged in these units. There are many auction shops for coconut, corn and cotton which facilitated the small business people for getting the raw materials. The major tourist spots like Bhavani Sagar Dam and Bannariamman temple are situated, which are 16 km away from the Panchayat area. The major communities of the Panchayats are Vellala Gouder, Okaliha Gouder, Thottiya Naicker and Adhidravidar. It is a multi caste and multi religious village. The people of the village has more opportunity for getting education because this Village Panchayat has both government and private schools and anganwadi. For higher education, colleges and technical institutions are located in Sathyamangalam and Erode.

Chlorinated drinking water has been provided through the water sources like individual house water connection, hand pumps and public taps. OHTs, mini sintex tanks are the major sources constructed for the provision of drinking water. In Konamoolai, one primary health centre and sub-centre are also available. The Panchayat has provided with proper drainage system and road facilities. Frequent transportation facilities facilitated the students to go for higher level education to different places. Individual and Public toilets were constructed in the Panchayat area, especially for the prevention of the open air defecation. Proper removal of garbages prevented the Panchayat from communicable diseases. Public distribution system highly satisfied the needs of the people below poverty line. The milk society in Konamoolai is economically well supportive for the people who have milch cows. Manual handloom units are more in the residential areas.

Removal of Encroachment

In Gandhi Nagar, when the Panchayat was decided to construct one OHT, there was no place for construction. But they came to know from the elders that there was one public park which has been situated long years back. Then she went to the village administrative office and clarified this doubt. The Administrative Officer referred the village map and foundout its location, which comprises six and a half cent, which was sold to a women by some culprits. Then this women was convinced by the President and the OHT was constructed in the same place.

Proper drainage channel was needed in Gandhinagar. There was no way to led out sewage water. The President realized the need of drainage canal and caution for the prevention of communicable diseases. Then it was decided along with the people, that suitable place for the construction of the canal might be purchased from the people, who are residing there. The place was finally identified and it was a patta land, the owner of the land accepted to provide the land for some amount but his neighbours did not allowed him to accept. People of the same area went to him and explained to him about the need of a drainage canal. At last he agreed to provide it for some amount. Then the beneficiaries of the area accepted to contribute the amount as financial contribution and one-fourth was from the Panchayat administration. Then pucca drainage canal was constructed, with full participation of the people. She lamented that this the monumental example of peoples participation in development activities.

Gram Sabha

The Gram Sabha meetings were organised in various hamlets. Around 500 members used to participate. Panchayat officials, MLA, District Chairman, Union Councillors, RETC Principal of Bhavani Sagar, traditional Panchayat leaders also participated. More women participated in the meetings and demanded their needs. The SHGs projected their needs especially SHG building, for discussing their group activities. The financial status of the Panchayat was clearly read out by the President in the meeting. Along with the subjects referred by the government, peoples demands were clearly analysed and they took decision on them

Gram Sabha

also. In the forthcoming Gram Sabha meeting the Panchayat has decided to take up solid waste management system, and provision of house patta and group houses for SC community. Under the demands several government departments were approached for further work. The Vice-President and Ward Members are well cooperative. They have attended all the meetings and put forth their area needs. The attendance register for the Gram Sabha was perfectly maintained. However, poor Panchayats are in terms of powers and finance, Panchayats can mobilize people for Gram Sabha and other developmental activities provided Panchayat leaders are people friendly, honest and committed she observed.

Preparation of Plan Document

The Panchayat, with clean roads without garbages, proper regular, clear drinking water supply, provision of street lights, group houses, etc. impressed the

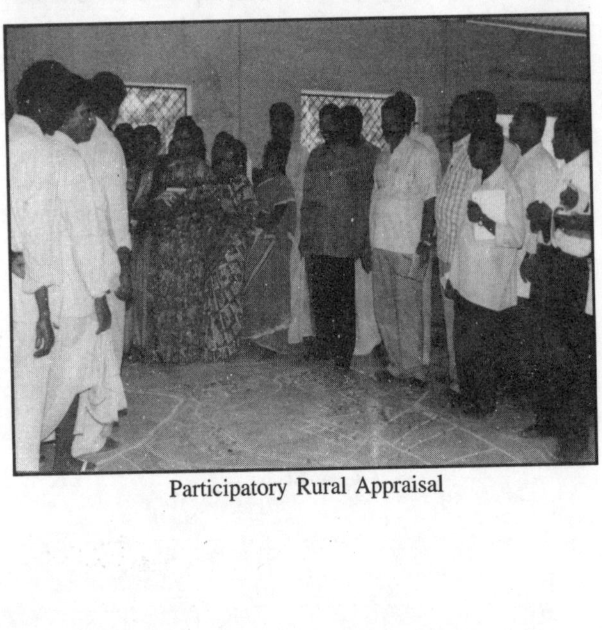

Participatory Rural Appraisal

government departments for making the Panchayat as a best one. Hence a village development plan was prepared with the cooperatives of the officials and village people. Participatory Rural Appraisal method was followed for gathering several informations from the community, need based demands were taken into consideration. She has received an award from the Collector for the eradication of plastic bags from the village.

The development report comprises the following details regarding Panchayat administration, land, water, population, important facilities available in the

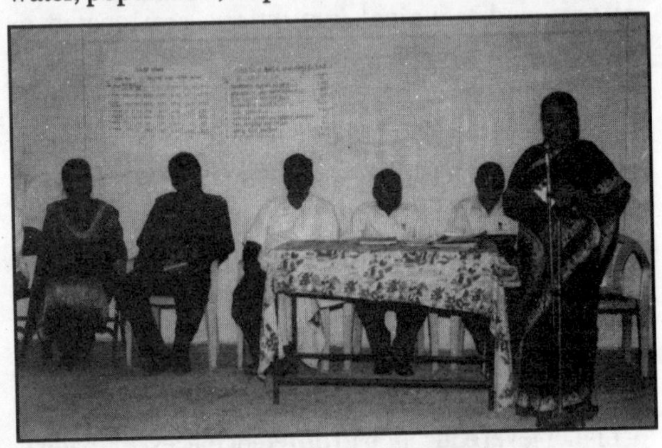

Preparation of Plan Document

Panchayat, educational institutions, drinking water facility, street lights, sanitation, women and child welfare, transportation, SC/ST welfare, maintenance of animal husbandry, milk society, industries and major occupation of the village, housing facility, cooperative society and other Panchayat related informations. The PRA exercise was done with the support of SIRD, Government Officials from each departments, self help groups, youth groups and other supportive voluntary organizations. The details were gathered with active support of the community. The President realized each and every needs of the Panchayat hamlets and have gained rich experience in approaching several department officials for fulfilling the peoples need. Based on the activities undertaken by the Panchayat, the officials appreciated her Panchayat administration and recommended her Panchayat for the national award under total sanitation programme.

Parents Teachers Association

Regular parents teachers association meetings were held in the schools. Several facilities were made for

Unemployed youth taught children during strike

the schools for enriching the students education. Prizes were provided by the President for the students during competitions on annual day. During the strike, which was done by the government officials, the PTA had decided to involve some unemployed educated youths for taking classes to the students. She used to visit the schools frequently and built up a good rapport with the headmasters and Education Department officials. She has given importance to girls education and increased the enrolment of students in schools and especially girls. A special drive was made every year to get the eligible children enrolled.

Sanitation

For her village, first preference was given to cleanliness, the garbages are properly cleaned by the sweepers in time and the drainages are also kept clean. The removal of garbages were altered into

Sugathara Pongal Varam

natural fertilizers, through composed pits for fertile lands. 'Sugathara Pongal Varam' programme introduced by the government which insists the importance of cleanliness. The self help group women and school students were fully involved in this programme with interest, and various cultural competitions were organised by the President and distributed prizes for them. The school students were involved in creating awareness among the villagers on the eradication of plastic covers and many campaigns, rallies were also organised regarding this theme. District Collector, MLA, Union Councillors were also invited to participate in these campaigns. This motivated several villagers for the eradication of plastic bags from the hamlets. She succeeded in all her attempts because of peoples involvement and participation.

Plastic Free Village

The Bhavani river which is the main water source of the entire district, which was also highly polluted by drainage water and the plastic covers which are

Plastic Bag Eradication Campaign

the major destructive elements and which blocked the flow of river water and reduce the level of ground water and affect the entire agricultural activities. She immediately wanted to take action on this matter and stressed the importance of the removal of plastic bags from the Panchayat areas with involvement of people. The Ward Members, the SHGs and youth groups welcomed such idea of the Presidents and immediately respondent to support it. Several rallies and campaigns were organised in the villages with the help of school students and youth groups. The Collector, MLA, Officials from DRDA and other traditional Panchayat leaders praised her and inaugurated the event by themselves by removing all the plastic covers from the village. The people are insisted to utilize paper covers and bags made of cloth. The Panchayat area became clean without garbages, maintenance of proper drainage system recommended the Panchayat for best Panchayat award. The Collector honoured her during the Republic Day ceremonies by awarded her Panchayat "as Plastic Free Panchayat". Even though this village Panchayat has more population, the President tried her best to fulfil the needs of every community without any discrimination. The collected plastic covers are gathered in a godown and decided to utilize it for the construction of roads. The President realized the importance of eradication of plastic bags, when the government insisted the destructions caused by the plastic covers especially its adverse affect against recharge of the ground water. Many voluntary organisations are also conducted rallies and campaigns against the utilization of plastic covers.

The sanitary complex in Konamoolai was maintained by four women self help groups. For the maintenance purpose, they have collected Rs.5 from the user group. All women and children of this area utilized the toilets and bathrooms. Bio-gas plant was also erected and the borewell motor was operated with the help of bio-gas. Both electricity and bio-gas facilities are available for taking water from the borewell. The wastes from the bio-gas plant was collected in a tank and that was utilized as fertilizer for agricultural lands. The schools are having separate toilets for both girls and boys.

The youth groups of this Panchayat were enthusiastically involved in the removal of plastic

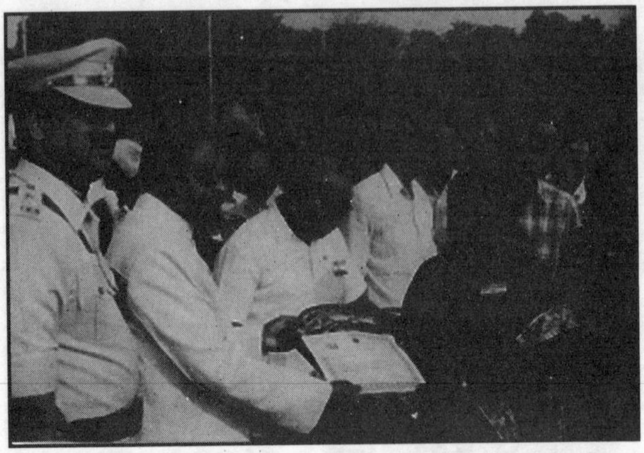

covers during campaigns. They have created awareness among the people on cleanliness and the adverse effect caused by the utilization of plastic bags through skits. They have actively involved in various Panchayat activities, solved many public problems and during Gram Sabha discussed Panchayat development activities. She makes it clear that her primary objective is to create awareness among the people to lead a decent human living. It is evident from the reality of life in the rural areas that many of the people and especially the poor are leading life in sub-human living conditions. Further natural resources are the life line of the people in the rural areas. They are to be protected.

SHGs Involvement in Panchayat Activities

The President has created a good relationship with the self help group women. Because she has frequently participated in their meetings, suggested solutions to their problems and collaboratively involved in Panchayat activities. Most of the SHGs families belonged to Telugu Chettiar community and whole family was engaged in manual handloom work. They have got the threads from some private concern and produced the Jakkard Cora Silk and handover it to that concern. For the production of each saree it takes two or three days and the amount varies according to the variety of designs.

Most of the SHGs got financial assistance from the banks, regarding this income generating activity. This Jakkard team of Gandhi Nagar went to Delhi for exhibiting their products, this trip was arranged by DRDA of Erode district. Weekly meetings of SHGs were held in anyone of the members house on Sundays, because of not having SHG building. Various personal and public problems were seriously discussed among the SHGs. The SHGs aimed to not to depend on the government, but everyone should have the tendency to equip themselves for their survival and tried to convince everyone to work towards Panchayat development. In all the activities she helped them and acted as a link between the people and the Departments of Government. The President realized the potentials of SHGs and hence she maintained a close link with SHGs.

Having seen the extensive pollution, she has decided to create awareness among the people. But people have a demand of setting individual tap connection for drinking water supply. When DRDA was approached for some help, the Project Officer of DRDA put a condition that the village maintain sanitary complex. She has agreed and on mutual basis, the Project Officer of DRDA provided necessary support.

The SHGs went to each house and canvassed the women for the utilization of sanitary complex and its necessity. They have also collected the peoples contribution for house water connection and hand pumps. Then the houses were provided with proper water supply.

The SHGs shared that many young aged destitutes and widows are residing in this Panchayat area, and they faced many problems due to lack of financial assistance or having no income generating activities. The President stated that their personal problems were solved among themselves but several welfare schemes implemented by the government for these vulnerable women have not reached them properly and also took more time for getting these facilities. The officials asked for various evidences and proofs for their clarification. The officials also took long time to implement the needed schemes and expected more relevant documents for reference. To get such individual benefits, they have to provide bribe. The frequent visit for the implementation of such scheme interrupted their day to day economic activities. It has not only taken more time but also cost as some of them are agricultural labourers and they have to lose their daily wage. She took a stand that on any account bribe should not be given for getting schemes to the Panchayats. Sometimes Panchayat took longer time to get such schemes yet she has not given any bribe. For individual benefits out of anxiety, they give but Panchayat cannot do it in the process. SHGs also have developed a healthy practice of avoiding such a kind of practice of giving bribe to the officials for getting assistance for the people. The President has decided to construct one marketing complex for the SHGs to sale their products.

The village health nurse visited the villages on Saturdays and Wednesdays and properly recorded the details of the reproductive health condition of mothers, distribution of iron tablets to teenage girls to control anemia and immunization treatments for the children were given to prevent communicable diseases. The deliveries were held in the Sathyamangalam hospitals. The anganwadi teachers were also recorded the details of reproductive mothers and children. Weighing machine, utensils and furnitures were provided for the anganwadi students by the Panchayat and SHGs. She visited anganwadi frequently and checked the noon meal centre. She used to supervise all the service institutions not authentically. But her visits helped the institutions to put things in proper shape. She felt that such a kind of supervision one can improve the service delivery.

Camps like legal awareness, agriculture, veterinary and health camps were organised by the President for the village people. Polio camps were done by SHGs along with youth groups. She has decided to create a roadside park for the entertainment of the children because it has tourist spots like Bhavani Sagar Dam and Bannari Amman Temple (situated 16 km. away from the Panchayat). Due to lack of rainfall, the agriculture activities are affected. It has started to establish the development of handloom units. To motivate several handloom unit holders, a cooperative society is being established and which would make easier for them regarding the purchase of raw materials like thread, cotton and marketing their products.

Drinking Water

For drinking water, overhead tanks, mini power pumps, hand pumps, individual water taps, etc., were provided and well sufficient water was distributed to every hamlets under shift system. At present, they have planned to establish joint water supply under sanitation project between Konamoolai and Ariappanpalayam Panchayats. They have decided to take water from Kondamuthur river through bio-gasifier plant. For this project, 10 per cent financial contribution was decided to collect from the village people, and this was approved from the Gram Sabha and the amount (Rs.42,000) was collected from the people by the SHGs.

Inauguration of Water Supply by MLA

Relationship with SC Community

The SC people were more supportive and demanded their needs whenever they face problems. The President has also visited their areas and their homes during festivals and without time bound. One land problem arised between Okilia Gounder and this community, which was changed into communal rivalry, this problem was solved by the President, without creating a peace committee, which was referred by the government officials. Hence there was no differential treatment among them.

Vision Behind Her Leadership

The following are the reasons for her success in her Panchayat :

- quick decisions are taken during crises.
- transparent administration.
- maintenance of proper accounts/financial transactions.
- regularly presence in the Panchayat Office and frequently met the people.
- first preference given to the really poor people below poverty line.
- good relationship with Dalit community.
- frequent supervision on Panchayat activities
- her openness and closeness with ward members.
- visited several departments for getting various development activities for the village.

In future, she wanted to become the Panchayat President through open contest in the election and make the village self-sufficient in every respect. She referred that the powers given to the Panchayat President, were not given to district, union councillors and the ward members. She insisted the government for providing capacity building training at the initial stage of the position given to the women as Panchayat President. Women should be aware of the outside world, and they have to be aware of what is happening in the outside world. She should be educated and came out of various cultural bonds and norms. Income generating opportunities and training programmes should be provided to women especially for poor women.

Source of Revenue

The sources of revenue for the Panchayat were house tax, sales tax, plan approval, advertisement tax, and 2C tree tax. The other sources were local cess, stamp duty, entertainment tax, house tax matching grant, and subsidies for street lights, hand pumps and motor pumps. Several government department officials were approached for getting scheme funds and other subsidies for village development activities. The financial transactions are transparent without any audit objection. The following are the financial transactions for the past three years.

For the Year 2001-2002

The major receipt of stamp duty income was Rs.1,95,422 and house tax was Rs.52,270. But the SFC grant for the year was Rs.21,626 only. The total income of the village was Rs.5,97,447. The Panchayat met out more expenses in the payment of EB charges as Rs.90,439, salary for the staff Rs.60,070, extension of street pipes constitutes Rs.66,708 and the maintenance of motor pumps Rs.24,875, Rs.53,189 was utilized for the maintenance of roads and small bridges. The major amount of Rs.98,708 was spent for the maintenance and construction of proper drainage system for making the village clean.

For the Year 2002-2003

An amount of Rs.17,652 was collected as entertainment tax for one old cinema theatre and the SFC grant received was Rs.1,58,478. For the plan approval Rs.28,903 has been collected. An income of Rs.40,460 was received from auction meat shop and Rs.14,370 as library tax. The total amount of income constitutes Rs.6,60,748. As for the expenditure, an amount of Rs.23,549 was spent for public sanitation, Rs.30,362 for the maintenance of street lights and Rs.49,289 for dinking water purpose. Rs.31,166 has been spent for the administrative expenses under 11th finance fund. Rs.500 was contributed for Red Cross and Rs.9,833 was utilized for the maintenance of Panchayat TV, totally the amount spent for this year was Rs.3,22,427.

For the Year 2003-2004

Rs.1,11,458 was received as SFC grant and other auctioning amount was Rs.43,843. Insisting the importance of sanitation during the Pongal festival an amount of Rs.2,500 was received as subsidy. Rs.2,025 was collected as licence fee. Rs.2,74,326 was the income of stamp duty. The total amount of income for the year 2003-2004 was Rs.5,99,560. Regarding the expenditures, an amount of Rs.34,350 was spent for public sanitation and Rs.57,238 for the maintenance of street lights. Rs.7,212 has been meet out the construction of drainages and Rs.6,500 for the cremation ground. For the maintenance of roads and small bridges Rs.1,97,795 was spent. Total expenditure costs Rs.5,81,572 and the unspent balance grant was Rs.6,16,209.49. Hence, enormous amount has been spent for public sanitation, maintenance of drainage and construction of roads and small bridges.

Annexure

President	:	S. Padmini
Vice-President	:	N.K. Krishnamoorthy
Ward Members	:	1. K.R. Ramasamy
		2. C. Rukmani
		3. V. Lakshmi
		4. Kaliappan
		5. S. Thilakavathi
		6. M. Rangasami
		7. P. Subramani
		8. Rajalakshmi

Evaluation

She is highly motivated and committed. Further she is always optimistic, despite the obstacles and barriers for good works and services. She has developed a perspective for Panchayat management. She has planned to mobilise people and for which she adopted a strategy of projecting herself as a humble, simple leader with a sense of commitment and transparency. Her approach drew the attention of all. She is careful in approaching people. She approached the people only through action. She felt that providing conducive environment for people to lead decent human living is the priority of the Panchayat. She is further committed on environmental sanitation. By her activities, she drew the attention of the government departments. Many departments extended cooperation to her to carry out their activities. She initiated the micro plan and through which she got the existing picture of the conditions of the village. Further through which she developed her vision for the development of the villages. She has evinced keen interest in adopting modern rural technologies.

Conclusion

She is the best example to demonstrate that a women leader with a passion for public service with a sense of commitment and honesty can deliver goods to the society effectively by realizing their worth. She had a vision for the development of villages. By taking up the sanitation, water supply and environmental problems in Panchayats she effectively addressed the issues of women and children. She is unequivocal that conditions could be created to make the people to lead a decent human living. She had realized, that people in the rural areas that too the poor are leading life in the sub-human living conditions and this condition has to be chased. Further she felt a Panchayat can work effectively only with the active participation of people and hence she started working in mobilising the people for development activities by conducting herself in administration transparently. She got awards incidentally. But she never dreamt of getting such awards.

CASE - 13

PEOPLE'S PANCHAYATS

Maravamangalam Panchayat is called a people's Panchayat. In a Panchayat where there is no support for the Communist Party of India, Annadurai, though a Communist, got the support of the entire community of the Panchayat area. All his activities are people centric. His idea of involving people in each and every action paid rich dividends. He created a citizen's centre for engaging the people. Whenever he felt that the actions of the government department were wrong, without any hesitation, he mobilized the people and fought against the government. His honesty, humility and courage made him very popular among the people. His motive in engaging citizens in all activities is to create enlightened citizens.

Mr. Annadurai, the President of Maravamangalam Gram Panchayat, Kalayarkoil Panchayat Union, Sivagangai District, is known for his capacity to mobilise people for community action through the Panchayat. He is 49 years old and belongs to the Yadava community graded as a Backward Class. He is tirelessly working for rejuvenating the village with the active participation and cooperation of the people. He is not very rich and not well educated and not highly placed in social hierarchy but he is highly valued by all because of his commitment to the public cause and his honesty in handling public affairs, which have attracted many. He developed a habit of working with the people for any action on any issue, which made him close to the people or made the people close to him. He does not belong to either the ruling AIADMK party nor the DMK but he is affiliated to the Communist Party of India, which has only seven members in his village. Both the AIADMK and the DMK are the prominent political parties which are present in the village. Maravamangalam is a big Panchayat, having 6000 people. It is a multi caste village with a dominant Scheduled Caste presence. His father, being a Congress Party member, earned a good name from the people for his dedicated service. Annadurai became the President of the Cooperative Society and he retrieved the society from total collapse and he made it vibrant. When he was the President of the Cooperative Milk Society, he enabled the poor to get loan, that too nearly 135 milch animals. He rebuilt the society only through the participation of the poor through their activities. He took earnest efforts to establish a Pandian Grama Bank at Maravamangalam after prolonged persuasion of the higher officials. In the first Panchayat elections in 1996, he contested along with the traditional Panchayat leader who was called Ambalam in vain. He could not get through because people did not want to defame the traditional Panchayat leader. As a result the traditional Panchayat leader won. But he did not perform his role well and he failed miserably in discharging his duties.

Working with the People

Further, when steps were taken to create a small bed dam in the waterway, Annadurai raised objection as this bed dam would stop water flowing to his Panchayat areas. He mobilised the people and informed them about the implications of the new proposal. But the then Panchayat President kept quiet without taking any initiative. Annadurai launched a series of agitations and went to jail. Finally, he went to court and got a judgment in favour of his village. This gave a name to him. He has developed a strategy of mobilising the people for all public actions. In a democratic society one can achieve whatever he wants provided the individual has got commitment, sincerity and honesty in his/her dealings, he observed. Honesty and commitment alone bring people towards the leader. Corrupt leaders can also mobilise by corrupt means but that cannot be sustained. He is not rich and he has only three acres of land. But he is able to manage his family within the income generated from his lands. Moreover he says that whenever he is in need of money, there are people in his own area to help him. Though he belongs to a party, he is able to attract all political party leaders because he has influence over the people.

In the second Panchayat elections held in 2001, he contested again along with four candidates, including the traditional Panchayat leader. All the four lost their deposits. His untiring public work with the participation of the public brought him to the Panchayat as President. His predecessor demonstrated his inability by his non-performance. Other candidates spent money for canvassing. He was determined not to spend money for the election. He did not have money also. He printed a hand bill projecting his promise; water supply, nothing more; non-performance to performance; corruption to corruption free administration; non-participative governance to participative Panchayat management. He further printed a hand bill asking the people not to sell their votes as, by selling their votes, they are selling their self-respect. He conducted a voter awareness campaign.

Micro Plan

When he was elected President, he decided not to receive petitions from the people. As per his observation, getting petition from the public would amount to reduction of citizens to the level of irresponsible dole receivers and petitioners. He did not want to do it. He wanted everyone as responsible citizens and active participants of development. Everyone should feel that they have strength to change their destiny and they can manage the government. He developed a vision for the total transformation of the village. It was only a wish list. When he developed such a wish list, he presented the same in the Gram Sabha and got the approval. He printed the same document with the contribution of the shop owners by giving advertisement. Even to print the wish list he mobilised money from the people. He said that mobilising money is not a problem provided people get something out of the exercise. He has an argument that even a poor person contributes for the temple festival as a share because he feels that it is his responsibility. Hence one has to make the people responsible for every act. It is possible and it is happening in his Panchayat, he said. In the wish list he had indicated the facilities the Panchayat needed, the services the Panchayat area needed. From the wish list he has developed a perspective plan for the development of his Panchayat.

Initially he prepared a vision document detailing only the activities to be carried out. After one year he constituted a Planning Committee consisting of Panchayat Ward Members, NGO representatives, retired government officials, representatives from youth group and representatives from SHGs. After having a thorough discussion with all segments of the society in the Panchayat area, he prepared a well developed plan in consultation with the Government officials. The plan document provides the following details:

- different committees involved in plan preparation
- methodology adopted to prepare the plan
- basic details about the facilities available in Maravamangalam
- conditions of the people (BPL)
- details about the needs of the community sector-wise
- financial details involved in implementing the plan activities
- steps taken to improve the internal resource mobilization

The total plan document is his creative idea. There are Panchayats, roughly 64, who have developed micro plan in Tamil Nadu with the support of the NGOs. But, in Maravamangalam, he initiated the steps for planning. He first dreamt of it and later he started the consultation process. Finally, he developed a plan. It is totally through a participatory process. A series of steps were taken to transform the plan into reality. The total outlay projected in the plan document is Rs.11 crores. He is taking earnest efforts to mobilise resources through various means. He printed the plan and circulated it among all the government offices. It is a 42 page document full of activities. He has given the document to the MLA, the MP, the Block Panchayat Chairperson, the District Panchayat Chairperson and the Ward Members. His priority is water supply and sanitation.

Committing Himself

Nattar Kalvai water is a main source for irrigation purposes to Maravamangalam. Water comes through the above channel and is being used for cultivating the lands in Maravamangalam. Water is being stored in a check dam at a distance of three kilometres. If another bed dam is constructed before Maravamangalam, it would help the Kannankundu and Siramam water tanks to feed water to other areas. When the new proposal of constructing a check dam for Rs.51 lakhs was announced the people perceived that it would affect eleven villages in Maravamangalam area. It was forcefully resisted by the people under the leadership of Annadurai. Subsequently they went to High Court. When the matter was subjudice again the Public Works Department initiated the construction plan and it was forcefully resisted by the people. 500 people were arrested under the leadership of the Panchayat leader Annadurai. Of the arrested the majority were women.

Finally, the High Court of Madras delivered a judgment in which it is stated that 90 per cent of the water from the proposed bed dam has to be given to Maravamangalam area. It was a prolonged struggle for a period of four years. The Gram Panchayat President Annadurai, took the lead in the struggle even before he became President of the Panchayat. Only through this struggle he became popular among the people. He continued the struggle even after he became the Panchayat President. The President involved all sections of the village in this struggle. In his opinion water will unite the masses. It is an instrument to integrate the people of different social categories.

Contact with Government Departments

Annadurai periodically gives demand letters to the concerned authorities to perform their roles. His pertinent demand is to desilt all the tanks in the Panchayat area. He feels that if a Panchayat looks after water bodies very effectively many of the issues could be tackled very easily. Water would solve many problems. Hence he is keen on managing common and especially natural resources. He used to consolidate the problems, demands and issues based on his personal visit to all the areas and segments of the society and the discussion in Gram Sabha. He used to classify all those issues and make them as demands of the people and he took them to sectoral departments for proper redressal as government departments are having enough resources and authority to solve them. His periodical visits to departments helped him to get many programmes implemented in his Panchayat area.

Alliance Building

Further he is a good organiser and as a result he organised the Gram Panchayat leaders of his block and put up their administrative problems to the officials for immediate redressal. He is having contact with all the 45 Gram Panchayat leaders. In many areas Panchayat leaders found it very difficult to manage the officials. Officials wanted to control the elected representatives of the people by using their ignorance and incapacity. Moreover the Panchayat leaders largely depend on the resources of the sectoral departments for Panchayat activities. To overcome the problems, he has developed a framework by which an association is formed at the block level. Whenever they face any problem in government offices, they jointly take decisions and organise protest meetings. By organising such collective meetings, Panchayat leaders are empowered. For many of the administrative problems created by the lower level officials, their federation has found solutions through their collective action.

Direct Democracy

His Gram Sabha mobilization is totally different from that of other Gram Panchayat leaders. For each Gram Sabha meeting he used to invite either a higher level officer or an elected representative. Further he keeps a number of issues of various strata of people in the agenda of the Gram Sabha to attract the members of the Gram Sabha. He comes up with challenges in

Gram Sabha Meeting

the Gram Sabha meeting. He allows people to speak and take decisions. For each decision he fixes responsibility also with regard to the implementation of the decision. The special invitees used to give some promises also. To follow up the promises, individuals are fixed. Literally he shares his burden with others. He used to invite some officials to create awareness among the people on certain issues.

Gram Sabha Meeting

He conducts the Gram Sabha meeting as a temple festival. While seeing the records, Gram Sabha attendance reaches 15 per cent and they are really active in articulating the problems of the people but also evolving solutions to the problems. He created a collective leadership. By conducting himself as a humble person and facing problems courageously he has given an image to the people that he is committed and honest in managing the Panchayat. Reaching the people is not a problem for him as his Ward Members, Committee Members and Self Help Groups leaders act as instruments to mobilise members for the Gram Sabha. Further he made it clear that the Gram Sabha resolutions are realized through the Panchayat, which made the people participate.

His Administrative Nuance

He uses two different designations. One is Gram Panchayat President and the other one is Panchayat Executive Secretary. While taking decisions he acts as President. While implementing the decisions he acts as Executive Secretary. He has a role clarity and as a result he performs his roles perfectly. For many problems created by antisocial elements, he strictly warned them by issuing notice. He formed a committee at the Panchayat level to monitor the activities of the Panchayat. Equally a strong committee he has formed to collect the taxes. He does not involve himself in collecting tax. He fixes the responsibility on a group. It is easy for him to collect the tax. He engages the Ward Members in organising the medical camps sponsored by various agencies. By giving responsibility to the Ward Members and sharing with them all the details of accounts and decisions, he ensures that all the Ward Members are cooperative. They take responsibility in every action.

He created a Citizens Centre in his Panchayat office. It provides information to the public. He created the Centre with the help of Catalyst Trust. His idea

Information Centre - Chiraag

Citizens Centre

of creating a Centre is to keep the people engaged. It not only provides information, but also provides opportunity to develop dialogue and discourse on development. With the help of Jan Shikshan Sansthan he provided needed skills to the women groups. He maintained a very good link with the higher level elected representatives, officials and the local NGOs. In this respect he is a good social mobiliser. He further created an information centre which is called Chiraag. It provides computer education to children and youth. It helps the people to get application forms downloaded from the system. It sends all kinds of applications and letters to various types of institutions. In order to protect the common properties, a committee has been constituted in which all prominent members of the community have been made members. They have been given power to deal with the issues arising out of misusing the commons. He made several such informal groups work as active participants. To cater to the needs of the people, a committee has been constituted and the committee has to bring to the notice of the Panchayat the needs of the people.

Rectitude

There is yet another issue—corruption in administration. Local body leaders are finding it difficult to get schemes and submit accounts in the corrupt administrative system in Tamil Nadu. Annadurai makes it clear that the present administrative system is corrupt. But it is corrupt only to the corrupt people not to the non-corrupt leaders. But if the non corrupt leaders work individually they cannot do anything and they will also succumb to pressure. But he said that he is working with the people and he is mobilising the people for development activities. His Gram Sabha is not a name's sake formality Gram Sabha. He made it a discourse Sabha and deliberation Sabha. He brings a lot of people's issues for discussion. Moreover, to protest against any wrong, he mobilises the people. In all his mobilization he mobilises more of women, Dalits and youth. It is a vibrant force. Even after he became President, he organised many protests and he succeeded. He never considered the President's post an office. He considered it a space to mobilise the people for development action.

Further he developed a control mechanism to minimize misdeeds in the villages. Villages are units of habitats with varying socio-cultural groups with different political backups. To manage the communities, one has to have a strategy. A Panchayat President is not a policeman or an inspector. He is only a leader facilitating development works in the areas of the Panchayat. At the same time, he has to create a peaceful atmosphere in the village settings to enable development works to be carried out. It could be done only through a committee consisting of members of various communities who have influence over the people of the respective communities. In this respect he has constituted such committees through which regulatory and supervisory activities are initiated.

Major Works Carried out

Clean Village Activities

Mr. Annadurai, to sensitize the community on sanitation and environmental protections organised several cultural programmes in all habitations. With the help of medical firms, he made arrangements for eye camp in the village and eye operations

Eye Camps

conducted by St. Joseph's Hospital, Trichy, to the needy persons. Further he made an attempt for a successful solid waste management. The wastes are segregated into bio and non-bio waste and from the bio waste, compost manure was produced. To transport the solid waste three bullock carts have been purchased from donation given by a local NGO.

Mr.Annadurai has done an innovation in environmental sanitation. The area around the Village Panchayat office was used for open defecation by

Parking Vehicles

the public. He discussed with public and they proposed a community toilet for both men and women.

Immediately he cleared all the thorny bushes and levelled the ground. There was an encroachment in the place and the same was also removed. Separate toilets for men and women were constructed and they were put into use. Further, to augment income to the Panchayat, banana saplings were planted in the cleared site. A bus shelter was constructed. In addition to that the Panchayat permitted public vehicle owners to make use of this site to park their vehicles. Now the area has become a clean business centre.

Provision of Drinking Water

Mr. Annadurai gave equal emphasis to supply of clean drinking water to all the hamlets by extension of pipe lines and construction of new OHT and regulating of water supply by fixing ferrule valve system in all public taps. Periodical cleaning of OHTs and chlorination were done regularly. Through public contribution he availed of Swajaldhara Scheme to ensure drinking water to all. Two OHTs with a capacity of 1,00,000 litres and 30,000 litres were constructed. Water supply connection is provided to all schools in the Panchayat. To ensure cleanliness around the public water taps a Vigilance Committee is formed in each habitation involving SHG members. As adequate water supply is available in the Panchayat it was proposed to give individual house connections. In this regard the Village Panchayat administration was seeking the technical guidance of the TWAD.

Over Head Water Tank

A *Dhobi Khana* was constructed at the main village Maravamangalam. To ensure regular supply of water for washing cloths a separate borewell was sunk near the Dhobi Khana and it was given electricity connection and so it is fully utilized by the community.

Information Empowerment of the Community

In Maravamangalam Panchayat already a computer centre is functioning which is very much useful to the community in gaining knowledge and information related to their socio-economic needs. Community members easily contact government officials through e-mail. And yet another centre 'Citizen Centre' sponsored by Catalyst Trust is also serving the community for their information empowerment. Mr. Annadurai decided to establish a permanent library for his villagers. With the help of local enlightened educated individuals, he collected contributions from the public and a public literacy centre was established in Maravamangalam Village. It is functioning well. Mostly young men are making use of the library regularly. It is in a new building with sufficient infrastructure facility. The library building was constructed from the fund allotted for local area development activities by the Member of Parliament, Mr.Sudharsana Nachiappan of Sivaganga Constituency.

Computer Centre

Library Hall

Educational Development Activities

There are three schools in this Panchayat area, of which one is a High School another a Primary Panchayat Union School and another an aided Primary School in Maravamangalam Panchayat. Mr. Annadurai has immense faith in the implications of education on the rural masses. He facilitated the functioning of Parent Teachers Association and its activities. Annual events like school day celebrations, sports and distribution of prizes to the academically bright students and improving the infrastructure facilities in the schools were the major contributions of Mr.Annadurai. In the Panchayat Union Primary School he arranged a pucca fencing, levelled the site for the play ground, and constructed a toilet from the allocation of TRSP scheme fund, SSA grant and also public contribution. In the high school, additional buildings and lab facilities were provided from the M.P. local area development programme fund. For one teacher employed in the high school, the salary is paid from the Parent Teachers Association common fund.

Common Property Protection and Management Activities

Mr.Annadurai, being a farmer, has given priority to agriculture development. His rapport with the traditional Panchayat enabled him to undertake improvement and maintenance activities in respect of common property resources. There are twenty-six irrigation tanks and three irrigation canals in his Panchayat area meant for agriculture. His association with the traditional Panchayat formed a committee to look after the protection and maintenance of common property resources. Periodical kudimaramathu activities were successfully carried out to maintain the water bodies. Whenever fund is available in the Village Panchayat under schemes like Jawahar Sampoorna Gram Swarojgar Yojana (JGSY), Namakku Namme Thittam and Employment Assurance Scheme (EAS), desilting and deepening works were undertaken in the irrigation tanks. Illegal felling of trees was strictly prohibited by social control. In distribution of irrigation water to the ayacutdhar equity is maintained by the committee.

Maintenance of CPRs

Vocational Training to Youth and Self Help Group Members

Mr.Annadurai evinced keen interest in human resource development. He encouraged the SHG activities and youth activities in the village. With the help of the Jan Siksha Sansthans (J.S.S.) Scheme implemented in the district, he availed of the vocational training programmes for his village youth and women. Training in mushroom cultivation, vermi composting, tailoring, camphor production, candle, soap, coir production have been provided to village youth and SHG members free of cost. Women trained in coir production started manufacturing of foot mats, ropes and other coir based products.

Tailoring

Soap Coir Production

Creation of Paddy Procuring Centre

Farmers in and around Maravamangalam used to raise paddy if adequate irrigation water was available. During 2004 the majority of the farmers had paddy cultivation and were fortunate enough to have a good yield. The Government of Tamil Nadu announced the list of places where paddy procuring centres would be located by which the farmers would get an incentive money if they came forward to sell their paddy to the Food Corporation of Tamil Nadu. In Sivagangai District when the government announced the scheme, Maravamangalam was not on the list. Mr.Annadurai organised a farmers meeting of Maravamangalam and neighbouring villages to discuss the issue. A representation was made to the government in this regard and there was a decision to organise a demonstration if the request was denied. He lobbied with government officials by providing various details like total extent of lands on which paddy was raised, estimated quantity of paddy crop available for sale to the government and also the extent of benefits small and marginal farmers would gain in the villages. Further he came forward to earmark a site and a building for the proposed centre and agreed to take the moral responsibility for the successful and smooth running of the centre. At last the government officials sanctioned a centre at Maravamangalam itself. The farmers benefited a lot. Mr.Annadurai shared that the position of the Panchayat President could be used to achieve many things provided the President is acknowledged by the people. His achievements were possible because of the people who reposed faith and confidence in his leadership and extended their support whole heartedly to all his actions.

Conclusion

His strength is honesty and working with the people. His strong belief is that approaching issues and problems with people's support would always bring positive results. He is known for his collective leadership. According to him people are the real strength for the Panchayats. Giving drinking water to all segments of the society, managing the commons by the community, looking after the well-being of the people by the committees of the Panchayat made the Panchayat unique. His identity with people for just causes made the people repose confidence in him. Further his selfless dedicated work for the cause of the community made the people listen to him. Though he is politically identified with a political party, his activities are never perceived as political. His strength is his responsiveness. He believes people immensely as they are the real support for all the activities.

Profile of the Panchayat

Village Panchayat President	:	Mr. P. Annadurai
Village Panchayat Vice-President	:	Mr. M. Periyakaruppan

Ward No.	*Members Name*	*Community*
1.	1. M. Periyakaruppan	General
	2. I. Abubekkar	General
	3. M. Velumathi	General
2.	1. K. Pandi	SC
	2. M. Panchu	SC
	3. Ramalingam	General
3.	1. K. Pandi	SC
	2. R. Rajeswari	General
	3. K. Muthuraman	General

Village Panchayat Activities Self-Evaluation Committee

1.	Name of the Village Panchayat President	Mr. P. Annadurai
2.	Name of the SC/ST Panchayat Ward Member	Mr. P. Pandi
3.	Name of the woman Panchayat Ward Members	Mrs. M. Panchu
4.	Name of the self-help group member	Mary
5.	Name of the trainer	Mrs. K. Anbuselvi SIRD (NGO)
6.	Name of the Animator	Mrs. Marikannu Junior Assistant Panchayat Union Kalayarkoil

General Details

1.	Name of the Village Panchayat	Maravamangalam
2.	Name of the Panchayat Union	Kalyarkoil
3.	Number of Hamlets	6
4.	Name of the Hamlets	1. Maravamangalam 2. Narangani 3. Boothagudi 4. Palkulam 5. Paluvakudai 6. Pappankanmai
5.	Number of Wards	3
6.	Number of Panchayat Ward Members	9

7. Revenue Division	Sivagangai
8. Revenue Circle	Sivagangai
9. Revenue Village	Palkulam Group
10. Parliamentary Constituency	Sivagangai
11. Assembly Constituency	Sivagangai
12. Village Panchayat Boundaries	*East:* Usilangulám Village Panchayat *West:* Siramam Village Panchayat *North:* Mudikkarai Village Panchayat *South:* Siramam, Sethambal Village Panchayat
13. Area	4.5 km
14. Permanent Houses	1222
15. Temporary Houses	-
16. Population	Not correct details given
17. School Details	
Anganwadi	1
Primary School	2
Higher Secondary School	1
18. Infrastructure Facility	
1. Library room	1
2. Bus Shelter	2
3. Ration Shop	1
4. Noon-meal Nutrition Centre	2
5. Community Hall	1
6. Play Ground	nil
7. Status of Village Panchayat office building	own
8. Type of roof of the Village Panchayat office building	pucca building
19. Length of Village Panchayat Road	
Thar Road (Black top)	392 m
Metal Road	1.236 km
Mud Road	5.4 km
Cement Road	350 m
Road to Burial Ground	2 km
Culverts	4
20. Details of street light	
Bulb	Nil
Tube Light	130
Mercury Lamp	6
Sunlight Lamp	Nil
21. Sources of drinking water	
Open Well	3
Bore Well	4
Hand Pump	17
Motor Pump	5
Overhead tank	2
Ground Level reservoir	5
Integrated Drinking Water Scheme	Nil
Drinking water facility for Schools	Hand Pump
Common Drinking water	42
House tap connection	Nil
22. Toilet Facility	
Public toilet	1
Individual household toilet	734
Toilets in school	5
Drainage facility	200 m
23. Sanitation	
Primary Health Centre	1
Sub-Health Centre	1
Private Clinic	1
Dispensary	1
24. Graveyard Facility	
Common Graveyard	1
Private Graveyard	1
Pathway to Graveyard	mud road 2 km
Graveyard with cremation facility	1
26. Total Houses with	
Television	500
Public Television Room	7
27. Information and public relation office	
Post office	1
Public Telephone	1
Houses with telephone	162
28. Bank	1. Primary Agricultural Cooperation Bank 2. Pandiyan Gram Bank

29. Land Development Bank

1.	Name of the Bank attached with this village	Land Development, Kalyarkoil
2.	Manure sales centre	1
3.	Pesticide sales centre	5

30. Details of Occupation

1.	Agriculture Labourer	
	Male	1578
	Female	1200
2.	(i) Small Farmers	473
	(ii) Marginal Farmers	990
	(iii) Big Farmers	25
3.	Cottage Industries	71

31. Water Sources

Tank Irrigation	Yes: 26 tanks
Open Well	Yes: 10
Bore Well	Yes: 5
Channel Irrigation	3
Other Irrigation	Yes

32. Type of Soil

Red Soil	Yes
Laterite Soil	Yes

33. Cattle Details

1.	Cow	1000
2.	Buffalo	500
3.	Sheep	3000
4.	Hen	2000
	Total	6500

34. Other Facilities

1.	Threshing floor	2
2.	Noon meal centre	2
3.	Anganwadi	1
4.	Biogas plant	1
5.	Ration shop	2

35. CBO Details

1.	Women SHGs	30
2.	SHGs operating for more than 6 months	15
3.	Economically benefited SHGs	10
4.	Adolescent girls group	6
5.	Children group	2
6.	Cultural group	10
7.	Village Development Committee	10
8.	Male SHG	6
9.	Male SHG operating for more than 6 months	4
10.	SHG which got revolving fund	8
11.	SC women SHG	6
12.	BC/MBC women SHG	Incense sticks, chalk piece, soap, phenoil
13.	SHGs Economic Activities	Production and Sales

36. Details of Electricity connection in SC residence

Houses with EB connection	50

37. EB connection details in public place

1.	Public toilet	1
2.	Community Hall	1
3.	Television Room	6

38. Electricity bill arrears to be paid by the Village Panchayat	From Rs.300000 to Rs.500000
39. Address of the Village Panchayat	Near Panchayat Union Bus Stop, Maravamangalam, Sivagangai Post Pin - 630 554

CASE - 14

A LEADER OF LEADERS

With the background of eighth standard education, Ponni Kailasam emerged as a Gram Panchayat leader and fought against the dominant communities while retrieving the commons from their clutches. She fought against illicit liquor and succeeded in her attempt with the support of the communities. Having realized the plight of the women leaders in the field, she has created a Federation of Women Gram Panchayat leaders and it became a support structure for the women leaders. Many times she set the agenda for many social development works. She did the basic work of creating awareness among the people and orienting SHG women. She motivated the ward members to work with her. She is thorough with Panchayat administration. She has travelled extensively in the country. She is responsible for getting the reservation of seats for women and Dalits extended for ten years. It is unique in Tamil Nadu and in the whole of India.

PART - I

PANCHAYAT ACTIVITIES

Ms. Ponni Kailasam, the President of Anaikuppam Panchayat of Nannilam Union, Thiruvarur District, has studied upto 8th standard and her age is 43. She belongs to the Thevar community and has four children. Her husband Mr.V.Kailasam is the owner of electrical goods shop and his main occupation is agriculture. He belongs to the AIADMK party and served as District Deputy Secretary. Ms.Ponni's first daughter got married. The second and third daughters are doing their graduation and her son has just completed his 10th standard. They have their own land for agriculture.

Ms.Ponni was allowed to study upto 8th standard, but was forcibly stopped from school, after the attainment of puberty. But her brother allowed to complete her graduation. In school days, she was always within the 5th rank and developed leadership qualities. At the age of 19 she got married to Mr.Kailasam. She admired her husband's mindset to do service and his close contact with people.

The former Panchayat President of this Gram Panchayat for the past thirty years engaged in illegal sand mining and felling of trees from Poramboke Panchayat lands. He himself auctioned several sand dunes and trees and took the income gained from such sources. People were made spectators and they never raised their voice against him in this village. When she came to this village after marriage she could not tolerate these atrocities. When she sounded other women they said that the President was a powerful and influential person. As District Deputy Secretary of the AIADMK party, her husband served the poor and got the support of the people. Yet he could not control such illegal activities of the traditional Panchayat leaders. They were only a few families.

In Nannilam, there was an election held for the President of the cooperative society. Her husband contested the same. A woman who was also a representative had to cast her vote. But the opponents threatened her and did not allow her to cast her vote. At this juncture, with the support of her husband, Ms.Ponni brought her to the spot and helped her to cast her vote. Watching this event, the AIADMK leaders wanted to give her the Union level party responsibility. This information was conveyed to her husband but she was not allowed to accept this block level party representation. At this juncture, the Village Development Committee of Nannilam Union, appointed her a convener through DRDA. She disseminated information about the available welfare schemes among the rural women and she was paid Rs.250 as salary by DRDA. She built up a good rapport with rural women and also visited several places along with the block conveners of Thiruvarur District.

When she was a housewife she wanted to study English to develop her vocabulary but she was provided with library books and she studied books like *Mahabaratha, Ramayana* and social novels. In the meantime, she felt that the MLAs had the power to solve any kind of problems. So she wanted to become an MLA. When she approached the AIADMK party, they refused to give her ticket but nominated two other candidates. Then she approached the Congress Party, which also refused. Then she contested as an independent candidate for the Vedaranyam constituency, but was defeated, though the deposit amount was refunded. She felt very sad and bitterly thought that without doing any service to the people, she could not attain the position of leadership. She also felt that she might choose an alternative constituency instead of Vedaranyam. She realized the non-acceptance of the community and the importance of the support of the party. The MLA seat could be achieved only with party influence.

The people had always followed the decisions taken by the traditional Panchayat leaders for whom they were asked to cast their votes. The traditional Panchayat leaders asked the people to promise on paddy and insisted on their not voting for some specific persons who contested the elections.

Then Ms.Ponni, along with her husband, decided to help the public by themselves and dropped their support for the AIADMK party. They helped the people by assisting them to get loans, provided shelter and food during natural calamities like floods and cyclones, provided furniture for schools, supported the farmers by providing seedlings, etc. Even though he came out of the AIADMK party he helped the members of the party who needed his support. The AIADMK party member who contested the 1996 elections, filed a case against her husband saying that he tried to murder him. This made him frustrated and he entirely withdrew from the AIADMK party.

When the 73rd Constitutional Amendment presented the opportunity to women, the AIADMK party asked her to contest and promised to provide complete support but she declined their offer and reminded them of the earlier incident. But the villagers belonging to the Vellalar, Dalit and Kallar communities compelled her to contest and assured their support. People themselves deposited money and nominated her. She affixed her signature on the form and did not even go to the nomination spot. One candidate with the support of the AIADMK party and another with the support of the Congress and DMK party, contested against her.

She went for canvassing in several villages along with seven youths and told the people that if they believed that she would fulfil the needs of the people they might cast their vote in favour of her. If they failed to choose the right person during that election, they would suffer a lot. She made it very clear that she was coming for delivery of services. She did not please anyone for getting votes. She distributed handouts to Dalit communities and sought their votes. She got honour and support from the womenfolk, because she was honest, bold and committed and they believed that she would surely fulfil their needs. She won the election by a difference of 100 votes. She felt very glad and happy when she won. She assured the people that she would transform the entire village, never bothering about any opponents and courageously facing any crisis.

Anaikkuppam Panchayat has nine hamlets. They are Anaikkuppam, Thalathankudi, Pidagai, Akkaraithennancheri, Moolamangalur, Thennancheri, Rajakalipur, Kalladimedu and South Adidravidar Street.

She built up a good rapport with the block and district level officials and got sanctioned the following for Anaikkuppam Panchayat: school buildings 3, Primary Health Centre 1, ration shops 2, library 1, Panchayat office 1, rice stockroom 1 and veterinary hospital 1. Among the above 10 facilities, 9 were allotted to Anaikkuppam Village and it was got approved through the Gram Sabha. One Ward Member, with the support of the Block Chairperson, tried to get sanction for the Panchayat office to be constructed in his area instead of Anaikkuppam. And he stated that he had made several arrangements to build up the basement, but Ms.Ponni filed a suit and got a stay of the construction. Then the judgment came in favour of the Panchayat. The people stated that there was no need to worry about a single Ward Member when the majority were with her. The people urged her to take necessary action against the Ward Member but she refused and convinced them not to take this issue very seriously.

Gram Sabha

In this Panchayat area, the traditional Panchayat leaders had indulged in felling of trees and selling them in an unauthorized way and it was found they used to pay a nominal sum by which they caused a great damage to the income of the Panchayat. The same group engaged in preparing illicit liquor and sold it in her Panchayat area and other places. She was determined to fight both. With great difficulty she managed to stop both with the help of the District Collector and police officials for which she faced a lot of problems.

Due to heavy rain the agricultural activities were disrupted. There was no other way for the farmers to engage in economic activities. The government assured to provide flood relief fund for the affected villages under the Namakku Naame scheme. The Gram Sabha decided to desilt all the ponds with the people's participation and the work was estimated at Rs.1 lakh and twenty thousand. When she approached the Panchayat Union office, they said that they would allot only forty thousand rupees. Then she decided to meet the Collector on this issue, and she met and spoke to the Collector. When she met the Collector and argued with him on this issue, the Collector, instead of discouraging her, encouraged her to maintain her assertiveness which, in fact, was a seed for her empowerment.

District Collector Visit

The District Collector, Mr.Umashankar, was known for his pro-active activities towards people, especially the poor and the Dalits. The Collector suggested that the Panchayat should give priority to strengthening the canal banks and the balance amount should be utilized for desiltation of ponds. Then he asked her to meet the Union officials and sanctioned an amount of fifty thousand from his own fund and motivated her to complete the work. She strengthened the canal banks and planted sixty thousand palm seedlings on the banks of the canals, which was done with the active participation of the people and continuous maintenance was undertaken by the Panchayat.

She stated that all this boldness and assertiveness was gained only due to the motivation given by a programme organized by the Social Welfare Board. In this three-day training programme, she had an opportunity to meet Dr.G.Palanithurai, Gandhigram Rural Institute and Ms.Kalapana Satish from HRF, Chennai. She came to know the logic of reservation of seats for women in Local Bodies from them and realized that women have to work vigorously to retain this position and do things which ought to be done. The reservation provided a political opportunity for women to participate in public activities. The Elected Women Representatives should speak out courageously without fear and shyness. They have to fight against the patriarchal society. They have to frequently approach government officials. Women have to work for the removal of proxy politics. The above were the ideas shared by Dr. G. Palanithurai, which increased the confidence of Ms.Ponni and initiated the idea for the formation of an association. When Dr. G. Palanithurai took class for the women leaders, he dealt at length on the need for a new kind of leadership to rejuvenate India. He also emphasized the importance of collective leadership. He further reiterated that in India unless the marginalized, weak and meak united and organized to raise their voice there wouldn't be any hope. She started thinking on this. She liked his words and wanted to learn more from Gandhigram Rural Institute. He also insisted on the Elected Women Representatives participating in all the meetings organized for them. She got a communication from Gandhigram Rural Institute and attended a 5-day programme along with her husband. After attending the five day training programme she came to know the full details of the Panchayat administration. If training is organized in the same manner as in Gandhigram in all other places, including SIRD, women's capacity can be built up within a short span of time. Having realized the importance of the training she requested the Gandhigram Rural Institute to organize training as well as follow-ups. So Gandhigram Rural Institute provided innumerable opportunities to Elected Women Representatives to participate in various programmes like training, seminars, consultancy meet, conventions and other meetings. As per her suggestion, the district administration of Thiruvarur provided an opportunity for the Panchayat Assistants to have capacity building training at Gandhigram Rural Institute along with the EWRs of Thiruvarur District.

In her family also there was no recognition for her, including from her husband. Her husband had faith in her when she was able to mobilize money through the bank for her husband's business. Initially her husband like others, thought that the Panchayat management could be carried out by him. She indirectly hinted that she had the capability to manage the Panchayat. Further she used to go to office regularly and contact the public and officials and thus she retained her space.

She was elected President for one more term because of the people who admired her boldness and fearless nature during the removal of encroachments and eradication of cheap liquor. Three persons who opposed her lost their deposits in the elections. She liked the position of leadership even though she had a dual burden—at home and outside.

Illegal sand mining was a regular activity in this area. Both politicians and the mafia, in collusion with officials, carried out this activity. She started opposing it and gave petitions to the Minister, and officials but none took steps to curb it. Finally, she stopped the trucks as they passed through the street where she lived and imposed a fine of Rs.800 per truck. It was paid but the officials objected that as such there was no such provision in the Panchayat rules. Nobody was ready to stop the illegal mining of sand. By making it public she arrested this practice. In this process she gained leadership. She received several threats.

Regarding the basic amenities she gave more preference to education than roads, street lights and others. She got two middle schools for Anaikkuppam and one primary school for Madamangalam. She provided the school with toilet facilities, drinking water, furniture and study materials. She attended all the Parent Teachers Association meetings without fail and also distributed prizes to the students during competitions.

As there was no road to the cremation ground, the people had to pass across a bamboo tree bridge and thorny bushes. The gravel roads had been encroached upon by several people. Due to her husband's membership in the political party she was not able to retrieve the road from the encroachers, who belonged to backward communities. When she approached the Tahsildar he refused to take up the issue and frankly said that he was not ready to fight against the influential people. Then she decided to leave the matter to the public. She called upon several people and widely discussed the matter. The people themselves assured her of their support, that they were ready to face any kind of situation. With the full support of the people she cleared the thorny bushes except the neem trees. She provided money to the parties who had reared the trees. The opponents filed a case against her. But she and the people never bothered or considered the opponents' attitude but courageously completed the work. She spent a full day in the court regarding this issue and won a victory. She was appreciated by the judge (who was a woman) in a public meeting because, without any lawyer or government officials, she was bold enough as a woman to succeed with the full support of the people.

Orienting Public for Namakku Naame Scheme

Receiving a flood relief fund of Rs.1,10,000, the Gram Sabha decided to utilize the fund for the desiltation of ponds and tanks. But they realized that the amount was not sufficient. Hence they decided to seek people's contribution and started to collect the money. Due to poor collection, they switched over to the Namakku Naame Scheme and combined the fund with flood relief fund and completed the desiltation work. A sum of Rs.17,500, being the balance, was deposited in the bank. The Thalathankudi Village people of her Panchayat required the money for the construction of a temple. When she suggested to them an alternative, they were not satisfied and complained to the District Collector along with the opponents, that the President had misused the amount. When she met the Collector, he asked her to meet the women of the village instead of their husbands and get their consent for the construction of a road instead of a temple. The Collector also assured his support for this process. The next Gram Sabha was organized in this village and convinced the people and finally, the road was completed with the consent of the people. The District Collector appreciated her in this regard.

Panchayat Vigilance and Public Action

There was a factory which produced raw materials for medicine, which engaged many labourers. There was no proper road between the village and the factory. The Panchayat decided to provide a gravel road of upto 5 kms. Then the work was entrusted to a local person who belonged to the SC community and who was the benami of an ex-MLA. But the person utilized only 8 loads of stones instead of 27 loads. When she warned him along with the people to ensure quality, he complained to the Police Department that she abused him in the name of his community. Due to the good rapport built up with the police officials, the police enquired into the same and told the opponents that she had the full support of the people. Then the person completed the work with good quality and now the people utilize this pucca road. The President shared that this happened only because of the entire people's support.

Welfare Activities for Women and Children

She emphasized the importance of education of girls from poor families. She referred to the marriage assistance scheme for the poor girls. She created awareness among the eligible couples of the significance of the small family norm and helped in organizing polio programme and ending alcoholism in the village. She organized various awareness campaigns regarding law, HIV/AIDS, health, agriculture and animal husbandry. The people of her Panchayat benefited by the camps.

Awareness Campaign

There are 25 women Self Help Groups which are involved in various economic development activities. They have formed groups on the basis of caste. They actively participate in the Panchayat and other public activities and approach the Presidents for many of the problems faced by them.

Awareness Campaign

A few SHGs belong to the Dalit community who served as labourers under wealthy Dalits. After forming a group they borrowed an agricultural land with borewell and engaged in agricultural activities. Some of them engaged themselves in goat and cow rearing and prepared roofing from coconut leaves. Some of the SHGs had undergone various income generating training programmes and started their activities with enthusiasm, but, due to poor marketing, they could not succeed and withdrew. At first the

Orienting SHGs

groups were formed by the President herself. Afterwards WARD, an NGO, continued the group formation processes. In the Gram Sabha, the SHGs asked for free house pattas, group houses, old age pension, training in income generation activities and, especially, a building for SHGs. Due to lack of SHGs building, they organized their meetings in their houses and under trees. During the eradication of cheap liquor, the SHGs actively participated in the agitation and supported the President and demonstrated against this menace and flashed it through the media. The cheap liquor packets were demolished on the roads. They never bothered about their husbands in this matter.

Orienting SHGs

They provided/sponsored furniture, tumblers, plates and other essential items to the schools and anganwadi. They distributed medicines to every house during medical camps organized for the eradication of various communicable diseases. They frequently visited the nutritious meal centre and checked the items along with the President. Under the Sanitation Committee, the SHGs, along with the VHN, organized meetings for the reproductive mothers and distributed iron tablets and nutritious food to for both teenage girls and mothers. They instructed the mothers about ANC, PNC and Child Health Care. They helped during the health camps and organized the provision of polio drops. For the 600 Dalit families the President distributed agricultural inputs and for the physically challenged she provided them with sheep and goats worth Rs.1000.

Youth Groups

Distribution of Agri. Inputs

The youth groups actively participated in every Panchayat activity. During the removal of thorns and bushes for the construction of a road to the cremation ground and during other critical situations they extended their help voluntarily. Under the Nehru Yuva Kendra they have been given sports ground and library. They have cleaned the temples and schools and desilted water tanks.

Award for Cent-per-cent Collection of House Tax

She was given an award by the District Collector for cent-per-cent collection of house tax and received the full house tax matching grant, which raised the

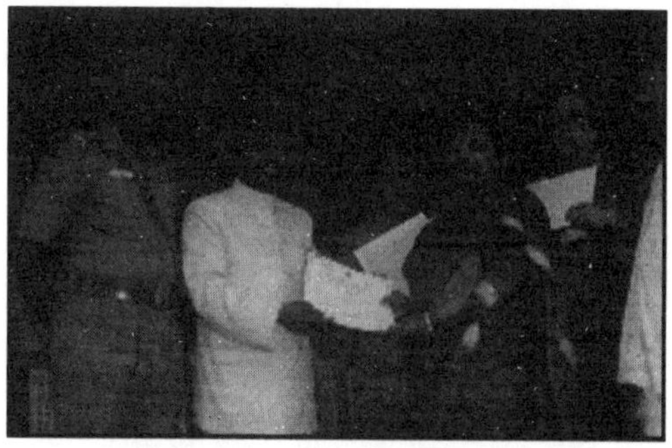

Honoured by District Collector

income of the Panchayat. She boldly announced that the people who have not paid the house tax would lose their free *dhotis*. This was accepted by the people and they paid the tax without fail. The house tax was increased with the approval of Gram Sabha. The District Collector appreciated her attending every meeting without fail and her active participation in Panchayat activities. She was honoured with a shield.

Formation of PHC

In her Panchayat, she identified a suitable site for the construction of a Primary Health Centre. It was in the custody of four families, but it was public property. She organized the villagers and informed them and finally, she met the families and persuaded them through government officials. When this failed to get a positive response, with the help of the villagers, she removed the encroachment and kept it clean for the construction. She met the Joint Director and appealed to him to commence the construction activities so that the expectation of the people would be realised as they themselves had been involved in the removal of encroachment. The health authorities acted quickly

Disilting Pond by SHGs

and the building was completed. The PHC is functioning well at present.

There was a bridge which connected Rajakalupour and Anaikkuppam. The bridge was old and in a damaged condition. The people have to cross the bridge to reach their place. This matter was seriously discussed in the Gram Sabha, which passed a resolution.

But the government agreed to provide only Rs.50,000 for the construction work. She directly met the Collector along with the people and explained the issue. The Collector appreciated her and sanctioned Rs.2 lakhs towards this construction process. Then the work was completed. In her Panchayat, the Panchayat roads are well laid. To avoid damages caused to roads due to rain, they raised the road at the centre and pipes were laid on either sides of the road to drain the water. They have planted 60,000 palm trees on the road sides, 200 trees for cattle feed and 100 tamarind trees. They have removed thorny bushes with full people's participation. The Panchayat gives preference to the maintenance of these trees. During the festivals like New Year, Adi-Perukku, Deepavali and Pongal the people themselves remove the thorny bushes and destroy them at the initial stage of growth. Trees have been planted upto 3.5 kms. For the construction of SHG building, sanitary complex and threshing floor, sites were identified with the support of the people. 200 road side encroachments were retrieved. To avoid rusting, they have provided copper gate valves and tap valves for the supply of drinking water. Among 1160 families, 246 families have no toilet facilities. They have decided to set right the same at the earliest.

Her Relationship with Ward Members

During the first term, out of nine Ward Members, three were women and four belonged to the SC. As she was apolitical and has faith in cooperation and partnership, she did not find it difficult to manage the Council. She was able to muster the support of all the Members and smoothly conducted Panchayat Council meetings.

Motivation to the Ward Members

Being a woman she considered the request of one woman Member and appointed her husband as the Panchayat Assistant. Moreover, she encouraged the Vice-President to get explanation from her for all activities as she wished to be transparent in Panchayat administration. This term there are 2 women Ward Members. One belongs to the BC and the other belongs to SC community. They have approached her for getting consultation during crises and sought various facilities for their people.

Creation of New Family Cards

She has prepared an elaborate permanent ration card which includes the entire details of the family. She listed the following merits of having this permanent family cards. They were Income Certificate, Birth Certificate, Death Certificate, Conduct Certificate, Tax due details, Community, Value of Property, Loan availed and Residential Certificate. She stated that this card will avoid unnecessary expenditure to the state. This card would be filled up with the support of the President, Vice-President, Council Members and the head of the family and she said that this card was sent to the Prime Minister of India along with details.

Her Development Perspective

She outlined the developmental perspective of her village as hereunder:

- Priority to desilt all ponds to store more water in tanks for recharge.
- Creating awareness on ecology and environment.
- Poverty alleviation through SHGs.
- Encouraging youth welfare activities as there is an immense potential in rural youth.
- Work for accelerating the process of public pressure in demanding 1/3 reservation in assemblies and Parliament as the womenfolk can play very effectively in rendering social justice and ensure gender perception in policy making.

Sources of Revenue

House tax, professional tax, stamp duty, cremation fund, house tax matching grant, 2C tree tax, plan approval fees, entertainment tax, advertisement tax and water tax are the main revenue sources of Anaikkuppam Panchayat. The Panchayat development activities carried out along with people's participation enriches the Panchayat income. It was honored as the best Panchayat, awarded for two years and provided with Rs.2 lakhs. The Panchayat financial transactions are transparent and every contribution is spelt out during the Gram Sabha. The President wisely approached the district level higher officials, narrated the positive and negative impacts of the problem and optimistically convinced them to allot the available financial resources and schemes for her Panchayat.

The Panchayat never met any audit objection and the Ward Members are also very cooperative in implementing various schemes and other public activities.

Financial Year 1996-1997

An amount of Rs.24,161 was received as stamp duty and an amount of Rs.5,840 was collected as house tax. Rs.5,489 was gained as house tax matching grant and Rs.772 was collected as 2C tree tax. The total income of the Panchayat was Rs.59,706. The Panchayat spent an amount of Rs.2,200, which was received as an incentive, for cremation. For the renovation work an amount of Rs.3,969 was spent and Rs.595 was spent for the maintenance of drinking water facility. Totally the amount spent for the year was Rs.71,886.

1997-1998

The SFC grant received for this financial year was Rs.1,79,420 and Rs.26,102 was collected as stamp duty. Rs.7,900 and Rs.590 were received as a profit from the coconut and tamarind trees. The house tax collected was Rs.8,610 and the entire income of the Panchayat was Rs.2,56,955. An amount of Rs.13,115 was spent for the salary of the OHT operator, the Panchayat Assistant, the TV operator and the street light operator. Rs.32,292 was spent as electricity charges for street lights. And most of the amount was spent for the purchase of materials for the maintenance of roads, street lights, OHTs and hand pumps.

1998-1999

The house tax was increased upto Rs.14,268 and Rs.12,057 was received as stamp duty. An amount of Rs.5,000 was received as cremation grant and totally an amount of Rs.1,88,476 was the income for this financial year. The Panchayat spent for the maintenance of OHTs, cremation ground, radio, television and road bridges. For sanitation purpose an amount of Rs.4,458 was spent. Rs.22,849 and Rs.26,956 were utilized for the construction of buildings and the maintenance of drinking water sources.

1999-2000

The Professional Tax collected was Rs.23,480 and Rs.15,017 was received as house tax. Rs.2,52,904 was the SFC grant received for the year 1999-2000. And most of the sources of income were from auctioning of trees, incentives for cremation ground, auction amount from the condemned old goods and stamp duty. An amount of Rs.84,100 was contributed for the Namakku Naame Scheme. The Panchayat workers' salary came upto Rs.24,981 and Rs.62,701 was spent for the electricity charges for the street lights. Rs.21,100 was spent for the creation of social forest and orchards. The total amount spent for the year was Rs.4,38,997.

2000-2001

Rs.2,61,507 was received as SFC grant, and Rs.40,907 as house tax matching grant and Rs.40,050 as stamp duty. Rs.1 lakh was got for the best Panchayat award and Rs.52,500 allotted the Namakku Naame Scheme. The total income was Rs.5,85,199. Rs.18,500 was utilized for the formation of social forestry. New street lights were provided for Rs.27,622 and for the extension of pipelines Rs.79,832 was spent. Most of the money was spent for the maintenance of water sources like ponds, water tanks and wells. Rs.14,263 was utilized for the construction of sports ground.

2001-2002

The total income for this financial year was Rs.6,41,104 and an amount of Rs,2,19,470 was got under the SFC grant. The house tax collection was Rs.17,989 and Rs.66,482 was received as stamp duty. This year also the Panchayat was provided with an amount of Rs.1 lakh as the best Panchayat award. Rs.52,074 and Rs.40,176 were spent for electricity charges for street lights and for motor pumps. For the construction of new roads Rs.2,08,000 was utilized and Rs.48,216 was spent for the extension of pipe lines. Towards sanitation purpose Rs.19,100 was utilized and totally the expenditure for this year was Rs.7,44,835.

Best Panchayat Award

Best Panchayat Award

2002-2003

An amount of Rs.2,91,015 was received as SFC grant and the stamp duty amount was Rs.70,699. Rs.18,845.50 was the income from plan approval and Rs.12,491 as local cess. Other income are house tax, 2C tree tax, water tax, advertisement tax and professional tax, the total income constitutes Rs.5,45,327. The total expenditure for this year was Rs.5,45,327. The major amount was utilized for electricity charges towards motor pump, building and maintenance of street lights and other expenditure sources are public sanitation, maintenance of roads, ponds and buildings, cremation grant and Panchayats contribution towards the work held under 11th Finance Commission.

2003-2004

The total income of this above financial year was Rs.4,95,745.68. Rs.34,322.50 and Rs.29,610 the income received from house and professional taxes. Rs.85,183 was got from stamp duty and Rs.30,000 was an income from drinking water scheme fund. Most of the income sources for this year was from auction, provision of licence, plan approval, advertisement and tree tax. The total expenditure constituted for this year was Rs.4,63,190. A huge amount of Rs.1,24,262 and Rs.5,109 was utilized for electricity charges and Rs.58,375 was spent for the maintenance of OHTs. Other exceeding expenditures were maintenance of roads, bridges, public sanitation purposes, social forestry and salary. For the maintenance of street lights Rs.66,976 was spent.

PART - II

ASSOCIATION ACTIVITIES

In the year 1996, Ms. Kalpana, the programme organizer of HRF, Chennai, organized a meeting for the Elected Women Representatives of Thiruvarur District, where at she asked Ms. Ponni to form an Elected Women Representatives Association which would exclusively enable women to voice their problems and motivate them to work independently without fear. But she stated that, due to familial responsibility, she was not able to take up the idea of the formation of an Association. The other Elected Women Representatives didn't respond regarding association formation. Then Kalpana urged Ms.Ponni to raise her voice as a representative of all Elected Women Representatives. This sowed the seed her mind. She analysed each and every situation related to work and to raise her voice against not only Panchayat issues but those of Elected Women Representatives who were all criticized by their male counterparts from home to public life. Then they formed the Association along with the other members of Thiruvarur District.

Even though she had not fully involved herself in the ideas of an Association, Gandhigram Rural Institute provided continuous opportunity to analyse the problems faced by women representatives. Gandhigram Rural Institute suggested that the Elected Women Representatives had to have their own organisation to voice their grievances. She was very much interested to learn how to tackle the complicated issues through the pro-Panchayat officials, especially with the support of Gandhigram Rural Institute. This encouraged her to challenge any kind of atrocities with the support and the full participation of the people. She analysed every issue and involved herself optimistically.

Discussion with Association Memebrs

Association Meeting

She realized the need for an association exclusively for women. When the women Presidents were criticized by the men during the union meetings. They criticised them and never gave them an opportunity to speak. If the women themselves tried to answer, they were discouraged by the males including the government officials. The government officials also did not consider the ideas given by these women. Before getting capacity building programmes from Gandhigram Rural Institute, the NGO (HRF) continuously approached her for organizing several meetings for women and motivated them to take up responsibility and raise their voice against the atrocities committed against women Presidents. When a Corporation Councillor, Leelavathy, was murdered, the supportive Institute staff member motivated the EWRs of Thiruvarur District to agitate on this issue. But it could not happen suddenly. The EWRs, who were expected to organize the meeting were a vulnerable target. Hence they planned to organize a meeting in the name of impacts caused by salt producing lands. The NGO struggled strongly to join them collectively and finally organized a meeting with 55 members among 432 Panchayat Presidents of

Meeting with other state representatives

Thiruvarur District. In this meeting they brought up the Leelavathy murder issue under the lights of the media and made the government take necessary action against the culprits. In this meet they selected the district representative and invited her for every programme held regarding local self governance to address the issue of Thiruvarur District.

Meeting with other state representatives

With the active support of Gandhigram Rural Institute, she has acquired various opportunities like participation in training, seminars, workshops, conferences, training of trainers programmes, media workshops, exposure visits, interface with higher officials and other programmes. With the support of Gandhigram Rural Institute, the women Presidents have a space for lobbying and linkages with supportive organizations. She has registered the Association with the guidance given by Gandhigram Rural Institute. She got adequate information from Gandhigram Rural Institute during several crises and also shared her experiences.

Interface with Prime Minister

Interface with Chief Minister

Likewise she has attended every meeting organized for both men and women representatives of local self-governance. She has boldly pointed out the problems faced by women in front of officials, politicians, experts, and media without fear. Even though she felt shy that she was not able to speak even in the Panchayat meetings at the initial stage of her leadership, now the situation is entirely changed. She frequently meets the EWRs of various districts,

Interface with Panchayati Raj Minister

Interface with TNCC President

has more interface with district administrators, officials, higher officials, political party representatives and media to project not only Panchayat issues but also highlight the demands of all the EWRs of Tamil Nadu.

Interface with DRD

Interface with DMK President

Observation

Even though the 73rd Constitutional Amendment provides the opportunity for women's participation in the political arena, many men decided to take up the leadership in the name of women as wives, mothers, daughters, etc. They wanted to handle the position behind women's leadership. Likewise, in the case of Ms.Ponni, who was timid, shy, and fearful to come out of the house and to raise her voice in front of males or the public, the entire village was tied up with cultural norms and traditional taboos.

Despite the traditional taboos, she tried to learn about the Panchayat administration along with her husband's support. She wanted to carry out Panchayat activities with people's participation and aimed at making her village self-sufficient with all basic amenities. She approached the government officials and pro-Panchayat members at the right time for getting financial aid for the Panchayats. The training undergone in Gandhigram Rural Institute, not only enriched her leadership quality but also facilitated a good rapport with the government officials, politicians and the media. Gandhigram Rural Institute provided a platform for her to meet several Panchayat experts and provided relevant information with support during severe crises. She was interested in visiting several states to enhance her leadership qualities and to share her experience with other state leaders and experts. Her motive is to become a Member of the Legislative Assembly. She tirelessly proposed herself to get an MLA or MP seat with the support of the political parties. She assumed that the powers were in the hands of politicians. She revealed her policy that if she becomes a politician, she will surely provide her entire support to Panchayats.

The Association gave her more experience with the support of the committee members from various districts. It has created a cordial relationship with the higher officials, who respond to them, whenever they point out issues. The politicians also highlight the Panchayat issues during the Assembly sessions. She is the role model for opportunity seekers.

Success Gained by the Association

The issues highlighted by the Association to the higher officials, politicians and the media brought success in certain issues after a long struggle. They are the following :

1. Extension of reservation of seats for women for one more term without rotating the seats every five years.
2. Eradication of cheap liquor.
3. The benamis of Women Councillors and Panchayat Presidents were arrested.
4. Government programmes were drafted with the support of the Elected Women Representatives.
5. Hike in Central Government Scheme Fund.
6. Rescue of Elected Women Representatives from Section 205 of Tamil Nadu Panchayat Act of 1994.
7. The Government issued an Order to District

and State higher officials to convene periodical meeting to sort out problems.

8. Scheme fund activities handed over to Dalit women Panchayat Presidents.
9. Interface with traditional Panchayat leaders to settle many of the issues.

Conclusion

It was learnt that if she could further improve her leadership she would be a successful candidate for the Legislative Assembly. She admitted that she will also opt for that position provided her husband extends the same encouragement and support.

She has identified her worth and potential and she has shut down all her inhibitions. She has developed her confidence in managing public affairs. More particularly she has developed a flaming aspiration to achieve something that provides needed energy to carry out all her activities. She had an advantage in the family. Her husband is always positive and cooperative in all her activities. It is proved through her case that the Panchayat is the nursery of our democracy.

THE TAMIL NADU WOMEN PANCHAYAT PRESIDENTS ASSOCIATION

(Activities Carried Out)

Sl. No.	*Date*	*Name of the Event*	*Place*	*Major Issues Discussed*	*Resource Persons*
1.	20.8.2000	State Level NGOs Network Meet	Gandhigram Rural Institute	Alliance building, periodical sensitization of EWRs on women issues, strengthening the association activities, inadequate skills and capacity, non-cooperation of the officials and party leaders and other state experiences were shared	GRI team, Dr.B.S.Bhargava, Senior Fellow, ISS, Karnataka, Thiru. Chidambaram (Retd. ADRD). Thiru. Vallinayagam (Retd. ADRD), Mr. Rajagopalan, Chairman, Administrative Committee, Gandhigram Trust
2.	26.8.2000	State Level Consultation Meet	Gandhigram Rural Institute	Dissemination of information to empower women, gender sensitization for both men and women, supporting women leaders for their effective functioning need for organisational support, women issues are identified from Public Distribution System, primary education, primary health care, environmental sanitation and family planning, overcoming personal hurdles, etc.	Dr. G. Palanithurai, Dr. G. Pankajam, NGOs and women activists
3.	18.10.2000	I State Convention/ State Committee Meet	Chennai	Formation of Association and selection of State Committee Members	—
4.	21.12.2000	Regional Level Meet	Madurai	Caste leaders never allowed to function EWRs belonged to SC community, obstacles caused by family members, discriminated by male members, dominate role played by illicit liquor political issues are sensitized rather development issues, non-cooperation of government officials, information are not properly disseminated by government officials, etc.	Dr.G.Palanithurai, GRI, NGOs like EKTA and RCPED, Madurai District
5.	2.2.2001	Regional Network Meet	Thirukkuvalai	Intensive training for EWRs, linkage with women's organisations and other supportive institutions, monthly salary for EWRs, reorganization of the Village Panchayat constituencies, handover sand quarry to Panchayats, rotation of seats effected once in ten years, etc.	Dr. G. Palanithurai, GRI team, SEVALAYA Thirukkuvalai

(Contd. ...)

(Contd. ...)

Sl. No.	*Date*	*Name of the Event*	*Place*	*Major Issues Discussed*	*Resource Persons*
6.	6.2.2001	Regional Network Meet	Chengalpet	Dalit EWRs are unaware of New Panchayati Raj System, GOs and other information are not reaching in time, officials are more dominated, interference of political parties, non-cooperation of caste Hindu members, inadequacy of funds to Dalit communities, threat on Section 205, etc.	Dr. V. Ragupathy, GRI and LRSA, Chengalpet
7.	17.2.2001	Selection of State Committee Members	Madurai	Problems faced by EWRs and selection of Association President Ms.Pankajam and Secretary Ms. Ponnikailasam	Tmt. Vasanthi Devi, the Former Vice-Chancellor of Manonmaniam Sundaranar University
8.	16.3.2001	II State Committee Meet	Chennai	Strategies for strengthening the local self-governance, extension of reservation for women for one more term, cooperation from the government officials, allocation of funds to Panchayat and devolution of powers over 29 subjects	Chief Minister of Tamil Nadu, Opposition Party leaders and Members of Legislative Assembly
9.	21.3.2001	Regional Network Meet	Aravanampet	Domination by male counterparts and caste leaders, ill treatment by various government department officials, proper information was not disseminated, lack of organizational support, obstacles due to dual responsibility, degradation of natural resources, lack of capacity building training, etc.	GRI team and NGO members from AREDS, Karur
10.	1.3.2001 30.4.2001	District-wise Meeting	Organized in Various Districts	Selection of District-wise Committees and office bearers, Issues discussed in each districts	District Collectors
11.	5.4.2001	Press Meet	Chennai	Urapakkam Panchayat President's murder	Rural Development Director and Media
12.	3.5.2001	District Level Meet	Nagapattinam	Illegal theft of silicon sand in Vanduvancheri Panchayat	Nagapattinam District Collector & Media
13.	9.5.2001	Workshop on District Development Planning	SSF, Bangalore	Shared Other State Experiences	Panchayat Presidents from Kerala, Karnataka and Andhra Pradesh
14.	25.6.2001	III State Committee Meet	Chennai	Sufficient funds to Panchayats, cooperation from government officials, devolution of power over 29 subjects	Rural Development Secretary and State Planning Commission Secretary and Media

(Contd. ...)

(Contd. ...)

Sl. No.	*Date*	*Name of the Event*	*Place*	*Major Issues Discussed*	*Resource Persons*
15.	27.8.2001	IV State Committee Meet	Chennai	Provision of several rights to Panchayats and fund allocation to Panchayats	Members of Legislative Assembly, Opposition Political Party leaders and Press
16.	19.12.2001	V State Committee Meet	Chennai	Selection of New Association President and Committee members. Like Kerala, rights over 29 subjects should be handed over to Panchayats, removal of encroachments, Police and Revenue Departments Panchayat friendly, proper fund allocation by Central and State Governments	Tamil Nadu Government officials and Press
17.	6.1.2002	Network Meeting	Thiruvarur	Need for the association, basic objectives of decentralized governance, multi-level planning, officials support during the removal of encroachments, issues of community and nativity certificate through Panchayats, periodical fund release, removal of cheap liquor, synergization of SHGs, etc.	GRI team
18.	22.1.2002 to 23.1.2002	Exposure Visit (first)	Kerala	Exchanging ideas and experiences with other state Panchayati Raj System	GRI team and Kerala Panchayat
19.	2.2.2002	Annual Mela	Gandhigram Rural Institute	Increasing the allocation of scheme funds by the Central Government	Central Minister of Rural Development Thiru. Venkaiah Naidu and Media
20.	8.2.2002	Exposure Visit (second)	Kerala	Exchanging ideas and experiences with other state Panchayati Raj System	GRI team and Kerala Panchayat
21.	19.2.2002 to 20.2.2002	Public hearing Meet	Chennai	Problem Faced by EWRs and the non-cooperation of government officials, more interface with District higher officials	Director of Rural Development and Media
22.	20.2.2002	Women Panchayat leaders meet	Gandhigram Rural Institute	Economic activities for SHGs, synergization between SHGs and Panchayats, exploitation of natural resources, increasing the SGSY earmarked fund, domination of bureaucrats, problems faced by Dalit women representatives, periodical funds to Panchayats, etc.	Dr. G. Palanithurai, Dr. G. Pankajam, Hon'ble Rural Development Minister Shri Venkiah Naidu, Thiru P. C. Panda, Rural Development Joint Secretary and Thiru. S. Aiyar, DRD

(Contd. ...)

(Contd. ...)

Sl. No.	*Date*	*Name of the Event*	*Place*	*Major Issues Discussed*	*Resource Persons*
23.	1.3.2002	Consultation Meet	Gandhigram Rural Institute	Problems faced by women and non-cooperation of government officials	Dr. G. Palanithurai, Gandhigram Rural Institute, DRD, Chennai
24.	13.3.2002	VI State Committee Meet	Madurai	Status of Village Panchayats, and hurdles for the EWRs during Panchayat administration	Legislative Assembly Members, Opposition Political Party Leaders and Media
25.	15.4.2002 to 16.4.2002	State Level Meet	Chennai	Allocation of funds to Panchayats, retrieval of common property resources, etc.	Legislative Assembly Members, Opposition Political Party Leaders and Media
26.	23.4.2002 to 24.4.2002	Exposure Visit (third)	Kerala	Exchanging ideas and experiences with other state Panchayati Raj System	GRI team and Kerala Panchayat
27.	9.5.2002	Second Annual Meet	Gandhigram Rural Institute	Discussion on the 15 point programme and the powers conferred upon Panchayats, strengthening the Tamil Nadu Council for EWRs and more importance given to social development issues	Dr. G. Palanithurai, Dr. G. Pankajam, Thiru. S. Ayyar, I.A.S., Director of Rural Development, Dr. Senthil Kumar, I.A.S., District Collector, Dindigul
28.	9.5.2002	Special Meet	Gandhigram Rural Institute	Critical evaluation on the possible role of Panchayats in the implementation process of the 15 point programme the expected barriers and obstacles, general Panchayat administrative problems, strategy for strengthening the federation, etc.	GRI team Dr. Mark Robinson, Ford Foundation, New Delhi
29.	29.5.2002	District Level Meet	Pudukkottai	Major Issues of the District	District Collector and Project Officer of Rural Development Pudukkottai
30.	20.7.2002	District Level Meet	Karur	Major Issues of the District	District Collector and Rural Development higher Officials, Karur
31.	30.7.2002	VII State Committee Meet	Madurai	Problems faced by EWRs and hurdles during Panchayat administration, condemned the removal of Panchayat Presidents under Section 205	District Collector, Madurai
32.	1.8.2002	Interface with DRD	Chennai	Condemned the removal of Panchayat Presidents under Section 205	Director of Rural Development, Chennai

(Contd. ...)

(Contd. ...)

Sl. No.	*Date*	*Name of the Event*	*Place*	*Major Issues Discussed*	*Resource Persons*
33.	6.8.2002	Consultation on Education	Chennai	Compulsory education to children under Tamil Nadu Education Act 1997. Schools should be brought under the control of Panchayats	Resource Persons from Human Rights and Research Insitute
34.	27.9.2002	District Level Meet	Trichy	Lack of sand rights to Panchayats, lack of auction income from quarries, retrieval of common property resources and problems faced by EWRs	District Collector, District Panchayat Chairman, and Media, Trichy
35.	11.10.2002	Campaign on Atrocities Against Women	Chennai	Atrocities against women, creation of rehabilitation centres for women and children and the performance of police officials	Resource persons from NGOs and Police Department
36.	28.12.2002	VIII State Committee Meet	Chennai	Strategies for the effective functioning of local self-governance and frequent interface with DRD	Director of Rural Development and Media
37.	18.12.2002 to 19.12.2002	ToT & NGO Network Meet	Chennai	Alliance building with NGOs	NGO persons
38.	8.2.2003	District-wise Meet	Nagapattinam	Problems faced by EWRs, non-cooperation of government officials in Panchayat activities, desiltation of ponds (like Andhra Government) to raise the ground water level, etc.	District Collector and Rural Development Department Officials, Nagapattinam
39.	17.2.2003	State Convention	Chennai	50 per cent of allotment of funds from the revenue to Panchayats, rights over the maintenance of local natural resources, removal of Section 205, power to take decisions on action plans, rights over 29 Subjects, reduction of Panchayat electricity charges, etc.	Dr.Vasanthi Devi, Chairperson State Commission for Women, Tamil writers like Tmt. Rajam Krishnan, Tmt. Vasanthi, Tmt. Rooth Manorama, Chairperson of National Women's Federation and Dr. Reginapapa, Centre for Women Studies
40.	3.3.2003	IX State Committee Meet	Gandhigram Rural Institute	The problems faced by the EWRs. Strengthen the federation as a registered body	Dr. G. Palanithurai, Coordinator, Rajiv Gandhi Chair for Panchayati Raj Studies, Gandhigram Rural Institute Team
41.	27.3.2003	X State Committee Meet	Chennai	Condemned the interference of Traditional Panchayat leaders and	Thiru.Sampath, Tamil Nadu State Minister of Rural

(Contd. ...)

(Contd. ...)

Sl. No.	Date	Name of the Event	Place	Major Issues Discussed	Resource Persons
				political parties in Panchayat activities and atrocities happened	Development, Members of Legislative Assembly and Opposition Party leaders and media
42.	24.4.2003 to 25.4.2003	Celebration of 73rd Amendment (came into force)	New Delhi	The success stories of Association was shared with other state EWRs	Resource persons, ISS, New Delhi
43.	26.4.2003	Put Forth Resolution to political party Leaders	New Delhi	Put forth the status of Tamil Nadu Panchayat report, increasing the allotment of SGRY scheme fund, and 10th Finance	Tmt.Sonia Gandhi & Media
44.	14.6.2003	District Level Meet	Thiruvarur	Problems faced by the EWRs	District Panchayat and Rural Development Officials, Thiruvarur
45.	11.7.2003	Interface with DRD	Chennai	Retrieval of common property resources, increasing the allocation of SFC grant, power over 29 subjects, and seeking for the submission of unpaid grant	District Collector with rural development officials Rural Development Director and Media
46.	30.7.2003	Meeting with the World Bank Officials	Gandhigram Rural Institute	Social development issues, community mobilization in social development activities	World Bank Team, District Collector, Director of WDC, Chennai
47.	21.10.2003	Consultation Meet	Gandhigram Rural Institute	Strengthening block level association, orientation on women's issues, alliance building with NGOs, SHGs, women's organizations and pro-Panchayat members, capacity building exercise, publication of newsletter, etc.	Dr.G.Palanithurai, various women organizations and NGOs
48.	27.12.2003	Regional Workshop	Thiruvarur	Problems faced by the EWRs during Panchayat administration, sensitization on gender and social development issues, alliance building, strategies for strengthening federation activities, etc.	EWRs of Nagapattinam, Tanjore and Thiruvarur, Dr. G. Palanithurai
49.	14.2.2004	XI State Committee Meet	Chennai	33.3 per cent reservation for women in Parliament, devolution of powers to Panchayats and the political parties should provide 33.3 per cent seats to women in their parties for MLA/MP	Media, Chennai
50.	14.2.2004	Interface with DRD	Chennai	8 per cent allocation of funds from the revenue and increasing the SFC	DRD, Chennai

(Contd. ...)

(Contd. ...)

Sl. No.	*Date*	*Name of the Event*	*Place*	*Major Issues Discussed*	*Resource Persons*
51.	16.2.2004	Interface with Higher Officials	Chennai	Reduction of electricity charges to avoid financial crisis, removal of section 205, MLA/MP Constituency Fund works should be intimated, retrieval of common property resources especially silicon sand and political parties are insisted to take up Panchayat issues in their party manifesto	Director of Rural Development, Political Party Leaders and Media
52.	17.2.2004 to 19.2.2004	Interface Programme	SSF, Bangalore	Experience shared with other state EWRs	EWRs from Kerala, Karnataka and Andhra
53.	11.2.2004 to 3.3.2004	Networking EWRs during capacity building training	Gandhigram Rural Institute	Problems faced by the EWRs during Panchayat administration, sensitization on gender and social development issues, alliance building, strategies from strengthening federation activities, etc.	EWRs of Tuticorin District, PRI team, Gandhigram Rural Institute
54.	21.4.2004	State Committee Meeting	Chennai	Support from the political parties for devolution of powers, 33 per cent of reservation for women in Parliament, eradication of proxy politics, strengthening the block level federation, cooperation from government officials, etc.	Ms.Kalpana Sathish and Media
55.	21.4.2004	XII State Committee Meet	Chennai	The political parties hesitated to provide more powers to local self-governance, the Central fund allocation to various State Government Departments not reached the Panchayats. Direct funds to Panchayats.	Prime Minister, Political Party leaders and Media
56.	24.4.2004 to 25.4.2004	Celebration of 73rd Amendment (passed Date)	New Delhi	The successful activities of the Association shared with other State EWRs	Resource Persons from ISS, New Delhi
57.	20.5.2004	Regional Workshop	Salem	Support from the political parties for devolution of powers, 33 per cent of reservation for women in Parliament, eradication of proxy politics, strengthening the block level federation, cooperation from government officials, etc.	Dr.G.Palanithurai, EWRs of Salem, Namakkal and Dharmapuri Districts

(Contd. ...)

(Contd. ...)

Sl. No.	Date	Name of the Event	Place	Major Issues Discussed	Resource Persons
58.	14.6.2004 to 18.6.2004	Networking EWRs during Capacity building training	Gandhigram Rural Institute	Panchayat Administrative skills, social development issues, village development plan, and Association of Elected Women Representatives	EWRs of Cuddalore District, PRI Team, Gandhigram Rural Institute
59.	16.6.2004	Honoring the Congress Party Leader for the Formation of Exclusive Ministry for Panchayati Raj	—	Praised the Central Government for creating a separate ministry for Panchayati Raj. Allotment of separate fund for education, sanitation and women development	Media
60.	21.6.2004	XIV State Committee Meet	Chennai	Devolution of powers to Panchayats	DRD, Chennai and Media
61.	21.6.2004 to 25.6.2004	Networking EWRs during capacity building training	Gandhigram Rural Institute	Panchayat Administrative skills, social development issues, village development plan, and Association of Elected Women Representatives	EWRs of Tirunelveli District, PRI team, Gandhigram Rural Institute
62.	11.7.2004	XIII State Committee Meet	Chennai	Reduction of EB charges from Rs.3.40 to Rs.1.60 per unit, requisition of unpaid SFC Grant for the year 2001-2002	DRD, Chennai and Media
63.	10.7.2004	State Committee Meet	Chennai	Implementation of all state government schemes through Panchayats, provision of computers to Panchayats, income generating training programmes for SHGs, reduction of EB charges, income from cable TV tax, birth and death records handed over to Panchayats, etc.	Demands sent to the Chief Minister of Tamil Nadu, and Media
64.	20.7.2004 to 21.7.2004	Exposure Visit	Coimbatore District	Utilization of available local resources, implementation of non-conventional energy sources, social development issues, Panchayat administration with people's participation, etc.	Odanthurai and Semmipalayam Panchayat Presidents
65.	1.8.2004	Media Workshop	Trichy	The problems faced by EWRs and the present status of Panchayats, condemned the political party for not supporting the provision of direct central funds to Panchayat accounts.	Media

(Contd. ...)

(Contd. ...)

Sl. No.	*Date*	*Name of the Event*	*Place*	*Major Issues Discussed*	*Resource Persons*
66.	7.8.2004	District Level Meet	Thiruvarur	Drought Relief Fund, prevention of drinking water crisis, hike in electricity charges, decreasing level of ground water level, insufficient allocation of funds blockade of day-to-day Panchayat activities	District Collector, Rural Development Department officials and Media
67.	29.8.2004 to 30.8.2004	Exposure Visit	Coimbatore District	Utilization of available local resources, implementation of non-conventional energy sources, social development issues, Panchayat administration with people's participation, etc.	Odanthurai and Semmipalayam Panchayat Presidents
68.	7.9.2004	Network Meet	New Delhi	Two Child Norm	Human Rights Law, Network Resource Persons, New Delhi and Press
69.	12.9.2004	Consultation Meet	Chennai	Tamil Nadu Government's non-allocation of funds to Panchayats, income from cable TV tax, tree auction, reduction of electricity charges, etc.	Media
70.	27.10.2004 to 28.10.2004	Exposure Visit	Coimbatore District	Utilization of available local resources, implementation of non-conventional energy sources, social development issues, Panchayat administration with people's participation, etc.	Odanthurai and Semmipalayam Panchayat Presidents
71.	24.11.2004	XV State Committee Meet	Gandhigram Rural Institute	Allocation of special funds for the maintenance of roads, reduction of EB charges, etc.	Media
72.	20.12.2004 to 29.12.2004	Networking EWRs during Capacity Building Training	Gandhigram Rural Institute	Panchayat Administrative skills, social development issues, village development plan, and Association of Elected Women Representatives	Dr.G.Palanithurai, PRI team and EWRs of Thiruvarur District
73.	30.12.2004 to 3.1.2005	Networking EWRs during Capacity Building Training	Gandhigram Rural Institute	Panchayat Administrative skills, social development issues, village development plan, and Association of Elected Women Representatives	Dr.G.Palanithurai, PRI team and EWRs of Erode District
74.	29.1.2005	Tsunami Consultation Meet	Chennai	The malpractices happened during the provision of tsunami relief fund and corruption	Resource persons from ISS, Chennai, The Central Minister of Panchayati Raj,

(Contd. ...)

(Contd. ...)

Sl. No.	*Date*	*Name of the Event*	*Place*	*Major Issues Discussed*	*Resource Persons*
				occurred during the adoption of orphans, the missed persons list should be taken by Panchayats	Opposition Political Party Leaders and Media
75.	5.3.2005	XVI State Committee Meet	Chennai	Devolution of powers to Panchayats, unpaid grant for the previous years, reduction of EB charges, etc.	DRD, Chennai, members of the Legislative Assembly, Opposition Political Party Leaders and Media
76.	21.3.2005	Interface with DRD	Chennai	Sufficient fund allocation to Panchayats, higher officials cooperation during the removal of encroachments, reduction of EB charges, etc.	Rural Development Department Higher officials and Press, Chennai
77.	21.4.2005	Interface with Political Party Leaders and President of India	New Delhi	Demands like increasing SFC grant, reduction of EB charges, retrieval of common property resources, power over 29 subjects, etc.	President of India and Tamil Nadu Congress Party Leader
78.	25.4.2005 to 26.4.2005	Celebration of 73rd Amendment	New Delhi	Association shared its experience with other State EWRs, Formation of All India Level Association and Strategies for Strengthening the state Federation	Resource persons from ISS, New Delhi, Hon'ble Minister of Panchayati Raj
79.	15.5.2005	Annual Mela	Gandhigram Rural Institute	Pollution Control, retrieval of common property resources, increasing SFC grant, EWRs meet with higher officials, computer to Panchayats, etc.	Dr.G.Palanithurai, DRD, ADRD, Chennai, Thiru. A.K.Venkata Subramanian, Director, Catalyst Trust, and Dr.Muthukumaran, Former Vice-Chancellor, Chennai
80.	22.5.2005	Regional Workshop	Gandhigram Rural Institute	Experience sharing with West Bengal Panchayati Raj Minister, Governance of Health, Governance of Education, Governance of Environment issues and marginalized are the issues elaborately discussed	West Bengal Panchayati Raj Minister and Dr. G. Palanithurai

Sl. No.	*Major Issues Discussed*	*Response*
1.	Extension of reservation for women to one more term	Achieved extension of reservation
2.	Brutal murder of Urapakkam Panchayat President	The culprits are arrested
3.	Increasing the allocation of scheme funds by the Central Government	The Scheme Fund was doubled
4.	Frequent interface with District higher officials	Got a Government Order for having interface with District higher officials every month
5.	Condemned the removal of Panchayat Presidents under Section 205	Rescue the Presidents booked under the Section 205
6.	Frequent interface with State higher officials	Got a Government Order for having interface with State higher officials every month
7.	Disiltation of ponds to raise ground water level	Nagapattinam District Administration ordered to desilt all the Panchayat ponds under the financial year 2003-2004
8.	Condemned the political parties' interference in Dalit women Panchayat activities with mafias	Scheme Fund activities was handed over to the Panchayat
9.	Requested the government for the provision of computers to Panchayat.	The Panchayat provided with computers.
10.	Demands put forth to the Members of the Legislative Assembly, Opposition Political Party Leaders	Various political parties and the Minister of Rural Development raised their voice during Legislative Assembly session
11.	Prevention of violence against women through the eradication of cheap liquor	Eradication of cheap liquor
12.	Implementation of 15 point programme by the State Government	15-point programme drafted along with the suggestions referred by the EWRs
13.	List of beneficiaries selected by the officials	The list of beneficiaries modified at the request of EWRs
14.	Unsolved district administration crisis take over to the notice of State Higher Officials	District Collectors were instructed over phone to take necessary action regarding their request.

CASE - 15

CLEAN VILLAGE

The Panchayat President of Tjamaraikulam is known for sanitation and a clean village. He made it a point that one has to take a difficult and challenging task and he or she has to achieve it by which one can become popular among the people. Hence he decided to take up sanitation work. He knew pretty well how difficult it is in the rural areas. Rainwater harvesting is yet another striking activity. He prepared a plan for the development of Tamaraikulam Gram Panchayat. For all his Panchayat works he fully relied on the support of the community. Government departments show this Village Panchayat as a model for the clean village concept. He involved the SHG members in Panchayat activities.

Village Setting

Mr. S. Sivalingam is the President of Thamaraikulam Village Panchayat of Mandapam Panchayat Union in Ramanathapuram District. It is situated 7 k.m. from Uchipuli on the Ramanathapuram to Rameswaram National Highway. The major caste groups in the Panchayat are Nadars, SCs, Thevars and a few others. Health and sanitation facilities are available in all villages and toilets are also available in all the houses. A public toilet with attached bathroom is available for women in Thamaraikulam Village. A number of public institutions are functioning in this Panchayat and they are Schools, Primary Health Centre, District Cooperative Bank, Library and Veterinary Hospital. There are 632 houses and 3952 population in this Panchayat area as per the 1991 census. Caste organizations function actively in this Panchayat and 16 SHGs have been recently formed. An NGO helps in the formation of SHGs and they are involved in economic and social development activities. SHGs have developed a good relations with the Village Panchayat. As he is in the Panchayat system both in the old and in the new, Mr. Sivalingam has a fervor to make this Panchayat a model Panchayat.

Socio-economic Background of the President

Mr. Sivalingam is 56 years old and he has completed pre-university course and belongs to a backward community, the Nadar caste. He has two sons. Both are married. One is working in a computer company in Malaysia and the other one is running an ice cream bar in a nearby town. He owns agriculture land and cultivates coconut. He also owns a printing press. His economic background is very sound. He belongs to the DMK party. In 1996, when the elections to the Village Panchayat was announced, his friends and well wishers advised him to contest in the elections. Since 1986 the villagers have elected him repeatedly in spite of some opposition to him.

Recruitment Process

The traditional village committee met to take a decision on the selection of a candidate unopposed. But there was opposition to this idea. So, the village committee did not take any decision. His elder brother told him to file his nomination and the majority of the members agreed to support him. The opposition candidate belonged to the AIADMK party. The villagers openly encouraged his candidature as he was better educated than the opponent.

Mr. Sivalingam and six other candidates for Wards joined together as a group. The opponent also belonged to his community and was also his relative. There was a tough competition but they observed peace and so there was no untoward incident.

Clean Village Campaign

When the government took the initiative for improving the sanitation of the village, Sivalingam decided to make his Village Panchayat a clean one. His effort to provide toilet to all families materialized after the construction of a new sanitary complex. When a few men failed to desist from the habit of open defection, the Village Panchayat formed a Monitoring Committee. This committee put up a notice board warning that open defecation is prohibited in the Panchayat area and any violation will be dealt with a fine of Rs.100. Four individuals were caught in this regard. The issue was brought to the notice of the

Clean Village

Gram Sabha and, as per the decision of the Gram Sabha, a fine of Rs.100 each was collected from them.

Approach Adopted

- To start the activity awareness campaign has been conducted and wall paintings, video programmes and cultural programmes have been conducted in various rural areas.
- Group discussions and training programmes for school boys and girls have been conducted.
- Mass contact has also been conducted by IEC to educate rural people towards hygienic habits.
- Special training programmes for Self Help Groups and hygiene workers have also been conducted.
- Many rallies regarding hygiene and sanitation have also been conducted to create awareness in the minds of the rural masses.

Innovative Approach

As per the present norms, the government provides Rs.600 to families to construct household latrines. Each family will have to purchase the building materials individually and this will cost more. So the President approached the District Collector and received the entire amount for all the 188 families with the idea of purchasing the building materials in bulk to reduce the cost. Thus he completed the construction of household latrines for all the 188 families within the limit with the help of a contractor. In the case of a few families who wanted different models he collected the additional cost from those families.

The President did this job with great difficulty. It is not so easy to convince the people about sanitation practices. It is part of the culture to keep the toilets away from the house and the place for defecation is also far away from the dwelling units. Since the President has got much recognition among the people he pacified the resistance of the people. Side by side, with the help of the IEC team he tried to influence the school going boys and girls.

Achievements

188 individual household latrines have been completed and put to use. Four school toilets have been constructed and all of them have been put to use. Two anganwadi toilets have been constructed and they have been put to use. Special training campaigns for anganwadi children have also been done. Thirty anganwadi school students have been given training to use the latrines. A Student Sanitary Club has been formed in all the schools and the school students maintain hygiene and sanitation habits in the best possible way.

Sanitary Complex

Sanitary Complex

The school children have also played a vital role in the total sanitation programme. The IEC group encouraged the students to wear footwear and all the students pressed their parents and got chapels. In the schools the children are trained to leave their chapels in an arranged manner outside the classrooms. With the help of the Parent Teacher Association (PTA) soaps have been kept in front of all the class rooms along with a bucket of water and the students are trained to wash their hands before and after taking meals. The PTA has also provides soaps in the toilets and students wash their hands after using the toilet.

Result

- The people are ready to construct latrines in their houses.
- A new sanitation culture has been created.
- Nowadays, a house with a latrine is becoming a prestige symbol.
- Open-air defecation has been discouraged and construction of household latrine encouraged considerably.
- People have started talking about this new culture.
- As for the Integrated Rural Sanitary Complex SHGs are coming forward to maintain the sanitary complexes.

The Concept of IEC and its Significance

Sanitation is a way of life. It starts with the baby. Inculcation of necessary behaviour and practice in maintaining personal hygiene and public sanitation by each individual has to be ensured for total rural sanitation. The toilet is a part. Safe disposal of solid and liquid waste, tree planting for pure environment, keeping common places neat and clean, equipping the villagers in health awareness and practice of better preventive care system, avoiding stagnation of rain water/waste water by rain water harvesting system, ensuring potable drinking water, toilet facilities in educational institutions, upkeep of roads, all these activities the components of total rural sanitation. The villagers of Thamaraikulam realized this in course of time after they got household latrines, Mr.Sivalingam said.

Tree planting was undertaken on roadsides and in public places. Shady trees were planted. To each house, tree saplings of guava, sappotta, mango, coconut, lime and papaya were distributed and most of the saplings have survived as the householders gave care. Medicinal plants were also distributed to the PHC. The villagers of Thamaraikulam are now well aware of the importance and the role of trees and green coverage in the promotion of total rural sanitation. Provision of institutional latrines in the primary and the middle school of Thamaraikulam was carried out by SSA. Students are properly oriented to make use of the school latrines. The Village Panchayat provides water facility.

Vermi Compost Building

Protection from Sea Erosion

In order to protect the people from the sea erosion casuarinas saplings have been planted in the seashore area. He distributed 2000 fruit saplings to the people to grow in the arenas of the villages.

Rain Water Harvesting

Rainwater harvesting has nowadays gained the attention of the government and the public. In general there is a perception that it has a limited scope in the case of hutments. But, in consultation with village elders, the youths made arrangements to collect the run-off water at a point so that it could be stored or let down into the ground for percolation. A movement was initiated for rainwater harvesting and in 539 houses, 224 hutments and 182 tiled houses the owners themselves installed 133 pucca rainwater harvest structures. The Chartered Engineer of the Village Panchayat helped in this regard. He offered technical guidance to the villagers. SHG members and Youth Association members spread the message to each household. The personal advice and attention of the Chief Minister in the promotion of rainwater harvesting is the chief source of inspiration and so the activities rolled on in 539 houses.

When the Government of Tamil Nadu emphasized the establishment of rainwater harvesting in all buildings, private and public, he proposed to install a drainage system to drain the rainwater from the rooftops of individual houses effectively by planting broken tiles in the front and backyard and, to collect the drained rainwater, a soak pit was dug at the side of the dwelling units. In about 100 per cent of the dwelling units the rainwater harvesting structure, i.e. a drain and soak pit, was established successfully. People joined together and worked as a team in this regard.

Cent Percent Rainwater Harvesting

I. Private Households

Thamaraikulam Panchayat became a role model for the entire district by becoming one of the first Panchayats to be totally covered by rainwater harvesting structures.

The village Panchayat has five hamlets

(i) Thamaraikulam
(ii) Thamaraikulam North
(iii) Keelamankundu
(iv) Melamankundu
(v) Valangapuri

There are total of 539 houses. All the households have rainwater harvesting structures. The details are:

Sl. No.	*Name of the Village*	*House Structure*			
		Hut	*Kutcha*	*Pucca*	*Total*
1.	Keelamankundu	54	43	30	127
2.	Melamankundu	31	22	28	81
3.	SC Colony	12	25	18	55
4.	Thamaraikulam	47	74	34	155
5.	Thamaraikulam North	24	12	19	55
6.	Valangapuri	56	6	4	66
	Total	224	182	133	539

II. Government Buildings

The Village Panchayat President and the Members have ensured that not only individual households, but also government buildings have rainwater harvesting structures. The following government buildings available in the Village Panchayat also have rainwater harvesting structures:

1.	School Buildings	4
2.	Community Hall	1
3.	Anganwadi Centre	3
4.	Noon Meal Centre	2
5.	Self Help Group Buildings	2
6.	Post Office	1
7.	Library Building	1
8.	District Cooperative Bank	1
9.	VAO Office	1
10.	T.V. Hall	4
11.	Veterinary Hospital Visitors Building	1
12.	Primary Health Centre	1
13.	I.T.I. Buildings	1
14.	Women and Children Sanitary Complex	1
15.	Panchayat Office Building	1
16.	Houses to Poor	40

Works Carried Out During this Tenure

Drinking Water Supply

1. Construction of overhead tank - 3 (Capacity 90,000 litres)
2. Valankapuri to Thamaraikulam laying of pipeline to provide water supply
3. Construction of Thamaraikulam pumping station - 2
4. Valankapuri to Keelamankundu laying of pipeline
5. Thamaraikulam individual water supply connection
6. Construction of water storage pump - 9
7. Water supply to schools
8. Water supply to SC colony

Link Roads

Totally 21 roads have been laid. Some of them are black topped and many of them are metal roads. A few of them are gravel roads. All the hamlets are well connected with each other. It enabled the transport corporation and fleet owners to operate buses and mini buses in these areas.

Parents Teachers Association

Regular Parents Teachers Association meetings were held in the schools. Several facilities were provided in the schools for enriching the students' education. The President provided prizes during competitions on the annual day. He used to visit the schools frequently and built up a good rapport with the headmasters and the Education Department officials. He has given importance to girls education and increased the enrolment of students in schools, especially girls. A special drive was made every year to get the eligible children enrolled.

Gram Sabha

In the Gram Sabha meetings women participate more than men, particularly SHG members, and ask questions related to their own development, issues of patta to the poor and loans. These are the people's expectations in the Gram Sabha meeting. For improving the Gram Sabha meeting transparency is essential both at Panchayat level and official level. Government grants are to be increased and regular employment sources should be provided for all people. The Gram Sabha adopted resolutions for the following:

Gram Sabha Meeting

(i) Ban on open air defecation
(ii) Total Rain Water Harvesting
(iii) Total water conservation and waste water disposal
(iv) Ban on littering of wastes and use of disposable plastics
(v) Imposition of penalty with punitive action against the offenders.

Preparation of Plan Document

The Panchayat, with clean roads without garbage, proper, regular, clear drinking water supply, provision of street lights, group houses, etc., impressed the government departments for making the Panchayat the best. Hence a village development plan was prepared with the support of the officials and the village people. Participatory Rural Appraisal method was followed for gathering information from the community and need based demands were taken into consideration.

Plan Document Preparation

The development report comprises details regarding Panchayat administration, land, water, population, important facilities available in the Panchayat, educational institutions, drinking water facility, street lights, sanitation, women and child welfare, transportation, SC/ST welfare, maintenance of animal husbandry, milk society, industries and major occupations of the village, housing facility, cooperative society and other Panchayat related information. The details were gathered with the active support of the community. The President realized each and every need of the Panchayat hamlets and gained rich experience in approaching several department officials for fulfilling the people's needs. Based on the activities undertaken by the Panchayat, the officials appreciated his Panchayat administration and recommended the Panchayat for the national award under the total sanitation programme.

Sanitation

In his village, the first preference was given to cleanliness. The sweepers properly clear the garbage in time and the drainages are also kept clean. The removed garbage is turned into natural fertilizers through compost pits. 'Sugathara Pongal Varam' programme introduced by the government, which urges the importance of cleanliness. The Self Help Group women and school students were fully involved in this programme with interest, and various cultural competitions were organised by the President who distributed prizes to them. The school students were involved in creating awareness among the villagers on the eradication of plastics and many campaigns and rallies were also organised regarding this theme. The District Collector, MLA, Union Councillors were also invited to participate in these campaigns. This motivated several villagers towards eradication of plastics from the hamlets. He succeeded in all his attempts because of people's involvement and participation.

The sanitary complex in Thamaraikulam is maintained by four women SHGs. For the maintenance purpose they collect Rs.10 from the user groups. All women and children of this area utilize the toilets and bathrooms. The schools are having separate toilets for both girls and boys.

Plastics Free Village

Another problem in the village was the spread of used polythene and how to clean and dispose of the same. He wanted to take action on this matter and stressed the importance of the removal of plastics from the Panchayat area with the involvement of the people. The Ward Members, the SHGs and youth groups welcomed the idea of the President and immediately responded to support it. He first sensitized the masses on the implications of polythene for the environment of the village. He further started acting on it. Villagers helped the Panchayat to clear polythene bags from the entire Panchayat. Students have been educated to deposit wastes in three different bags. Thus he made waste management easy by educating the people.

Several rallies and campaigns were organised in the villages with the help of school students and youth groups. The people are urged to utilize paper covers and bags made of cloth. The Panchayat area has become clean, without garbage and with maintenance of proper drainage and system. The collected plastic covers are gathered in a godown and decided to utilize it for the construction of roads. The President realized the importance of the eradication of plastic bags, when the government exposed the destruction caused by the plastics especially its adverse affect on the recharge of the ground water. Many voluntary organisations also conducted rallies and campaigns against the utilization of plastics.

The youth groups of this Panchayat were enthusiastically involved in the removal of plastics during campaigns. They have created awareness among the people on cleanliness and the adverse effect caused by the utilization of plastic bags through skits. They have actively involved themselves in various Panchayat activities, solved many public problems and, during the Gram Sabha meeting, discussed Panchayat development activities. He makes it clear that his primary objective is to create awareness among the people to lead a decent human living. It is evident from the reality of life in the rural areas that many people, especially the poor, are living life in sub-human living conditions. Natural resources are the lifeline of the people in the rural areas. They are to be protected.

In all the streets the Panchayat has provided two dust bins and the families dump all the garbage only in those dustbins. But, whenever outsiders pass through the village to the temple, they sometimes throw away waste papers in the street. Immediately on seeing these waste papers in the street, the residents of the street pick them up and put them in the dustbin and thus the streets always appear neat and clean.

Desilting of Tanks and Ponds

Tanks and ponds are the essential sources for storage of water and the lifeline of the people. Hence their maintenance, protection and enrichment will help the people to secure their livelihood. Almost all the twelve tanks have been desilted and deepened. As a result the water level of the subsoil is maintained. Further all the channels which bring water to these tanks have been cleared and are maintained in such a condition that as and when it rains, even the smallest amount of water will reach the tanks without any wastage.

Committee System

Along with the statutory committees, he formed an other three committees to supervise the activities of the Panchayat and the activities of the sectoral departments in this Panchayat area. This committee system enhances the level of participation of the people in the Panchayat management.

Helping the Widowed, Aged and Poor

He constantly monitors the widowed, poor and marginalized who are getting assistance from the Government with the help of the Ward and Committee members. He is keen on getting government assistance to the needy. In that respect all the aged and the widows are getting the needed assistance for their livelihood.

SHGs Involvement in Panchayat Activities

The President has created a good relationship with the self help group women because he has frequently participated in their meetings, suggested solutions to their problems and collaboratively involved them in Panchayat activities.

Production of Palm Mats

Most of the SHGs got financial assistance from the banks for their income generating activity. Weekly meetings of SHGs were held in the SHG building on Sundays. Various personal and public problems were seriously discussed among the SHGs.

The SHGs aimed at not to depend on the government, but to equip themselves for their survival and tried to convince everyone to work towards Panchayat development. In all the activities he helped them and acted as a link between the people and the Departments of the Government. The President realized the potential of SHGs and hence he maintained a close link with SHGs.

The SHGs went to each house and canvassed the women for the utilization of the sanitary complex and its necessity. They also collected the peoples contribution for house water connection and hand pumps. Then the houses were provided with proper water supply. SHG members have been authorized to check the PDS shops and it is being discussed in Gram Sabha also. As a result the PDS functions perfectly well without any problem.

The village health nurse visited the villages on Wednesdays and properly recorded the details of the reproductive health condition of mothers, distribution of iron tablets to teenage girls to control anemia and immunization treatment for children were given to prevent communicable diseases. Deliveries were held in the Thamaraikulam PHC.

The anganwadi teachers also recorded the details of reproductive mothers and children. He visited the anganwadi frequently and checked the noon meal centre. He used to supervise all the service institutions though not authoritatively. But his visits helped the institutions to put things in proper shape. He felt that through such a kind of supervision one can improve the service delivery. Camps on legal awareness, agriculture, veterinary and health camps were organised by the President for the village people. Polio camps were organized by SHGs along with youth groups.

There are 16 active SHGs of women in this Village Panchayat. Most of the SHGs got financial assistance from banks for their income generating activity like palmyra products.

Connectivity and Communication

He perceived that connectivity is imperative for development and accordingly he has laid roads from the fishers colony to the sea, from all streets to the crematorium. All service stations are linked with the hamlets. Pucca connectivity has been created. In the same way 30 bus trips from different places have been created through community transport system. All important towns are connected for mobility. Phone connection was given to the village through an STD booth.

In this Panchayat 85 per cent of the houses are provided with individual tap connection for supply of drinking water. Water supply is a very sensitive and basic entitlement of the people as per the Panchayat President's perception and hence it is attended to with utmost seriousness.

Protection of Public Properties

The President made it a point that all public properties have to be protected and then only they can be maintained well. Hence construction of compound wall for all public buildings was made mandatory. So he constructed compound walls for all buildings. Likewise in all tanks protection walls have been constructed.

Drinking Water

Drinking water, overhead tanks, mini power pumps, hand pumps, individual water taps, etc., were provided and sufficient water was distributed to every hamlet under a shift system.

Education Development

There are two schools (one Primary and one Middle) in this Village Panchayat. For high school the students go to the nearby village of Irattaiyurani (High School) as well as Kadukkavalasai (Hr. Sec. School). He has given importance to the enrollment of all eligible children. The Village Education Committee (VEC) and the Parents Teachers Association (PTA) are not effective but, with the help of a few teachers and villagers, Sivalingam was able to draft an annual plan for the welfare of the school students.

- Prizes were awarded to the outstanding students.
- Essay and oratory competitions were organized.
- Toilet facilities were provided in all the schools and balwadies.
- Separate bore well and motor connection were provided to each school for water facilities to toilets.
- Enough care was taken to ensure that the toilets were being used.
- Parents are motivated to send their wards at least up to the eighth standard.
- Additional teachers were appointed
- By donating money to the Nadar Mahajana Sangham, he organised an ITI for the youth.
- SHGs are entrusted with responsibilities in the implementation of the student welfare activities.
- Students are encouraged to engage in village welfare activities like cleaning of bushes along the school campus and roadside, assisting in transporting of trees for planting, arrangement for fencing and awareness programme on rain water harvesting.
- Two anganwadi buildings have been constructed with toilets for kids.
- He helped to organise a library in his village by sparing a small room in his own house.

Perception of the President

He has a clear understanding of the role of the New Panchayati Raj System in Tamil Nadu as per the 73rd Amendment to the Constitution of India. But, as per the Tamil Nadu system, he observes that the Panchayat is an effective implementing agency. He perceives that the Panchayat can do well even if it is only an implementing agency. His perception is that one has to work effectively as per what is at hand instead of talking too much on what is not available.

The Panchayat President feels that people can lead a happy life if they use their potential. He felt that if health governance is done perfectly by the Panchayat with the active participation of the people, people can be saved from disease. People need not spend money for hospitals.

The Panchayat, by taking steps to maintain cleanliness in the village, providing safe drinking water, maintaining good sanitation, can protect the people from diseases. It should be a health movement like the literacy movement.

Nirmal Gram Puraskar Ceremony

Vision Behind His Leadership

The following are the reasons for his success in his Panchayat:

- quick decisions are taken during crises.
- transparent administration.
- maintenance of proper accounts/financial transactions.
- regular presence in the Panchayat Office and frequent meeting with the people.
- first preference given to the real poor below poverty line.
- good relationship with Dalit community.
- frequent supervision of Panchayat activities.
- openness and closeness to Ward Members.
- visited several departments for getting various development grants for the village.

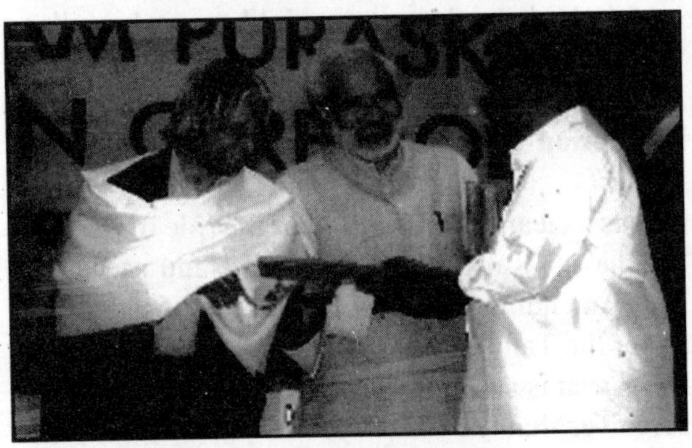

Received the Award from the President of India

Orientation to Public of Thamaraikulam

A public meeting was organised to explain to the villagers the project and its various components. A good number of women turned out and they accepted that a toilet was very much necessary. At the next meeting many women came forward to talk of the scheme. Here and there toilets came up. Witnessing the physical structure and its utility the scheme was speeded up. The villagers spent additional money for better facility in the toilet. About 421 household latrines have been constructed under the Central Rural Sanitation Programme (CRSP). And through the Total Sanitation Programme (TRSP), an additional 188 toilets have been provided to the rest of the villagers.

The inhabitants of small houses expressed their inability to find adequate space for the construction of toilets in their houses. A public toilet was constructed with the assistance of the TRSP where six toilets and six bathrooms have been provided. About seventy families are utilizing the toilets.

Basic Details of Thamaraikulam Village Panchayat

President	: S. Sivalingam
Vice-President	: V. Murugeshan
Population	: 3592 (Male 649 + Female 741)
Total No. of Household	: 539
Total No. of Wards	: 5
Total No. of Ward Members	: 6 [Male 4 (General 3+SC 1)+Female 2]

1. V. Murugeshan
2. M. Gunarathinam
3. K. Kannan
4. T. Periyathurai
5. G. Indirani
6. A. Saraswathi

Total No. of Hamlets : 6

1. Thamaraikulam
2. Keelamankundu
3. Melamankundu
4. Valangapuri
5. Thamaraikulam SC Colony
6. Thamaraikula North

MLA, MP and District Panchayat Fund Works Carried Out

Sl. No.	*Works Carried out*	*Fund*
1.	Library	M.L.A.
2.	Women and Children Sanitary Complex	"
3.	Thamaraikulam Middle School Compound Wall	"
4.	Keelmankundu Primary School Compound Wall	"
5.	Keelmankundu Community Hall-1	M.P.
6.	Thamaraikulam PHC Compound Wall	"
7.	Veterinary Hospital Visitors Building	Dist. Panchayat
8.	Valagapuri Street Light -3	"
9.	Melmankundu Street Light -3	"
10.	Keelmankundu Street Light -2	"
11.	Melmankundu Community Well -1	"
12.	Keelmankundu Bus Shelter -1	"
13.	SHGs Building -1	"
14.	Thamaraikulam Middle School Auditorium -1	"
15.	Thamaraikulam Bus Shelter (in front of PHC) -1	"

Sl. No.	*Schemes*	*1997-1998*	*1998-1999*	*1999-2000*	*2000-2001*	*2001-2002*	*2002-2003*	*2003-2004*	*2004-2005*
1.	IAY Group Houses	2	5	3	10	-	5	5	-
2.	JGSY Group Houses	-	5	-	-	-	-	-	-
3.	BMS Group Houses	-	-	5	-	-	-	-	-
4.	Kutcha Group Houses	-	-	-	-	-	8	5	-
5.	Individual Toilets	-	-	195	-	38	-	188	-

Evaluation

The Thamaraikulam Gram Panchayat President is a leader with extraordinary commitment and sincerity towards service to the community. He has very rich experience in managing the Panchayat and administering development. His rapport with the people is extraordinary. He has got a clear cut perception of the New Panchayati Raj System and its implications. He knows the existing limitations in the system. Yet the limitations never bother him in discharging his duties. He feels that the present Gram Panchayat is under the influence of the state government and particularly under the influence of the bureaucracy. It is almost an implementing agency to implement the schemes and programmes of the State and Central governments.

He further informed that resources are not scarce. They are adequate but Panchayat Presidents have to identify where resources are lying. Resources are not with Panchayats. They are with sectoral departments and the Panchayat Presidents have to make use of them. Many Presidents do not have the acumen to tap the resources. Having realized the fact that resources are not with Panchayats, Panchayat leaders have to cultivate good rapport with officials to tape all those resources available with them. He said that he is able to do all the works in the Panchayats because of the cooperation of the people and the officials. He is able to get the cooperation of the people because of his performance and attending to the works of the people.

Officials are cooperating because the Panchayat President is able to implement the schemes and programmes within the stipulated time and helps the officials to achieve their target and get name from their higher level officials. His talent is exhibited through synthesis of the government schemes and programmes with the demands of the people. His success lies in his responsiveness and responsibility in meeting the needs. He said that meeting or strengthening the demands of the people with government schemes and programmes is not so easy. It needs skill, capacity and capability to manage the officials and there are lot of risks involved in it.

The Panchayat President can take a risk if people are with the President. The success of a President depends on many factors of which forward and backward linkages are more important along with the skill, capacity and capability of the Panchayat leaders in managing crowds and the Panchayat. It is proved from his case that if, even with the limited powers and resources he is able to make this much of progress, he will achieve much more if adequate powers are devolved to Panchayats. He feels that on many occasions the Panchayat President has to assume responsibilities and carry out activities and thereby assume power. Finally, one can come to the conclusion that for grassroots governance and achieving development and social justice leadership matters much.

Thamaraikulam Panchayat
Income and Expenditure Details for the year 2001-2002

Account No. I

Sl. No.	*Details of Income*	*Amount (Rs.)*	*Details of Expenditure*	*Amount (Rs.)*
1.	House Tax	24,035.00	Panchayat Assistant - Salary	18,000.00
2.	Library Tax	2,524.00	Sweeper - Salary	9,680.00
3.	Professional Tax	13,560.00	OHT Operator - Salary	9,680.00
4.	Bank Interest	2,018.00	Electricity Charge - Light	16,752.00
5.	State Finance Commission Grant	43,024.50	Electricity Charge - Motor Pump	4,655.00
6.	Land Tax	1,225.00	Electricity Charge - Bldg.	2,872.00
7.	Licence	665.00	Light Maintenance	92,693.00
8.	Water Tax	94,805.00	Motor Pump Maintenance	49,400.00
9.	House Tax matching grant	11,027.00	Other Expenditure	1,695.50
10.	Small Savings	5,050.00	Cable TV	100.00
11.	Registration Fees	67,666.00	Library Tax	6,510.00
12.	Tender Fees	6,953.00	Dhoby Work Place	7,675.00
13.	House Plan Approval	1,200.00	Group Insurance	7,700.00
14.	Grace Grant	525.00	Travelling Allowance	5,620.00
15.			Cement Concrete Road	48,702.00
16.			Record note	3,097.00
17.			Road Work - Refund of Deposit	5,165.00
18.			Ayyan Thiruvalluvar Library	3,000.00
19.			Income Tax	12,482.00
20.	Total	2,73,076.50	Turner Expenses	3,750.00
	Initial Balance	41,292.00	Total	3,09,228.50
	Total	3,14,368.50	Final Balance	5,140.00
			Total	3,14,368.50

Account No. II

Sl. No.	*Details of Income*	*Amount (Rs.)*	*Details of Expenditure*	*Amount (Rs.)*
1.	Bank Interest	1,720.00	Funeral Grant	500.00
2.	Ayyan Library	3,000.00	Bank Commission	10.00
3.	Funeral Grant	500.00	Total	510.00
	Total	5,220.00	Final Balance	22,713.58
	Initial Balance	18,003.58	Total	23,223.58
	Total	23,223.58		

Account No. III

Sl. No.	*Details of Income*	*Amount (Rs.)*	*Details of Expenditure*	*Amount (Rs.)*
1.	IAY	23,400.00	IAY	77,726.00
2.	Village Development Fund	11,300.00	Cement Road	17,550.00
3.	Cement Road	48,702.00	Toilet - 38	21,594.00
4.	Bank Interest	2,654.00	Bank Commission	85.00
	Total	86,056.00	Total	1,16,955.00
	Initial Balance	34,673.00	Final Balance	3,774.00
	Total	1,20,729	Total	1,20,729.00

Thamaraikulam Panchayat Income and Expenditure Details for the year 2002-2003

Account No. I

Sl. No.	Details of Income	Amount (Rs.)	Details of Expenditure	Amount (Rs.)
1.	House Tax	31,205.00	Panchayat Assistant - Salary	12,760.00
2.	Library Tax	3,120.50	Sweeper - Salary	9,600.00
3.	Professional Tax	23.620.00	OHT Operator - Salary	10,350.00
4.	Water Deposit	57,000.00	Electricity charge	70,809.00
5.	Water Tax	25,140.00	Street light Maintenance	1,125.00
6.	House Plan Approval	4,300.00	Other Expenditure	4,521.00
7.	Scheduled	550.00	TV Maintenance	1,200.00
8.	Earnest Deposit	1.410.00	Library Tax	2,524.00
9.	Bank Interest	567.00	Group Insurance	3,245.00
10.	State Finance Commission Grant	88,070.00	Travelling Allowance	6,440.00
11.	Registration Fee	5,322.00	Record Note	4,131.00
12.	2½% Deposit	100.00	EB Deposit	4,740.00
13.	Income	18,850.00	Street Light Maintenance	74,770.00
14.	Other Income	1,825.00	Tender Work	59,776.00
15.	Total	3,29,834.50	Local Communication Charges	400.00
16.	Initial Balance	5,140.00	Water Tap Extension	9,034.00
17.	Total	3,34,974.50	Bank Commission	403.00
18.			Approved Expenditure	1,498.00
19.			OHT Maintenance	950.00
20.			Depavali Bonus	2,000.00
21.			Turner Expenses	1,712.00
22.			Post Office Deposit	15,000.00
23.			EB Deposit (Street Light)	32,175.00
24.			Panchayat Building Maintenance	4,547.00
			Total	3,33,710.00
			Final Balance	12,64.50
			Total	3,34,974.50

Account No. II

Sl. No.	Details of Income	Amount (Rs.)	Details of Expenditure	Amount (Rs.)
1.	11th Finance Commission Grant	45,144.00	Bank Commission	125.00
2.	11th Finance Commission Panchayat Matching Grant	11,286.00	Amount transfer to Planning Account	16,000
3.	Bank Interest	868.00	11th Commission Graveyard road	28,200
4.	Deposit	2,003.00	Turner Expenses	1,073.00
	Total	60,814	New Streetlight Establishment	28,215.00
	Initial Balance	22,713.58	Total	73,613.00
	Total	82.897.58	Final Balance	9,284.58
			Total	82,897.58

Account No. III

Sl. No.	Details of Income	Amount (Rs.)	Details of Expenditure	Amount (Rs.)
1.	JGRY	12,486.00	Bank Commission	169.00
2.	IAY Group House	86,000.00	Cement Road	28,300.00
3.	State Finance Commission Grant	16,000.00	Group House - IAY	53,745.00
4.	Deposit Income	708.00	Turner Expenses	2,913.00
5.	Adi Dravida House Maintenance - IAY	84.744.00	IAY-SC house maintenance	78,000.00

(*Contd.*)

Sl. No.	Details of Income	Amount (Rs.)	Details of Expenditure	Amount (Rs.)
6.	SGRY - Income	34,400.00	Total	1,63,127.00
7.	Adi Dravida - 2½ deposit	2,000.00	Final Balance	81.789.00
	Total	2,41,142.00	Total	2,44,916 .00
	Initial Balance	3,774.00		
	Total	2,44,916.00		

Thamaraikulam Panchayat
Income and Expenditure Details for the year 2003-2004

Account No. I

Sl. No.	Details of Income	Amount (Rs.)	Details of Expenditure	Amount (Rs.)
1.	House Tax	1,12,390.00	Panchayat Assistant - Salary	30,600.00
2.	Library Tax	11,239.00	Bank Commission	884.00
3.	Professional Tax	21,760.00	President - Sitting fee	6,360.00
4.	Registration Fee	94,226.00	Panchayat Writer - TA	1,800.00
5.	Water Tax	22,085.00	Group Insurance	3,300.00
6.	Land Tax	923.00	Other Expenditure	10,678.50
7.	Transfer from Post Office	14,000.00	Extension of drinking water tap	5,719.00
8.	Drinking water deposit	33,000.00	Extension of street lights	34,701.00
9.	SFC	51,259.00	Urgent meeting - sitting fee	200.00
10.	Interest income	855.50	Record note	2,515.00
11.	House Plan Approval	3,200.00	Maintenance of Motor	7,150.00
12.	2½% Deposit	2,063.00	Electricity Charge	23,502.00
13.	Mines	80,675.00	EB Deposit	425.00
14.	Scheduled	300.00	Approved Expenditure	2,425.00
15.	Earnest Deposit	7,850.00	Rainwater saving - advertisement	1,000.00
16.	Penalty	1,800.00	Gate-valve cement cover	1,300.00
17.	Other sources of Income	1,992.00	Maintenance of office room	555.00
18.	Licence	665.00	Public Health	48,694.00
19.	Total	4,64,311.50	Sweepers Uniform dress	1,492.00
20.	Initial Balance	1,264.50	Advertisement in *Dinathanthi* daily	8,070.00
21.	Total	4,65,576.00	Festival Advances	2,400.00
22.			Streetlight maintenance charges	1,000.00
23.			New Gravel Road	1,55,000.00
24.			Library Tax	3,121.00
			Total	3,52,891.50
			Final Balance	1,12,684.50
			Total	4,65,576.00

Account No. II

Sl. No.	Details of Income	Amount (Rs.)	Details of Expenditure	Amount (Rs.)
1.	Interest Income	716.00	Bank Commission	184.00
2.	11th Finance Commission Grant	45,144.00	Funeral Grant	500.00
	Total	45,860.00	Total	684.00
	Initial Balance	9,284.58	Final Balance	54,460,58
	Total	55,144.58	Total	55,144.58

Account No. III

Sl. No.	Details of Income	Amount (Rs.)	Details of Expenditure	Amount (Rs.)
1.	SGRY Grant	43,700.00	SGRY	76,310.00
2.	2½% Deposit	1,702.00	Bank Commission	621.00
3.	IAY Income	1,07,055.00	IAY House	75,165.00
4.	Interest Income	987.00	Private Toilet	1,12,500.00
5.	IAY	50,000.00	IAY houses	49,305.00
6.	Private Toilet	1,32,162.00	Total	3,13,901.00
	Total	3,35,606.00	Final Balance	1,03,494.00
	Initial Balance	81,789.00	Total	4,17,395.00
	Total	4,17,395.00		

Thamaraikulam Panchayat
Income and Expenditure Details for the year 2004-2005

Account No. I

Sl. No.	Details of Income	Amount (Rs.)	Details of Expenditure	Amount (Rs.)
1.	House Tax	1,13,975.00	Panchayat Assistant - Salary	28,200.00
2.	Library Tax	11,397.50	Daily Allowance	3,960.00
3.	Professional Tax	31,020.00	President - Sitting fee	2,400.00
4.	Scheduled	1,100.00	Travelling Allowance	7,707.00
5.	Earnest Deposit	16,800.00	Electricity Charge	26,981.00
6.	Audited income	200.00	Record note	5,036.00
7.	Other source of income	7,770.00	Public Health	92,032.00
8.	House Plan Approval	17,200.00	Finance Transformation	29,927.00
9.	Deposit	936.00	Other Expenditure	11,695.50
10.	House tax matching grant	39,006.00	Advertisement Board	7,600.00
11.	Mines	44,200.00	Street light maintenance	375.00
12.	Interest income	1,025.00	Drinking water tap maintenance	488.00
13.	Registration Fee	62,571.00	New Gravel road	2,14,339.00
14.	State Finance Commission Grant	70,865.00	Bank Commission	1,308.00
15.	Nirmal Gram Puraskar Grant	2,00,000.00	Electricity Charges	38,384.00
16.	Total	6,18,065.00	Library Tax	11,239.00
17.	Initial Balance	1,12,684.50	Festival Advance	2,400.00
18.	Total	7,30,749.50	News Advertisement	32,264.00
19.			Telephone Deposit	2,500.00
20.			Approved Expenditure	2,804.00
			Total	5,24,939.50
			Un received Bank Cheque	12,064.00
			Total	5,12,875.50
			Final Balance	2,17,874.00
			Total	7,30,749.50

Account No. II

Sl. No.	Details of Income	Amount (Rs.)	Details of Expenditure	Amount (Rs.)
1.	Finance Transformation	11,286.00	Library Compound Wall	25,984.00
2.	Commission Interest	1,265.00	Graveyard road maintenance	25,984.00
3.	11th Finance Commission Grant	11,286.00	Bank Commission	151.00
4.	Income from Garbage	15,360.00	Total	52,119.00
	Total	39,197.00	Final Balance	41,538.58
	Initial Balance	54,460.58	Total	93,657.58
	Total	93,657.58		

Account No. III

Sl. No.	Details of Income	Amount (Rs.)	Details of Expenditure	Amount (Rs.)
1.	IAY	1,57,199.00	IAY House	1,09,435.00
2.	SGRY	2,30,082.00	Individual Toilet	13,200.00
3.	Interest Income	3,987.00	Bank Commission	1,286.00
4.	Total	3,91,268.00	Maintenance of Well - 2	25,387.00
5.	Initial Balance	1,03,494.00	Desilt of ponds	66,280.00
6.	Total	4,94,762.00	Building - women	1,37,600.00
7.			Garbage Shed	58,480.00
			Total	4,11,747.00
			Final Balance	83,094.00
			Total	4,94,762.00

CASE - 16

MOVING BEYOND PANCHAYAT

Grandline Gram Panchayat is known for many activities of which working for the marginalised and the aged is one and significant. His work for the SHGs and Dalits made him popular. Eviction of encroachment, creating public library, establishment of park and garden got him recognition among the people. Transforming waste into wealth brought a name to the Panchayat President. Desilting of ponds and creation of hydraulic gym, drew the youth close to him. He introduced a new scheme, feeding the poorest of the poor and it is this scheme which attracts everyone. In his Panchayat a provisional store is being run by the Gram Panchayat. It is also unique in this Panchayat.

About the Village Panchayat

Grandline is a Village Panchayat in Puzhal Union of Thiruvallur District located 16 km distance from the Chennai City. It is a multi-caste village where the Vanniar caste is numerically larger than the other caste groups, namely, Adi Dravidar, Mudhaliyar, Yadhavar and Thevar.

There are three hamlets, including the main village of Grandline. Samiyarmadam and Thandal Kazhani are the other two hamlets. About twenty years back the village had been engaged in agriculture as irrigation water was received from the nearby big tank named Puzhal Lake. As the water stored in Puzhal lake was earmarked for the metro drinking water supply to Chennai, cultivation in agricultural lands became impossible and they became barren lands. Slowly the same were converted into housing sites and commercial plots. Now there is no cultivation at all. The Village Panchayat area is now a part of the suburb of Red Hills which is the nearest town.

Background of the Village Panchayat Leadership

Mr. N. Jagatheesan, aged 39, married, belongs to the Mudhaliyar community. Basically his father was a farmer. Jagatheesan is a postgraduate in Tamil literature. He studied B.Sc. Mathematics in Pachaiyappa's College. After his graduation Jagatheesan worked in some business firms and also studied part time M.A. in Tamil literature.

After his school education his exposure through college education shaped his personality. He used to spend his leisure time in libraries where he learnt a lot from the books authored by Gandhiji, E.V. Ramasamy, Anna, Karunanidhi. Further he was attracted towards the writings of Dr. M.S. Udayamoorthy. His readings of the writings of the great leaders made him engage himself in public welfare activities. Mostly the ideology of Periyar E.V.R. influenced Jagatheesan since 1991.

In the meantime Jagatheesan and some friends of his community organized themselves as V.O. Chidambaranar Youth Association and actively engaged in social welfare activities. They celebrated the Tamil New Year day in a grand manner by arranging lectures by personalities like Dr. M.S. Udayamoorthy and Ms.Thilagavathy. Further he became a youth member in the DMK party. He had won a prize in an oratory competition held in Sri Vivekananda College when he studied in Pachaiyappa's College.

He got married in the year 1994 and, at that time, he worked in a company for his livelihood. When the Constitutional Amendment was enacted to establish the new Panchayati Raj System, Jagatheesan, along with other youth members of the Makkal Sakthi Iyakkam, undertook a yatra in Thiruvallur District to create awareness among the voters.

His association with the DMK party helped him to became a good orator, very effective in communicating his ideas pertaining to village, society and its development. He trained himself to talk more efficiently, quoting attractive examples and short stories.

Panchayat Elections 1996

When the election to the Panchayati Raj Institutions was held in 1996, the members of the VOC Youth Association encouraged Jagatheesan to file his nomination. Though Jagatheesan himself was also interested to contest, he wished to avail the support of the DMK party so that he could get more votes than as an individual. Hence he met the concerned party officials of the DMK and pleaded with them to extend their support. At that time he did not have the support of the party officials as he could not get recognition from the party workers. At the same time another person who also belonged to DMK demanded the candidature. The DMK Party Secretary of Puzhal unit evaluated the merits and the demerits of the candidates and finally decided to extend support to the young and energetic new leadership of Jagatheesan.

Though the Village Panchayat election was not on political basis, political personalities projected themselves through their party identity so as to gain more votes, Jagatheesan claimed.

Jagatheesan was a new entrant to politics. Hence others thought that he would not be able to muster enough votes. There were four candidates in the fray. One was the former Vice-President. There was a tough competition. The youths of the Panchayat area cutting across castes and extended their support to Jagatheesan in recognition of his welfare activities for youths through the VOC Youth Association. These youngsters had a unique propoganda technique of publishing bit notices in many forms declaring the significance of youth power, dream and mission of youth to transform the village etc. The opponents could not counter this style of propaganda adopted by the youths. Moreover door do door canvassing, frequent visits and group efforts turned the result in favour of him. Jagatheesan won by a 75 vote margin. It was a joint and dedicated effort of friends, Jagatheesan said. Moreover the public had faith in the leadership of youths, he added.

Panchayat Administration

"Our Panchayat Council Members wholeheartedly support all initiatives undertaken by me," Jagatheesan claimed. First he focused his attention to work for youth welfare and to improve the basic amenities to the villagers. But there was no piece of land available for any new construction. Sanction was accorded to construct a TV room and an overhead tank in the village. But the individuals who had encroached upon Panchayat lands refused to vacate the lands. Hence in spite of the sanctioning of the construction of a TV room and an overhead tank it was not accomplished, Jagatheesan felt.

A Helping Hand from Revenue Official

The VAO Thanikasalam was very much helpful in identifying the poramboke lands under the jurisdiction of the Village Panchayat. In one poramboke site, there were twelve encroachers who had constructed houses on the land. They were warned officially but no response came from them. With the help of Ward Members and a few youngsters, the encroachment was cleared using a JCB machine. There was a threat to the Village Administrative Officer and the Panchayat President. The issue was widely covered by the media. This bold action brought a name to the Panchayat administration. From then onwards Jagatheesan launched attempts to bring welfare schemes to his villagers.

Periyar Thidal

The site redeemed from the encroachers was named Periyar Thidal where the office of the VAO and the sanitary complex for women and children were constructed. Jagatheesan, being a cadre of the DMK, easily met the sitting MP and got Rs.10 lakhs for the construction of a community hall in the Periyar Thidal.

Community Hall - Periyar Thidal

Further when a multi-functional building for SHGs was allotted, the same was also housed in the Periyar Thidal. Once it was an encroached site, now it was worth millions. It was possible because of the Panchayat Ward Members and youth groups.

Park — Periyar Thidal

Establishment of Rural Library

Providing library was one of the main promises made by the team of Jagatheesan. Hence efforts were made to provide the library facilities. Furniture, books and personnel were mobilised. But the site for the construction was always an issue in Grandline Panchayat. There was a public space where a village temple and the Village Panchayat office were located. When the proposal for the construction of the library building was announced, the members belonging to one community who manage the temple refused to surrender the site.

Earlier, also, when a ration shop building was sanctioned, there was opposition to the construction of the building in the empty space near the temple. Hence, it was shifted to the Dalit colony area. But the library building should be located very near to the public for easy access to all hamlets. In this context, the proposed site near the temple area was most suitable, Jagatheesan told.

Hence in spite of opposition from one section of society, Jagatheesan and the Panchayat Ward Members jointly determined to establish the full time library at the public place where the Panchayat building and temple were located. They mobilised one hundred membership, four philanthropists and necessary furniture to start the library. It was commenced to function initially at the campus of the Village Panchayat office.

Library Building under MP Fund

In the meantime, the MP had sanctioned Rs.1.70 lakh rupees for the construction of the library building if it would be a full time library. Jagatheesan and his Panchayat Ward Members succeeded in getting sanction for a full time library. The next assignment was finding the site for the construction of the building. Jagatheesan tried his best to get a site free of cost from a house owner who owns a site at the side of the public place where the temple is located. The community which manages the temple did not expect this proposal. They agitated against the proposal and they complained to the police. The Village Panchayat administration handed over the document related to the disputed site and it was not in the public site. Moreover there was no record even for claiming the temple site. Hence the compound wall near the proposed site for the library building constructed by the temple administration was knocked down and a pucca building for the library was constructed. There was of course misunderstanding between the two groups. But realizing the significance of the necessity of the public library, the differences melted away.

Library

The library is properly utilized by all the age groups and the understanding of the public has also improved, Jagatheesan claimed. As his activities are always in the interest of the public and his decision making process was on consensus support to his activities has been increasing day by day in the Panchayat area.

Eviction of another encroachment

There was a land of 75 cent of poramboke which was included in the house sites promoted by real estate owners. This was unnoticed by the earlier administration of the Panchayat as well as government officials, as the site was referred to as space for public utility.

Panchayat Garden

But the real position of the land was known to the VAO. When the Village Panchayat was struggling to identify public land for providing various amenities to the public, the VAO helped by identifying this 75 cent as poramboke land which was illegally held by the real estate promoters.

The Village Panchayat administration passed a resolution to evict the encroacher and commenced its work through proper channel. As a precautionary measure, a caveat was obtained to prevent any move of the encroacher through a court of law to delay the action. It was a risky one as the real estate promoters were very powerful. But the villagers and Village Panchayat Ward Members stood firmly with Jagatheesan. At last the site was redeemed. Its local value is Rs.50 lakhs. The land was reclaimed and a garden was established. Banana, vegetables were raised. Tree planting was also done. A compound wall was constructed enclosing the site of the extent of 75 cent from the Panchayat fund account.

Solid Waste Management

In the exposure visit to a Village Panchayat in Vellore District where Exnora is engaged in solid waste management, Jagatheesan decided to commence such work in his village also. With the approval of the Panchayat Council, a bullock cart was purchased and a bull also purchased. Necessary orientation programme was organised to educate the public. The cart had two divisions the red coloured for inorganic waste and the green coloured for organic waste.

Compost Manure

Segregation of Wastes

In the village farm a separate manure yard was prepared where organic wastes were further segregated into various items, recycled ones among polythene based goods, glasses, tins, irons, cardboards etc. There were forty sets of boxes in this area. The inorganic wastes were after segregation kept in these boxes accordingly. Nearly there were four brick structured tanks where the organic wastes collected daily were dumped for compost making.

Further Self Help Group members of Jhansi Rani Group were engaged in vermiculture. There were long beds of brick construction where the vermicompost was produced. The women members sold the vermicompost to the public. There is a proposal to raise a nursery in the Village Panchayat garden for herbal gardening was also established.

Road Improvements

Jagatheesan and the Ward Members joined together in mobilizing resources to improve the condition of the roads in the Panchayat. From the MP Local Area Development Fund a CC Road in the Dalit Colony at an estimate of Rs.5.00 lakhs and another CC Road from the MLA Fund at a cost of Rs.1.70 lakhs were provided in Samiyar Madam hamlet. The amount allotted under the SGRY was also spent for road improvement and so all major roads in the Village Panchayat were converted into CC road or bitumen road, Mr. Jagatheesan told. Totally all the hamlets are well connected through roads.

CC Road

Construction of New Balwadi

Out of three hamlets, in Samiyar Madam, there is no Balwadi whereas there were about forty children in that hamlet. The Village Panchayat Council moved the higher officials for obtaining sanction for the provision of Balwadi, requested the SHG members to make improvised arrangements in this regard.

Balwadi Inauguration

In the meantime the government sanctioned a Balwadi for Samiyarmadam but there was no adequate space to construct the Balwadi. Jagatheesan, with his Panchayat Ward Members, met the office bearers of the Association of Wholesale Rice and Paddy Merchants and with their donation an extent of 5 cent (local value of Rs.40,000) land was purchased from a patta holder.

The MP came forward to allocate Rs.1.50 lakh for the construction of a building for Balwadi. Now the children of Samiyarmadam are in the new environment of learning. Thanks to the public and private partnership initiated by the Village Panchayat, a good Balwadi was established.

Youth Welfare Activities

The President and many of the Ward Members of Grandline Panchayat were youngsters. They encouraged youth — both students and non-students — to associate themselves through sports and games. Sports/games equipments like cricket bats, Volley balls, Basket Balls, Footballs, Carom board, Chess board etc. have been provided to village youths. Further the gym/bar equipments provided through government grant were also properly put to use. But the youth requested the Panchayat Council to help them to have a full-fledged gym in the village. Jagatheesan approached the Sakthi Oil Mill which is functioning in the jurisdiction of the Village Panchayat. The proprietor was kind enough to give donation for a full-fledged hydraulic gym-equipment costing Rs.75,000.

Hydraulic Gym

Immediately the Village Panchayat made arrangement for locating the hydraulic gym at the campus of the village farm. To ensure a sound mind along with a sound body, Jagatheesan made arrangements with the mission of Vedathiri Maharishi Yoga. Meditation classes were arranged for all including youths.

Public Private Partnership

Jagatheesan is always keen in making use of the potential of Panchayati Raj Institutions. As a number of activities have been carried out in the Village Panchayat jurisdiction, the developments are visible to all. Step by step attention like provision of drinking water, street lights, motorable road facilities, other infrastructures like community toilet, community hall, children's park, SHG building and Library are being provided, the Grandline Village Panchayats reputation is known to all. He gained name and recognition. Jagatheesan is serious in converting benefits to the Panchayat rather than aiming at personal gain. Hence for any innovative proposal he could mobilize private support. There are modern rice mills, oil mill, metal company and polytechnic institute whose managements are readily available to help the genuine efforts undertaken in the Grandline Panchayat Council in utilizing the village panchayat fund for better utilization and for support activities when innovations are initiated. For example, Yoga classes are handled by the Vedathiri Mission in the SHG centre. But there was no carpet for the comfortable seating of practioners. Immediately Jagatheesan consulted the Panchayat Council and purchased the required number of carpets from the Panchayat fund.

Public Contribution

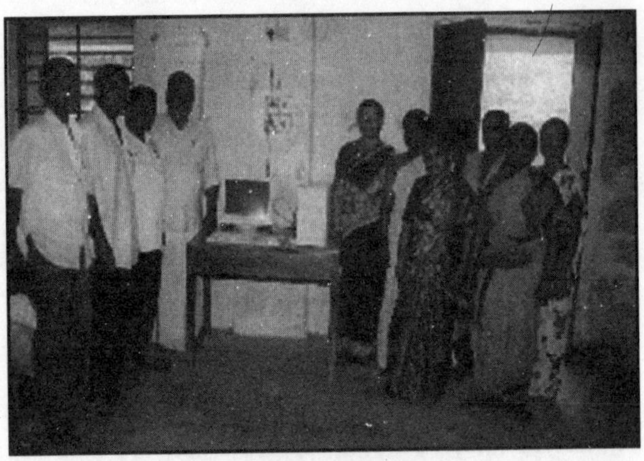

Public Contribution

Likewise there are various items of expenditure incurred by the Village Panchayat. In this respect the procedure of tender calling, obtaining of quotation, obtaining administrative/technical sanction have to be adhered to by the Village Panchayat administration. But it is a cumbersome one and always delaying in nature. But it is the legal duty and responsibility of the Village Panchayat President as he has to perform the role of Executive Authority for the Village Panchayat administration. Mr. Jagatheesan undertakes all activities after properly consulting all members during the Panchayat Council meetings. Moreover important subjects are discussed and decisions are taken in the Gram Sabha meetings also.

Awareness Camp

Further there is a considerable level of decentralization of power exercised by the Village Panchayat administration. But now and then legal powers entrusted to the Village Panchayat are unnecessarily restricted by the officials. Jagatheesan

Desilting of Pond

Vermi-Compost by SHG

had taken the risk of bypassing the bureaucratic control but he respects and consults Village Panchayat Council and Gram Sabha. Though there are several objections in the audit of accounts in Grandline Village Panchayat, development officials after personal verification and clarification cleared several objections raised in the audit. The understanding between the Village Panchayat administration and the block officials is very much necessary for the smooth and successful functioning of the Village Panchayats. Mr. Jagatheesan realizes the significance of this rapport and establishes contact with officials properly and whenever necessary meets the concerned officials for any clarification. But Jagatheesan feels that the degree of control and authority of bureaucracy exercised over the Village Panchayat administration is against the letter and spirit of law.

Promotion of SHG Activities

Jagatheesan informed that during the first tenure he seriously engaged in the formation and strengthening of Self Help Groups. He recollected the efforts of the then Assistant Collector Mr. Santhosh Babu of Thiruvallur District in orienting the SHG members providing exposure to various types of enterprises. The exposure visit to Gandhigram was very much useful, Jagatheesan claimed.

There are eighteen SHGs and almost all of them availed of economic assistance. But there is not any single group involved jointly in any production or trade activities. Most of them are engaged individually in petty business. Jagatheesan opined that NGOs role in improving the group morale and equipping them to manage an enterprise jointly, is yet to materialize practically.

SHGs in the Grandline Village Panchayat are yet to be motivated by the NGOs. But Jagatheesan was not ready to throw the ball in the court of NGOs. He with the approach of all ward members constructed a workshed from village panchayat fund for SHG members and procures 10 nos. of sewing machine so that the young women who know tailoring could engage themselves in production of readymade garments. He helped them to get an order from a wholesale trader. Recently the Secretary of the Departments of Rural Development visited the Grandline panchayat and after assessing the scope of the readymade garment business, sanctioned an amount of Rs.3.80 lakhs to provide a pucca training-cum-production centre to the SHGs of Grandline Village Panchayat. The building is coming up in the campus of Periyar Thidal, Jagatheesan shared.

The relationship between the SHG members and the village panchayat administration is very cordial. The SHG members are very much cooperative and participate in the developmental activities like rainwater harvesting, construction of individual toilets environmental sanitation and tree planting initiated by the Village Panchayat, Jagatheesan explained.

But Jagatheesan does not feel happy over these developments alone. His aim is to end poverty and under development among the villagers. He has immense faith in the power of Self Help Groups. If they are properly oriented and equipped they could venture into any type of micro economic activities,

Jagatheesan argued. But make them to believe in joint ventures is a hard and challenging task, he added. He is an optimist that if the village panchayat is entrusted with powers finance and responsibility to eradicate poverty through SHG activities, there would be sure developments in the arena of the SHG activities. In the context of urbanization of Puzhal union as it is located on the Grand Link Road connecting northern India, there would be many opportunities to the enterprising SHG members, Jagatheesan opined. He suggested a special plan especially by the village panchayat to enhance the income of families who are below poverty line.

Employment Opportunities to Educated Youth

In Grandline Panchayat generally most of the families wanted to get employment to their young men immediately after higher secondary education. Only very few families send their sons to higher studies in Industrial/Technical institutions. To find employment in the industrial units situated in and around the village panchayat area, the parents of young men approached the village panchayat President, Jagatheesan. Jagatheesan used to maintain good support with all the industrial and business firms and tried his best to get employment to the village youths. So far about twenty youths have employment in various firms functioning in and around Red Hills area. The proprietors respect the President and agreed to engage the reliable youths recommended by the president, Jagatheesan told.

Welfare of the Marginalised Section

Motivation and encouragement are the two major things which kindled the activities of the aspirants. Jagatheesan used to get motivation from the achievers. Once he came to know about the innovative action of the village panchayat president who made arrangements for the feeding of poor elders. Jagatheesan decided to help poor elders in his village. Mostly elders belong to poor families in general and among the Adi Dravidar in particular cannot get necessary care and attention as the other members of their families have to engage themselves in breadwinning activities.

Feeding the aged

Hence Jagatheesan, with the support of local philanthropists, started a free feeding centre for elderly poor in Grandline village panchayat. He used to collect rice from the surrounding rice mills and use the vegetables available in the Panchayat farm and so the feeding was immediately organized at the Periyar Thidal.

Women are engaged in the preparation and distribution of rice to the needy elders. To ensure self-respect to these elders Jagatheesan did not formulate any strict rules for the entry and to avail of the food. Anybody who is in need of a meal can come straightaway to the centre. The sundry expenditure in running the old age feeding centre is met from the village panchayat fund, Jagatheesan explained.

SC Welfare

Housing is the most serious demand put forth by the poor families of the SC community in the Grandline Panchayat. The provision of basic amenities in the SC habitation was properly attended to. Formation of roads, Cement Concrete road, water supply, street light, individual toilet, employment opportunities to the SC youths have been provided by the village panchayat. The demand of housing to the SC could not be met as the Government does not provide *patta* to their house site. The issue has been continuing for more than 20 years.

Jagatheesan is trying to take the issue to higher officials but yet his efforts to get *patta* could not succeed. It was told that the government is considering the removal of ban ordered on the transfer of poramboke land in urban areas into house site area so

Park in Dalit Colony

that group housing schemes could be implemented for SC communities in the bordering area of Chennai metro city.

In the SC colony at Grandline main village there was a public space. The vacant site could be protected by establishing a public garden as there is a statue of Dr. Ambedkar on the site. A few individuals objected to the proposal of a public park but the others agreed. Flower plants, grass beds, shady trees and decorative plants have been planted there by the Village Panchayat. The SC youths came forward to look after and to maintain the same. Jagatheesan encouraged their leadership in this regard. Now a beautiful public park has developed around Dr. Ambedkar's statue. It gives an aesthetic look and sense, Jagatheesan claimed.

Augmenting Panchayat Income

Jagatheesan realized the importance of financial resources, especially the village panchayat income through taxes and licences. He enhanced the house tax and property tax for the industrial firms. The income in this regard has improved from merely Rs.30,000 to Rs.4.00 lakhs. He used to collect development charges when approval is sought for new housing in extension area.

All India Football Tournament

Further, he mobilized resources from the public interested in philanthropy. The proprietor of Sankar Panner Thirumana Mandapam donated 100 chairs for the community hall. 100 plastic chairs were donated by the management of a Polytechnic and 20 chairs by a metal box company.

His positive thinking and service mindedness always bring benefits to his village. A Christian missionary institution, dedicated to youth welfare, named Don Bosco, functioning in the jurisdiction of Grandline Village Panchayat, is training youths in sports and games. As there is constant support and encouragement given by the Village Panchayat Council, the management of the missionary successfully organized an All India Football Tournament during the month of January 2005. It was a big event. Hundreds and thousand of nearby villagers witnessed the play and it was a matter of pride for the youth. The Secretary of the Don Bosco institution accorded respect and recognition to Jagatheesan during the prize distribution ceremony. He was treated equally with other chief guests. If Presidents of village Panchayats are committed to their service, name and fame would come to them, Jagatheesan said.

Jagatheesan's Continued Leadership

After the completion of his first tenure in 2001, Jagatheesan once again contested for the position of the village president. His five years' service was counted by the public and so he faced only one opponent during the second election. He declared that if he was elected he would continue his leadership to concentrate further on the activities of poverty alleviation. The innovations and other achievements of Grandline Village panchayat under the leadership of Jagatheesan were projected during the election campaign. People's faith in his leadership brought him success. He sustained his leadership winning by a 450-vote difference. Moreover all Ward Members fielded by his team were won in the election. The present village panchayat council of Grandline consists of the following office bearers:

Vice-President	:	S. Vasudevan
Members	:	N. Moorthy
		P. Devaki
		S. Manakaron
		M. Lakshmi Muniasamy
		Kamuthi Arasu
		R. Saroja Ravi
		G. Vadivel
		R. Mariammal Ramakrishnan

Provisional Store

All members show real interest and concern in the overall development of the Village Panchayat. This unity is the strength of Grandline. Due to the existence of mutual understanding and harmony among the ward members as well among the caste groups, it was possible to establish a common burial/funeral ground in Grandline Panchayat. Earlier there were different locations for different caste groups for funeral activities. In his second tenure, the common burial ground was established; a beautiful garden was formed with high quality grass planted along the compound wall. Water Supply, seating arrangement and shady trees for rest were also developed. An unanimous decision was taken to forbid construction of any monument in the graveyard earmarked for burial of dead bodies.

The whole site is covered with green bushes, trees, plants, grass land and a variety of flower plants coming up beautifully inside the campus of the funeral/burial ground. It gives an impression to the visitors that it is like a moghul garden.

Jagatheesan's Future Agenda

The development and growth accomplished in Grandline Village Panchayat was possible due to the cooperation and involvement of the Panchayat Ward Members, Mr. Jagatheesan said. Further, with the support of youths and SHG members, activities like environmental sanitation, tree planting, solid waste management etc. have been successfully undertaken. "The guidance and counselling of development officials of Thiruvarur District and training exposure given by the SIRD, RIRD — S.V. Nagaram, Gandhigram University, Vivekananda Kendra, Exnora and Kuthambakkam Model Village shaped my development vision," Mr. Jagatheesan said.

His future agenda is to plan for poverty alleviation programmes involving SHG members. His attempt to establish and run a provisional store by a partnership of the Village Panchayat and an SHG is now coming to shape, Jagatheesan claimed. Likewise there are several possible opportunities to harvest the available resources in the village through enterprising activities — Dairy, Nursery, Poultry, Catering, Readymade Garments Unit. He decided to give a proper motivation to SHG members to make them realize the scope of joint venture. Individually one SHG member is able to earn very nominal money only. The SHG members have in general a fear of the joint approach. This fear has to be removed through proper and professional guidance and constant support structure, Jagatheesan felt. Hence Jagatheesan prepared himself and his team of panchayat ward members and other volunteers to establish contact with various institutions and agencies concerned with the strengthening and equipping of SHGs. As he has a vision and begins to work for making the vision a reality, it is sure he is going to be a path finder in these respects also.

His leadership is extraordinary. His commitment is appreciable. His openness, his dedication, his honesty, his partnership, his participation and his farsightedness brought this much of success. His achievements beyond the scope of the Panchayat brought name to him. His retrieval of encroachment of common properties worth about several lakhs gave a message to the people that he is an extraordinary leader known for his integrity. His activities are audited by the public. He relies on social audit. He does not bother about the departmental audit.

His activities are based on demands. Officials have responded positively to the demands of the Panchayats. He wants to be responsive and responsible to the people. His attention is always towards the people rather than towards the bureaucracy. He believes that by working with the people the Panchayat can achieve anything whether powers are given to the Panchayats or not.

CASE - 17

A NEW CULTURE FOR CLEANLINESS

Veerapandiapattinam is known for cleanliness. The President hailing from the fisher community, wanted to transform the Panchayat into a clean Panchayat as it is fully dominated by fisherfolk. With great difficulty he made it possible. Now the entire area is clean, neat and tidy. He wanted to create a new culture of cleanliness. By establishing a management system for delivery of services, he started delivering services according to the needs of the people. Having realized the potential of the Panchayat, government departments extended their full support to this Panchayat. His aim is to create a sanitation culture, not merely providing toilets. In his attempt he has succeeded. The people have been conscientised on hygiene, sanitation and cleanliness.

Veerapandianpattinam is a Gram Panchayat known for its cleanliness and it draws the attention of all who go to this area. One would find the streets and public places in Veerapandianpattinam clean and tidy as if it expects the visit of some VIPs.

It has become the culture and behaviour of the people to keep the place neat and clean. Another wonder takes place in this village which is unique in character. There is no drainage system in the entire village. Instead, in every house, there is an arrangement to manage the waste water.

Panchayat Building

In all public places soakpits have been created to absorb the waste water. In every house one finds a kitchen garden and flower saplings. There is no waste water either in the street or in the house yard. It happens in a Village Panchayat wherein 75 per cent of the people are fisher folk. There is one dominant argument projected that the majority of them are Christians and so the sanitary culture has been imbibed by the people. But the question is why did it not happen four years ago? There is yet another argument projected that the nature of the soil is sandy and hence it has got the capacity to absorb the moisture and waste water and hence it is clean. Again the same question, why did it not happen four years ago?

This question made us visit Veerapandianpattinam and analyse the factor. In our analysis the leadership in the Panchayat made the difference. T. Babiloas Gorge is the Panchayat President who came to the Panchayat area after spending 36 years in Rameswaram in fishing. Veerapandianpattinam is his native place. But he went to Rameswaram only for earning his livelihood. In the first period he did not show any interest in the Panchayat as he was not aware of the potential of the system. His predecessor assumed office and ran the administration for five years and yet nothing moved in the positive direction.

When the second election for local bodies was announced, he made up his mind to contest in the election. He decided to contest after knowing fully well the potential of the Panchayat system. He perceived water supply and removal of waste as the two gigantic tasks one had to do in this Panchayat. People were travelling 3 kilometres everyday for bathing through a town bus and everywhere people dumped waste material which was a challenge to the Panchayat administration. He gave two promises to the people that he would give water regularly to the level of their need and remove the waste from the streets to the dump yard. He secured more votes than the others and got elected and started the work.

This Village Panchayat was in Kayalpattinam integrated drinking water supply system and got water supply regularly for which the Panchayat had to pay money periodically. Since the arrears had accumulated to the tune of several lakhs, water supply was stopped. Petitions were given to get water but nothing moved. After assuming office he went to the TWAD Board

Opening Ceremony — OHT

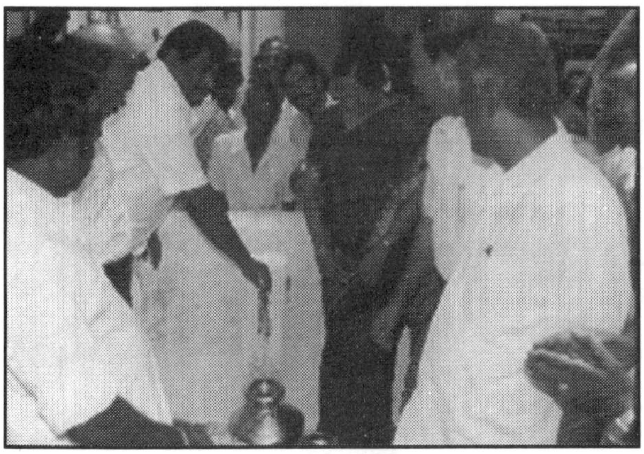

Opening of Public Tap

office and enquired about the problem and he was informed that if the Panchayat cleared the old arrears, the Panchayat could get water from this scheme. But the Panchayat was not in a position to pay the arrears and hence some new formula had to be worked out. He argued with officials and he came to a negotiated settlement with the officials that then onwards there would not be any delay in payment. This was the arrangement projected by the President. The officials mooted a new proposal that an advance of Rs.88,000 (six months' water charge) has to be remitted and every month the actual charge has to be remitted, by which water supply could be regularized. With this arrangement he convened the meeting of the Gram Sabha and explained the position to the people and asked for their opinion.

Everyone agreed to the proposal of the Panchayat President to pay six months advance and pay regularly the water charge and from that pool water can be given to all families to the level of their need. He explained the financial position of the Panchayat by showing the entire accounts and asked for their suggestions. His way of dealing with things is totally different from that of others. In every village there is a temple committee that is convened by the President of the committee. They will discuss informally as everyone feels that they are partners and owners. In the same way, without making it either ritual or official, he makes it an informal but stakeholder forum. He never takes positions. He gives options leaving it to the members of the Gram Sabha. By appearance also he is unassuming, simple and decent in his dealings. He allows everyone to talk and argue. Hence decision making is easy for him. People themselves suggest ways and means for every problem. But his role is to facilitate the discussion of the group. For this financial crisis many suggested that house tax could be increased. He asked everyone about hiking the house tax. He made a suggestion that the hike for the poor should be very low, but, for the rich, it should be high. This proposal was meant to avoid opposition from the poorest sections of the society. Everyone agreed. By hiking the house tax, he brought the revenue up from Rs.56,000 to Rs.1,66,000. He informed the people that he would remit the amount for water charges advance from this collection. Every month they had to pay the charge and which they had to devise a new mechanism. This was the next agenda discussed in the Gram Sabha. People suggested the same old water charges. Irrespective of poor and rich, everyone agreed. With this proposal he started the work. He remitted the money in the TWAD Board office and restored the water connection.

While connecting the water supply he regulated the entire water supply through a water connection card just like the EB card. He has given 276 house connections for which a charge is collected every month. There is no problem in collecting money from the people for water use. It is a boon to them as they were in distress. As he fulfilled his promise of water supply, people started believing him. By restoring the water supply he got money from the Government to construct overhead water tanks. He added 5 tanks (OHT) to the existing two. When water supply was regularized and distributed he provided a cell phone to the OHT operator from his own money. Every morning the Panchayat President used to cover the entire area of the Panchayat to check whether water supply was proper. Whenever people need the service of the OHT operator he gives the cell number of the OHT operator to all and they can call him and ask him to get the service done. He made the water supply a system. He is collecting fines from the defaulters also. When he was asked about the reaction of the people towards the water charge and the fine levied against the defaulters, he said that the decision was not the decision of the Panchayat President. He made another interesting observation that people are ready to pay for the service which they get from any agency provided the service is good and of good quality and precisely meets their demand. In this Panchayat people have struggled to get water which made the job easier to the Panchayat President.

Secondly he started attacking the waste. He witnessed many times conflict over dumping of waste. It was the second promise he had given during the election.

Cleaning the Streets

Normally, in any place, fishermen's settlement will be considered for dumping yard, especially for the waste. Here also this was the practice. On many occasions conflicts arose among the people over dumping the waste in the fishermen's area. His primary concern was that fishermen should be sensitized on decent human living as others are leading. Since he belongs to fisher folk he had the feeling that fisher folk should also lead a decent human life in the society. Hence he wanted to remove the waste and classify it and make it compost manure. Profit making is a secondary thing for him. How to make the village clean and how to sensitize the people is the major problem. He felt that unless people are sensitized and people are involved, whatever step the Panchayat takes will last only for a few days and a few months. Hence he took a series of steps to sensitize the people. He sought the help of an NGO and got two vehicles to remove all classified waste from every house and every street by using the sanitary staff. Needed boxes have been given to all the families. People themselves classify and give it to the staff.

Removing the garbage from Streets

Collecting the Waste

Clean Streets

Everyday all the classified wastes are collected and dumped in one place and now they make it into manure. A contract is made with a group to take all the manure for a long period. They have fixed Rs.150 per truck. Everyday the Panchayat can sell at least four to five loads of manure by which Panchayat can earn money. While doing this exercise the "Total Sanitation Scheme" and "Namathu Gramam Scheme" were announced. Incidentally these schemes were helpful to perfect his activities which he had initiated. All IEC activities for water supply and sanitation have been done by making use of the scheme. While seeing the entire village one can find it advertisement for sanitation and clean village. By his personal effort all IEC activities were carried out meticulously and he personally supervised them.

Sanitation

A test case is a school going boy who repeated the ten commandments for sanitation. A student undergoing fourth standard from a tuition centre and we asked him to say list the ten commandments of sanitation, he did that just like mantra. It is called sanitation mantra. He made everyone internalize the sanitation practice. When we asked him to narrate and explain the other activities carried out by the Panchayat, he said that there are several activities that have been carried out in this Panchayat. But they are all sectoral development activities. They have earmarked the allocation and they have to spend it and hence they are doing their activities. Of course, Panchayat leaders have to take the initiative to get the schemes implemented in their area. But these activities are not so difficult. If a Panchayat leader has got negotiating skills, he will manage the officers and get things done in the Panchayat area, he observed. Because the sectoral departments' schemes do not have space for people's participation. Moreover, the Departments carry out their work whether the work is needed by the people or not. There is no challenge in it.

Sanitation

There is yet another striking activity he has done in his Panchayat. While taking stock of the Panchayat finance, he found a lapse on the part of the transport corporation. The road transport corporation which has to remit professional tax to the Panchayat. But it has not remitted it for several years. The earlier Panchayat leader also ignored it. When he approached the manager of the Depot, he said that the corporation is running at a loss and that if it gains profits, definitely the amount will be remitted. Then the Panchayat President approached a lawyer with the Panchayat Act book. The lawyer advised him that the Panchayat has got a right to collect the dues. Based on the opinion, he informed the manager of the depot that he was going to court.

The manager approached him and assured him that he would remit it in installments. But the Panchayat President told him that collecting and remitting the professional tax is the responsibility of the corporation office and officials working in the office have already paid the money, but the office has not remitted the same. So there was no question of remitting the money in installments. This was the reply given by the Panchayat President. Against this background the manager of the transport corporation depot remitted the entire 7 lakh rupees in one installment. He felt that this a great achievement he has made.

There is an issue which is being faced in all Gram Panchayats, namely, the identifying of beneficiaries for Government schemes under the BPL list. In all Panchayats everyone wants to become a member in the BPL list. It is almost a political exercise. On many occasions, more number of ineligible families are included because of political considerations and eligible families are excluded as they have no political base.

In his Panchayat he did that exercise differently. He collected the list and presented the same in the

Gram Sabha and asked the people to finalize the list. The people discussed the names and eliminated many names from the list by doing wealth ranking analysis. Finally, he asked the members to arrange the families according to the level of intensity of poverty in an ascending order. The poorest of the poor would be number one and accordingly the numbering was done for all families. According to the observation and approval 282 families are under BPL list. They belong to the Dalit community. The others need no support from the Government. A plan has to be prepared for 282 families for their livelihood security. In this Panchayat 70 per cent are fishermen, 27 per cent are Dalits and 3 per cent constitute other categories. For each and every scheme, he has prepared a list and got it approved in the Gram Sabha. He maintains a seniority list among the beneficiaries. Once a benefit is enjoyed by a family, it cannot enjoy another again. It has been decided so in the Gram Sabha.

Clean Street

Clean Street

Having got training in training institutions, he has extreme role clarity on his role and responsibility. His way of conducting the Gram Sabha is totally different from that of other Panchayats. Having made the system transparent, he conducts the Gram Sabha like the traditional Panchayat. He never collects petitions. Instead he brings up issues for discussion and taking decisions. He never allows the Gram Sabha to pass resolution as in other places. What could be done in the Panchayat is allowed to be discussed in the Gram Sabha. Sometimes the passed resolutions might not have been implemented. He used to explain the reality to the people. He made the Gram Sabha vibrant because he has acted on the direction of the people. He is not collecting petitions from the people and he made it clear that the Gram Sabha is not for the Government or its officials. It is for the people. He openly discusses all matters and he informs what can be done and what cannot be done. Needed publicity is being given to Gram Sabha meeting and hence he attracts a large number of people for Gram Sabha meetings.

There is yet another striking work he has carried out in his Panchayat area. There is no drainage system in his Panchayat. In many villages there is a provision for the Panchayat to construct a small channel to remove the waste from the streets. But, unfortunately, in the absence of sensitization of the people on sanitation and hygiene, the drainage channel constructed out of the scheme stores enough waste to breed mosquitoes. Ultimately instead of keeping the street clean it makes it dirty and filthy. In this Panchayat he adopted a totally different strategy. Each household has to formulate a device by which the waste water has to be absorbed. If there is excess water, it has to be drained into a soak pit. Through this devise in each and every house kitchen garden has been developed. It is a unique feature of the Panchayat. There is no smell or excess stagnated water in his Panchayat area. All people have created such a device without any problem.

It is a hundred per cent sanitized village and rain water harvesting structures have been created in the entire village. In his Panchayat area, there is a hostel meant for fisher folk students. When he became the Panchayat President the hostel was defunct.

Rain Water Harvesting

Rain Water Harvesting

He revived the hostel by getting support from the Church. Apart from the above work, he approached the District Collector for assistance to run the hostel. He helped the Panchayat leader to revive the hostel. For a specific question "what have you done for women and children?" he said, by providing water to all to their requirement during their convenient time, he helped women. Their worry and tragedy was over. In fact he said that he gets more support only from women for collecting water charge. If water problem is solved one fourth of the problems of women are solved. If the water is clean, purified another one-fourth is solved as they do not have any sick person in their family due to the supply of good drinking water. By keeping the streets and public places clean, by providing toilets to the school, by creating a toilet complex for women, the Panchayat is helping women and children. He argues that health governance and education governance will facilitate many of the problems of the community being solved very easily.

He maintains that his Panchayat office is open from 9.30 a.m. to 5.30 p.m. everyday. A Gram Panchayat office functions as Block Panchayat Office. Both the President and the Clerk will be in the office. People used to come to the Panchayat to submit petitions, remit money and see the accounts.

Conclusion

It is demonstrated unequivocally that a leadership with vision, commitment, mission, honesty and passion for service can deliver service however poor the Panchayats are. These leaders are change agents. By merely applying their mind with a sense of service the whole system can be geared up. People are willing to cooperate provided the needed leadership is demonstrated to deliver service and goods. Even tough decisions can be taken and people will accept the decision provided the leader is honest and sincere. There are a large number of essential activities to be carried out in the villages which require no money. By changing the mind set, many can work together and transform the village. But the initiative has to come from the leader. He has demonstrated his ability to mobilise the people for community action. He is the solid example for grassroots governance. Health governance is the solid work of this Panchayat. By mere supervision and partnership many of the government institutions can deliver services effectively and in good quality. Finally, the Panchayat President made a remark that people should feel that they are getting services regularly and they should feel that they are a person in the Panchayat with responsibility and responsiveness. At every level one has to see the outcome, not the output, finally observed the Panchayat Presidents.

Anganwadi

SHG Building

Public Distribution System

Fisherman with his net

Bus Shelter

Shopping Complex

Shopping Complex

Clean Street

EERAPANDIANPATTINAM PANCHAYAT

General Particulars

1. Year of Panchayat started on	1923
2. Total Area	10 SK
3. Total Population	4652
4. Male	2114
5. Female	2558
6. Total houses	1253
7. A.P.L.	4387
8. B.P.L.	285
9. No. of Hamlets	5
(i) Veerapandianpattinam	
(ii) Kurinji Nagar	
(iii) Pradesh Nagar	
(iv) Fisheries Colony	
(v) Raj Kanna Nagar	
10. No. of Streets	41
(i) Veerapandianpattinam	10
(ii) Kurinji Nagar	8
(iii) Prasadh Nagar	12
(iv) Fisheries Colony	8
(v) Raj Kanna Nagar	3
11. Public Taps	110
12. Tap Connection for houses	276
13. OHT	6
14. Sintex Tanks	7
15. Combined Water scheme	1
16. Public Well	3
17. Waste Box	2
18. Sweepers	10
19. Women Sanitary Complex	1
20. School Toilet	2
21. Anganvadi Toilet	2
22. Individual H.H.Toilet	1190
23. Noon meal building	2
24. Anganvadi Building	2
25. Private Hospitals	2
26. Arivozhi Buildings	1
27. Private Arts College	1
28. Private Teacher Training School	1
29. Higher Secondary School Private	1
30. Government I.T.I.	1
31. Nutrition Centre	1
32. Government Transport Department	1
33. T.V. Room	2
34. V.A.O. Office	1
35. Community Hall	1
36. PDS Shop	1
37. Street Lights	
(i) Tube lights	305
(ii) Sodium	4
(iii) Solar, Sun lights	1
38. Private Bank	1
39. Post Office	1
40. Road details	
	Length
(i) Caravel Roads - 4 nos.	1.10
(ii) Metal Road - 5 nos.	1.40
(iii) Tar Road - 8 nos.	1.80
(iv) Cement Road - 12 nos.	2.85
41. No. of wards	9

42. Ward Allotments

Reservation (General)	6	
General (Women)	2	
S.C. (Women)	1	**9 nos.**

43. President and Ward members details

1. Thiru T. Pabilas Kuna	President
2. Thiru Jeyels Raj	Vice-President
3. Thiru Anigia Prinster	Member
4. Thiru Rani Jortar	Member
5. Thiru Mani	Member
6. Thiru Giyotter Pris	Member
7. Thiru Jeya Kumar	Member
8. Thiru Joat Phin Tennosha	Member
9. Thiru Edisen Burnandhu	Member
10. Thiru Edvij	Member

44. Panchayat Clerk Thiru P.M. Meeran Panchayat has got TSC Award for 2003-2004
    - ★ Activities for Total Sanitation Programme
        - IEC print Materials
        - Mass Media Campaign
        - Street Texture
        - Mass Rally
        - Door to Door Campaigns
        - Anganwadi Training
        - Special Training
        - Construction of Latrines
        - Individual House Hold Latrines
        - Integrated Women's Sanitary Complex
        - Total Sanitation Festival
        - Sanitary Corps
    - ★ Clean Village Campaign
    - ★ Solid Waste Management
    - ★ Rain Water Harvesting.

CASE - 18

SHOWN THE WAY FOR STATE GOVERNMENT

Ms. Jesumary went up to Washington D.C. at the invitation of the World Bank to explain how she transformed her Panchayat into an instrument to guide the state government, especially on rain water harvesting. Having seen the plight of the people in getting water for drinking and other purposes, she resolved to solve the problem on a priority basis. Her intention was to find out answers not from outside. Hence she thought that by establishing rain water harvesting structures, water could be saved and the same could be made to percolate into the soil. By carrying out this activity with great difficulty she demonstrated the implications in the next year itself by raising the water table. This made her popular among the people and the bureaucracy and she received several awards. This is yet another model Panchayat. By quoting her achievement, the Chief Minister has written letters to all Gram Panchayat Presidents to adopt rainwater harvesting following the model of Michalepattinam.

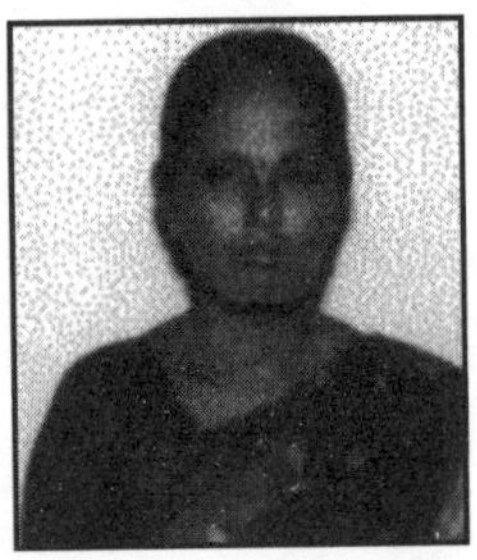

Ms. Jesumary (49) is the President of Michalepattinam Gram Panchayat in Mudukulathoor Block Panchayat in Ramnathapuram District. She studied upto PUC. She was born in a small village near Kilakarai and got married in Michalepattinam. She has four sisters and a brother. Her father was a businessman. Her father got her married to an agriculturist and her husband is the only son of her in-laws. Both her in-laws carry out all the activities—both agricultural and household—after her marriage.

So she took the responsibility of taking care of herself and her children. She has three sons. She joined as a teacher in an Adult Education Centre after her marriage. She worked as an Adult Education teacher for fifteen years. She used to interact with village women and they used to come to her to share their grievances. She acted as a counsellor. Sometimes she even settled their family problems. When she was doing all these she did not envisage a role for herself in Panchayat.

She wanted to contest the Panchayat elections immediately after her marriage. In the previous Panchayat system, as per the Tamil Nadu Panchayat Act, 1958, there was no reservation for women as we find now through the 73rd Amendment. Her father, a businessman, used to actively participate in all village development activities. As the only daughter she lived with her parents and she closely involved herself and supported her father in all his activities and thus she automatically got oriented in public work. Her in-laws opposed her wish to contest in elections. So she waited nearly thirty years to contest in an election. During the 1996 election, though her father in-law had died and her mother in-law opposed her contesting in any election, because she had a very bad opinion about elections and electoral politics. Her perception was that individuals would be killed in Panchayat elections and candidates would have to spend a lot of money for the election.

In the meanwhile the entire village community supported her candidature in the Panchayat elections. The reason for extending support to her candidature was that she was the only woman who had studied upto PUC and she had already involved herself in many community development activities, actively supporting women, especially poor women. With the support of her husband she agreed to contest and won the election. She contested again in 2001 and won the election based on her performance. Her father was a source of her inspiration. She reflected only her father's qualities.

Social Backdrop

Michalepattinam Panchayat is in between Mudukulathoor and Paramakudi. The Panchayat is two kms away from the main road. The entire area except Michalepattinam is covered by bushes and thorns and hence the Panchayat has to put up street lights on both sides of the road from the main road up to the entrance of the Panchayat. The entire community of the Panchayat belongs to the Christian Udaiyar community. After assuming office she used to go to the Block Development office and the Collectorate on her own. Her husband and her three sons never accompanied her. At the same time, she saw to it that her family commitments and her family agricultural activities should not be affected because of her new assignment. She considered this new position an opportunity to serve the people. She belongs to the Indian National Congress Party. She considers this space as a development one not a political one. Her family is not rich and not so poor either.

She emerged as a successful Gram Panchayat President because of the District Collector Mr. Anand. She remembers him as a gender sensitive officer. He always encouraged women leaders to perform their role and responsibility perfectly. He encouraged them to act independently. He also advised them that they should have self-confidence. As far as she is concerned, there is no relationship between education and administering Panchayat activities.

Emergence of Successful Panchayat Leaders

When she contested the Panchayat elections, she promised the villagers that after assuming office as Panchayat President, her first and foremost priority would be to solve the drinking water problem and to desilt the tanks to increase the agricultural activities. The entire village depends on agriculture for livelihood. Only educated youths have migrated to cities and abroad for employment. After assuming office, she took the initiative to desilt the tanks and water ways. But the nearby Gram Panchayat President objected as he considered all the water ways part of his Panchayat. He threatened that he had a plan to get a stay order from court. Ms. Jesumary approached the Public Works Department. The PWD engineer informed her that all the water ways and the oorani belong to the neighbouring Panchayat. She knew very well that they all belong to her Panchayat as she has seen the map of the village with the Village Administrative Officer. She approached the District Collector in this regard. The District Collector constituted a Peace Committee headed by the Paramakudi Sub-Collector. She wanted to discuss the issue with the people before going to the Peace Committee meeting. She convened a Gram Sabha meeting. The entire village community attended the Gram Sabha meeting. They realized the importance of desilting the tanks and constructing check dams. They decided to construct them by themselves overnight. The Panchayat President had to attend the Peace Committee meeting the next day.

Desilted Tank

Michalepattinam is a very dry area. They depend on rain to do farming activities. Only a few families possess wells. So she explained to them that the water ways should be cleaned before the rain comes and desilting of tanks also has to be done. She also told them that desilting of tanks would not only help them to do agricultural activities but also help their cattle. The Makiti Panchayat President planned to stop the work with the help of the police. Both complained to the police. Her villagers worked overnight and they cleaned the water ways and strengthened the check dams. It was a shock to the other Panchayat President and officials including the Collector. Everyone realized the potential of the community. It was a breakthrough in her work which has raised her image among the people.

She learnt from a reliable sources that many village people from Makiti Panchayat were waiting near the Sub-Collector in Paramakudi with lethal weapons to kill her. Ms.Leelavathi, Councillor, Madurai Corporation, was killed by *goondas* during that time because of the water distribution problem in her ward. She decided to take all cautious steps. She went to the Taluk Office through the back door for the Peace Committee meeting. The Peace Committee decided to stop all work till the Collector gave orders. But she informed them that already she had completed the work. The officials immediately decided to send police personnel to guard the water ways and ooranis.

Again a meeting was convened by the Collector the Sub-Collector and the Tashildhar. They verified all the records and informed the Makiti Panchayat President that all the water ways and ooranis belonged to Michalepattinam Panchayat. The Makiti Panchayat President had no option but to obey the government orders. They planned to disturb her. She was very cautious and hence she stayed out for more than a month. She took up this issue because every year the people of both the Panchayats fought each other to share water for agricultural activities during the months of September, October, and November. She had watched this problem for more than 30 years. She wanted to find a solution to this problem. So she acted and succeeded. This incident made her gain more strength without spending a single paise. People started believing her and started supporting her. Problems which could not be solved over decades have now been solved. It is all because of her initiative. She remembered that all the officials, including the then District Collector Mr. Anand, came to the village to settle the dispute between the two Panchayats. She also felt that mere ego clash between two Panchayats left the problem unsolved. The community leaders never reared women as leaders. They won't accept women as leaders and they openly tell everyone that women does not have the capacity to lead the Panchayat. Now she is very happy that she has disproved their stand. But still many have the same opinion.

Receiving Awards on various occasions

She felt that women have a very big role to sensitize men on gender issues. She is doing this among Gram Panchayat Presidents belonging to Ramnathapuram District. She also keeps sensitizing the husbands of women Gram Panchayat Presidents who are not allowing their wives to perform their roles and responsibilities.

She felt good governance and gender are her priority. Reducing poverty is her another agenda. She felt women have the capacity to administer and govern. But men are not allowing them to act due to fear of losing their traditional place and respect. They thought that women lack the mental and educational qualifications' for political participation. They also have a crude notion that the public sphere belongs to men. She felt that men react very jealously when women achieve something more than men. Sometime this leads to extremely unpleasant harassment towards women. She felt that the same feeling led the Makiti Panchayat President to show hostility towards her. According to her, foes always make us realize whether we are in the right path or not. Even if we have no friends, even if we have ten foes, we can succeed easily, because we will be always cautious in taking decisions and doing things.

Meeting with EWRs

Panchayat Management

After assuming office as Panchayat President, she started learning Panchayat administration. She attended many training programmes conducted by the Government of Tamil Nadu and Gandhigram Rural Institute. She found that the capacity building exercise given by the Gandhigram Rural Institute helped her to understand the Panchayat administration in the right perspective. She learnt the following aspects from Gandhigram Rural Institute to run the Panchayat successfully:

- how to speak in front of large gatherings.
- how to conduct herself in a public place.
- how to manage a crowd.
- available Rural Development schemes.
- administrative nuances.
- how to maintain Panchayat records.
- difference between Government Orders and notifications.

She felt that she got self-confidence after attending meetings regularly. She felt that capacity building for women Gram Panchayat leaders and gender sensitivity training to their husbands and male counterparts are very important. They encourage men to support women leaders to perform better with an understanding that they have also a role to play in household activities. She also feels when women become effective local body leaders automatically transparency and delivery of goods will improve. Gender sensitive training to their husbands will begin to change their perception of female leaders.

She is running the Panchayat without a clerk for the past six month. She has the ability to write all accounts in a proper manner. Her Panchayat is considered the best Panchayat in all aspects including maintenance of records. The Block Development Officer of Mudukulathoor Block and the Personal Assistant to the Collector of Ramnathapuram District felt the Michalepattinam Panchayat records are the best maintained ones. She never paid a single paisa as commission or bribe till now to anyone in the administrative set up. If the Panchayat President is honest nobody can touch him/her.

She gets up at 3 O'clock every morning. She completes all her household activities before 6.00 a.m. She does agricultural activities up to 10.00 a.m. in her fields. Afterwards she takes the responsibility of doing all the Panchayat activities from 10.00 a.m. to 6.00 p.m. She breaks her routine only on Sunday. She attends prayer in church upto 1.00 p.m. and afterwards she takes up all family related engagements.

Her family members are very cooperative and supportive. She lives with her two sons and husband. Whoever goes home first in the night will take up the responsibility of preparing dinner. She said that she succeeded in all her endeavour because of her husband. Her husband takes up the family responsibility whenever she goes out of station for Panchayat work. Her family members have a very good understanding among themselves. They never have food in hotels.

Performance

Michalepattinam is a very dry area and hot area. She wanted to cover her entire Panchayat with trees. She distributed saplings to each and every household with the slogan "veetukku oru maram". Now in each and every house in Michalepattinam a tree is growing. The Panchayat planted trees on both sides of the roads and wherever common lands were available. Her Ward Members are very cooperative and whatever idea emerges she discusses in the Panchayat meeting and she implements all schemes with the support of the Ward Members. She never allows contractors to carry out any work. The Panchayat does all the work to ensure 100 per cent quality. She felt that even if she allow contractors, they don't take up work in Michalepattinam, because of her expectation of quality. If it is individual work, the particular household itself implements the work.

Rain Water Harvesting

One priority is to reduce poverty by increasing agriculture production. Her main thrust is that each and every person should earn his/her livelihood. She works as Panchayat President with the aim of achieving the following:

- Every family should get a pucca house with toilet facility.
- Every adult should get engaged in livelihood activities.
- She wanted to make her Panchayat hunger free. After the government announcement of rainwater harvesting, she regarded this scheme as a poverty reduction scheme. She convened the Gram Sabha and she explained all the positive points about the installation of rainwater harvesting structures and everyone agreed. She convened the Panchayat meeting again to discuss among the members how to install this structure and how to enable people to do this. They decided to help each and every house to install a pucca rainwater harvesting structure. The Panchayat provided sand and stones to each house. The Panchayat purchased PVC pipes for the entire village and distributed to them to ensure quality.

Rain Water Harvesting

She created an innovative technique of connecting all the side pipes from all the houses to a common pipe to harvest the rainwater. This rainwater harvesting device has been put up in such a way that the entire rainwater will be stored without any waste. The rainwater from the roof of the house falls into a PVC pipe and all such PVC pipes from all the houses on both the sides of the street are connected to a large sized PVC pipe which has been sunk in the middle of the street. The PVC pipes from all the streets are connected to a large size pipe which takes the entire rainwater to a public tank. Through this every drop of water will go to the tank without any waste.

Sanitation

While constructing rainwater harvesting structures, she urged the villagers to construct toilets also. Each and every house in Michalepattinam Panchayat has a toilet and a pucca rainwater harvesting structure. She encouraged people to construct toilets not only in their

Segregation of Wastes

houses but also at the tail end of the village, where elders can use it. Elders usually do not have the habit of using toilets in their houses. She could not change their mindset. So she decided to construct a few individual toilets separately for men and women. Now the elders are using them. She also constructed a women sanitary complex with incinerators. She learnt this technique from Kerala. In the corner of the building she has created a structure, i.e. she has covered the open space with a wall and has let two holes — one at the bottom and other at the upper side, just above the bottom hole she has put some steel net. Women can throw napkins and waste into it. Through the upper hole Panchayat drops fire in the hole of the structure once a week and thus the wastes are burnt. She also constructed toilets in the balwadi and the schools. She encourages children to use the toilet in the balwadi by giving chocolates to them as incentive. She announced among children that they have to inform her if anybody indulges in open defecation. She also announced to them that whoever uses toilet regularly will get chocolates, pen, notebook and such small gifts. This has created a tremendous impact among the children. They even insist on their parents using toilets. She has completely stopped open defecation.

Common Property Resources

She found three acres of Panchayat land available. There are no Scheduled Caste people in her Panchayat and hence the government SFC grant is very little for her Panchayat Rs.8,000 only. So she has to augment the resources. She wanted to cultivate jatropa in three acres to get resources. But the condition of land was very bad. The Panchayat did not have the capacity to spend for cleaning the land. She requested SHG groups and they agreed. They cleaned the land by cutting the trees, bushes and thorns in their free time. The villagers helped her to plough the land. She planted jatropa seeds. She is now confident that she can earn a good amount for the Panchayat next year onwards.

She also constructed a manure godown at a cost of Rs.85,000 to prepare bio-manure. She appointed a sweeper exclusively for collecting bio-degradable waste. They have sold bio-manure for Rs.500 till now. The people of her Panchayat are contributing Rs.20 to collect waste from their houses and cleaning toilets. She pays a salary to the sweeper from the people's contribution. In her Panchayat every family has a pucca house with rainwater harvesting and toilet. She has also constructed the cement roads. Michalepattinam has a very good drainage system. She has desilted all the tanks in her Panchayat.

She is planning to celebrate seed week festival in the school and the balwadi to drive home the importance of growing trees among children. She is planning to distribute seeds to students. They are to plant them in their school premises. She wants to establish a garden in the balwadi and the school with the help of the children. The Panchayat also planning to create gardens on many themes. These would be handed over to each class and the entire class should maintain the garden. Every month an external agency will assess the gardens and give marks for maintenance. Prizes will be given to best maintained garden. She has given buckets, mugs, towels, soaps to the balwadi. She has also given two bags (green and red) to collect non-degradable and bio-degradable

Encouraging School Children

Visiting various places

wastes. All the children in her Panchayat are going to the school or the balwadi. The youth are engaged in work. No one is idle.

Only one ultra poor person lives in her Panchayat. She has a plan for her also. She gave her a new life on the Independence Day by setting up a new house, providing all household items. She wants to create a regular income for her.

Her Future Plan

She wants to transfer her skills to someone in her Panchayat. She does not have a plan to contest in the next elections. She has a plan to bring many women to public life. She wants to actively involve herself in the Elected Women Representatives Association activities to strengthen the same after the completion of her tenure as Panchayat President.

Personal Achievement

She not only attended rural development training but also attended training programmes conducted by the Ministry of Food and Consumer Affairs, Tamil Nadu Agriculture Department, Gandhigram Rural Institute, RIRD, T. Kallupatti, The Hunger Project, ISS and others. The Tamil Nadu Gram Panchayat Leaders Association conferred on her the award Seva Ratna for the best performing Panchayat President. The Rotary Club of Ramnad conferred on her the title of Mangaiyar Thilagam in the year 2003 for her achievements.

She is the first Gram Panchayat President to achieve 100 per cent rainwater harvesting structure in all houses and Panchayat buildings. The NGO named WIN came to know of this achievement. It nominated her for the award of the World Bank in the category called Development Market Place. She won the award and she travelled to Washington along with her District Collector to explain her strategy. She put up a stall to explain about the relationship between poverty reduction and rainwater harvesting. She also won Rs. five lakhs as cash award for achieving 100 per cent rainwater harvesting.

Tamil Nadu Elected Women Representatives Association

Ms. Jesurathinam from SNEHA (an NGO) approached her after the 1996 elections. Ms. Jesurathinam travelled the entire district of Ramnathapuram and collected all the women leaders and they convened a meeting in Ramnathapuram with the help of the Ramnathapuram District Collector. All the elected women Panchayat Presidents attended the meeting. They selected Ms.Jamruth Beevi as the Elected Women Representatives Association district leader. Ms.Jesumary acted as Vice-President in the beginning. They also elected representatives for each block. HRF, Chennai, SNEHA and other NGOs convened Elected Women Representatives Association meetings regularly. But they did not bear the travel cost of the Gram Panchayat women Presidents. The Department of Political Science in Gandhigram Rural Institute also supported Elected Women Representatives Association. She felt that after Gandhigram Rural Institute's intervention the Association got strengthened and many Gram Panchayat Presidents realized there role, why they were elected to local bodies and how to address issues of women, children and the marginalized. They started proving that they were able to perform. Many Panchayat Presidents started acting independently after attending the Elected Women Representatives Associations meetings regularly in Gandhigram. They had interface with government officials regularly with the help of Gandhigram.

She felt that the Elected Women Representatives Association is working for the transformation of the society through the women leaders. To strengthen the Elected Women Representatives Association the following steps should be taken immediately :

- All Elected Women Gram Panchayat Presidents should realize that the Association is theirs, not Ponni Kailasam's or whoever leads the Association.
- Every member should contribute some amount as membership fee.
- Elected Women Representatives should create a permanent office either in Gandhigram or in some NGO's office premises, i.e. whoever supports them in the long-term without imposing their ideas and agendas on them.
- Whoever leads the Association should possess good leadership qualities to make everyone feel that its their Association.
- Elected Women Representatives should regularly organize meetings at block level and district level.
- Association members should regularly meet the state level higher officials to do policy advocacy.
- Association members should get specialized training regularly, e.g. gender sensitive training.

Panchayat Information

Name of the Panchayat	Michalepattinam
President	J. Jesumary
Vice-President	V. Irudhayaraj
Members	1. V. Arul
	2. V. Susai Irudhayamary
	3. T. Michael
	4. S. Jesammal
	5. V. Irudhayaraj
	6. A. Vedamuthu
Total Population	921
Men	447
Women	474
Office	1
Tube light	43
Sodium Vapour Light	1
Women complex (SHG building)	1
Self-Help Groups	1
Women Sanitary Complex	1
Community Hall	1
Ration Shop	1
Primary Health Centre	1
Jeevan Jothi Hospital	1
Post Office	1
Cooperative Bank	1
Anganwadi	1
RC Middle School	1
School Toilet	1
Waste dumping shed	1
TWAD OHT	1
Computer	1
RC School - total Students	96 boys and 102 girls
Teachers	3 men and 3 women
Gober Gas	1
Tube store	100
Street tape	16
Hand pump	3
Individual toilets	270
Church	1
Small pond	4
Water channel	2
Panchayat road	2
Streets	9
Cement Road	4
Drainage canal	1
Bridges	6
Vehicle	1 (to collect waste)

Income and Expenditure for the year 2004-2005

A/c I Income

House tax	7550
Library tax	755
Professional tax	3189
SFC grant	50537
Stamp duty	3391
House tax matching grant	33971
Other income like lease	12950
Deposit	930
Shop licence fee	300
Taxes from other sources	2440
Interest	354
Income from tamarind trees	210
Total Income	86,003
Open balance	3,404
Total	89,407

Expenditure

President's permanent fee	3960
Sitting fee	2400
Clerk salary	9600
Sweeper salary	4800
TA for President and Clerk	11850
Panchayat contribution for 11th Finance Commission Work	9458
Premium for group insurance	1650
Library tax	1510
Purchase of electrical goods	6253
EB charges	9777
Others	14101
Xerox	469
Stationery	717
Hand pump repair	6980
Bank commission	336
Total	83841
Closing Balance	5566
Grand total	894071
Open balance	3404
Income	86003
Total	89407
Expenditure	83841
Balance	5566

A/c II - Earmarked Fund

11th Finance Commission	19848
Panchayat Contribution	9458
Savings	414
Employers Health Fund	50
Interest	161
Deduction	1167
Income from purchase of vehicle for cleaning	7680
DD with cash	268
Total	39046
Open balance	5308
Total	44354

Expenditure

Maintenance of girl children sanitary complex	6000
Maintenance of sanitary complex	8033
Savings	414
Employers health fund	50
Repairing of hand pump	8039
Amount paid for last cremation	500
Commission	94
11th Finance Commission work	10766
Deduction	1167
Amount send it back	268
Deduction	114
Total	35445
Closing balance	8969
Grand total	44354

A/c II - Scheme Fund Income

Indira Awas Yojana	34277
PM Welfare Fund	28968
Sampoorna Gram Welfare Fund	403400
______________________	387297
Interest	3324
Jatropa Plantation amount	1512
Total	858778
Opening balance	182438
Grand total	1041216

Expenditure

Expenditure on SGSY	402676
11th Finance Commission i.e. has deposited wrongly in different account and again deposited in scheme a/c	13176
IAY	151542
Expenditure on Prime Minister Welfare Fund	63493
Deduction	387297
Interest send it back	924
Bank interest	1116
Amount sent it PA Ramnad	193
Total	1020417
Closing balance	20791
Grand total	1041216
Open balance	182438
Income	858778
Total	1041216
Expenditure	1020417
Remaining balance	20719

Conclusion

Seeing the performance of this Gram Panchayat leader one can make the following observation: When a leader with a commitment looking for opportunity moves into public space, for her the transformation is fast. Opportunity came in the form of reservation of seats for women. She has used this opportunity very effectively. To establish herself and to get recognition, she touched upon a vital issue of common interest which was a bone of contention for several decades between two villages. After winning the case she gained the support and solidarity of the community. She started another work, that also related to water. She did the rainwater harvesting and sanitation programmes innovatively which brought name to her. Her leadership was well recognized by the community and the district administration. She is the most sought after person for training institutions and the district administration as she has been projected as a model and her Panchayat has been projected as a model. Her linkage with the community, the Ward Members and the officials brought continuous success for which her leadership was responsible. Her grip over the administration made the officials act properly. Even in the corrupt administrative system she is able to manage without giving any bribe. This Panchayat serves as a model for others. Her alliance with NGOs, academic institutions, government departments and other leaders of the Panchayati Raj is strong. Her vision and her communication ability are extraordinary. She initiated activities first and then she drew the support of the government for completion of her efforts. She has demonstrated her credentials, ability and commitment which makes everyone extend support to her. Despite the negative trend in devolving powers to the Panchayat, she assumed responsibilities and acted on them. Her initiative in rainwater harvesting was quoted by the Chief Minister in her letter. For many she gives guidance. She is an effective trainer not only for women leaders but also for men leaders. Her capability to convince others is extraordinary. Her manners, approach, pleasing personality have helped her to be in the limelight, close to media, the government and development organizations.

CASE - 19

PANCHAYAT LAUNCHED A SCHEME

Mr. Nattuthurai is the President of Keeranur Panchayat. He first worked out a strategy of mobilizing the people for social action, for which he started his work in the temple. Being a progressive farmer, he knew the problems involved in mobilising people for social and political action. His Panchayat is known for water works, common property resource management and work for the marginalised. By attending to works related to the livelihood of the people, delivering proper health services and attending to the marginalised he won a name and support. He has also launched an innovative programme to distribute rice to the poorest of the poor. Nattuthurai emerged as a role model and hence Panchayat Presidents of his district and other districts are visiting this Panchayat.

Socio-Economic Background of the President

Sri. A.M. Nattuthurai, aged 57, is married and has two children. He is the President of K. Keeranur-Kondarangi. Keeranur literally means where the clouds come down. There is a tall hill named Sri Mallikarjunamalai, about 3850 feet high. During the rainy season clouds gather around atop the hill. The village of Keeranur used to get adequate rain during the monsoon.

Nattuthurai hails from a farmer family. His father was the President during the earlier system of Panchayati Raj and also served as the first Block Panchayat Chairman of Ottanchatram Block. His father is still alive. His father is so healthy as to walk independently even at the age of 94 years. Nattuthurai informed that his father is an inspiring force. His father is a multifaced personality—a community leader, a progressive farmer, a team leader of a local artistes group which used to stage dramas during the temple festival. Nattuthurai has got training on the stage. He recollected that during his boyhood days he was taught to sing songs from the Ramayana along with a few other boys. Further he acted in the role of women characters also. Nattuthurai said that since his boyhood days he has had many opportunities for socialisation.

His Schooling

Nattuthurai had his schooling at Saint Mary's High School in Dindigul and did his Pre-University course in Pope College, Sawyerpuram of Thoothukudi District. During those days he was a hosteller. The hostel life in the Christian missionary institution shaped his perception and understanding, Nattuthurai claimed. He said that he learnt to be a disciplined student with social understanding. The surroundings of the school and the hostel campus and the attention given by the Church authorities to the protection and maintenance of trees and other plants was always a good learning for him with regard to the significant role played by natural resources, Nattuthurai recalled.

His Village Life

His interest in nature and agriculture brought him to his village. He helped his father in agriculture. His father is a big farmer and owns about 100 acres of land. During the 70s, when the election to the Village Panchayat was held, Nattuthurai's paternal uncle contested in the election. The Village Munsif of K. Keeranur used his influence in opposing the paternal uncle and he could not win. This incident made an impact on the young mind of Nattuthurai, who decided to become the Village Munsif. He prepared well and appeared for the new post of Village Administrative Officer when the age old system of Village Munsif was abolished. He passed in the examination and served as the Village Administrative Officer of Thottanoothu and Sirumalai Village of Dindigul Taluk. But he was not able to continue to work as the Village Administrative Officer for various reasons. Mainly he had to be away from his family and the issues like bureaucracy and red tapism in the system of village administration were not easy to adjust to Mr. Nattuthurai felt. Hence he resigned his job. But he learned the administrative system of government machineries, he claimed.

Nattuthurai As a Progressive Farmer

The background of college education and the experience in government service moulded Nattuthurai to become more scientific in his life. He engaged himself in intensive agriculture. He used to establish good rapport with the officials of agriculture department and learnt from them modern techniques in agriculture operations. He adopted the modern techniques recommended by the officials in the agricultural activities, especially in seed processing, planting, irrigation management, inter-cropping, and marketing. He learned the functions of the private market system and the regulated market system located in Vellakoil and Ottanchatiram.

When poultry was introduced as a supplementary activity, Nattuthurai established a poultry unit consisting of broiler and leghorn variety for eggs. He availed of the credit assistance from the Canara Bank of K. Keeranur for this venture. Due to fluctuation of the price of eggs, Nattuthurai switched over to contract poultry form of selling broilers to the suppliers who supply the chicken and feed for chicken. The maintenance is the responsibility of the farmer. Nattuthurai said that there is a profit in this system of poultry farming.

Village Background and His Community Leadership

K. Keeranur Village Panchayat is moderate in size, a multi caste one with a total population of more than 5000. Apart from the main village of Keeranur, there are five hamlets, namely Idayan Valasu, Chinnakaliappa Goundan Valasu, Velliyan Valasu, Perumal Goundan Valasu and Cheriyan Nagar. Mirasu Nagar, Anna Nagar, Malleegapuram are the extension areas. Among the communities, Kongu Vellalar is the numerically dominant caste. There are other castes like Mudaliyar (weaving community), Devanga Chettiyar, Naicker, Scheduled Caste and Boyer (who engage in stone-cutting activities). Among the Scheduled Castes the sub-group of Sakkiliyar is dominant. Parayar is the other sub-group who are the minority.

Sri Mallikarjuna Hill and Temple

The temple atop the Sri Mallikarjuna hill is a cave temple. The deity is Lord Siva in the form of Lingam. It is said that it is one of 108 temples constructed by

Temple Celebration

the Pandiya King Sundara Pandiya of the later Pandiya period. There is a perennial spring at the top of the hill. Chitra Pournami (Full Moon of Chithirai month) is the main celebration which attracts thousands of devotees from all over the district. Free meal is provided to all irrespective of caste and religion during the celebration. The celebration is institutionalized for the past twenty-seven years through a Temple Celebration-Executive Committee representing Vellala Gounders from seven nearby villages. Nattuthurai is one of the seven members. He replaced his father due to his age. Nattuthurai is an active member. Nattuthurai, through his involvement in various social activities, became a known personality. Moreover his orientation in the DMK political party and its activities added name to him. He is one of the members in the district level unit of the DMK party.

Nattuthurai is an artist. He has been interested in drawing since his boyhood days. He developed himself in this art. Later he joined the famous drawing school 'Maya' and successfully completed the diploma through correspondence. He used to present his drawings to VIPs when they came to the village.

His Entry into Panchayati Raj

Election is the democratic process which provides opportunities to the citizen to participate in governance. But sometimes, it brings about an unwarranted situation of enimity between the contestants and their supporting groups. K. Keeranur is not an exemption. Once, during the Panchayat elections, due to a straight contest between two candidates who were relatives, there was dispute and enmity, besides spending of huge money by each candidate. After this, the village elders realized the need to avoid any further misunderstanding among the family members. They decided to select the President unanimously in future. When the election was declared during 1996, Nattuthurai was unanimously selected by the villagers. One individual from the SC community opposed him. But Nattuthurai won. For the second term also he was selected unanimously. But there was a close relative of Nattuthurai who was determined to contest, though his parents did not encourage him to contest against Nattuthurai. As expected, the opponent of Nattuthurai was defeated. Nattuthurai said that there was no enmity with the opponent. The candidate who opposed was a close relative. He used to come to the Panchayat office and freely mingle with all. He used to offer his suggestions and always extend his help in executing the Village Panchayat activities, Nattuthurai said. This is possible as Nattuthurai never shows enmity with anyone, he claimed.

Village Development Activities during the First Tenure

As many poor families of the Boyer community used to migrate to Kerala and other cities where employment/income generation activities are available in stone quarries, they are not able to get ration cards. But a ration card is a very important document for many reasons. The issue of non-availability of ration cards was raised in the Gram Sabha meetings. Hence the Village Panchayat administration undertook a survey and made arrangements for applications. All the families who had migrated to Kerala were identified and ration cards were given to them. The Village Officer's and the Civil Supplies Department Officials cooperation was the main support, Mr. Nattuthurai claimed.

In the SC community there are many families living in small huts. It was proposed to give proper shelter to these poor Dalits. Details on the availability of house site, non-availability of patta were collected and steps were taken to get house sites and pattas to eligible families in the SC community as well as to the poor among the BC community, he added. It was found that more than four hundred families needed house sites as they could not live as joint families within a small dwelling. Necessary steps were taken to procure land. An appropriate site was identified but the cost of the land was higher than the value of the guidelines fixed by the government. As the families were economically poor also, they could not contribute. The District Collector was approached and he helped to get additional sanction to meet the cost of land. 22 acres of land was purchased and 434 plots were earmarked for 434 poor families. For the Dalit families, 6 acres of land was purchased at Periya Goundan Valasu where 91 house units for 91 SC poor families were distributed, Nattuthurai said.

During 2004-05, 10 houses were allotted to the eligible poor families in K. Keeranur Village Panchayat; 3 beneficiaries from BC community and 7 from SC community were selected in the Gram Sabha meeting. The beneficiaries proposed their intention of changing the design of the house as the conventional type was not an attractive one. Nattuthurai discussed the proposal with the Union officials. The Union engineer informed that the cost would be more if the design of the roofing was changed. The beneficiaries agreed to spend the additional amount in one way or the other. Nattuthurai ensured by regular monitoring and guidance the completion of the construction of the houses in time. The house design was very appreciable and it gave a sense of pride to the beneficiaries as they staked their ownership in the building, he added.

Yet another 45 poor families were left out. With the help of the VAO of Keeranur, a government poramboke land was identified at Cheriyan Nagar and five acres of land was earmarked for house sites. The 35 house site pattas were allotted to poor families. As there was remaining land available, another 45 pattas were distributed to poor families. Nattuthurai said that almost all the poor families were provided with house sites. Though it was a tough task, the same was successfully achieved with the help of government officials. Frequent meetings, proper follow-up, close monitoring and effective organizing of poor families and joint efforts of the all Ward Members of the Village Panchayat were the factors which helped to succeed, Nattuthurai shared.

Power Tiller

Overall Welfare of the Marginalized

Nattuthurai said that as the SC population is in considerable number, the welfare of this community was focused upon mainly. During his first tenure provision of house site and patta was given much attention. And in the second tenure construction of houses for poor families was attempted. So far sixty colony houses and 35 tiled houses under IAY and 8 houses under Katcha House Scheme, have been provided to SC families.

To improve the approach roads to the AD colony, encroachments along the roadside were removed, cement concrete road was provided in the South Colony of K. Keeranur, Idayan Valasu, AD colony and Cherian Nagar Colony area. 16 additional street lights were provided in these habitations, Nattuthurai said. Under the Million Wells Scheme, one open well and four borewells were provided for SC farmers. To get electricity for these irrigation wells, frequent reminders were sent to the authorities and the EB was taking necessary steps to extend electricity connection, Nattuthurai claimed.

Alliance with the Non-Governmental Organization

Nattuthurai said that it was the duty of the Village Panchayat President to get assistance and help from various agencies as the Panchayat finance was limited. He established a good rapport with the NGO World Vision of India and extended all assistance to the activities implemented by the NGO in the village. With the help of the NGO scheme, land improvement activities and maintenance works in the AD Colony old houses were undertaken.

Management of Common Resources — The Water Bodies

The main village Keeranur and other hamlets are located at the foot hills of the Malleswarar hill. There are twenty-seven ponds/tanks under the jurisdiction of the Village Panchayat. As agriculture is the major occupation and the majority of the lands are rainfed, protection and maintenance of all water bodies is very important, Nattuthurai expressed. Hence the Village Panchayat administration decided to give priority to improving the ponds/tanks, canals and streams so that the ground water level will improve, Nattuthurai pointed out. Nattuthurai acknowledged the training given by the Rajiv Gandhi Chair for Panchayati Raj Studies, Gandhigram Rural Institute as then only he

Community Participation

got more sensitization with regard to the significance of scientific management of the village commons. Hence it was decided in the Village Panchayat Council not to spend scheme funds on activities other than the watershed activities, he added. Though the expectation of the villagers was generally like provision of sodium vapour lights, CC road, drainage, etc., the reasons for the priority given to the watershed activities were explained to the villagers in the Gram Sabha meetings. Further, with the financial assistance of World Vision of India five watershed works at a cost of about Rs.13.50 lakhs have been successfully carried out, Nattuthurai reported.

NSS

Medical Camp

In association with the Christian Fellowship Hospital, Ambilikkai, activities to promote the health and welfare of the village community were undertaken. Periodical health camps for general diseases and leprosy were organized. The Village Panchayat administration actively took part in the propaganda about camps, mobilization of the community and also in the arrangements. Further the medical team used to give advice to him on what the Village Panchayat should do to improve the environmental sanitation in the village and the personal hygiene of the children. Nattuthurai said that the guidance and motivation of the Ambilikkai Hospital and their field staff was very much useful to the community. Moreover the Ambilikkai Hospital implemented a rehabilitation programme for leprosy patients. Seven families in the Keeranur Village Panchayat received loans at marginal interest, he added. Further the facility of free hostel for poor students available at the Ambilikkai School run by the hospital management was also properly utilized by the community. The Village Panchayat administration used to identify the eligible poor students and recommend them to the hospital management. As the list of students referred by him was always genuine, they got admission, Nattuthurai pointed out.

Nattuthurai never misses the opportunity of availing of help from any sources for the benefit of the village community. With the help of Canara Bank he organized AIDS awareness camps and also observed World Health Day. With the joint effort of the Ambilikkai Hospital and Canara Bank, involving the nursing college students, a survey was conducted to assess the status of women in respect of their weight; anemic level, blood test and maintenance of personal hygiene. It was found that the majority of them suffered from anemia and blood pressure. All those concerned got treatment, Nattuthurai explained.

Rapport with the Primary Health Centre

Nattuthurai is very keen on tapping all the resources available in all directions. His family donated 5 acres of land for the establishment of a Primary Health Centre (PHC) at Keeranur. The PHC was established during his father's tenure. Nattuthurai made attempts to improve the infrastructure facilities in the PHC. The Village Panchayat provided the water tap in the

Awareness Generation

centre. When the Siddha unit was housed within the same building as allopathy, Nattuthurai did his best to get sanction for the construction of a building from the MP Local Area Development Fund to house the

Siddha unit separately. The medical staff of the Siddha unit informed that they used to get invitation for the Gram Sabha meetings and in the Gram Sabha meetings awareness songs and talk on the importance of balanced diet, personal hygiene, and RCH activities were disseminated. The paramedical staff Arulraj said that the Village Panchayat administration was very much cooperative in promoting awareness on Siddha system of medicine. A garden of medicinal plants has been established with the involvement of the Village Panchayat, he added.

The medical officer of the PHC appreciated the administration of the Keeranur Village Panchayat for its responsiveness in various activities related to the PHC. She pointed out that there were cases of anemia with very low level of hemoglobin among the women and all were advised to report to the hospital during delivery. The medical officer further informed that there were cases of suspected heart diseases, cervical

AIDS Awareness Campaign

cancer, ANC severe anemic, referred to the higher hospital. The medical officer suggested that the Village Panchayat Health Committee must periodically come to the PHC if the PHC is situated at the Village Panchayat or meet the VHN during her visit to the villages to learn about the various types of diseases prevailing among the members of the community. In Keeranur the Village Panchayat President helped in organizing polio camps, meetings for adolescent girls and general health camps. But apart from these, the Village Panchayat administration should ensure the effective functioning of the Health Committee, the medical officer added. Moreover the health condition of womenfolk is always subject to the level of awareness on and practice of personal hygiene. There were cases of scabies, impetigo and dermities among the rural children. These are all the diseases spreading due to poor maintenance of personal hygiene, the medical officer pointed out. She further informed that if the health committee was more effective, STD, HIV, and AIDS could be easily controlled and prevented through periodical sharing with the health officials and field staff. Promoting the status of health and family welfare is a joint effort wherein the role of Village Panchayat was significant, she pointed out. Nattuthurai who was also present during the discussion with the medical officer promised to try his best for the effective functioning of the Health Committee of Keeranur Village Panchayat.

Linkages with the Agricultural Engineering Department

Being a progressive farmer and already oriented in the activities of rainwater harvesting through the NGO programme, Nattuthurai gave focus to tap the technical knowledge and financial resources available in the line departments of the government. Especially with the help of the Department of Agricultural Engineering, percolation ponds were constructed by widening the inlet canals/streams wherever space was available, Nattuthurai said. Further in the poramboke lands adjoining the streams were also converted into rainwater harvest structures with the provision of retaining wall, sluice and other necessary devices in the structure. Due to these structures the ground water level has improved in the irrigation wells and borewells meant for drinking water, Nattuthurai claimed.

Soak Pit

Check dam

At the OHT source of Chinnakaliappa Goundan Valasu the ground water was not adequate to cater to the drinking water demands of the public. Hence it was decided to construct a check dam near the OHT source. But the land available for the check dam was not sufficient. As there was patta land nearby, the farmers who owned the patta land were contacted and the proposed work of check dam was discussed with them. They came forward to give permission in writing to make use of their land for the catchment of rainwater. And with the help of the Department of Agricultural Engineering, a percolation pond was constructed. So far, at a cost of Rs.6 lakhs, four structures have been established from the allocation of the Agricultural Engineering Department, Nattuthurai explained.

Further from the Village Panchayat Scheme Fund as well as from its own resources at four places rainwater harvest structures/percolation ponds/check dams have been constructed at a total cost of Rs. 4.50 lakhs. As more number of works were carried out to improve the groundwater level, with a spell or two of rains, the level of groundwater has increased in the village, Nattuthurai explained. Any further rain water is properly stored in the check dams/tanks as the inlet canals leading to these storage tanks are also properly maintained, he added. And there is improvement in the drinking water supply as the five bores are located near these structures, Nattuthurai remarked.

Improvement in the Provision of Drinking Water Supply

Nattuthurai said that for provision of potable water to the Village Panchayat, a planned approach was taken in consultation with the TWAD officials. During the year 1997, 2000 and 2001 one open well and two bore-wells were provided. But due to the sinking of a new borewell by yet another Village Panchayat near the above mentioned referred bores, the yield was limited. It was proposed to deepen the open well after discussing with the TWAD officials. With the help of the District Councillor's Fund the open well was deepened in the year 2002 at a cost of 0.60 lakhs. When he assumed office there were only four OHTs of which one was in a damaged condition. Now, with the help of TWAD, 3 new OHTs and 8 mini power pumps have been provided. Further, when the NGO World Vision of India proposed its readiness to contribute for the drinking water supply, the contribution from the public of Rs. 25,000 was added to the contribution of World Vision of India of Rs.1.50 lakhs and another OHT was constructed. At Idayan Valasu, from the Village Panchayat's own sources at a cost of Rs.1.50 lakhs one new borewell was provided.

As the number of devotees visiting Malleswara-malai temple has been steadily increasing, to cater the needs of the devotees as well the inhabitants of the area, with the TWAD assistance of Rs.9.0 lakhs a new bore well, OHT and pipelines have been provided. The source is the PWD tank 4 km away. It caters to the water supply demand of the public through 110 public taps and 40 household services. Due to delay in the monsoon, at present water supply is provided on alternate days in the main village of K. Keeranur and, in the hamlets, once in two days. There are now 8 mini power pump projects completed and properly utilized. The total cost of Rs.3.20 lakhs was allocated from the TWAD fund. Now in all the villages there are OHTs as well as mini power pumps which will ensure sustainable and equal distribution to all, Nattuthurai shared. He acknowledged the assistance extended by the MLA in this regard. He said that the MLA contributed from the MLA Local Area Development Fund. The MLA also helped in availing of Rs.10 lakhs from the Rajya Sabha Member who belonged to the DMK party. As he was a member in the district unit of DMK party, he was able to influence the MLA.

Resource Mobilization from the Higher Representatives

Since 1997-98 till 2004-05, Nattuthurai was able to mobilize Rs.20-95 lakhs for various activities like, open-air theatre, borewells, street lights and improvement of roads and one hand pump.

From the MP Local Area Development Scheme Fund one OHT, and two bus shelters have been constructed at a total cost of Rs.2.45 lakhs. A new proposal was given to the MP to improve three major roads. From the Rajya Sabha Member's fund, through the influence of the MLA, Rs.10 lakhs was availed of and three bridges have been constructed. By the assistance of the Union Councillor and the District Councillor, retaining wall work, replacement of earthen road by metal road were undertaken at a cost of Rs.4.04 lakhs. Though he belongs to the DMK party, he never projects himself as a party man. He projects the felt needs of the villagers to the higher representatives and he is lucky enough to get assistance from all members of different communities.

Contribution to the Development of Education

There are three primary schools and one middle school in K. Keeranur Village Panchayat jurisdiction. Of these in the primary school of Perumal Goundan Valasu, the majority of the students belong to the SC community. The middle school is located in the main village of K. Keeranur. There are two balwadis. Nattuthurai realized the importance of education to rural children. With the help of the Ward Members and other educated volunteers, he actively worked for the enrolment of all eligible age group children. He encouraged the public to contribute mats, play materials, vessels and weighing machine. From the District Councillor's Fund, a kitchen shed was constructed at a total cost of Rs.1 lakh. Except in one school, toilets and drinking water are provided to all schools.

Sarva Siksha Abhiyan is a innovative scheme, Nattuthurai claimed. As there is a freedom to have a plan at the village itself by the Village Education Committee, public involvement and contribution was mobilized through this scheme. With the contribution of public of the Rs.0.50 lakhs added to the SSA Scheme fund of Rs.4.50 lakhs, an additional school building was constructed wherein the headmaster's room was provided with more space than in any other school. Further for the storage of water a masonry tank was also constructed. Nattuthurai has established a good contact with the DIET (District Institute of Education and Training) and with their help training students were allotted for teaching in the middle school for a period of one year. And after that, under the sponsorship of the NGO World Vision and the community, a young disabled SC woman was employed as additional teacher in the middle school. These arrangements helped to improve the educational standard of the school children.

Nattuthurai as a Role Model

Nattuthurai is a born artist. He improved his talent further through a professional course. Being an educated person he himself wanted to render assistance to the school students. Every Friday afternoon, he spares his time with the students of class 6, 7, and 8 standard. Nattuthurai explained the concepts of rainwater harvesting, health and environmental sanitation and used to tell moral stories besides teaching the students the principles of drawing. Celebrations of nationally important days and school annual day are very grandly organized every year at the middle school. Even parents are encouraged to participate in the competitions. Nattuthurai acknowledged the cooperation and support of the headmaster and school teachers in this regard. Nattuthurai said that he used to give sufficient attention along with the headmaster to ensure discipline and character among the students.

Nattuthurai said that the students of the SC community were showing interest to continue their study. Almost all the boys of the SC are pursuing the high school education in Ottanchathiram, Ambilikkai or Kallimanthayam high schools. The free pass, hostel facility and the general awareness among the SC are the major reasons for this development. With regard to the students belonging to the BC community, several of them discontinued their study after completing high school, opting for self-employment or wage employment, Nattuthurai observed.

Establishment of Public Library

As there are many educated youths in K. Keeranur Village Panchayat, the youths put forth a demand for a library. After the construction of the additional school building and the upgradation of the primary school into a middle school, the old building in the primary school was repaired and a public library was established by the government. The NYK youth helped in planting of trees in front of the library building. There are four hundred members in the library.

Moreover as there is sufficient space in the above said building apart from housing the library, Nattuthurai encouraged the SHG women members to conduct their monthly and weekly meetings there. Usually during Sundays these groups meet there. The old building is now put use for public purposes. Nattuthurai shared his happiness in this regard.

Support to SHG Activities

Nattuthurai realized the importance of SHG activities through his involvement with the NGOs. There are 15 SHGs promoted by two NGOs, namely, DMSS Dindigul Multi Purpose Service Society and World Vision of India. The SHG multi-purpose building was constructed during the year 2002 at the main village of K. Keeranur. The building is very much useful as the meetings are usually organized by bankers, hospital authorities and NGOs. The Village Panchayat decided to provide a toilet in the SHG building from its own fund. The Village Panchayat improved the surroundings of the SHG campus. A medicinal plant garden is established here and also rain water harvest structure is properly constructed at the SHG building.

Sanitary Complex

Gram Sabha

Apart from the activities of micro finance, the SHG women members are making use of their group's strength in solving their family problems and issues in the Public Distribution System, school activities and other issues in the provision of basic amenities. The SHG members actively participate in the Gram Sabha meetings. There are many positive developments in the aspects of personal hygiene, food and dress habits, child rearing and leadership qualities among the SHG members, Nattuthurai observed. Moreover many of the SHG members have taken LIC policy and opened RD account, he added.

Now-a-days the SHG women members have developed confidence to deal with their alcoholic husbands. Earlier they used to go over to their parents' house. Now they take the issue even to the police station, Nattuthurai remarked. Television is available in the majority of the houses irrespective of variations in income. Women have awareness in many fields, thanks to the mass media, especially TV, Nattuthurai explained. The majority of the SHG women have availed of revolving fund. And 3 SHGs got economic assistance. Animal husbandry is the major economic activity of the SHGs as most of them are less educated, Nattuthurai said. Marketing is not a problem as Ottanchathiram is very famous for milk based goods.

SHG

Namathu Gramam

Apart from the cooperative milk society, there are private companies who are marketing their milk with brand names. Moreover there is lot of common land for grazing. Hence the SHG members prefer animal husbandry. Among the SC youths many are getting employment in the Ottanchathiram market, earning about Rs.100 per day. They used to freely mingle with the other youths of all castes. Communal harmony prevails, Nattuthurai said. Youths do shramdhan periodically. With their labour contribution environmental sanitation has improved, Nattuthurai shared.

Welfare of the Aged and other Marginalized Sections

Nattuthurai said that his father, aged 94, is the source of inspiration in understanding the problems of elders. Nattuthurai shows immediate attention in claiming eligible assistance from the government social security schemes meant for aged persons, widows and differently abled persons. Pension assistance has been got for to 10 aged person. Under the free rice scheme 23 eligible widows, elders and very poor families have been covered.

An Innovative Programme of 'Kalanchiam'

Training is an effective tool to improve the perception of any individual. Nattuthurai had undergone training in many centres like SIRD, RIRD, Gandhigram Rural Institute and Vivekananda Kendra of Kanyakumari. During the training at Bhavanisagar an idea of organizing free noon meal for those who are very poor and destitute by the community itself was mooted to the participants. Nattuthurai got the message and he decided to work it out in his village. Nattuthurai met the SHGs and other public spirited individuals and shared this idea. Though all SHGs did not come out in favour of the experiment, 3 SHGs agreed to contribute. It was decided to contribute a handful of rice/paddy everyday in a pot (Kalanchiam) kept in the house of the contributor, and once in a month the collected quantity has to be put into the another Kalanchiam a big bucket kept in the Village Panchayat office. The Village Panchayat discussed the modalities of providing the free noon meals with the self help group members. It was proposed to handover the collected rice to the beneficiaries. All agreed to that arrangement. At present there are twelve persons, mostly aged destitutes, who are receiving the rice every month. Among the beneficiaries there are lepers also. There is one beneficiary disabled in both legs. The Kalanchiam is implemented from 01.03.2005. On 15.08.2005, during the Independence Day Gram Sabha meeting, the District Collector Mr.Murugiah participated and distributed the collected rice to these poor persons. Witnessing this activity of feeding of destitutes from the village contribution, especially from the SHGs, other people also came forward to contribute. Without any setback the programme is going on and Nattuthurai showed his happiness. With regard to the social security of differently abled persons, Nattuthurai tried his best to get the government scheme benefits. There are 18 in the category of physically disabled and one mentally retarded person. Two individuals have been provided with tri-cycle, Nattuthurai said.

Linkage with the Department of Agriculture

Nattuthurai, during his visit to the Union office at Ottanchathiram, used to go over to the agriculture department office which is also located in the campus of Panchayat Union. His frequent visits and contacts with the officials helped him a lot. He was able to

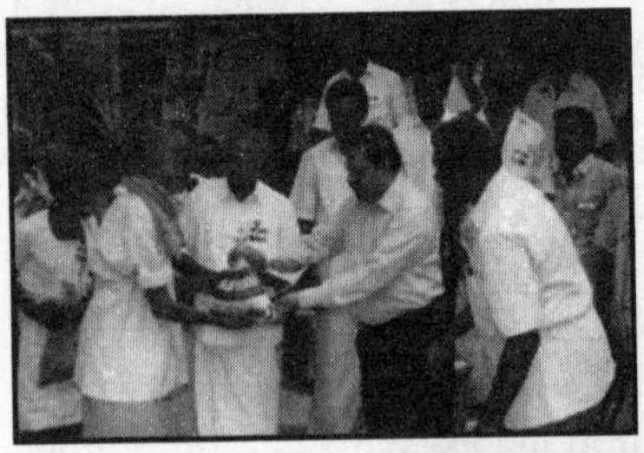

Kalanchiam

know of the available schemes/allocations for farmers and he immediately counselled his village farmers to avail of the scheme benefits. Activities like installation of drip irrigation system, purchase of certified seeds, hybrid fodder grass shoots, tree planting, construction of farm ponds and techniques in pest control have been effectively carried out in consultation with the officials. For eligible farmers subsidy was availed of.

Linkage with the Department of Forests

Afforestation activity was carried out on the bunds of all the water bodies. Forest Department officials helped a lot by identifying the suitable tree variety. Saplings were procured from the forest nursery with subsidy. Moreover they used to give guidance during the construction of rain water harvest structures.

Task yet to be Completed

Nattuthurai showed that as more attention was given to the watershed activities, he was not able to allocate

NSS

necessary funds for the maintenance and improvement of village roads. There are earthen roads and metal roads and the same have to be improved.

Further tree planting has to be concentrated on along the roadsides and around the tanks/ponds. He proposed to prepare a nursery exclusively for his Village Panchayat and in consultation with the forest/ agriculture officials to undertake afforestation in all the hamlets. After witnessing the effect of check dams and percolation ponds, many farmers demanded the same provision near their fields. It was identified that yet another 10 water harvesting structures could be constructed. And also to ensure sustainable drinking water supply, wherever possible it was decided to deepen the bore along with proper maintenance of the catchment area. Two ground level reservoirs for the inhabitants of Cherian Nagar have been proposed.

To extend the street light facilities to the extension area, it was calculated that 15 additional street lights have to be installed. To ensure total sanitation, Nattuthurai proposed construction of 100 household latrines and some families requested the World Vision of India to compensate the additional expenditure in the construction of pucca latrines. There is a demand from the males to construct a community toilet for men at K. Keeranur and Malleswaram areas. In the campus of the middle school tree-planting was proposed involving SHG men.

Proposal of Making K. Keeranur a Pilgrimage Centre

The hill top temple of Sri Mallikarjuna Swamy is attracting thousands of devotees during the important festival days. Moreover devotees used to visit during weekends and other auspicious days every month. The celebration of Chitra Pournami (Full Moon Day of Chitrai month) is a very big one drawing more than twenty thousand people. Cutting across caste and religion, all community members visit this temple. Hence it is necessary to provide needed amenities and infrastructure in the temple area. These amenities could not be provided by the Village Panchayat administration. Hence he proposed to the government to declare the place a pilgrimage centre by which special funds could be allocated to improve the facilities. The harmony among the communities would also improved, he added. He proposed the following steps to improve the campus/foot hill of the Mallikarjuna Swamy hill temple:

1. Fencing of foot hills - planting of trees to generate income.
2. Park.
3. Lodging facility for pilgrims.
4. Shade arrangements along the way to hill top.
5. Construction of small percolation pond on the hill sides.
6. Electricity.
7. Additional drinking water facility.
8. Improvement to the open-air theatre.
9. Cement floor-in the shade of trees.

Conclusion

Nattuthurai is emerging as a popular leader. His plain and humble approach inspires the officials and so he is able to mobilize support and resources for the development of the village. His free and easy access to the villagers strengthens their faith in him. He is always available at the Village Panchayat office except during his visit to government offices and to inspect the progress of the works in his village areas. He used to accept any suggestion from anybody to improve the functioning of the Panchayat administration. Apart from Ward Members, youth volunteers, farmers, SHG members and village elders come to the Panchayat office as the office is located very near to the library. His artistic talent attracts the youth. He cultivates hope in the minds of farmers by encouraging scientific farming. Without any reservation he used to visit the police station or any other office for the benefit of his villagers. He is a full time President-cum-executive authority. He is careful in his Panchayat administration. He periodically consults the officials with regard to the administration of the Village Panchayat. His constant touch with the other representatives like Union/District Councillors, MLA and MP yields fruits regularly. In these ways Nattuthurai is a model.

CASE - 20

DEVELOPMENT THROUGH FORWARD AND BACKWARD LINKAGES

The Melachindalachery Gram Panchayat President is conscious of his forward linkages with officials and other representatives of the people at other levels and his backward linkages with the people for all development activities. The Panchayat President identified school related activities as the major work from which he could move further with the support of the communities. His school work paid rich dividends. He worked closely with the youth. Sanitation and water supply are yet other achievements of his Panchayat. He kept the people active in participating in many of the programmes organised by the Panchayats. His multifarious activities made him close to the community and government officials.

About the Village Panchayat

Melachindalacherry is a Village Panchayat in Uthamapalayam Block of Theni District. It is a multi caste village. The population of the Panchayat is 7000. The village economy is not so prosperous. Being a rainfed area, agriculture is not a profitable occupation at present.

The former President of the Gram Panchayat was a businessman. He did not pay much attention to the Panchayat activities. The felt needs of villagers were not properly attended to by him. Even the very basic need of drinking water was not provided to the needy. The young men of Melachindalacherry could not get brides as the womenfolk of this Panchayat are suffering due to shortage of drinking water and women have to suffer a lot to fetch water for their daily use. This was the position of the past before Mr. Durairaj assumed office.

New Panchayati Raj System and the New Leadership

The New Panchayati Raj System promised that it would bring many things to the village provided a leadership is there. The traditional leader who headed the Village Panchayat had been defeated for his failure to address the people's felt needs. The present incumbent was elected because of the failure of the traditional leader.

Mr.Durairaj belongs to Okkaliga Gounder community. He has two children who are in school. Basically he is a progressive former. He owns land in the village and he has a cardamom plantation in Kerala State. As the role and responsibility of the Village Panchayat President demands full time and dedicated attention, he felt that he would not be able to give necessary attention to his farming as well as plantation which resulted in poor income from those sources, he added.

His interest in public welfare brought him to the attention of the community leaders who encouraged him to involve himself more in the public activities. He was selected as the secretary of the committee of his own community. Further he gained the respect of all other communities by his real interest in serving the community and his simplicity. He became the treasurer of the Village Welfare Committee. He demonstrated his honesty and sincerity while he was serving in the community organisations.

Mr. Durairaj defeated the traditional leader in spite of his strong traditional hold. He won by a margin of 240 votes. For the second tenure also he contested and defeated the candidate fielded by the traditional Panchayat President.

His first attempt was to look into the issue of drinking water. The ground water level has gone down. The norm of the government with regard to the creation of bore well was limited to 100 metres. He personally met and explained the problem of severe drought/ ground water level position to the District Collector and availed of a special sanction to have a 200 metre deep bore. Money was made available. But when the sinking of borewell commenced after verifying the availability of water by a water diviner, the farmers of the nearby site objected to the borewell. They were persuaded and then the bore was sunk successfully. Further, with TWAD assistance, two new OHTs were constructed and four mini motors with Sintex tanks were provided and water supply was ensured to all. The total cost was Rs.13.50 lakh. This is the achievement of the New Panchayati Raj System, the President Sri A.S. Durairaj claimed. This gave a name to him. This was the long felt need and dream. It was the concern of the women of this area.

Educational Development

School compound wall, with people's contribution

The next task Durairaj attempted was educational development. There is a middle school under the administration of the Panchayat Union. The school is located in the middle of the village. There was no compound wall or any other fencing arrangement and hence the environment of the school was not kept clean and tidy. Moreover the village children made use of the campus for open-air defecation. The villagers complained about that but they would not come forward with a solution to rectify the problem.

The Panchayat Council decided to arrange for an improvised fencing by erecting a wire mesh instead of a compound wall, though construction of a compound wall was the best solution. But the public did not come forward to donate as they considered it the duty of the Government. The Panchayat President met each and every parent, village key persons and rich men and explained to them about the status of the Village Panchayat funds. Later the public responded positively. At a cost of Rs.25,000, all from public contribution, the fencing was completed and the environment of the middle school is now clean and there is no open air defecation. It was relentlessly pursued by the Panchayat President without losing hope.

During 1997-98 he realized another dimension of education. After completing middle school, the children have to go out to other villages for high school as there was no high school in his village. The villagers, especially from one dominant community, the Okkaliga Gounders, came forward to give necessary funds as per the government norm. Accordingly, Rs.60,000 was donated by the above said community and necessary steps were taken to obtain government sanction to upgrade the school. There was undue delay in getting permission to upgrade the school. The bureaucracy took such a long time to process the file. In the meantime the norm of the government for the local contribution for upgradation of school was enhanced from Rs.60,000 to Rs.1.00 lakh. He took earnest effort to mobilise another Rs.40,000 from the MLA and, with the help of the MLA, the Panchayat got the order for upgradation. It was another dream of the people realised through his efforts.

Daily School Prayer with Panchayat President

A high school needs adequate space to meet the requirement of more number of class rooms, laboratory, play ground and other infrastructure facilities. Steps were taken to acquire land. A few individuals, namely Sri Nagaraj, Sri Ramaraj, Sri Suburaj and Sri Jeyaraman, local farmers, came forward to donate their land to the extent of 2.10 acres to the school. As more space was needed additional land of 2.40 acres of land was kept ready to establish the proposed High School and a Hostel for BC students was also planned. An extent of 0.60 acre of land was earmarked for the proposed hostel.

In the meantime, the upgraded high school was run at the campus of the middle school itself as the construction of building was not complete. A considerable number of students, after completion of middle school education, for want of a good school, joined the schools located in nearby villages. The parents of those pupils were met and assurance was given to them that quality education would be ensured in the newly upgraded school. Accordingly special coaching classes were arranged during the evening hours and two additional teachers have been appointed by the Parents-Teachers

Rally on Public Awareness

Association, Consolidated payment was given to those teachers. Parent also came forward to pay Rs.15 per student per month and so another teacher was also appointed. Dropouts were brought down in the school. With all these efforts, the result touched 98 per cent. Now the pass rate is 100 per cent pass from 1999 to 2004.

Sarva Siksha Abhiyan (SSS) is a very significant scheme, as funds are readily available for the construction of school buildings. At a cost of Rs.4.50 lakhs under the SSA a building was constructed on the new site. From the donation of the Spices Board Rs.20,000 and a public contribution of Rs.5,000, toilet facility was provided in the school. Under the NABARD rural infrastructure development scheme, at a cost of Rs. 24.00 lakhs, additional class room buildings with lab facility were sanctioned and the construction was completed and the buildings are in use.

The Parents-Teachers Association and village public join together and every year organise 'Education Day'. Teachers are honored and meritorious students are awarded cash prizes. In extra curricular activities, competitions are arranged and prizes are distributed. It is just like a mela, the villagers said. Education has drawn the attention of the people.

Under the "Namakku Naame Scheme" Mr. Durairaj personally contributed Rs.25,000 and Rs.75,000 was obtained from the government from which one computer was purchased and given to the middle school. Benches are provided from class one to all classes through public donation. School uniform is distributed to all the students and shoes and ties are provided for them. This practice was developed in the Panchayat Union School.

Students have now improved themselves in education and extra curricular activities in Melachindalacherry Village as the atmosphere is encouraging. One girl of the third standard memorized 500 couplets of the Thirukkural; songs and dance performances are done efficiently by the students; oratorical skills are developed by many; and these developments of the students of poor families attract the attention of the public. Four students of this school got entry into teacher training schools in open merit system, Durairaj claimed. But all these achievements were made with several difficulties. He is able to succeed because of the cooperation of the people. Hurdles are set at different levels in the government.

The Village Panchayat was able to bring about these educational developments within a short span of seven years. If more power and responsibilities are devolved to the PRIs in the sector of education more and more successful events could be conducted. The government must realize this and take necessary steps towards this, Durairaj pointed out.

Panchayat Administration

Environmental Sanitation

Mr.Durairaj after he came to position again, decided to augment the income to the Panchayat. During the Gram Sabha meetings he explained the financial position and the necessity of enhancing the house tax as per the instructions of the government. During 2000-2001 the house tax collection was Rs.30,702. From 2001-2002 it was enhanced to Rs.43,365 and the collection of house tax was cent percent continuously from the year 2001-2002 and the district authority appreciated his efforts in this regard and awarded a merit certificate. For this tax collection people cooperated with Panchayat as the Panchayat delivered the promised services.

Improvement in Water Supply and Sanitation

From the Village Panchayat's own resources he spent money for the improvement of the village sanitation, maintenance of streetlights and extension of drinking water supply lines to the new habitations coming up in the main village Melachindalacherry. He improved the water supply system by providing 4 mini pumps,

Prompt Maintenance of Road Warning against Open Air Defecation

2 hand pumps, 2 over head tanks additionally. Water supply connections for Union and High School were also provided. Altogether he spent about Rs.7.0 lakhs to improve the water supply during his second tenure.

From the scheme funds received from 2001 to 2005, the activities like construction of group houses and repairing work on the old houses, construction of small bridges, formation of new roads, provision of cement concrete roads, drainages have been executed. Further, he was able to mobilise funds from the MLA's local area development fund for the construction of three public sanitary complexes which

Solid Waste Management

are in use involving the self-help groups. The sanitary complexes are kept very clean. Mr. Durairaj said that once the Collector visited the village and inspected one of the sanitary complexes and found it very so neat and clean that he suspected whether it was in use or not. He later sent the RD Engineer who broke open the Septic tank and found that it was full of human waste. Then only the claim of the Village Panchayat on the use and maintenance of the public sanitary complex was accepted, the President added. Moreover 450 individual household latrines were also constructed under the special incentive of Rs.1500 per unit.

To ensure cleanliness in the public areas, a warning board was erected banning open defecation and slowly the public extended cooperation in this regard. Provision of cement road with pucca drainage system provided a face lift to the streets and lanes. The villagers after experiencing the comfort of the CC road and drainage facility came forward to undertake maintenance also. They are cooperating very well with the Panchayat administration. So far the Village Panchayat has spent Rs.23.46 lakhs in improving the village streets and lanes. The environment is very much improved.

Road Improvement

With regard to road improvement, he has given preference to the roads leading to the burial ground and major streets in the two villages in the Village Panchayat. In this regard Rs.6.0 lakhs was spent to convert earthen road to metal road and tar road. Further in the burial ground street lights and water facilities were also provided.

Rural housing

Yet another major work carried out in Melachindalacherry Village Panchayat is rural housing. Mr.Durairaj realized the necessity of rural housing as many number of poor families are living together within a small living area. He listed those poor families who needed house site/patta. He was able to obtain 450 free house site pattas for the deserving poor families in the village.

Because of his continuous leadership since 1996, Mr. Durairaj was able to improve the housing condition of the poor belong to Scheduled Caste and Backward Communities. So far 30 SC families have received new houses under the IAY. In 40 SC houses repair/ maintenance work was carried out at a cost of Rs.4.50 lakhs. With regard to the backward communities 20 new houses under the IAY and five houses under the Katcha House scheme have been provided. Of the above houses, five were allotted to physically disabled persons.

As many new houses are constructed through government scheme and by the initiative of individual families in the extension areas of Melachindalacherry, the Village Panchayat is bound to provide basic amenities like road, water supply and street lights in the areas, Durairaj felt. Hence much attention is given in this regard as in the main habitations located inside the village, necessary basic amenities have been already provided, he claimed. It is proposed to give new names to these extension areas. To avoid any misunderstanding among the public it was decided to select names of flowers like Malligai, Mullai and Rivers like Vaigai and Cauvery to the new habitations coming up in the extension area, Durairaj stated.

Afforestation

Sectoral linkages — Forest Department activities

Mr. Durairaj stated that the hamlet of Keelachindalacherry was located near the foothills of the Salamalai. He was able to succeed in improving the natural resources and the dry land of farmers through the Forest Department. The Forest Department adopted Keelachindalacherry village. Seven women groups and one youth group were formed under the aegis of the Village Forest Council. Training in trades like canning, fruit processing, driving and tailoring were given to the 43 members belonging to these groups. World Forest Day was observed and tree plantation was undertaken. Around assets like Village Forest Council building, borewell, afforestation in 250 hectares 77,000 seedlings were planted. It was found that the survival rate is 75 per cent as people extended cooperation in the protection of saplings. Further soil conservation works through construction of skin walls, check walls, micro check dams and percolation pond were carried out. This helped in the augmentation of water. Now the ground water table has improved. The economy of the villagers has also improved as from the revolving fund of Rs. 4.17 lakhs earmarked in the Village Forest Council Budget, the families of Keelachindalacherry are engaged in tailoring, cloth vending, apart from agriculture, Durairaj added. The total outlay of the Forest Department Programme including people's support activities was Rs.6.0 lakhs, Durairaj said.

Development of Waste Land Project

Under the waste land project, Rs.6.0 lakhs was sanctioned (of which Rs.3.00 lakhs was subsidy) to reclaim the waste land of marginal and small farmers. The women heads of these farming families were organised into Self-Help Groups named Semparuthi, Neelamalarkal, and Mullai. They have been oriented in the activities of floriculture which was new to them. Now the members of these Self Help Group are raising flower crops successfully.

THADCO—Project

To ensure the livelihood of poor Dalit families Durairaj initiated steps to have a tie-up with the cooperative milk society functioning in the Village Panchayat jurisdiction. Apart from availing of the groups' economic activities scheme fund from SGSY, Durairaj contacted THADCO and for one Self Help Group of Dalits credit facility was availed of for rearing milch animals by 15 women members with a tie-up arrangement for marketing of the milk produced by them.

Self-Help Group Activities

There are 21 self-help groups in the Village Panchayat. Mahalir Mennertra Sangam, the NGO, is very actively associated with the Village Panchayat administration. A Self Help Groups building was constructed to enhance the activities of the groups. Periodical meetings are organised in the building. Credit facilities were availed of by 15 self groups. The groups major economic activities are rearing of milch animals and goats, readymade garments, cloth-vending and one group runs a retail shop where cattle feed is sold.

Adi Dravidar Welfare-cum-Humanism Day Celebration

Awareness generation activities to improve the participation of women in Gram Sabha meetings, for making use of free legal aid, eradication of child labour and empowerment of women were carried out with the help of NGOs. The Free Legal Aid Society and

Women's Development Corporation helped the Panchayat. World Women's Day rally is organised every year on the 8th of March.

As the women empowering process is becoming progressive, thanks to the Self Help Group movement, issues like dowry, harassment of women by alcoholic husbands, misunderstanding between husband and wife are brought out for reddressal. The executive member of the Village Panchayat level federating SHGs and the President of the Village Panchayat join together in dealing with these issues. Counselling and awareness building measures are adopted in solving the problems successfully.

A Case of Challenge

In spite of the upward mobility of society, there is a slackness of gender sensitization especially in the rural areas. During 2002 an incident occurred in the village. A Dalit male eve-teased a school girl of a backward community. The issue was brought to the notice of the community leaders and the Village Panchayat President. They conducted an enquiry but the accused failed to admit the charge. Hence a case was registered against him with the police and the case is now in the juristication High Court, Chennai.

In the meantime the accused filed a false complaint against a few relatives of the girl and the Village Panchayat President charging that they attempted to misbehave with his wife, abusing her by her caste name. The complaint was against the members of the BC community and the case was registered under the Personal Civil Rights Act. The President appealed to the higher officials of the PCR enforcement wing in Chennai and the DIG of PCR Wing came to the village to verify the facts. The Village leaders of the Dalit community deposed and informed the authorities that the reported incident of misbehaviour was not true and they further informed that the Village Panchayat President was a pro-Dalit person. After a detailed enquiry the authorities did not proceed and the complaint was declared false. But the eve-teasing case was yet to be heard and the accused came out on bail.

Agriculture Development Activities

Mr. Durairaj himself is a progressive farmer. He has a good rapport with the field and higher level officials of the Department of Agriculture and its allied activities. Schemes under agriculture development like drip-irrigation, distribution of seeds, tools and equipments, and facilities at subsidized cost, training and exposure were properly tapped. Women got training in crop protection, demonstration for hybrid seeds, compensation for the failure of coconut trees during drought and training in the preparation of vermi-compost. He felt that even in the existing arrangement Panchayat Presidents can make the Department of Agriculture work in the villages provided the leaders have enough knowledge of the schemes available in the Department and build up rapport with the officials of the Department.

Organising of Camps

Mr. Durairaj is always waiting for the opportunities to serve the community. Realising the importance of health he associates with institutions like Aravind Eye Hospital and the government machinery, organises free eye camp, health camp for women, leprosy identification, female infanticide camp, veterinary camp, polio immunization camp, dental camp, Students health scheme, AIDS awareness camp etc. in the village itself. The series of camps organised in his Panchayat area have created awareness among the people on health. The health sub-centre is properly functioning in Melachindalacherry because of his intervention to ensure the minimum facilities. He repaired the toilet and the pipeline for drinking water at the health sub-centre. The VHN is very cooperative. The scheme 'Namathu Gramam' was very much useful as it provided opportunities to involve various departments. As the VHN is permanently staying in the quarters itself, the delivery of services in the HSC is very effective.

Improvement of the Highway Road

A rural highway leads to Pannaipuram-Pulikuthi. From the hamlet of Keelachindalacherry, there is a stream which stood as a hurdle to the free and safe movement of vehicles. Accidents took place many times there. The issue was brought up during the Gram Sabha meeting and the Village Panchayat administration took

Retaining Wall to Ensure Road Safety

necessary steps with the department of highways — rural work. Mr. Durairaj appealed to the higher officials and to the concerned Minister. He personally went to Chennai and met the concerned Minister and succeeded in getting an allocation of Rs.10.0 lakhs from the NABARD scheme. A retaining wall of a length of 200 metres was constructed and now the vehicles are freely moving on the road. There was a well along the side of this rural highway. Hence an additional amount of Rs.8.40 lakhs was obtained to construct a retaining wall near the well. Thus safety was ensured on the highway to vehicles as well as pedestrians, because of the initiative of the Village Panchayat administration under the leadership of Durairaj.

Students NSS Camp

The NSS volunteers of the higher secondary school from Kombai, a nearby town, visited the Village Panchayat of Melachindalacherry during the year 2004. They engaged in environmental sanitation improvement activities, for which awareness generation programmes were conducted. *Kudimaramathu* activities were also carried out along with the village youths. The NSS volunteers staged cultural programmes and street plays on AIDS awareness.

Rain Water Harvesting

Mr. Durairaj is very sensitive to the problems of farmers. He is very much involved in programmes like afforestation, soil conversion and water shed activities. When the Chief Minister of Tamil Nadu, Selvi J.Jayalalitha, announced the importance of construction of rain water harvesting structures in all buildings in both rural and urban areas, Mr. Durairaj decided to carry out the message very practically. He sensitized the public by organizing a public rally in which leading personalities like Members of Parliament, Members of Legislative Assembly and the District Collector and the Councillors of the Union and District Panchayat participated. It created a strong impact on the minds of the villagers and so they came forward to construct RWH structures in their houses. It was a 100 per cent successful achievement in the Village Panchayat area and the district authorities gave a certificate of merit acknowledging the sincere efforts of the Village Panchayat administration. About the impact of the RWH activities, Mr.Durairaj said that the groundwater level in the village was coming up. The yield in borewells for irrigation as well as of drinking water supply system has increased.

Step in the Protection of Historical Monuments

There is a temple at the top of the Jagajalamalai. The height of the hill is 1500 feet. The deity of the temple is Lord Perumal. Devotees from all over the Theni District visit this temple to worship the god. There are no facilities like transportation, electricity and street lights, road and drinking water in that area. Mr. Durairaj appealed to the district authorities and to the Government of Tamil Nadu to take necessary steps to meet the felt needs of the devotees. Since the year 2000 the issue has been brought to the notice of all concerned but nothing was done by the government, as the area is controlled by the Forest Department. He said that if the necessary facilities were provided, it would be a popular pilgrimage centre attracting thousands of devotees from all over Tamil Nadu. He is pursuing the matter further.

Welfare of the Disabled Persons

Mr. Durairaj, in consultation with the district authorities, organised a special medical camp for disabled persons. Hearing aids and calipers were distributed to the needy persons. To those who needed special care, a monthly pension of Rs.200 was arranged. There are sixteen disabled persons who benefited in this regard. To a disabled person from the Dalit community a

Rs.10,000 credit with subsidy was obtained from THADCO for his self-employment.

Youth Welfare Activities

Mr. Durairaj encouraged youth activities. He guided the village youth to organise themselves into Self Help Groups. He donated munificently to the sports activities of the youth. From the Village Panchayat fund, sports goods and other equipments have been provided to the youths. He used to invite dignitaries during the village sports meet organised by the youth cricket club members.

The Success of His Leadership

When Mr. Durairaj contested for the second term, it was a tough challenge. It was possible for him to succeed because he gave preference to the areas of the downtrodden and the underdeveloped. He gave necessary attention to improve the hamlets where the community of the opponent candidate was living during the first tenure. He projected the activities so far done cutting across caste/habitation. Hence he was able to get more votes than in his earlier tenure from the Keelachindalacherry hamlet.

He is of the opinion that as the position of President is very close to the public he can succeed provided he attends to the needs of the people. It is necessary to understand the aspirations of the public. The Village Panchayat President should act fairly and justly cutting across political party or caste. Further respecting and recognizing the role of the representatives of the other two tiers and members of legislative and parliamentary constituencies should be very much adhered to by Presidents of Village Panchayats as they have to work for the whole village. They should not project their personal identity with political parties. Personal character also counts when assessing the Village Panchayat leadership. Durairaj said that he does not have any bad habits like smoking or alcoholism. This is very much helpful to identify his uniqueness from the group of unwanted elements, he claimed.

With regard to ensuring the cooperation of the Ward Members and the Vice-President in the context of joint signature when transacting the Panchayat funds, Mr. Durairaj encouraged the members to personally carry out the development works by which one could understand the challenge of successful execution without compromising on quality. Further Durairaj involved all my Ward Members in finalizing the selection of works, selection of beneficiaries and meeting the higher representatives. All the nine members of his Council and the Union Councillor are jointly functioning, he stated. Further Mr. Durairaj gave due space for the functioning of the PTA, the community leadership, the Self Help Groups federation, the youth group, NGOs and field officials of the government departments in the Village Panchayat activities.

He encouraged public to register their demands both personal and general in writing during the Gram Sabha meeting to the discussed one by one with the participants prioritizing the most necessary, involving the participants and deciding the further course of action at the Gram Sabha meeting itself. All this process was undertaken in front of the public transparently. Sometimes, due to paucity of time, works have been referred to the higher officials when they urgently called for particulars to implement some special scheme. Even for this reference, works discussed in the Gram Sabha only were taken up. Hence the villagers never complained that the President acted with personel interest, Durairaj explained.

To sustain honesty, Presidents have to lose their pocket money. Durairaj said that the Village Panchayat Presidents are easily accessible to the public and the public demand donation from Presidents for various social functions. Moreover many individuals extended invitations to attend their family/personal functions for which also he has to donate. Mr. Durairaj reported that he had to sell one of his properties after he became the President. Expenditure during election is also a unavoidable one in the context of the expectations of all concerned.

His Future Vision

Mr. Durairaj felt that after becoming the Panchayat President he was able to enhance his leadership. Though he is one of the notable leaders of the community, the position of Village Panchayat President provided opportunity to move very closely with government officials/departments and other public institutions and individuals. It helped to sharpen his vision of the public welfare activities.

He does not have any idea of contesting again in the Panchayat elections. He tried for Legislative Assembly. Out of 27 individuals who applied for a ticket under the AIADMK, he was one of the three selected for personal interview by the party higher-ups. Though he was not selected, he was happy to learn that his leadership got high recognition. He is an optimist with regard to his higher moves in the public. At the same time he is content with the public welfare activities at the local level through his own community committee and the village committee as he still serves as the secretary and the treasurer in the respective institutions.

Further he is the President of the District Association of Village Panchayat Presidents of Theni District and the Vice-Chairman of the State Association of Presidents of Village Panchayats. He stated that he would be able to fulfil the many basic needs of the villages within a short span of a decade after the introduction of the New Panchayati Raj System in Tamil Nadu. He thanked the training institutions, namely Gandhigram Rural Institute and SIRD, which brought out his talents and assisted in transforming his village.

Conclusion

For him his honesty paid rich dividends. At the same time he had to lose his hard earned money. He has been made to work in the corrupt system. In the past six decades people have been oriented to receives doles at the cost of self-dignity and self-respect. People have been made to swallow any amount of misdeeds in government. He started working on the demands of the people. But he established rapport with all the three tier representatives of the Panchayat System along with the MLA and the MP of his constituency. Likewise he was able to develop good relationship with the officials of the Departments of Government. He has attended to the needs of all segments of the society. He discussed the entire activities of the Panchayat in the Gram Sabha. He never failed to consult the members of the Panchayat. Likewise he used to contact the MLA and the MP constantly and tap resources from them also. His performance, management and transparency brought him again as President through the election. He is building a track record of performance in the Panchayat to make a claim in his party for a ticket to contest in the Legislative Assembly elections. He knows the nuances of tapping resources from the sectoral departments through schemes and programmes to the Panchayat. He had taken up both hardware and software works that will help the panchayat to achieve social development. For all his excellent activities his leadership is imperative. So leadership matters in governance whether it is in Delhi or at Chennai or at the grassroots.

CASE - 21

WOMEN AND CHILDREN ARE PRIMARY

Communal harmony, delivering services to the marginalised, mobilizing the citizens for public action, creating awareness among the people about development, working for children and women are the priority areas on which she worked mainly. Her firm faith is the activities relating to children and women. She feels that attacking malnutrition and anemia is the major activity of the Panchayat. Being a Dalit woman she is conscious of the conditions of the Dalit children and the Dalit women. Hence all the time she works in school, balwadis and primary health centres. She is a role model for achieving the millennium development goals. In a caste ridden Panchayat, she is able to maintain communal harmony and provide services to the Dalits very effectively.

Her Background

Ms. M. Kala, the Noothulapuram Panchayat President, is the daughter of an inter-caste married couple. Though she was educated upto 10th standard, she worked as a coolie. With the help of an NGO, namely ASSEFA, she received training in health education and served in villages in and around Nilakottai. She also served as a promoting agent for the small savings scheme. Her husband runs a travel agency after getting a bank loan. When the Panchayat elections were declared in the year 1996, Noothulapuram Village Panchayat President's position was reserved for Dalit women. The villagers of Noothulapuram encouraged Kala to contest and her husband also did so. Hence she contested and won in the election. She is associated with the Tamil Manila Congress (now it has merged with the Tamil Nadu Congress Party).

Kala's candidature under Dalit reservation was challenged in court. But the case was dismissed and her candidature under Dalit reservation was upheld because even though her father belongs to a non-Dalit community her mother is a Dalit. In Noothulapuram Village, there are 11 hamlets and the total population is 5000. The Dalit community is more in number than the caste Hindu communities.

Communal Dispute and Intervention of the President

Goddess Chelliamman shrine is the village temple and both Dalits and Thevars jointly celebrate the 3-day festival. The Thevar community enjoys the right to the sanctum sanctorum. This is the traditional practice. During the recent festival the Dalit youth got into the sanctum sanctorum. It became a communal dispute. Government officials intervened and it was settled peacefully through negotiation. The Dalits and the Thevars were to celebrate the festival separately. The first day was reserved for the Thevars and the second day for the Dalit community.

Recently, in the year 2001, when the celebration was declared, anticipating communal clash police officials did not permit the celebration. Kala met the Police officials and explained the practice earlier adhered to. The representatives of the non-Dalits who were present during this meeting appreciated Kala's the leadership as she took a neutral position and explained the truth. She assured the police that no dispute would arise during the celebration. The Police as well as the leaders of non-Dalits accepted this assurance and permission was granted for the celebration and it was completed without any dispute. The youth of the Dalits felt very much about the unfolding of the truth in the Police Station Kala as she referred to the earlier practice of privilege to the Thevar community. But President Kala convinced the youth that during the celebration this practice could be removed in the presence of the police and the Dalits can also enjoy the privilege of going into the shrine. Since any further difference created would disturb the communal harmony. Most of the youth agreed to Kala's advice but a few radical youngsters did not agree. Yet Kala conducted the celebration successfully.

When Kala contested for a second term, she felt that the Dalit youth particularly men, entertaining enmity for caste Hindus, would work against her. But the village women has got socialized through SHGs. Women of Dalit and non-Dalit communities joined together through SHG activities and eliminated the differences between these two communities. The power pump of the drinking water system is being operated by women of both communities through an SHG. There is no dispute between these groups on any aspects. Wherever necessary, the women of both community work jointly for the common cause. Being a woman hailing from the Dalit community occupying the post of Gram Panchayat, Kala encourages understanding among the womenfolk in Noothulapuram. Kala contested in the election again as the Government of Tamil Nadu ordered that the reservation of seats for women to continue for a second tenure also. Though huge amount of money was spent by the other candidates in the election, Kala projected the activities carried out by her, cutting across castes and won the election by a margin of 380 votes. Kala said that she served fairly, treating all communities alike, and so she won in the election.

Panchayat Activities

The scheme fund earmarked for the welfare of Dalits is more than the fund earmarked for non-Dalits and so a large number of work have been carried out in the hamlets of Dalits. During the Gram Sabha meeting she explained the fact that since more Dalits live in the Panchayat, the panchayat gets more for the Dalit community. To provide necessary basic facilities for the habitations of non-Dalits, Kala mobilized funds from other sources like the MLA fund, the District Councillor's fund, the MP fund and the Union fund. In this way she is able to retain the support of all the communities.

People's Expectations

Irrespective of caste, lower middle class and poor families demand loan facilities for economic activities, patta for house sites, group houses and improvement of facilities in their streets. In the Gram Sabha there is good participation by the non-Dalit community. Available funds position and priorities of work are properly deliberated upon the Gram Sabha meeting. It is only through the Gram Sabha she has proved herself a genuine and sincere President.

Disunity among Dalit

Kala feels that the people of the Dalit communities do not function as a unified force. The families of the Dalit are divided in the name of clan and traditional positions followed by their forefathers. Recently the Dalit community representatives brought about a change in these systems and selected responsible individuals from other non-traditional Dalit families who did not hold any traditional positions. In reaction to this unexpected decision, a few people encouraged an individual who had encroached upon panchayat land and prevented the formation of a road through that site.

Relationship with Officials

Kala says that officials in general encourage the women Presidents when they shed their inhibitions. She herself never feels inferior to men and her husband used to visit the block office to question any unwarranted reactions of the officials in the respect of her Panchayat activities.

Reservation of Seats for Dalits

According to Kala, reservation of seats for Dalits and women is the right approach to empower them. Through the position of elected representatives, individuals belonging to the so called marginalized sectors got exposure and established contacts with officials by which they have enhanced their leadership qualities.

Only those women Presidents who are able to get the support of their own families and womenfolk in general could sustain their leadership. The socio-economic conditions of Dalits could be improved only if they are oriented in many activities other than farm sector activities, as the scope for employment in agriculture is shrinking now-a-days. Economic background, group support, caste association support, encouragement given by family, educational background and patronage from the general public are the enabling factors determining the upward mobility of Dalit leadership emerging through reservation. The NGOs are not fully involved in the election campaign even though they support their own

SHG members. Political parties in general do not work seriously in Village Panchayat elections whereas in the case of the other two positions, namely Union Councilor and District Ward Member the candidates depend mostly on the political parties. When the Presidents of Village Panchayats gain popularity political parties try to draw them into their party and encourage them to contest for higher positions. Through the Panchayats, Dalits have come to understand the system of governance and avail of their entitlements and now psychologically they feel better. The community will be benefited by interlinking panchayat with the sectoral department particularly the Dalit community for whom plenty of schemes and programmes are available.

FOCUS OF ACTIVITIES DURING HER FIRST TENURE

Provision of Water Supply

Improvement in the basic amenities especially provision of drinking water supply, road, street light and public sanitation was the major expectation of the villagers from the Panchayat administration, Mrs. Kala observed. When the election to Panchayati Raj Institutions was held in the first tenure, during election campaign, residents of all eleven hamlets of Noothulapuram Village Panchayat complained about the non-availability of adequate water in the hand pumps. Moreover in many hand pumps the water table has gone down to more than two hundred feet depth. People demanded protected water supply from the river source as the taste of ground water in Noothulapuram was not good. Hence she made a promise to the villagers that she would definitely solve that issue, Mrs. Kala referred.

Rain Water Harvesting Campaign programme

After becoming the President her first effort was to get a comprehensive drinking water supply system from the river source. She met the then MLA Mrs. Ponnammal and through her contact brought the issue to the attention of the TWAD officials. At last a comprehensive drinking water supply scheme was carried out covering all eleven hamlets of Noothulapuram Village Panchayat. Ten overhead tanks have been constructed of which 8 OHTs have the capacity of 10000 litres each and the remaining two tanks have a capacity of 15000 litres each. About 50 public taps were also provided in the hamlets.

Though the comprehensive water supply scheme was successful in resolving the issue in water supply system, due to variation in the slope of supply pipe route, in three hamlets the pumped water from the river source did not reach the overhead tanks. Mrs. Kala took up that issue with the TWAD officials. But it was delayed a lot and she could improve the water supply to these three hamlets only during her second tenure. The problem was solved by constructing a sump to store the water received from the river source and then water was pumped into the overhead tanks of three hamlets. Now there is adequate water supply even during summer, Mrs. Kala claimed.

Issue with the TWAD Officials

Mrs. Kala shared that the line departments do not give much importance to the Village Panchayat administration. The officials of TWAD engaged a contractor in the water supply works meant for the three hamlets where the water did not properly reach to the overhead tanks. There was no official communication from the TWAD to the Village Panchayat administration in this regard. The contractor also did not meet the Village Panchayat in connection with that work. But after executing the work, TWAD official demanded resolution of the Village Panchayat administration. Mrs. Kala sent a reply to the TWAD officials in which she made an observation that the works was carried out by the contractor without the knowledge of the Village Panchayat administration and so the village Panchayat was not able to carry out the monitoring of the quality of the pipes used. Moreover the old pipes replaced with new ones were not returned to the Village

Panchayat. She replied that in that circumstance the Village Panchayat was not ready to pass resolution on the works completed, Mrs. Kala explained. She was not happy with the mindset of the officials, who were still in the perception that Panchayats were only implementing agencies.

Challenges in the removal of encroachment

Thanks to the callous attitude of government machineries, a vast extent of village commons was encroached in villages. Due to lack of coordination between the Village Panchayat administration and the revenue administration, the encroachers are left in free movement, easily escaped from the legal action. But recently the High Court in Tamil Nadu ordered for a detailed survey on all the encroachments and instructed the local bodies to take necessary steps to remove encroachments especially in the water sources area. The communication in this regard was received by Mrs. Kala. She immediately discussed the issue in the Village Panchayat Council and it was decided to take legal action against the encroacher who encroached a vast extent of land along the Kanmoi at Chinnamanaickankottai. The encroacher was given 'B' memo by the village administrative officer and it was told that it was under encroachment by him over a period of more than twenty years. The encroacher erected a borewell and raised 85 coconut trees over the land encroached by him. Mrs. Kala brought the truth to the attention of the taluk officials. The taluk officials made enquiry and issued an order of cancelling of the 'B' memo with the instruction of surrendering the land encroached to the Village Panchayat administration. But the encroacher who was a resident of the nearby Village Panchayat challenged Mrs. Kala and even threatened her. Mrs. Kala made resolution in the council to do numbering the trees so as it could be auctioned to augment income to the Village Panchayat. In the assignment of numbering of trees she engaged workers along with her husband. But the encroacher abused the workers and her husband by mentioning their caste and threatened to kill.

The numbering of trees was disturbed and both side made complaint against each. Mrs. Kala informed that in spite of court instruction, there was no prompt co-operation or assistance from the development officials to the Village Panchayat administration. But at last the development officials used to come and made accusation that the Village Panchayat failed to adhere the rules and regulation and even the officials resorted to take serious action in these regard, Mrs. Kala complained. She referred an example with regard to the mindset of officials, in dealing with Village Panchayat administration. The development officials initiated enquiry proceedings against the complaint made on the administration of Mrs. Kala. The main complaints were that she acted individually in selecting beneficiaries for IAY housing schemes and failed to pay insurance premium due to the workers of her Village Panchayat. Mrs. Kala had proper explanation to these accusation. The selection of beneficiaries was discussed in the Village Panchayat council meeting and all members including the Vice-President (who was the complainant) who attended the meeting put their signature after the selection. With regard to the non-payment of insurance premium, for the past six months there is no fund available even for salary to the workers. How could she make payment of insurance premium to the workers. The officials show interest in punishing the Village Panchayat Presidents than to comprehend the situation before taking action, Mrs. Kala felt.

Mrs. Kala expressed that there is a lack of civic sense among the members of the public and the government officials are in bureaucratic nature. Moreover due to non-orientation, the Village Panchayat ward members insist to do many works in their wards instead of planned and priority based activities. Against this backdrop, the work atmosphere in the Village Panchayat is not a conducive one. In the midst of pressure and strain, the Village Panchayat President looses their interest to serve, Mrs. Kala felt.

The Importance of Capacity Building and the Service of the Supportive Organisations

Mrs. Kala recollected her days during the period of first tenure. Though she had an orientation in public activities, she felt very difficult in handling the affairs of the Village Panchayat. It was the capacity building and frequent refresher trainings extended by the institutions like Rajiv Gandhi Chair for Panchayati Raj

AIDS Awareness Programme

Studies, Gandhigram Rural Institute and Rural Extension Training Centres, Government of Tamil Nadu equipped her leadership. She outlined moreover the federation activities of Human Right Foundation, Chennai and Tamil Nadu Women Presidents Association, under the aegis of Gandhigram University helped a lot in enhancing the perception of the women leadership and their potentials, she observed. Mrs. Kala is serving as the District President of Tamil Nadu Women Presidents Federation as well as President of the Dalit Women Leaders of Southern Region.

Panchayat Role in Promoting Health and Hygiene

Mrs. Kala realizing the importance of the health properly made use of the opportunity given for the establishment of a Primary Health Centre in the jurisdiction of her Village Panchayat. She mobilized public contribution for the purchase of 5 cents land required for the construction of the Primary Health Centre. Now the PHC is functioning well. She is having good rapport with the medical officers of the PHC. There is a mutual understanding between the Village Panchayat administration and the hospital administration in promoting health and hygiene. The medical officers used to guide the Village Panchayat in maintaining cleanliness in the provision of water supply. Mrs. Kala had the practice of visiting the PHC periodically. She told that she verified the out patient register and came to know that majority of the patients with complaints like fever, stomach pain, were from the nearby village. The number of delivery in the hospital has also increased, she observed.

Eye Camp

She referred that the medical officials showed much and immediate attention when the outbreak of Cholera was noticed in one of the hamlets, namely Chinnamanayakkenkottai. It is told that due to the failure of motor meant for water supply, some of the villagers fetched water from a public well which was not put into use at that time. Moreover they did not boil the water. Hence Cholera occurred. Immediately steps were taken to treat the patients at the PHC and water from the public well was removed and chlorination was done. All public places were cleaned and villagers were advised to drink water only after boiling. In the meantime the repair work in the motor was attended and the water supply from the usual source has been commenced. The doctors took all efforts in checking the water tanks and other public area in all hamlets and it took a week to bring normalcy, Mrs. Kala observed. Mrs. Kala had served as Balwadi teacher and had the experience of organising women sangams when she was with the NGO, ASSEFA. After she became the President, she made use of the services of Balwadi teachers and village health nurse in promoting the health and welfare of women and children. She joined the nurse in creating awareness among the pregnant women and lactating mothers regarding the intake of nutritionally rich ingredients in their food.

Women Sanitary Complex and the Mindset of Rural Populace

When a women sanitary complex was allotted to Noothulapuram Village Panchayat, Mrs. Kala after discussing with ward members selected Thummalapatti hamlet being a bigger in size and approached the villagers to earmark a suitable site for the construction of the sanitary complex. The villagers of Thummalapatti did not had the mindset to make use of the same. Moreover they were of the opinion that the proposed women complex should be far away from the habitation. The women did not come forward to give their opinion in this regard in spite of availability of women ward member in that village. As there was no other way, the sanitary complex was constructed at the site identified by the village elders which was far away from the habitation. Women are not yet utilizing the toilet. Some anti-social elements removed the pipes and bulbs of the complex. But the village elders were not at all concerned about on this issue, Mrs. Kala felt.

To sensitise the women, Kala with the help of Nilakottai Government Women College students of NSS organised a camp in Thummalapatti village. The girls of NSS stayed in the village and they used the women sanitary complex. Door by door campaign was carried out to disseminate the importance of personal hygiene and public sanitation. Folksongs and dramas were also staged during the evening. Mrs. Kala was of the opinion that only by promoting individual household latrine, the issue would be solved. She had an idea of coercing those householders who had drinking water supply connection to construct toilet in their homes. There are thirty householders who came forward to have individual latrine. Kala is waiting to get eligible subsidy available under Total Rural Sanitation Programme in this regard. There are two hundred household toilets constructed under TRSP. About 50 householders spent additionally and made their latrine as pucca. Remaining householders are persuaded to make use of the latrine. Kala felt that among the villagers, awareness was generated with regard to wearing of Chappel, wearing of clean cloths, keeping of children clean and neat; but it is very hard to change the mindset of villagers with regard to their habit of open air defecation, she added.

Village Panchayat and the Self Help Group Activities

Kala enabled one women ward member to organise women self help groups in association with NGOs. There are about fifty self help groups in Noothulapuram Village Panchayat promoted and guided by four non governmental organisations, namely ASSEFA, KALANCHIUM, CENTREDA and SEDWIN. Recently MMS is also formed two groups, Kala informed. The self help group members are serious in micro finance than in venturing into group enterprises, Kala remarked. She felt that there was lackness among the SHG members in respect of public services. During Gram Sabha meetings, she properly informed all SHGs and about half of the participants were women who attended Gram Sabha meetings with an expectation of individual benefit, Kala explained. She remarked that due to the Self Help Groups movement, the villagers of Nilakkottai taluk have been relieved to a some extent from the money lenders who charged abnormal interest, Kala added.

TRSP Household Toilet Campaign

Contribution to the Educational Development

When Kala assumed position as the President of the Noothulapuram Village Panchayat, there were four union schools, one school under Kallar reclamation and seven balwadis catered to the educational needs of the society. At that time the Operation Black Board scheme was under implementation in the district of Dindigul. She made use the scheme properly for the infrastructure development in these educational institutions. She could able to mobilise fund for the construction of two additional buildings in two union

New School Building

schools and compound wall was provided to the Kallar reclamation school. For Balwadi children from the contribution of the mill owners and other traders, she provided mats, plate and tumblers.

During her present tenure, when a new and innovative scheme namely "Sarva Siksha Abhiyan" was introduced, Kala has been nominated as a member in the district level committee solely representing Village Panchayat Presidents in her block in monitoring the SSA implementation. It is a honour given to her recognizing her active cooperation with the officials of the education department as well as with the teaching community during the implementation of operation Black Board Scheme. Under SSA, Kala fulfilled the need of infrastructure development in the remaining two primary schools. Compound walls and flooring works were provided to the schools. Further she assisted the headmaster of all the five schools in her Panchayat to carryout whitewashing of building to provide furniture, teaching materials and playing materials. The couplets of Thirukkural were written on the walls of schools to motivate the students and public. Toilets and drinking water tap was also available in schools.

Mrs. Kala pointed out that the efforts taken by the community to establish a government college for women was fulfilled. She assisted the government authorities in identifying the suitable site in the jurisdiction of her village Panchayat and meaning fully negotiated with the landowners to part off their land. She further rendered assistance to raise tree saplings in the campus of the college. She is maintaining good rapport with the college administration. Two times she was able to get the support of the NSS unit of the college and organised NSS camps in Noothulapuram village Panchayat. She joins with all those who work for the development of the college. She opinioned that the socio-economic standard of the villagers would be changed as the expenditure spent on the higher education of girls was less as the college for women was available at local area itself.

Improvement in Road Facilities

During her first tenure, approach roads in all hamlets had been improved into Bitumen roads. In streets, CC road was provided. There was a long pending demand to improve the rural highways road which was formed about thirty years back. She consistently took follow-up with the district authorities and succeeded in her attempts during the second tenure. At the cost of Rs.5.00 lakhs the road was newly formed. She assisted the contractor of the rural highways in removing the encroachments so as the road would be as wide as possible. From the NABARD assistance at the cost of Rs.5.75 lakhs road improvement work in 5 KM distance was carried out during her first tenure. She appreciated the NABARD officials for their immediate response to her request.

Improvement in Rural Housing

Kala understood the system in the block and the district administration with regard to the execution of development schemes. She used to complete the works given to her Panchayat in time. Moreover she equipped the beneficiaries of individual scheme with all needed information so as the works have been up

IAY House — New Model

to the satisfaction of the inspecting officials. Hence she was able to get more number of houses under IAY. During her first tenure she recollected that about 100 houses have been provided to poor SC families. And now so far 80 houses have been successfully constructed in her village Panchayat. When the innovative housing with cost effective roofing under Prime Minister Housing Scheme was introduced she was able to get 15 houses and successfully completed. Under Kutcha House scheme also about 60 huts were replaced with tiles. In the above housing schemes almost all the beneficiaries belonged to Dalit community. Kala has concern for the poor among the other backward communities also. When the district administration sanctioned houses for poor families of backward class, she provided three kutcha houses and three colony houses to the 6 poor families. Further from the village Panchayat fund, she provided cement concrete road facilities in all the streets of BC habitation. Other facilities like provision of thrashing floor was also given in priority to the farming community belonged to BC. Two open air theatre stages were constructed in two hamlets where the temple celebration was observed in grand manner.

When the credit-cum-subsidy scheme for housing to the poor families was announced by the Nationalized Banks, Kala assisted six families belonged to BC to avail each Rs.40,000 from the bank for the construction of house. Out of the total Rs.40,000 the subsidy component was Rs.10,000 and the balance amount had to be paid in easy annual instalments. It is learnt that she was the only president who assisted poor families to avail the credit-cum-subsidy scheme for housing.

Management of Common Property Resources

There are five Kanmois in the Village Panchayat of which two are coming under the jurisdiction of PWD. Desilting works have been undertaken in all five tanks. The height of the tank was also raised. Repair work at sluices of tanks was also carried out apart from the maintenance of inlet channels.

From the allocation of union general fund, two new ooranis have been formed at two hamlets, namely Thummalapatti and Sirunayakkankottai, at a total cist of Rs.4.50 lakhs Ms.Kala identified Panchayat poramboke lands where ooranis could be formed. She submitted a list of twenty works for next work including four new oorani's under the management of Common Property Resources. Her Panchayat is the second graded one due to less income. Hence she pleaded with the district administration to allocate fund for the planting of trees in the tanks like social forestry scheme. The district administration replied that there was no such scheme existed in the government. Kala recollected that the social forestry was a good scheme as there were two benefits — one, income from the sale proceedings of the trees and another benefit which was most important one that the protection of tanks from the encroachment. During the implementation of social forestry schemes extention the boundaries of all tanks have been measured and planting of tree saplings were undertaken at the whole extent of tanks. Hence any attempt to encroach the tank area would be immediately known to all, she added. She regretted that wherever more number of tanks are available in the village Panchayats, the officials should help the village Panchayat administration to scientifically plan for the improvement in the management of tanks so as income could be augmented to the Panchayats.

Her Assistance in Eradication of Poverty

Being a Dalit, Kala has a good rapport with the THADCO officials. Economic welfare schemes targeting poor individuals like jeevandhara wells, self employment loans for activities like rearing of milch animals, vending, petty shop, brick kiln, mike set operation were properly availed by the eligible poor families belonged to Dalit community with the intervention of Kala. She proudly referred that about twenty poor families have promptly repaid the loan and availed the second time loan from the bank, she added. During 2005, she approached the Aavin Milk Society management and got sanction to run a collection centre-cum-branch society in her village Panchayat as owner of about twenty milch animal agreed to sell milk to Aavin. She complained in spite of the assistance there were a few who restored to the practice of cheating by showing milch animals of others instead of purchasing milch animals by themselves, when the loan was given to them.

Her Association with the Officials of Agricultural Departments

Kala is a member in the committee constituted by the Assistant Agricultural Officer (AAO). She used to get invitation to attend the meetings convened at the office of AAO where guidances given for farming according to season and she helped marginal farmers of her village to get hand sprayers, seeds and other inputs available for subsidized cost. She organized farmers meeting at Thummalapatti and Sirunaicken-patti hamlets to discuss various issues in agriculture. She told that staff of village knowledge centre run by

Removal of Blocks in the inlets of Kanmois

M.S. Swaminathan Research Foundation at Sempatti attended the Farmers meets and disseminated information sought by the farmers.

During the north-east monsoon of 2005, she mobilized all farmers of Kulathupatti to discuss as the rain water was not reaching properly to the tank in spite of good rain. It was decided to check the route of the inlet channel which originated from the Sangaharikottai Karadu, the catchment area of the tank. It was found that there was a block purposefully made by some other villagers in the inlet channel meant to Kulathupatti and the rain water was diverted to other area. Kala and her village farmers removed the block and successfully brought the water. In the meantime bushes in the inlet channels were cleaned so as water flows easily. She happily pointed out that one tank at Thummalapatti was filled and the excess work reached the tank of Kulathupatti and very soon it would also be filled. All farmers irrespective of castes responded to her call for Kudikaramathu. "Now they are enjoying the fruits of their hard labour", she remarks.

Monitoring of Public Distribution System

There are three PDS shops in the jurisdiction of Noothulapuram Panchayat. Kala used to periodically visit the shops for checking the quality and quantity of the commodities distributed in the shops. Once sub-standard quality of rice was distributed to the villagers who straightaway came to the Panchayats and made complaint. Kala took the rice distributed in the PDS and went to the taluk office and brought it to the attention of the officials. The taluk officer immediately went over to the concerned shop, instructed the staff not to distribute the sub-standard quality rice. He made arrangement at once for the replacement with good quality rice to the villagers. Realising the bold step taken by the Panchayat administration the staff of the PDS shops took caution in the procurement of rice from the common pool, Kala shared.

Rapport with the Higher Level Representatives

Kala though belongs to the Congress party she never projects herself as a mere politician. In respect of development of her village, she duly met the higher level representatives, MP, MLA, Union Chairman and district and union councillors. Almost all higher level representatives except the member of parliament are from the AIADMK party. But she maintains cordial relationship with them. The MLA contributed Rs.3.50 lakhs for the channel maintenance, and union councillors contributed for the erection of borewell and hand pumps. The District Councillors allotted Rs.1.75 lakhs to construct open air theatre stage. Union Chairman sanctioned fund for the provision of mini power pump in 6 hamlets. The member of parliament Mr.Sithan contributed Rs.10.00 lakh for the construction of building in the Government Women's College and Rs.1.35 lakh for the construction of Open Air Theatre in Noothulapuram.

Her Outstanding Leadership

Mrs. Kala, a decade ago was an ordinary housewife of a Dalit family. Reservation in PRIs brought a new change in her life. Constant support of her husband and cooperation from her son and daughters are the main factors which contributed for her onward march in the public life. During her first tenure she faced oppsition from four candidates and won in a small difference of 22 votes. Her hard works to improve the socio-economic welfare of the villagers and her contribution in bringing peace and harmony between the members of Dalit and Other Backward communities spoke her talents and leadership qualities. She was encouraged to contest again when the Panchayat election was held in the year 2001. Kala remarked that in the earlier election, votes of backward community were distributed to all candidates. But during the second tenure, the village community who witnessed her performance, defeated the four candidates who opposed Kala. Kala won by the difference of 389 votes. It is possible as the majority of the members belonging to backward community casted their votes in her favour, Kala pointed out.

Her Future Course of Action

Kala remarked that role of village Panchayat President was very challenging one to perform. As it demands physical presence in all times, women Presidents are not in a position to look after their family. Moreover there is no salary to the President of the village Panchayat in spite of full time engagement. Issues like dominance of bureaucracy, lack of orientation among the ward members, absence of real decentralisation power to village Panchayat and lack of finance in village Panchayats have to be encountered fearlessly, Kala pointed out. She opined that honesty and straightforwardness is not sufficient enough to run the village Panchayat administration. Courage, muscle power and finance are needed to manage the affairs in the context of threat from the encroachers, selfish individuals and political opponents, she felt. She acknowledged that the Capacity Building and consistent guidance of the Gandhigram Rural University are the major factors enabling to continue her public life besides the motivation and support of her husband.

Being an active cadre in the congress party, Kala proposed to enter into active politics and decided to make an attempt to get a seat for the MLA election in the incoming election to the legislature. She opined that it was a tough time in the village Panchayat administration. She felt that she was under constant pressure and tension as she had to fulfil the expectation of the villagers. But the role of MLA is different from that of a village Panchayat President, she pointed out. Moreover the pension given to the MLA is considered as an allowance for good subsistence in the public life without any weary, she observed. Further she shared that in the position of MLA she could contribute more in the development of the constituency as she had sufficient experience as a village Panchayat President consecutively for a decade, she claimed.

Leadership Process of Kala

Kala's background was a simple one. Her association with the NGO, namely ASSEFA after her marriage changed her lifestyle. Earlier she even has been engaged in manual labour. But orientation given by NGO improved her understanding on her own-self as well as about the society. She served as a health educator in the NGO activities. She used this opportunity to move freely with the villagers. Her husband being a member in the Indian National Congress Party, had a perspective with regard to women empowerment. He at his capacity used to serve villagers in availing credit assistance from THADCO and from other line departments of the State Government. From these interventions also Kala learned issues in public life.

The reservation of seats for women in Panchayati Raj Institutions was a boon to her. Kala's husband though disappointed on the declaration that the President position in Noothulapuram Village Panchayat was reserved for SC (Women), he quickly decided to field his wife and encouraged her to function independently.

The occurrence of communal dispute in Noothulapuram Village Panchayat was successfully managed by Kala. Without any prejudice she involved in the negotiation process for mutual understanding cutting across caste, and people understood her leadership potential. She duly got the recognition and right to serve to the Dalit community with regard to temple celebration. Her close interaction with youth helped her to analyse the mindset of Dalit youth. She was able to pacify them to sit across for negotiation. She has developed a conflict resolution methodology in her village. The process can be studied.

Her association with women self help group cutting across castes won recognition to her. She had used this opportunity to assist women belongs to BC community wherever possible using her good office. Further to improve the basic amenities in the habitations of BC, she contacted MLA and MP and representatives of higher tiers of Panchayati Raj System. She made use of the Village Panchayat source for the welfare of Dalit habitation. She realized the importance of fair deal though she belonged to SC community.

Her close association with the Congress Party helped her to understand the major dimensions of politics and governance. She had opportunity to accompany the local MLA Mrs. Ponnammal and participated in the party meetings. Steadily she gained insights and equipped her leadership through better relationship with the supportive institutions like Rajiv Gandhi Chair for Panchayati Raj Studies, Human Right Foundation and State Institute of Rural Development. She never missed any events of training or other programmes meant for Village Presidents. Her public speech in stages was focused on reality rather than creating pipe dream.

Kala gained knowledge and understanding of the functioning of government machinery. She never hesitated to make visits to various departments and availed the details of schemes and assistances executed by those line departments, and made use of the same for the development of her villagers. She moved steadily from the activities of providing basic amenities to the economic assistance to eligible poor.

She equipped her capacity in the system of Panchayat administration. She herself used to verify the entries in the records made by the Panchayat clerk. She used to line out the ways of sending communications to queries made by the officials. If necessary she used to avail the support of Rajiv Gandhi Chair for Panchayati Raj Studies. Her interest to learn the system pushed her to the position. Her ambition raised to a height, she started realizing the scope of a potential SC women leader in politics due to emerging trend of accommodation of women leaders by the political parties. She made use of all the opportunities to associate with the activities of the Congress Party. She wished to contest in the MLA election as the constituency is reserved to SC. A consecutive period of 10 years equipped her leadership through the process of Village Panchayat administration, SHG activities and political activities. The capacity building improved her vision. Her perspectives, understanding, approach, commitment towards delivery of services, access to people, interface with officials developed his capability, skill and capacity. Without antagonizing the caste Hindus, she delivered all services to the Dalit hamlets. She is a role model for women leaders in Panchayats. She fought with officials to maintain her dignity. She is sensitive towards the issues of Dalit and Women. Her interest is to move further in the ladder of power from Panchayats to Parliament or State Legislative Assembly.

CASE - 22

A ROLE MODEL FOR DALIT WOMEN LEADERS

Ms.Pappa is a rural revolutionary leader known for her fight against the existing social order and bureaucratic system and she has emerged as a force to reckon with not only in the Panchayat area but also among the Gram Panchayat women leaders. She moved into social service much before she moved into the Panchayat. Setting right the public institutions is the first step in ensuring delivery of services to the poor. She responded to the challenges from the upper caste and the bureaucracy and on all the occasions she fought against them. She is the President of the Dalit Women Gram Panchayat Leaders of Tamil Nadu. She is a good trainer and she takes classes in training programmes. She is a role model for Dalit women.

Her Background

Mrs. Pappa aged 33 is a science graduate. She hails from the Dalit community. Her father is a progressive farmer who preferred Pappa to be an educated woman. To ensure proper and conducive atmosphere for her study, Pappa was sent to a Government Arts College, Palani where she stayed in the hostel. During her college days she was in sports and she acquired proficiency in athletics and games. Her college education helped her to understand the sufferings of the Dalit community, Pappa recollected. Being a cadet in the NCC unit in her college, Pappa had the opportunity to live in villages other than her own. Pappa informed that the plight of Dalit in the villages around Palani was agonising. They lived in sub-human living condition. Moreover they lived in abject poverty, completely depending on the caste Hindus. Pappa expressed her concern for that status of the Dalits. She was longing for an opportunity to help Dalits.

After successfully completing of her graduation — B.Sc. (Zoology), she learned computer also. In 1995 her marriage was arranged with her close relative. Family of her in-law's is a reputed one. Her father-in-law was the ex-President of Athankaraipatti Gram Panchayat three times. Being aged, he withdrew from public life and paved way for the entry of his son, the husband of Pappa. Pappa's husband served as an employee in the local cooperative. Moreover he is a key member in the Traditional Committee which looks after the social activities of the caste group. Of the four key members in the Committee, her husband is 'Kaladi' a traditional position meant Secretary/ Treasurer in the activities of the Committee. The other three positions are Kudumban, Varian and Nattanmai. This is the practice of the 'Pallar' community of SC in Athankaraipatti. Thus Pappa has a strong support base besides her education and family.

Pappa as a Social Worker

Pappa did not want to sit idle in the house. She is a highly motivated, committed and educated woman among the members of the Dalit community. She used to render assistance to her neighbours by offering guidance and counselling in their family affairs. In the meantime she came to know the activities of Dr. Ambedkar Development Society functioning in Perungudi near Madurai, which called for the service of young and dedicated, men and women to contribute for the advancement of education of the Dalit students. She applied and got the post and served as animator. She conducted coaching classes for school students in her house. Further she used to mobilize adults and elderly women, shared their concern and created awareness among them about the conditions

Associating with youth

of the poor and especially women. She helped them to acquire literacy which considered as a main factor for empowerment. Realizing the potential of Pappa, many women used to visit her and get her guidance for many matters relating to their family. She was paid for these activities also by Dr.Ambedkar Development Society. Her in-laws expressed happiness over the development. They even appreciated her for her approach and method of doing services. Her husband also encouraged her activities. Being a politically oriented person of the Congress Party, her husband used to involve her in the public welfare activities also. Thus Pappa slowly prepared herself to shoulder higher responsibility in the public in the ensuing days. Her family stood as support structure for her public activities.

In the service of our animator, Pappa had a good company of students and youths. She spent from her pocket to meet the educational needs of poor Dalit students. She organized excursions and picnics to the students to the nearby mountains, religious places, and dam sites. Parents of these children witnessed the attitudinal and behavioural changes among the school students and used to frequently visit Pappa and express their gratitude. Pappa became a significant woman in the village of Athankaraipatti. She has come to the public space already on her own.

Panchayati Raj Election in 1996

Athankaraipatti Village Panchayat had two hamlets, namely Subbulapuram and Kamatchipuram. Athankaraipatti and Kamatchipuram are exclusively Dalit habitation. In Subbulapuram hamlet families of backward class communities are living. The major communities are Thevar, Naicker, Vellalar and Brahmin. When the election under new Panchayati Raj System was held in 1996, a middle aged Dalit woman became the President as the seat was reserved for Dalit women. She was a proxy. Her father was the Union Councillor at that time. The woman President was not approachable to the public also. The delivery of services were not effective during her administration. Moreover there was misuse of Panchayat funds and she was dismissed at the fag end of her tenure after the enquiry conducted by the district administration. Villagers stood in solidarity against the misdeed of that woman President.

Pappa as a citizen used to attend Gram Sabha organized in her village. She recollected that she was just attending along with other women, as the proceeding of the Gram Sabha was not so serious. In the meantime, she became an agent in the LIC and actively engaged herself in that assignment. Within a short duration she achieved high position among the agents of LIC as she achieved the highest target. Her approach and sincerity in follow-up, with regard to LIC works as well as her counselling and guidance in the family affairs of those premium holders who sought her opinion were very much useful to her to gain recognition among the public. Moreover she learned a lot as an insurance agent, she claimed, which helped in the administration of Village Panchayat after she became the President.

Panchayati Raj Election in 2001

When the election to Panchayati Raj Institutions was held in 2001 villagers, suggested to Pappa to file her nomination. Though Pappa had the mind to serve community, with regard to contesting in election she had some reservation. The villagers influenced the in-laws of Pappa. The family members of Pappa finally agreed to the suggestion of the villagers. There were four candidates in the fray who were not at all oriented in social activities. Moreover they were less educated than Pappa. The villagers suffered a lot during the first tenure in the hands of ill-equipped leadership. So they were determined to elect a potential woman this time. Pappa and her team of women and young men projected the necessity of a better qualified, independent and easily accessible leader in the Village Panchayat. The propaganda worked successfully. Pappa won the election in the four-cornered contest. Pappa told that she was able to get more votes from the backward community also.

Pappa as the Village Panchayat President

Pappa shared that though she was not well versed with the Panchayati Raj System, and she had her own perceptions over the issues of underdevelopment. She proposed to do activities under on three important areas, namely (i) education; (ii) women development; and (iii) economic development as she realized that her villagers did not encourage girl children to continue their studies after schooling and most of them have been living in abject poverty. Due to rainfed irrigation, there is no successful agricultural practice and so poor landless labourers and marginal farmers used to go over a distance of 20 km to get employment in farms or to fell down trees in the forest area so as they could earn for their livelihood from the sales proceedings of wood as fuel, she informed. Moreover due to the lack of awareness, women failed to make use of the services like pre-natal and post-natal care available in the health centre. They did not have the practice of prompt reporting and registration of pregnancy. They did not adhered to the small family norms. There were many couples who have five children and even eleven children. Further there was the practice of female infanticide especially among the community of Pallar and Kallar, Pappa pointed out. She decided to work against these issues and hoped that the Village Panchayat will be a suitable place for those activities.

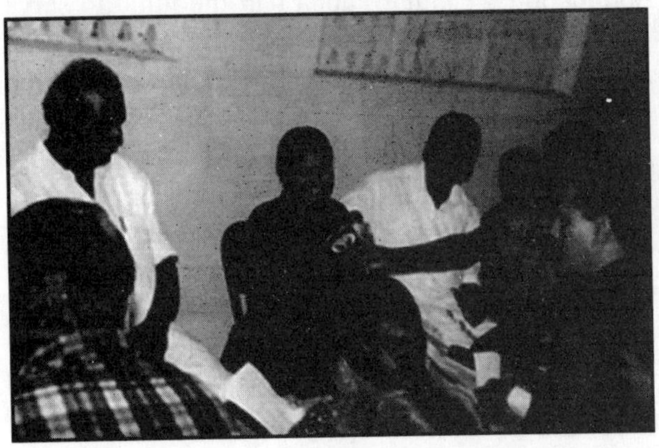

Pappa with Media Reporters

But in practice Village Panchayat Presidents were asked to carry out the plan programmes drafted at top level, she complained. Moreover the villagers were also of the opinion that the basic amenities like drinking water supply, roads, other infrastructure facilities had to be carried out by Village Panchayat, she remarked. There are a large number of issues and problems in the rural areas which were not discussed in public fora and she has decided to discuss all those issues with the people. She is of the opinion that unless the poor, dalit and women are sensitized and concientized, social transformation cannot be achieved.

Improvements in the Basic Amenities

*1. **Drinking water supply*** : Availability is not adequate in the Panchayat when Pappa assumed position. There were only six public taps. Pappa in consultation with the development officials was able to get TWAD assistance and two borewells have been sunk. From the village fund three mini power pumps and a sintex tank for storage have been provided. Now there are 23 public taps in the Village Panchayat, Pappa claimed. The drudgery of women has reduced a lot, she added.

*2. **Road and Transportation Facility*** : From the village fund, at a total cost of Rs.5.35 lakhs, five road works have been carried out in the Village Panchayat jurisdiction. Priority was given to the replacement of gravel road into metal road and to provide CC road in streets and lanes, Pappa pointed out. As a large number of young girls and youths came forward to take labour works in the Panchayat. In the road improvement and other labour intensive activities, village youths were given employment. Athankaraipatti is located in a remote area. There was no public transport facility. Public pleaded with the district administration and transport corporation officials, succeeded to get bus facilities, two trips a day from Peraiyur and Usilampatti, she told.

Removal of encroachment

*3. **Educational Development***: Pappa's family is closely associated with Indian National Congress Party. Her husband is serving as the Vice-President of the SC cell of the Madurai District Congress Party.

She along with her husband assisted the candidate, in the election campaign of Lok Sabha election 2001 and personally known to the sitting M.P. She availed fund from MPLADP and a school building was constructed at the cost of Rs.2.60 lakhs. From the MLA fund toilet and water supply facilities were provided to a Balwadi in her Panchayat. Further the women sanitary complex, and village community centre 'Chavadi' were also provided under MLA constituency development fund at a total cost of Rs.3.15 lakh in her Village Panchayat.

4. ***Common Property Resources — Maintenance***: The supply channel for Manickapuram Kanmoi meant for Kamatchipuram farmers had been desilted at a cost of Rs.1.60 lakhs. The work was successfully completed with the involvement of farmers. In about fifty irrigation wells the water table has been improved as the rainwater properly reached and was stored in the kanmoi which resulted in the percolation of ground water into nearby irrigation wells, Pappa claimed.

After witnessing the improvement in the water table, villagers suggested to make a new oorani as a porambokku land was available in the hamlets. A suitable place was identified involving the farmers of Kamatchipuram. During the discussion the farmers suggested to have a retaining wall at the side of the proposed new oorani so that it will be a pucca arrangement. It was decided to form the oorani first and in the meantime approach the PWD to get fund for the construction of retaining wall. When the formation of new oorani was in progress, the PWD officials inspected the site and agreed that they themselves would construct the retaining wall. Accordingly with people's participation from planning to the stage of implementation, an oorani was successfully formed at a cost of Rs.0.70 lakhs, Pappa explained. Livelihood of the poor is so important and hence natural resource management was given priority that too water bodies are so important. She is conscious of the world to be done for poor by the Panchayats.

Her Struggle for Entitlement

Athipatti is the nearby Village Panchayat of Athankaraipatti. There is an irrigation kanmoi, benefiting the ayacatdhars of these two Village Panchayats located in that area. When they experienced severe drought during 2003-04 the government decided to undertake maintenance work in that kanmoi. Accordingly at a total estimate of Rs.2.60 lakhs the work was given to Athankaraipatti Village Panchayat by an administrative sanction earmarked to that Panchayat. But in the meantime, the work of desilting and strengthening of bunds have been executed by a contractor without the knowledge of the Athankaraipatti Village Panchayat. Hence Pappa raised her objection against the contractors work. Moreover the work was very unsatisfactory as the desilting was done only to a limited extent. It was easy to observe for any ordinary person that a cost of Rs.2.60 lakhs work was not really carried out when compared to the quantum of work and removal of earth which existed there. The issue was brought to the notice of the union as well as the district officials. But it was unnecessarily dragged to find out the truth, she complained. In the meantime, due to poor and sub-standard work, there was a breach in the bank and the rainwater flooded into the field causing a heavy damage, Pappa added. When the issue of damage was highlighted the union administration just engaged the contractor who did a surface work instead of strengthening the bank. Till today the administration played the hide and seek in the issue of giving the work to a contractor by the union administration despite of administrative sanction to the Village Panchayat, Pappa remarked. The bureaucracy used to play second fiddle to the ruling party men, Pappa commented.

Issue in Selecting the Beneficiary of IAY

Pappa used to show real concern in selecting the eligible poor families under IAY. The allocation and the details of norms, procedure and rules and regulation were properly explained to the villagers in the Gram Sabha meeting with regard to all schemes and programmes assigned to the Village Panchayat, she informed. So far about 40 poor families (34 SC and 6 BC) have been provided with the IAY house. There was no procedural lapse in this regard and the work was completed successfully, Pappa shared. But during the year 2005-2006 it was told that 10 houses have been allotted. But a list of beneficiaries was sent by the union administration instead of the written rule that the selection had to be in the Gram Sabha meeting. Hence Pappa did not yield to the pressure made on her to pass resolution in this regard.

In the meantime, the Gram Sabha was convened at the marriage hall owned by the backward community and Pappa sought police protection. Pappa had the practice of availing police protection whenever she convenes Gram Sabha meetings as there would be anti-social elements or drunkards who tried to disturb the proceedings. On that day of Gram Sabha where the issue of list of beneficiaries sent from the union administration, was taken for discussion, Pappa availed police protection.

Pappa maintained the procedure with regard to the seating arrangements during the Gram Sabha meeting, and there by avoided any special importance to anybody. But the officials resorted into breach of the customary practice. When the Union Chairman came to attend the meeting (he is a local resident) the officials arranged seating especially to him and his accompanies. Pappa refused to have a break in the system and the proceedings of that Gram Sabha was disturbed. She was instructed to convene another Gram Sabha. In the meantime Pappa discussed the issue of denying the legal right entrusted with Village Panchayats and Gram Sabha in respect of selection of IAY beneficiaries, with institutions like Rajiv Gandhi Chair for Panchayati Raj Studies, and at last she decided herself to seek the direction of the court in this regard. She moved the petition in the Madurai bench of High Court of Tamil Nadu and the court ordered the stoppage of activities in this regard, Pappa informed. Realizing the consequences of legal action, the union administration and the Union Chairperson agreed to adhere to the list of beneficiaries selected by the Gram Sabha. Among the ten beneficiaries proposed by the union administration six of them were found ineligible and they have been replaced with 6 eligible families identified by the Gram Sabha, Pappa told.

Issues in the 2004 Parliament Election

In 2004 when the election to the Parliament was held, Pappa joined her husband and assisted in the campaign for the success of Congress candidate of Periakulam Parliamentary Constituency. It was told that the Congress candidate pooled 6000 votes more than the AIADMK candidate in the union of Sedapatti, she told. After a few days, a group of opponents gathered and forcefully entered into the house of Pappa, assaulted their in-laws and her husband was beaten when he was in a tea shop and was hospitalized. A false case on Pappa was also registered by her opponents. But Pappa went to the local police station and explained the furious attack made by the opponents and demanded to register her complaint. As the local police officials delayed Pappa approached the district officials in the police department and Pappa resorted into *dharna* with a majority of her villagers. Then the case was filed and two among the accused were sent to jail for further investigation. The case was registered only after an agitation and a *dharna* by Pappa and her relatives and villagers. The case is still pending, Pappa shared.

Panchayat By-election to Fill the Vacancy in her Panchayat

As a SC woman ward member expired, a by-election was held in the Athankaraipatti Village Panchayat. To challenge the leadership of Pappa, her opponents fielded a SC woman in the by-election as their proxy. But Pappa identified a woman volunteer who really showed interest in public life. It was the toughest election. Heavy expenditure was incurred by the opponent party of Pappa, she explained. But the local villagers knew the potentials of Pappa and the significance of her team. So majority of villagers in that Ward casted their votes in favour of the candidate supported by Pappa. At last in 40 votes margin, opponent was defeated, she added. Pappa reiterated that it was the politics which stood against the decentralization and women empowerment. Money and muscle power play an important role in Panchayat election. But she courageously faced and tackled all these threats successfully. She acknowledged that it was the confidence building and guidance received from Gandhigram equipped her to withstand against all the hurdles. She claims that support structure is very important for the women and Dalit leaders.

Her Contribution to the Welfare of Women

Pappa explained that she was constantly working to create a social climate in which her village women would be in a better position. She told that she could observe a change in the mindset of her village women. They never used to come in front of unknown male visitors and always shown inhibition in conversation. They won't come to undertake journey independently even to nearby cities and towns. They never individually visited government offices and other public institutions like banks etc., Pappa pointed out. Self help group activities and personal encouragement given by her brought a new life to the majority of womenfolk in her village, Pappa claimed.

The number of girl students who continue their studies after primary school increased, the practice of early marriage has decreased, the participation of women in SHG activities is enhanced, girls are permitted to undergo professional courses like nursing and computer study, and the women in general courageously express their opinion in families as well as in public forum; Pappa listed out the attitudinal and behavioural changes occurred among women of her village within a short span of five years, thanks to the reservation to women especially SC women in Panchayati Raj Institutions, she reiterated. She herself is role model and she constantly interacts and facilitates women to move further in the public space.

Pappa further cited the process of transformation among the women. Pappa recently organized a women's meet under the aegis of the Catalyst Trust a non-governmental organization promoting the civil society activities through establishing 'people's centre' in villages. Pappa is running one such centre in Athankaraipatti Village Panchayat. In the women's meet, response among the women was so intensive, Pappa quoted. The women cutting across age mingled themselves and keenly participated in folk songs and games programmes. They shared their feelings and aspirations frankly and without any inhibition they staged cultural programmes. The rural women are coming away from the routine life of manual labour, cooking and eating, and personal time with husbands. Now-a-days they spare time for SHG activities. Moreover in that connection they used to go over to various places from the local area for training and exposure. They undertake entrepreneurial activities, discuss profit and loss, market, stock and registers etc. They visit banks, government offices and fearlessly meet authorities and share their opinions, with them, Pappa remarked. The women sanitary complex is in full utility. Even elderly women are taught to make use of the toilet properly and without hesitation Pappa spends her time in early morning and late evening to motivate and to create awareness about public sanitation and personal hygiene. Informal discussions are held on the topics like reproductive health care, HIV-AIDS, waterborne diseases, importance of literacy and education to girl children, Pappa explained. It was found that there were four dropouts. The parents have been contacted and after coaching the children were admitted in the same school to continue their study.

Witnessing the involvement of Pappa in creating awareness through formal and informal gathering of women, the union officials made use of her voluntarism in the IEC activities on AIDS awareness and ills of alcoholism. In all the 31 Village Panchayats of Sedapatti Union, Pappa participated and influenced the women participants in the above topics. These experiences capacitated Pappa and she mobilized women of her village at once when the government introduced sale of liquor in the rural pockets, through TASMAC, and showed stiff opposition against the TASMAC officials to open and run a retail liquor shop in their Village Panchayat. She met the District Supply Officer in this regard and succeeded in their attempt. There is no TASMAC retail liquor shop in her village, Pappa shared.

Pappa herself was instrumental in the formation of a self-help group in her habitation. The name of her group is Saryodaya Women Group No. 56. There are twenty members in that group. The members have a system of mutual help and assistance for the social activities of the fellow members apart from their joint venture in enterprising activities. It is told that during the events like marriage, puppetry, death, hospitalization, etc. each members contribute 200 rupees and the consolidated total Rs.4,000 is used to procure useful household utensils, furniture and jewel. It is a lottery to the recipient member, Pappa remarked.

Moreover Pappa used to spend her time on the promotion of SHG activities in all hamlets of her

Village Panchayat. She assisted a few women to undergo training in marketing of articles of companies like Hindustan Lever. Rearing of milch animal is economically viable to rural women, Pappa observed. There is a cooperative milk society at T. Ramanathapuram, a nearby Village Panchayat and so marketing of milk is easily done, Pappa added.

Promoting Social Harmony

Athankaraipatti is a multi caste Village Panchayat. The relationship among the various communities of Athankaraipatti Village Panchayat is a cordial one. It is told that there is no communal clash in this area. Pappa shared that there is a village temple Samathi Pattaiya situated in a site belonged to SC community, but the temple affairs are managed by Naicker and Vellalar community. There are common temples, Mariamman Temple and Vinayakar temple where all the communities participate in the celebration. Moreover each member of SC community contributes to the *pooja* activities during the annual celebration where meals prepared from the contribution of paddy by each SC member and all communities irrespective of castes part-take in the food commonly. It is a grand celebration of two days. Villagers from 18 villages located around the area used to participate in the celebration. The temple *poojari* belongs to Naicker community. In spite of a huge congregation of people from different castes, the celebration adhered peacefully, Pappa explained. Pappa told that as the President of Village Panchayat she was very much serious in promoting the communal harmony in her Panchayat area as many villages are witness communal conflict among the castes.

She used her good office and position when dealing with issues which involve more than one community to ease the tension by her personal visit to the houses of both community members, freely shared with men and women and assessed their feelings and emotions related to issues and instead of projecting the negative feelings if any shared, Pappa used to project positive feelings of the opponents. Hence she acted wisely to reduce tension and contributed for the promotion of communal harmony. Pappa opined that it was all possible because, being a woman President it is easy to get into touch with the female and youth members among the disputed families, she pointed out.

Her Contribution to Social Reform Activities

Pappa has another dimension as an agent of Life Insurance Corporation of India. In connection with enrolling policy holders she maintains a wide contact with a large number of families in many Village Panchayats of Sedapatti Union. Pappa shared that it was a great opportunity to mingle with family members and able to lend her ears to their emotional sharing especially of women members, she added. She facilitated for successful widow remarriages. In one incident it was a widow member in her group with one child, got married. It took about two years to pacify the parents of the bridegroom. Now that women is pregnant and Pappa and her group members participated in the celebration. Another marriage was for a widow of backward community with two children. Both couples are living happily, Pappa remarked. Being a woman she was able to realize emotional problems of women, Pappa pointed out.

Promoting Small Savings Account among Rural Populace

Pappa, through personal contacts explains the significance of small savings among the poor families. With the help of the local postal department staff, she made 400 families to open small saving account in the post office. Appreciating her efforts in mobilization of small savings account, Rs.3.0 lakhs was awarded to her Village Panchayat, as an incentive.

Her Achievement in Namathu Gramam

When the innovative scheme of 'Namathu Gramam' was introduced in all the Village Panchayats of Tamil Nadu, Pappa with the cooperation of villagers undertook activities to accomplish the seven components targeted in Namathu Gramam. She had given attention in the following activities:

1. Maximum utilization of women's sanitary complex.
2. Cleanliness in streets and lanes.

Receiving award

3. Segregation of wastes—organic and inorganic.
4. Tree planting in all houses, public lands, school campus and tanks.
5. Cent per cent School enrollment.
6. Education of girl children.
7. Eradication of child labour.
8. Creating awareness about the age of marriage.
9. Prevention of female infanticide.
10. Transparency in Panchayat administration.

Pappa informed that all details of finance, works proposed to carried out, and even the details of her tour programme have been written in the notice board. Her Village Panchayat was graded as 'B' and Rs.1.0 lakh was awarded under Namathu Gramam incentive. Pappa during the interview engaged in improving further in the above areas anticipating to achieve 'A' grade.

Welfare of the Marginalized Section

Pappa is quickly acting in assisting the eligible persons among the marginalized section to avail their entitlements. She personally involved in getting marriage assistance earmarked for daughters of widow, widow's remarriage, old age pensions to 12 elderly persons, disabled assistance to 7 persons and under the free rice scheme to ultra poor for 35 families, Pappa listed out.

Pappa informed that in her Village Panchayat a hostel-cum-training/production centre for persons with special needs is under construction. She assisted the union administration in conducting camps for persons with special needs and distribution of identity cards for them in other Village Panchayats of Sedapatti Union.

Pappa as a Winner of the Heart

It is a well known that female infanticide is in practice in the area of Sedapatti Union of Madurai District. Government of Tamil Nadu has taken series of steps in preventing the inhuman cruelty of female infanticide. Law is also enacted to give punishment apart from programmes like creation of awareness, cradle scheme of adoption of unwanted female are implemented by the government. Pappa being an educated woman as well as in the capacity of woman President took much efforts in this regard. She used to associate with the village health nurse in meeting mothers who delivered female children and offered guidance and counselling to rear the female children. Pappa narrated her experience in this respect. In a family there is a delivery of one female child. The above said mother already has two female children. Having a third female child, the grandma of the child advised her daughter to desist herself from feeding the child and let it die itself naturally avoiding the accusation of female infanticide. Pappa having known that informed the village health nurse and accompanied her to that house with an intention of getting the female child admission under cradle scheme for adoption. But the family members refused to give the baby and even resorted to react angrily towards Pappa and the nurse. The grandma of the baby threw away the loincloth on the nurse. But nurse showed patience and both advised all the members of the family to immediately save the baby otherwise they had to face legal action. Further Pappa family persuaded the mother to feed the baby. At last she won the heart of mother. The mother fed the baby and as the baby eagerly waited for the mother's love and care enjoyed her feeding. A lamp is protected to burn, Pappa quoted.

Pappa used to share that she herself was a successful woman and so she assured the rural womenfolk that there was a great scope to all women in ensuing years provided they are empowered. She learnt to drive motor bike and she was known as 'bike lady'. It is an inspiration to several young girls, Pappa observed.

Linkage with Line Departments

Pappa maintains good rapport with the officials of line departments. She helps her villagers to avail services from Agriculture Department, THADCO, Electricity Board, Education, PWD, Women Development, Social Welfare and Revenue Departments. She successfully availed the Land Purchase Scheme of THADCO and 4 landless agricultural labourers in her village and 6 landless labourers from nearby Village Panchayat were benefited in this regard.

Creating awareness

In consultation with the government doctor, she helped a poor wage earner to undergo operation in his brain at Chitira Thirunal Hospital, Tiruvananthapuram. She accompanied the patient to the hospital and pleaded with the committee of doctors regarding the case of the patient. Now after the operation, he has returned to normalcy. The family of the concerned person thanked much in this regard, Pappa shared.

Creating awareness

Ulder the scheme 'Single Light to Hut' in 40 hutments electricity connection was obtained by her efforts. The Parent Teachers Association activities are strengthened. The school children adhere to the ten commandments of personal hygiene promoted under Total Rural Sanitation Programme, Pappa highlighted. The distribution of free noon-meal was monitored and the quality of food was ensured. Additional building for school have been provided by the Union Chairman.

Pappa informed that various trainings and exposure she had at the aegis of institutions like Gandhigram, Vivekananda Kendra, RETC, SIRD, ISS and training given by Women Development Corporation for SHG animators helped to shape her personality. Further her service as an agent of LIC was very much helpful in sharpening her approaches in dealing public affairs, she added. She used to organize legal awareness programme under the aegis of Department of Law and Justice and helped women to get justice by the intervention of Women Commission, and Human Right Commission, she pointed out.

Activities in the Federation of Women Panchayat Presidents

Pappa is serving as the President of Madurai District unit of the Association of Elected Women Representatives of Panchayati Raj Institutions. She is the treasurer in the union level committee of Village Panchayat Presidents of Sedapatti Union where both men and women Presidents were members. She is the Secretary of the Dalit women Presidents District unit, Madurai District.

Pappa informed that though education is very much essential to the empowerment of women, it was her active involvement in public affairs brought her to limelight. Her struggles and achievements have been featured in many newspapers and electronic media. She opined that even less educated women could perform well provided they got needed orientation and guidances whenever they demanded. It is by performance only women Presidents could get recognition in the community and the society. In this regard she acknowledged the services of supportive institutions functioning in the State of Tamil Nadu.

Honour on Pappa

Pappa's struggles have been brought to the wider public through media. In several newspaper, and magazines the details of her struggle and her courage to uphold the truth and commitment in public life were

Honorary Doctotrate from Colombo University

published frequently. Colombo University of Sri Lanka recognizing the struggle of Pappa come forward to honour her by offering honorary doctorate (D.Litt) on her. She has been invited to go over to Colombo to accept the doctorate. Pappa visited Colombo University along with her husband and she recollected that it was an ever green memory. She shared that she came to realize the power of media in the contribution of grassroots democracy. She expressed her heartfelt thanks to the media.

Her Future Vision

She is seriously contemplating on the ways and means for the socio-economic advancement of the villagers of her area. She pointed out that they needed support to start self-employment ventures and by vocationally trained youths could get employment elsewhere, she added. She proposed to have youth centres, meant for physically and mentally challenged persons.

Villagers assured to extend their support if Pappa contested in the next election to Panchayati Raj Institutions. If opportunity is available, Pappa is ready to move further, to be the Member of Legislative Assembly in her constituency. She gained popularity by her bold and courageous steps which she carried out after planning and in the support of all concerned, she added. She has a positive feeling that the future is bright and full of scope for her active involvement in the public space in the context of under development and poverty in her area.

Conclusion

Primarily she is an educated and motivated individual who has a passion for public service. Even before contesting in the election, she has come out for public service with the support of the family. Moreover the family has got political connections. Her husband is also supportive. One important factor which helped her to assert herself as leader is that she has gone to police station, she has gone to court and she went to different offices. Finally, she won in all her ventures and that provided confidence. She got strength from her family external agencies like Rajiv Gandhi Chair to overcome the barriers created by a political class and bureaucracy. But she was always on the right path. Her moral strength and community support made her to face all ordeals. Many popular articles have been written about her struggle and success and some of the articles got awards also. Her story is both a struggle and success. The moment she got success, she begins another struggle. In the whole process, she has built up her capacity. She is conscious of Dalit problems and her commitment towards the issues of Dalit is visible and yet her approach is that Dalit problems could be solved with the support of the Caste Hindus. She said that it is possible and it is happening in her Panchayat.

She has moved further frontiers in socio-political transformations of the villages. She has not confined her activities only in her Panchayat areas. She has expanded her activities in and around the Sedapatti Block Panchayat areas. She is not looking into the powers assigned to Panchayats. She has a tendency to respond to the demands and calls of the people. As her administration is transparent, non-corrupt, she has been fighting against injustice. She is being supported by the community. Her movement with higher officials and support agencies helped a lot to strengthen her position in Panchayats. She is a role model for other Dalit women leaders. She is the head of many associations including Dalit. Her multifaceted role enhanced her capacity and capability.

CASE - 23

PANCHAYATS IN TSUNAMI RELIEF AND REHABILITATION

It was a major criticism against the state government that it wilfully ignored the local bodies in the relief and rehabilitation work after the Tsunami disaster in the coastal areas. Here are four Panchayats which have demonstrated their ability to carry out relief and rehabilitation work on their own. Their activities were supported by government officials. These Panchayats are role models for disaster management by the Panchayats.

Role of Gram Panchayat in Relief and Rehabilitation of Tsunami Disaster

December 26, 2004 is a black day to the coastal villages of Tamil Nadu State, especially to the districts of Nagapattinam, Cuddalore and Kanyakumari. The tsunmai has created a major damage to the life and livelihood of the people in the coastal area. To manage the damage created by the tsunami, an organised effort is needed with partnership. The Panchayat is the nearest responsible responsive and representative institution which has to act swiftly and firmly to save the people, and carry out relief measures jointly with the government to recover the people from trauma. The machinery required for relief and rehabilitation is huge. In Tamil Nadu there was an argument that in the relief and rehabilitation activities Panchayats were not involved and consulted. Even seminars were organised in which Government officials were criticized as they acted upon their own perception and data projected by officials. But, in the same seminar, a few Panchayat Presidents narrated their activities in tsunami relief and rehabilitation work. They made a point that the government officials came to the scene only after two days. Wherever Panchayat Presidents were committed, they started their work immediately with the active involvement of the youth. The officials and NGO volunteers joined them the next day onwards.

First responsibility of the Panchayat is to take a responsible position in managing the crisis for which enormous will-power is needed. Wherever the Panchayat expected direction from the government, many players started their own work and kept different kinds of statistics on death and damage to property. Having realised the dispute over the statistics by the people of the respective villages, Government officials took a decision that they would have to collect data on their own. Against this background Panchayats were marginalised. Whenever Panchayats took the lead, government officials followed the direction of the Panchayats. In this context, we are interested in knowing the role of Panchayats in tsunami relief and rehabilitation measures. Four case studies have been conducted and they are presented hereunder.

Case Study - I

V. Chandran, President of Kothattai Gram Panchayat of Parangipettai Panchayat Union, Cuddalore District, has been hailed by many as he managed the crisis created by the tsunami in his Panchayat area. Basically a marine engineer (38) hailing from the fisherfolk community he was in the Middle East for some time to earn his livelihood. He was back to his village and contested in the Panchayat election and won. He carried out the Panchayat activities very effectively with the participation of all despite the opposition from some of his own community men since the election. It was purely election fund. When he heard the news of tsunami he was in a bus. Pudukkuppam was the worst affected area. The total death toll came to 126. Only six persons were in the village. Others totally vacated the village after the tsunami hit that area. The six were involved in removing dead bodies. In fact people living in other villages had the courage to visit the seashore and involved themselves in the rescue operation. Fishermen who lived in Pudupattinam who saw the tsunami waves refused to go the village again. They had such a kind of trauma after witnessing the tsunami waves. The rescue team saved twelve persons. He went to village and bodies were removed and identified. The Jammath came to the rescue of the villagers. They provided food and first aid to the affected families.

When all the dead bodies were brought to one place, the villagers refused to bury the dead bodies. Finally, officials requested the Panchayat leaders to accept the dead bodies. People were in an agitative mood and refused to accept the bodies. They refused to either burn or bury the dead bodies. Finally, he convinced the people. Since he took the responsibility to bring more number of people from outside to help the victims, people started believing him. Before the government started the rescue operation, the Panchayat President took the lead and, as a result, government officials followed the President and he was supported by the government in attending to the needs of the people. The Panchayat President, with the help of the youth and the clerk, collected the data. While doing this exercise he consulted the traditional Panchayat leader on every aspect of relief, rescue and rehabilitation. When he received relief material he openly maintained a note book and the entire responsibility was given to the traditional Panchayat leader. In fact the traditional Panchayat leader who was instrumental in opposing him in his Panchayat area right from the days of his election.

When the data pertinent to the loss of life and property was consolidated, the Gram Sabha was asked to approve the same. As such there was no dispute over the data as a pucca record system was maintained. He created an information centre in the Panchayat office to disseminate information relating to relief and rehabilitation works of the government and other donor agencies.

The Panchayat leader identified the location for a temporary shelter. Necessary facilities were provided at the temporary shelter by the Panchayat. Reboring was done by which good drinking water was supplied. Identity cards were prepared and issued to the affected 427 families. The Panchayat never allowed any agency to deal with the affected persons directly and, in the same way, the Panchayat never allowed the government officers to deal with the affected families directly. In all tsunami affected areas, data management became a big issue. In many of the Panchayats everyone was keeping a list of affected families and approached the donors and the government. But, in this Panchayat, there was only one list which was approved by the Gram Sabha and, endorsed by the traditional Panchayat leader. He maintained a very good relationship with the traditional Panchayat leaders and he was always in consultation with the traditional Panchayat leaders.

Collection of material, storing of material and distribution of material for relief were done in a scientific way. He created a transparent system by which he distributed all the materials to the needy. He saw to it that no body other than the affected families got any relief material. His involvement in all the activities was from day one. He formed many committees for all activities in order to involve more number of people. Every activity was carried out through a committee. Even in the Gram Sabha convened on 10th February 2005 to approve the beneficiaries list, he allowed the people to examine each and every name included in the list. He invited higher officials including the District Collector. He carried out activities in a transparent way.

He took special care of children and widows affected by the tsunami. Since affected persons were getting huge sums from the government, relatives showed keen interest in those individuals. To settle all the disputes in the best interests of the individuals, a lengthy dialogue was adopted with the involvement of the traditional Panchayat. Safety measures were taken to save the money given by the government to the affected persons, especially widows and children. All the money which the government gave has been deposited safely.

He established a good rapport with the people and won their confidence which enabled him to have a firm contact with the government officials and NGO representatives. NGOs played a key role in clearing the entire village and now they are providing permanent shelter. In his village all are the poor fishermen. He demonstrated his leadership by maintaining his cordiality with the traditional Panchayat leaders and all the other groups including his opponent who contested in the election. Further he proved his transparent administration by constituting a committee for relief and distribution of relief material by incorporating more number of individuals from the traditional Panchayat leaders group. On all occasions he went to the houses of others and never called anyone to his house. He was always responsive to the call of public, NGOs and government officials. He took responsibility in managing the affairs. He has been firm though he has maintained transparency.

Case Study - II

Manickappangu is a coastal village in Kollidam Block of Nagapattinam District. It is a moderate village in size. There are 10 hamlets in Manickappangu, of which four are fisherfolk habitations, namely, Puthupettai, Perumalpettai, Vellakovil and Kutiyandiyur. Mr. Manimaran is the President of Manickappangu Village Panchayat. He is 45 years old, married and has two sons. His wife is a school teacher. Manimaran's family is basically identified with the DMK party. Manimaran from his boyhood had been a fan of MGR. When MGR started the AIADMK party he joined the AIADMK. Now he is in the DMK because he does not like the style of the present AIADMK leadership.

Manimaran's life is different from that of the other youth in the fishermen community. He was motivated by those educated and employed persons who belonged to fishermen community. His parents were economically well off. So they encouraged him to study instead of engaging in fishing. Manimaran's longing for study moved him further even after he completed his post graduation. He did his M.Phil., B.Ed., Diploma in Labour Laws and another Post Graduate Diploma in Tourism Management from the Distance Education wing of the Annamalai University.

His father was in Singapore where he engaged in some work and had good earnings. Manimaran's brother worked on a ship. Hence there was no poverty in their family. The socio-economic background of his family made him different from other youth in the fishermen community. In reality, Manimaran does not know the nuances of the fishing avocation. Manimaran is now a progressive farmer. Along with his 3 acre own land, he used to get land for lease and did farming. With his wife's salary and earnings from agriculture, Manimaran is economically in a sound position.

His Entry into Village Panchayat Affairs

During 1996, when the first election under the New Panchayati Raj System was held, he contested for the position of Village Panchayat President. But he could not win. As the State Government was in the hands of the DMK party, Manimaran helped the villagers to avail the eligible benefits from the State Government. He waited for his turn. Once again he contested in the 2001 Panchayat election and won by a good margin of 350 votes. There are nine members in the Manickappangu Village Panchayat of which five belong to the fishermen community. There is only one member from the Scheduled Caste. Though the Village Panchayat is a multi-caste one consisting of Padayachis, Parayars and Christian Vanniyars, the fishermen community is numerically a stronger one than the others.

The Significance of Temple in the Fishermen Community

The fisherman has strong faith in God. Moreover the temple celebration enables the community to get together and so there was a change in the mindset of the fishermen community with regard to temple affairs. Earlier the temple was located near the seashore. In course of time the community realized the importance of a pucca and big building structure for the temple. So the fishermen community relocated the temple site from seashore to a place near the main habitation. A big temple, spacious enough to accommodate the community was constructed. In Manickappangu more than forty lakh rupees were spent to complete the construction of the temple for goddess Chinthamani Amman at Puthupettai. Moreover it serves as a community shelter during natural calamity. Further individuals suffering from contagious diseases like smallpox used to stay during the period of cure in the temple premises. The temple priest is usually from one of the families of the fishermen community. In Manickappangu village there is also a priest in the Chinthamani Amman temple. But the heirs of the priest's family failed to adhere to the expected norms and procedures in the temple's day to day affairs. Hence the system of engaging priest from the traditional family was discontinued. Now a person from Brahmin community is engaged as priest in the temple, Mr. Manimaran explained. It is learnt that the Sanskritization process is spreading fast among the fishermen community.

From Poverty to Prosperity

Mr. Manimaran shared that the socio-economic status

of the fishermen community is undergoing a big change recently, thanks to the modernization and technological innovation in the fishing avocation. Earlier the fishermen did not venture up to long distances in the sea for fishing. They had only kattumarams. Moreover they did not have different sizes and patterns of fish-net to catch different kinds of fishes in different seasons. But the Pattinavar, i.e., fishermen community is in a better position now. Possess different types of boats and fish-nets and so they go to deep sea and catch different varieties of fishes, Mr. Manimaran explained. Sales by auction is the system of marketing of fishes. Even a non-fisherman can participate in the auction, Mr. Manimaran explained. Thanks to the availability of facilities like transport and communication, fish marketing is a profitable business as fishes can be sold in other area markets and even sent to other states like Kerala where they are processed and packed for export, Mr. Manimaran explained.

Being an educated and socially oriented person, Mr. Manimaran shared that he served to the expectation of both groups, fishermen as well as non-fishermen communities. He further said that the community affairs of the fishermen is wholly looked after by the traditional Panchayat. He said that he does not feel any one against the social recognition accorded to the traditional Panchayat instead of the constitutionally recognized Panchayat. Mr.Manimaran gave emphasis to activities like promotion of health and hygiene, upgradation of schooling, provision of toilets, street lights, drinking water facilities to all hamlets etc.

The disaster of Tsunami and the Response of the Village Panchayat Administration under Mr. Manimaran

Ensuring the timely distribution of water supply is one of the important tasks the Village Panchayat administration is expected to do, Mr. Manimaran said. On 26th December, Manimaran woke up early morning and proceeded to switch on the power pump — OHT water supply system. Though there is an operator to do this, Manimaran did not wait for him. Then, as usual, he went to his field. Near the field there was a tea-stall and in front of the tea-stall there was a pond. Passersby crowded round it and saw that the water in the pond rose up and down around 8.45 a.m.

He then returned home. The houses of the fishermen were located within 200 metres of the seashore. When he was returning, there was an alarming sound. He saw waves from the sea rise upto 10 metres and the water was very thick and dark. Thorny bushes, thatches, broken logs, debris of damaged houses and other buildings all rolled on along the flood water. He immediately shouted at his sons and his wife to run away from the house. He got into his house and brought out his bike and drove to the nearby power plant office to contact the District Collectorate. He came to know that the Collector was already out to attend to the call of the public in this regard. Hence he drove back his bike to the habitation against the flood water but could not. He fell down in the speedy flow of water and he was able to hold on to a tree and escaped.

The villagers ran towards the bamboo bridge over the flooded river to escape from the chasing waves. Though the water was up to level of the bamboo bridge, the bridge was fit enough to cross over. It was so fortunate that just four days back, the bamboo bridge had been repaired. Otherwise there would have been no way to escape, Manimaran said.

Manimaran, with the help of other villagers, enabled others to climb over the bridge and to cross over to the other side, one by one. The youth of Anaikoil Village, which is a non-fishermen village, rushed immediately and helped to rescue the children and the old. In the meantime, the thorny bushes and debris struck against the bamboo bridge and it was later found that there were two dead bodies of children. The corpse of the children were removed and then Manimaran, with others, visited the habitation where they found dead bodies of children and adults. The dead bodies were removed by all and kept at the side of the local temple. Till 4 O'clock in the evening the rescue operation and removal of dead bodies was attended to, Manimaran said. After 4.00 p.m., he thought about his sons and wife. Immediately he visited Thirukadaiyur temple where all the people were staying. On his way, he was told that only one of his sons was seen. He is heart beat rose. With the hope that his family members would be alive, he moved towards Anaikulam in Thirukadaiyur, i.e., 7 kms from Manickappangu. He found his two sons and his wife there. Immediately he returned to his habitation in Manickappangu and engaged in burial activities.

During the rescue operation, it was very hard to walk freely. There were thorns and broken logs which struck against feet and fingers. It was a tough. Ordinary persons could not withstand such a struggle, Manimaran said. Only able bodied individuals could engage in relief work like tsunami relief, he said. When they all engaged in identifying dead bodies, they found one woman trapped between a gate and a wall and the wall fell on her and squeezed her to death. To remove the body, the cement gate had to be lifted up. But it was not easy to do so due to its weight. Manimaran and some youths jointly made an attempt and they were able to remove the dead body of that woman. Manimaran felt that it was a horrible scene to recollect. Manimaran shared that the rescue and relief operations initiated by the government was not to the expected level. The survey and collection of data by the government officials was not seriously carried out. The relief packages were not properly reached to the real sufferers, he complained.

The members of the fishermen community, though in fear of recurrence of tsunami like disaster, had a lesson and were getting ready to face the challenge, Manimaran explained. Manimaran suggested the following arrangements to be provided in coastal villages to handle the threat of tsunami:

- Construction of a tall tower like building structure within 500 metres of the sea so that villagers can climb up and escape from the chasing waves.
- The construction should be sound enough to withstand the challenges like tsunami/heavy rain etc.
- The habitation layout should be planned so as to have sufficient space between houses, broad streets, so that all can run away at the time of any threat.
- Thorny bushes should be removed from every directions. Standing trees are not dangerous. On the contrary, they are saviours.
- There should be a big and spacious community centre with all infrastructure facilities. This should not be any type of temporary shelter. Guidance and further backward and forward linkages to those who are ready to have a new avocation other than fishing should be provided. As it is a customary practice in the fishermen families to engage any one of their sons, if there are more than one son in the family, in fishing, it is possible to counsel these families to encourage other young men to go to new avocations.

The tsunami made them realize the concern of humanity towards fellow beings, Manimaran told. There were a large number of relief and rescue activities which were in unexpected quantum. The fishermen had never thought that the world would come to their side at this level. The compensation to the dead was very much a consolation to the concerned family. But there were cases of wasteful expenditure by the family members, Manimaran observed. Due to the availability of money, the habitual drunkards spent lavishly, some others purchased motorbikes, and only poor families deposited it in banks, Manimaran said. The tsunami had a lot of impact on the culture of the fishermen community. There are now occurrences of early marriage and the mindset of the youth has changed and they have came forward to marry with less dowry. After the tsunami, the youth wish to engage in a settled life, Manimaran felt.

Further, as the period of rehabilitation is a long one, the lifestyle and will-power of the youth and adults among the fishermen has changed. Due to monthly doles, provision of household articles free of cost, free supply of rice and other necessary commodities to the affected families, a type of laziness has developed in the minds of the fishermen community. They have failed to muster courage to venture into the sea for fishing, Manimaran observed. Though the role of non-governmental organizations in relief and rescue activities was commendable, the standard of works they undertook was poor. Particularly works like food for work schemes were carried out for name's sake, Manimaran complained. Manimaran felt that there was confusion on the side of the government with regard to the drafting of permanent rehabilitation plans. Moreover there was heavy damage to the farmers also. The agricultural land to an extent of one kilometre from the shore had been filled with salt. The reclamation of these degraded lands has not yet been seriously taken up for discussion by the government, Manimaran felt. But, being a farmer as well as a fishermen, Manimaran is serious enough in providing all eligible assistance, both monetary and goods to all families in the villages of Manickappangu Panchayat, irrespective of are farmers, fishermen or farm labourers.

He was of the opinion that due to lack of proper coordination among the NGOs and GOs the implementation of relief and rehabilitation activities was not in an orderly manner. He suggested that in every coastal village there should be a standing committee consisting of all stakeholders, i.e., representatives of the government machinery, non-government institutions, traditional Panchayat committees and the Village Panchayat. They should meet periodically or whenever necessary and convey to the higher level authorities the experience of fishermen at sea during various seasons, the speed of wind, the magnitude of waves, the rainfall details, erosion of sand dunes, mangroves and other natural vegetation along the coastal area. This committee will not only be a disaster management committee but also work for the protection and promotion of coastal based socio-economic livelihood of all sections of the coastal area, Mr. Manimaran explained. Special orientation, exposure and training should be given to the members of this standing committee in this regard. The State and the Central Governments should allot a special fund for the execution of the plan drafted by the Village Panchayats through the standing committee for the overall development of the coastal zones, Manimaran opined.

Case Study - III

Selvi Manimegalai is the President of Cauverypoompattinam Village Panchayat of Kallidam Panchayat Union. She belongs to the fishermen community. She is unmarried. Even at the age of 50 years, she moves fast at the call of the public. The interview was interrupted due to the visit of the revenue officials who came over to the village with regard to the complaint of Selvi Manimegalai against an encroacher. She just sat on a two wheeler behind the driver and urged him to drive quickly to the spot. It was only after half an hour that she returned and resumed to the interview.

Selvi Manimegalai recollected the worst day, December 26, 2004. On that day she was watching the TV around 7.30 a.m. and the news about the tsunami hit in Indonesia was flashed. She immediately rushed outside and ran to Chinakuttai (small pond) to check for consequence in the village. Manimegalai informed that during the Gujarat earthquake, there was a sensation of body movement in Cauverypoompattinam. Hence, on December 26 after viewing the TV news, she went to the pond side and witnessed that the water in the pond had risen up to two feet and there were bubbles. To alert the villagers she ran to the seashore were the habitation of the fishermen community was located. Immediately she telephoned to higher officials from the police station. In the mean time sea water had come to the shore and within fifteen minutes the water rose to neck level. Children were struggling in the flood and were saved by youths. The walls of houses broke down and the flood water forcibly drew away everything around the habitation.

Earlier six huts had been constructed across the area by the community to house the larger families. Just three days earlier, Manimegalai had evicted all the inhabitants of the six huts and removed the thorny bushes/trees and cleared the approaches to all the roads leading to the shore-habitations. When the tsunami wave hit on that day, it was through that passage the community members ran fast and escaped from the attack of the killer waves. But mostly women and children who could not run quickly became victims, Manimegalai shared her experiences with tears in her eyes.

The northern side of Cauverypoompattinam is the Chinna Cauvery Pattinam where about 300 huts are located very near to the sea. Here 87 deaths occurred, Manimegalai said. She telephoned to various government departments and the District Collector. In the meantime, the Block Development Officials came to the villages and facilitated the relief works. The fishermen community handled the removal and burial of dead bodies. Several bodies lay underneath collapsed buildings and constructions. A JCB machine was brought to remove the debris and the bodies were recovered, Manimegalai said. The Village Panchayat administration arranged for refreshments to the community members. Biscuit and milk were provided. Lunch was also given by the Village Panchayat administration.

The non-fishermen community of Manthekarai volunteered for relief activities. The nearby villagers of Mangamadam and the merchants and traders of Sirkali Town came over and distributed food packets, Manimegalai explained.

Manimegalai said that the life of the fishermen community was very peaceful and joyful. They used to lie down on the shore fearlessly and allowed their little children to run and play on the shore. At the age of twelve years, the boys used to accompany their fathers and happily ventured into the sea. Steadily they learned the lifestyle, customs and techniques of life inside the sea. The boys became full-time bread winners of their family at the age of seventeen or eighteen and would get one share of the fishes collected at sea. In the fishing trade there is no master-servant relationship. It is mere sharing of catches based on a basic rule. Whatever they get they share it. They enjoy their life with what they have. Their life is always entwined with nature.

Life in the sea is always a struggle. It is always uncertain and yet they enjoy their life. They have witnessed several challenges in their life. Yet this tsunami has created an irremovable fear among the fisherman. Even if there is a small change in the height of the tide, they imagine so many evils from the backdrop of the tsunami. The tsunami taught many lessons to the fishermen. Now one could find a change in the mindset and behaviour of the fishermen.

When a memorial was constructed in Poompukar for Kannaki, fishermen felt that it is only a protection wall for the memorial. But now they felt that because of the protection wall many saved their lives. But everyone in the seashore area felt that a protection arrangement has to be made either by creating natural barriers or an artificial barrier. Over a period of time the natural barriers have been removed by the people and the government for their advantage. Now the time has come to create such a barrier by planting saplings of different varieties of trees as per the advise of experts. People have witnessed that whenever natural barriers were created people had been saved as the velocity of the tide had been reduced. Now the community has realized the importance of natural barriers and this is stated by the people themselves.

To meet any such disaster, Manimegalai proposed a system. A community-cum-relief hall with pucca construction is very much needed, she explained. Further there should be availability of vessels, utensils, bedding and other livelihood facilities inside the proposed construction, she said.

Life in Temporary Shelters

It was after a period of one month, spent at temples/ schools, temporary shelters were provided. The role of NGOs in this was noteworthy, Manimegalai said.

The killer waves destroyed everything, they lost their near and dear ones, houses and other properties, it was a total loss, Manimegalai felt. It was only in the past two or three decades that the life of fishermen had taken the path of progress and prosperity owing to science and technology, Manimegalai said. Due to the availability of boats, the availability of varieties of nets, oil engine, consolidation as a sangam, cooperative venture in fishing, the income was high. Hence the comforts and enjoyments increased. But due to the tsunami everything was destroyed.

The life in the temporary shelter was a horrible one and was very pitiable. Hence the Village Panchayat administration took steps to provide protected water supply, build roads, remove debris and clean roads and passages, protect environmental sanitation, health of women, immunize children and persuade the government to identify a suitable site to relocate the affected houses, Manimegalai explained.

Manimegalai expressed gratitude to the services and assistance rendered by the government and non-governmental organizations. But she felt sorry for their attitude towards the community. Instead of discussing with the community to identify the felt needs among the youths and children and other stakeholders of the community, the NGO staff just provided what they chose. For instance, to a child of a victim family was given four bags from four NGOs, but nobody bothered to find out what could be kept inside the bags. People wanted more interaction from the people who came from outside but people who came here distributed material and took photographs and disappeared. Donors and the government provided material relief but not psychological relief. This is the feeling of the community.

She suggested that there should be a disaster management committee at the village level, Panchayat level and taluk level in the coastal areas. She was of the opinion that farmers and farm labourers should also be compensated from the government relief packages and NGO assistance. It is the whole coastal economy, environment and the sustainable livelihood which was affected. Hence development should be holistic covering all stakeholders, Manimegalai reiterated.

Case Study - IV

Prathamarapuram is a Village Panchayat located near the Velankanni Church. Seruthur is the fishermen community village under the jurisdiction of Prathamarapuram Village Panchayat. The President, Sri R.V. Swaminathan, explained the details of the relief activities undertaken by his Village Panchayat administration.

The Day of Disaster

The President, hearing the news of the tsunami the local community, informed the Police, Fire station, RDO and the District Collector over the phone. Since he is a well informed person, he had all the phone numbers. He made arrangements to move the affected people to the hospitals. At the same time, all the families from the coastal area came out and fled to safer places. The President helped them to go over to safer places, far away from the coastal area, by making arrangements with private transport companies, lorry and tractor owners. He found it very difficult to bring transport to this village. Most of them were put into the marriage hall and schools located in the village itself. The President arranged for preparing breakfast and lunch with the help of local community volunteers.

In the meantime, he made arrangements for visiting Seruthur Village. A team of youths and other volunteers from the main village Prathamarapuram joined the youth and elders of the fishermen community, started the identification of dead bodies, and removed the same for burial. In the meantime government officials started to go over the affected area and collected various details and so the President assisted them by providing the necessary details through verification and clarification from the concerned families and the community. The Panchayat President established his control over the entire activities and left no room for government officials to act on their own. In the beginning he did not wait for the arrival of the officials.

Association with NGOs

The second and third day after the disaster, a number of NGOs came to the site and distributed various items of relief materials. The President helped them to identify the victim families and assisted in proper disposal of relief materials to the concerned families. By then the Government formed a team of various sectoral officials and the relief work was systematized—removal of debris, restoration of electricity, drinking water supply, link road and connectivity to the affected area. The President joined the official team and assisted them. At the camp site, medical check-up and medicines were also provided by the team.

Various NGOs, volunteers and social institutions visited and a lot of activities were undertaken by them like counselling, distribution of provisions, play materials and other essential materials like blankets, buckets, vessels etc. to the affected families. In general, the NGOs used to meet the President and sought the help of the Panchayat Administration to contact the right persons or community leaders. Without any confusion the relief activities were properly carried out. The President informed that some NGOs, when they directly contacted the affected families, faced a lot of problems in distributing the materials. The presence of the Village Panchayat President brought some order, Swaminathan claimed. Further the President helped in identifying and establishing a temporary shelter with necessary facilities like drinking water supply and toilet and electricity connection.

When the Government arranged the dole and other cash benefits to the affected families, the President assisted the Village Administrative Officer in listing the eligible families in this regard. He gave an impression to the officials as well as the members of the community that he is a person with leadership and sense of commitment. He maintained the exact data with regard to death and damage to properties. He did not permit anyone to take advantage of the misery. He demonstrated his leadership in managing the situation very effectively. In many places the communities were divided on caste lines for distribution of relief material. But in his Panchayat he maintained harmony among various segments of the society.

Role in the drafting of Micro Level Plan

The President assisted the local NGO engaged by The Hunger Project, Gandhigram Rural Institute, to carry out the Micro Planning exercise. He assisted in identifying the local volunteers, farmer groups and SHG groups, helped in the baseline survey, focused group discussion, in conducting PRA exercise, and drafting the developmental plan for the Village Panchayat. Swaminathan explained that generally the fishermen community was very traditional in nature: they used to come to the Village Panchayat to stake their entitlements, namely, drinking water, road, street lights etc. For other needs, they used to seek the help of the traditional Panchayat leaders. But tsunami created a new atmosphere and interface with all sections of the community, Swaminathan said. It is a normal tendency among the poor, whether they are affected or not, where there is any opportunity to get any assistance from the government, they utilize it by any means. This is being exploited by all from politicians to officials. This, in fact, created a whole lot of problems in the communities. But Panchayat leaders, with their responsible action could avoid many of the unpleasant situations. The elected Panchayat leaders have to act responsively with a sense of commitment.

Conclusion

It is a major complaint that in the tsunami relief and rehabilitation activities, Panchayats were not involved and they were not consulted. The state government believed only the officials and not the Panchayats. It is further argued that even the government officials established contact with traditional Panchayat leaders and not with the constitutional Panchayats. But the cases analysed in this study have amply established the fact that wherever the Panchayat leaders took responsibility and responded to the situation without expecting direction from the government officials, they established control over the community. They did not allow the external agencies to divide the community. Panchayat leaders have established good rapport with traditional Panchayat leaders. It is not the power and resources that matter it is only the leadership that matters.

CONCLUSION

From the cases presented above one can make a few observations. In all the cases an aspiration fire for achievements has worked very well. Some are role models. Their humility, capacity and capability have brought many close to them. They have emerged as icons. They have a penchant for innovations. Their passion for responding to challenges is remarkable. Their responsiveness and their transparency in Panchayat administration have made the people repose confidence in them. Their readiness to take risks have attracted many of the government departments to experiment with many new and innovative projects in their Panchayats. For many social service is a major passion in life which made them feel interest in doing their work. For a few, delivery of service is the foremost essential duty. Protecting the self dignity of the Dalits is the major mission in life for Ponnuswamy of Semmipalayam Gram Panchayat. He did the job very effectively and to the satisfaction of the Dalits. Basically MGR is a role model for him. Water supply is the basic service and even this basic service was not delivered to this Dalits so far. Only after he became the President he did this work by which their self dignity was protected.

Some of them have emerged as successful leaders by carrying out the schemes and programmes of the government. By their doing so both the government departments and the people are happy as target is achieved and the people are involved. They are always set in a Win Win mode in all the activities of their Panchayats.

Global warming is debated and resolutions are passed internationally, nationally and regionally, but who will act on the resolution? It is only the community and the grassroots institutions that have to act on resolutions. Creating a green village and a clean village are the visions of the grassroots leaders. It has been mentioned in the Act that the Panchayat leaders have to carry out certain activities mandatorily. Apart from the mandatory activities, they have to act in certain areas discretionally. In the latter case, they have set an agenda for themselves. They have found ways and means to provide services and carry out development works.

In fifty years of democratic governance not even a single village was declared hutfree. But now a Panchayat President has made it possible in Koothampakkam Gram Panchayat. Neither any MLA nor any MP undertook such a kind of exercise. Gandhians has been preaching. But Koothampakkam Panchayat has acted. Koothambakkam Panchayat has created an academy for Panchayat leaders. It is a practice based academy.

Normally the Central Government and the State Government announce schemes and programmes. Panchayats are only to implement programmes and schemes. Nobody has heard about Panchayats launching schemes and programmes. Here in Tamil Nadu this has happened. Some of the Panchayats have launched new schemes and nobody has stopped them. Those who are left out of the BPL list are being provided with noon meals. Feeding centres have been functioning in Panchayats and a provisions store is being run by a Panchayat. All these activities are possible because of the support of the people.

There are leaders at the grassroots concerned about communal harmony. They work hard to maintain communal harmony. As per the observation of the Panchayat leaders, communities are not communal; they are secular but our politicians are communal; and, hence, Panchayats have to work for communal harmony. Natural resource management is the major concern of a few leaders by which they save the livelihood of the poor. For many water supply is the basic work and it is the need of all.

In the absence of public discussion on many of the social development issues, India is low in Human Development Indicators. But now Panchayat leaders are concentrating on anemia and malnutrition and it is something unique and interesting. MLAs or MPs never discussed anemia or malnutrition or global warming. But Panchayat leaders discuss with people on all the above subjects.

In order to solve the problems of the women leaders in Panchayat administration the women leaders have formed a federation for which one leader is responsible all the time. Many times, they have sorted out problems by their collective efforts. The

Women Leaders Federation has gone up to policy advocacy and changed the policies also. The women federation leaders met the Chief Minister and convinced her on reserving two terms consecutively for Dalit and women leaders. The Chief Minister agreed and did it. Just like a trade union movement, the women federation set an agenda and fought. It is a role model for other states also. The women federation leaders went up to the Prime Minister and the President of India with a petition against the state government.

Creating linkages and achieving synergy is a very difficult task. The above cases have demonstrated the ability of the grassroots leaders to establish forward and backward linkages. Generally leaders are interested in establishing forward linkages with people's representatives, government officials and political party leaders. But they do not link up with the stakeholders. Leaders are interested in a link up with the people only during the time of election. Very rarely they meet people and discuss their problems for articulation in the authoritative bodies for decision making. But the cases which we have studied are known for their achievement in creating linkages with officials, youth, women, school children and people's representatives. Their linkages are always to get the needed support either in the form of material resources or in the form of human resources.

The above leaders have realized the strength and value of traditional Panchayats and they have drawn the support of the traditional Panchayats. In all their actions one finds a synergy between the constitutional Panchayat and the traditional Panchayat. They have paid great attention to training. For follow up, they keep in touch with the training institutions.

The Dalit leaders, by their transformative action, have made the Dalits repose faith in the institutions. It is proved that social frustrations have been eased to some extent because of the involvement of the stakeholders in the process of development.

Some of the leaders are creating records by their activities and they show the way to the state government. The state government has recognized them as models and they are being referred to continuously for others' benefit.

All these leaders have gained strength from within. The women leaders have acted very aggressively, based on their moral strength. All the leaders are on the job continuously and training, for them, is on the field. Their continuous participation in programmes enhances the skill and capacity of the leaders.

They have attended training programmes in many places and got their doubts clarified. It is like an immersion programme. They have got immersed in Panchayat administration. The level of equanimity is very high and, as a result, they have gained respect and recognition among all segments of the society. One notices the high calibre of the Panchayat leaders when they speak on public platforms on development issues. Some of them are highly informed and energized. They are always in the process of evolving themselves as leaders.

Their honesty has paid rich dividends. Many of them waged struggles against sand mafia, officials, politicians and dominant caste leaders. In all the struggles they have succeeded and emerged victorious because they have maintained their rectitude in their dealings and administration. Their honesty is a major source of strength. The leaders have their own strategies to work on issues. Everyone is interested in water supply and by this the community is mobilized. When the community is mobilized and prepared positively difficult work like sanitation can be taken up.

Despite all the barriers in the political system and the administrative system to proper devolution of powers, the Panchayat leaders, by their commitment, sincerity and honesty, have made it possible to activate the Panchayats vibrantly. The above leaders are Change Makers. These leaders have shown that a grassroots level movement has to be initiated to demand proper devolution of powers. They have instilled confidence among the people that the Panchayat will deliver goods and services to the people to a satisfactory level.

All over the world it is proved beyond doubt that four conditions are imperative for the success of grassroots institutions and decentralization of powers. They are: (a) sufficient powers to fulfil the responsibilities on development activities; (b) sufficient financial resources to fulfil the felt needs; (c) adequate capacity to manage the Panchayats and to administer development; and (d) a mechanism to ensure accountability to citizens.

In Tamil Nadu the condition of devolution of powers is contradictory to the principles of success of the devolution of powers. Despite all the negative factors, the Panchayat leaders are emerging as models as they built up downward and upward accountability. They worked with the people and they involved the people in implementing the programmes and schemes of the government. Thus they have mobilized the people for social action and kept them in fact. This grassroots mobilization drew the attention of the bureaucracy, the MLAs, the MPs and other higher level representatives. For them money was not a problem. They mobilized resources from MPs and other local body representatives. Their managerial and negotiating skills have immensely contributed to their emergence as leaders.

INDEX